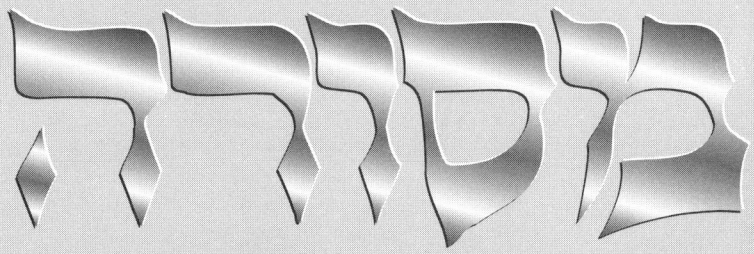

ArtScroll Series®

Rabbi Nosson Scherman / Rabbi Meir Zlotowitz
General Editors

Rav

by
Yonoson Rosenblum

Published by
Mesorah Publications, ltd

Dessler

The Life and Impact of
Rabbi Eliyahu Eliezer Dessler
the Michtav M'Eliyahu

FIRST EDITION
First Impression ... May 2000

Published and Distributed by
MESORAH PUBLICATIONS, LTD.
4401 Second Avenue / Brooklyn, N.Y 11232

Distributed in Europe by
J. LEHMANN HEBREW BOOKSELLERS
Rolling Mill Road / Unit E
Jarow, Tyne & Wear
England NE32 3DP

Distributed in Israel by
SIFRIATI / A. GITLER
10 Hashomer Street
Bnei Brak 51361

Distributed in Australia and New Zealand by
GOLDS BOOK & GIFT SHOP
36 William Street
Balaclava 3183, Vic., Australia

Distributed in South Africa by
KOLLEL BOOKSHOP
Shop 8A Norwood Hypermarket
Norwood 2196, Johannesburg, South Africa

ARTSCROLL SERIES®
RAV DESSLER
© Copyright 2000, by MESORAH PUBLICATIONS, Ltd.
4401 Second Avenue / Brooklyn, N.Y. 11232 / (718) 921-9000 / www.artscroll.com

---

ALL RIGHTS RESERVED
The text, prefatory and associated textual contents and introductions
— including the typographic layout, cover artwork and ornamental graphics —
have been designed, edited and revised as to content, form and style.

No part of this book may be reproduced
IN ANY FORM, PHOTOCOPYING, OR COMPUTER RETRIEVAL SYSTEMS
— even for personal use without written permission from
the copyright holder, Mesorah Publications Ltd.
except by a reviewer who wishes to quote brief passages
in connection with a review written for inclusion in magazines or newspapers.

THE RIGHTS OF THE COPYRIGHT HOLDER WILL BE STRICTLY ENFORCED.

ISBN:
1-57819-506-3 (hard cover)
1-57819-507-1 (paperback)

Typography by CompuScribe at ArtScroll Studios, Ltd.
Printed in the United States of America by Noble Book Press Corp.
Bound by Sefercraft, Quality Bookbinders, Ltd., Brooklyn N.Y. 11232

This volume is dedicated to the

קדושי קעלם זצ״ל הי״ד

The holy martyrs of Kelm

ה׳ וכ״ח מנחם אב, תש״א

Kelm — the name still evokes visions of uprightness, of purity, of devotion to Torah and Mussar, of love of Hashem and *Klal Yisrael*, of integrity and purity, of a tabernacle whose memory remains a tribute to the greatness of the heavenly soul that the Creator blew into mortal man. Kelm was like the sun, a source of an unearthly light, whose rays illuminated and ennobled all who were privileged to enter its orbit.

Rabbi Dessler wrote, "I remember the night of Simchas Torah in Kelm. The rabbis went through the street and danced with all their strength toward the city, with joyous ecstacy, singing exuberantly אַשְׁרֵנוּ מַה טוֹב חֶלְקֵנוּ, *We are fortunate — how good is our portion!*"

Forty years later, when the precious tzaddikim of Kelm were destroyed in Churban Europe, they sang and danced again. Even their final hour testified to their incomparable spiritual brilliance. And again Rabbi Dessler wrote. "The time of the terrible destruction arrived. At the gate were the murderers ... They took every man, woman, and child out to the street, driven and beaten with cruel, unrelieved blows. These holy people strengthened their hearts and firmed their spirits, with enthusiasm and fervent joy to perform the commandment of קדוש שם שמים, *sanctification of the Hashem's Name* ... They danced with all their strength and sang that same joyous song: *We are fortunate — how good is our portion!* How fortunate that we are Jews! How fortunate that we merit to die because we are Jews! So they went, with dancing and enthusiasm, as the joy became stronger and stronger, going further and further upward ... until they arrived at the killing field on the outskirts of the city... where they surrendered their lives to their Master, cleaving to Him with the joy of the mitzvah."

With these words, the gaon and tzaddik Rabbi Eliyahu Eliezer Dessler זצ"ל described the last moments of the great Talmud Torah of Kelm. He was its product and it survived in him, in his teachings, and in his talmidim.

This volume is his biography, and in a deeper sense it is a biography of Kelm, because, as Rabbi Dessler taught constantly, spiritual accomplishments never die. Kelm never died. It lived on in him, as he lives on in his writings, his example, his teachings, and the generations he still inspires and elevates.

תנצב"ה

Table of Contents

Acknowledgments   i

Introduction   v

1 Childhood   11
The Dessler Family / The Dessler Home / His Father's Influence

2 Arrival in Kelm   25
Kelm – the Town / The Legacy of Kelm

3 The Alter   36
Educator

4 Chochmah U'Mussar   46
The Beis Medrash of Avraham Avinu / Chochmah / Mussar

5 Kelmer Chinuch   58
A Spiritual Elite / A Framework for Perfection / Discipline and Order / Menuchas HaNefesh / Combating Self-Love / The Quest for Perfection

6 Budding Torah Scholar   74
Rabbi Tzvi Hirsch Braude / Rabbi Nachum Velvel Ziv

7 War and Poverty   88
Emunas Chachamim / Reversal of Fortune

8 Marriage — 99
Rabbi Doniel Movshovitz and Rabbi Gershon Miadnik / Failure in Business

9 Stranger in a Strange Land — 113
A Spiritual Wasteland / The Rabbinate / Separation from Family / Continuing Spiritual Aliyah / Reunited with Family / Reb Reuven Dov Dessler's Petirah

10 Teacher of Youth — 139
Rabbi Solomon Sassoon – the First Talmid / The Circle Widens

11 Drawing Close With Cords of Love — 155
A Reluctant Critic / A Relationship for Life / Casting His Net

12 Separated Once Again — 173
Farewell to Reb Nachum Velvel / Separation from Wife and Daughter / Escape / Australia / Chesham

13 The Founding of Gateshead Kollel — 190
An Implausible Dream / Reb Dovid Dryan / Gateshead / Working Out the Details

14 The Opening of the Kollel — 202
Rabbi Dessler's Role in the Kollel / Rabbi Dessler's Schedule

15 In His Image — 216
The Ideals of the Kollel / An Exemplar in Middos / A True Giver

16 Builder of Torah — 232
The Gateshead Teachers' Seminary / In His Footsteps

17 Transitions — 250
War's End / Meeting the Ponevezher Rav / First Visit to Eretz Yisrael / Return to England / Back to America / Leaving Gateshead

18 The Power of His Word — 278
A Speaker Nonpareil / His Impact Within the Yeshiva / A New Derech

19 The Power of His Example — 296
Not a Mashgiach / The Beauty of His Ways

20 In the Public Eye 310
Spreading the Word / Efforts to Uproot Religion Among the New Immigrants / Peylim Is Born / Rabbi Dessler's Involvement in Peylim

21 The Final Years 337
Michtav Me'Eliyahu

Appendix / Meeting the Challenge 353
Uprooting Materialism / Combating Superficiality / Against the Worship of Science

Glossary 371

Acknowledgments

Without the ongoing involvement of RABBI ARYEH CARMELL and RABBI NACHUM VELVEL DESSLER, I would not have had the courage to offer this volume to the public. Rabbi Carmell and Rabbi Dessler both reviewed the entire manuscript several times.

Rabbi Carmell first became a student of Rabbi Eliyahu Eliezer Dessler at the age of 15, and he remained an intimate of Rabbi Dessler's until the latter's passing in 1953. In the nearly half-century since then, Rabbi Carmell has done more than anyone else to perpetuate Rabbi Dessler's teachings as editor and co-editor (depending on the volume) of the five-volume *Michtav Me'Eliyahu*.

Rabbi Nachum Velvel, Rabbi Dessler's son, taught me a great deal about the refinement of speech instilled in Kelm. For him the biographer's normal standard of truth was not sufficient. He insisted on asking repeatedly: Is this instructive? Could it be misunderstood or hurt someone? Is there a gentler way of phrasing the point?

But for the generous support of the entire project by MR. REUVEN DESSLER, this biography of his grandfather would never have come into being. The present volume is one more in a long series of works he has sponsored to perpetuate the legacy of a world that is no more.

RABBI ELIYAHU ELIEZER DESSLER, Mashgiach of Ponevezh Yeshiva and editor of the four-volume *Kisvei HaSaba Mi'Kelm*, added immeasurably to my understanding of Kelm. For decades he has collected material concerning Rabbi Dessler, after whom he was named, and has spoken to as many people as possible in *Eretz Yisrael* who remember Rabbi Dessler. He guided me to most of the key interviews with *talmidim* of Rabbi Dessler in Ponevezh Yeshiva.

RABBI MORDECHAI MILLER, the long-time principal of Gateshead Seminary, is the other surviving *talmid* of Rabbi Dessler's London circle. In over five decades of teaching young women, he has introduced thousands to Rabbi Dessler's thought. Through his students and many *sefarim*, he has played a major role in making Rabbi Dessler's works a staple of today's Torah education. Rabbi Miller not only shared many fascinating recollections concerning Rabbi Dessler's London years, he also generously consented to read those sections of the book dealing with the London and Gateshead years.

RABBI ZUSIA WALTNER is the only surviving original member of the Gateshead Kollel, and his memories are central to my account of the Gateshead years. Rabbi Dessler maintained his residence in the attic of the Waltners' apartment for nearly four years during World War II and shortly thereafter.

Other members of the Gateshead Kollel who provided valuable information about the Gateshead years are: RABBI ALTER HALPERIN, Rosh Yeshiva of Yeshivas Toras Emes (Schneider's Yeshiva) in London and co-editor of the first volume of *Michtav Me'Eliyahu*; RABBI ELIEZER ZAHN, Rosh Yeshiva of Sunderland Yeshiva; RABBI BETZALEL RAKOV, Rav of Gateshead; RABBI DOV STERNBUCH; RABBI WOLF KAUFMAN, Rosh Kollel in Manchester; and RABBI ELCHANAN KARNOVSKY.

I had the opportunity to interview RABBI NAFTALI FRIEDLER, one of the first *bachurim* in the Gateshead Kollel, just a few days before his passing, and I will not soon forget the warmth with which he and Rebbetzin Friedler spoke of those years, including Rabbi Dessler's efforts as a *shadchan* on their behalf.

Mrs. Miriam Dansky's *Gateshead* was the source of much useful background information on the Gateshead community.

Among Rabbi Dessler's close students in Ponevezh Yeshiva the following offered many important insights and memories: RABBI DOV WEIN, Ram in Yeshivas Be'er Yaakov; RABBI YAAKOV EDELSTEIN, Rav of Ramat Hasharon; RABBI DOV LANDAU, Rosh Yeshivas Slabodka; RABBI MEYER MUNK; RABBI SHALOM ULMAN; RABBI BERL POVARSKY, Rosh Yeshivas Ponevezh; RABBI SHMUEL SHULSINGER, Rav of Kiryat Ata; RABBI DOVID HILLMAN; RABBI MENACHEM COHEN; and RABBI DOV YAFFE, Mashgiach Yeshivas Chazon Chizkiyahu (Kfar Chassidim).

RABBI SHLOMO NOACH KROLL, and *lbch"l*, RABBI SHALOM BER LIFSHITZ provided a great deal information about the early days of Peylim and Rabbi Dessler's role in the organization.

Unfortunately RABBI SOLOMON DAVID SASSOON, Rabbi Dessler's first and closest *talmid* in London, and RABBI CHAIM FRIEDLANDER, his closest disciple in Ponevezh Yeshiva, passed away prior to the commencement of my research. But I benefited greatly from conversations with members of both the Sassoon and Friedlander families. RABBI NATAN SASSOON opened up for me a treasure-trove of letters from Rabbi Dessler to his grandfather.

RABBI EMANUEL FELDMAN, RABBI ELIYAHU MEIR KLUGMAN, RABBI MATTISYAHU ROSENBLUM, RABBI MICHAEL MARKSON, and MR. ERIC PINES read and made valuable comments on an earlier draft of the manuscript.

RABBI MENACHEM GOLDBERGER meticulously checked hundreds of citations and offered many important insights. I greatly benefited from the vast knowledge he has acquired in the course of preparing the general index to *Michtav Me'Eliyahu*. MRS. AVIVA GORDON located many parallel citations between *Michtav Me'Eliyahu* and its English adaptation *Strive for Truth*.

RABBI MEIR ZLOTOWITZ and RABBI NOSSON SCHERMAN are wise mentors and trusted friends. A decade ago, they welcomed me to the ArtScroll family, and since then everything I have achieved has been inextricably bound to their warm support. This book is a product of their friendship and the dedication of the staff at ArtScroll, particularly DANNY KAY who designed the cover, HINDY GOLDNER who typeset the book, and MRS. FAYGIE WEINBAUM who proofread.

My parents, PAUL and MIRIAM ROSENBLUM, continue to be sources of boundless love and wisdom. They freely confess to being completely prejudiced as far as their children are concerned, and I have been the beneficiary of their unconditional love and support all my life.

Everything I do is only possible because of the wonderful home created by my wife Judith. The biography of Rabbi Dessler is no exception. It is our prayer that by virtue of my three years of involvement with Rabbi Dessler something of his spirit has entered our home and left its imprint on us and our beloved children, Micha David, Naama, Elisha, Yechezkel Mordechai, Chananya, Zecharia, Yaakov, and Elimelech Gavriel שיחיו.

No words can convey my gratitude to *HaKadosh Baruch Hu*, Who granted me many years in the *beis medrash* devoted to the study of His Torah, and Who has enabled me to remain in the presence of great men even after leaving full-time learning.

Yonoson Rosenblum

Jerusalem
Iyar 5760

Introduction

IN THE LATE SUMMER OF 1941, A LETTER ARRIVED IN Chesham, Buckinghamshire at the lodgings of a middle-aged rabbi. The rabbi in question was a distinguished product of the famed Talmud Torah of Kelm. For the preceding thirteen years, he had served as a congregational rabbi in London — a position that provided him little satisfaction.

With the beginnning of World War II, the recipient of the letter found himself completely cut off from his family. His wife and two teenage children were in Lithuania when the war broke out, and they barely managed to escape — the wife and daughter to Australia and the son to America.

In the wake of the German Luftwaffe's nightly bombings of London, many Jews, including some of the rabbi's closest *talmidim* (students), evacuated London and sought refuge in the countryside. The rabbi now joined them. What the future held for him he had no idea.

He was then in his fifty-first year and had but twelve more years to live. Though he had already formulated many of the ideas that would one day make him a household name in every Torah home, and some of his best-known essays were already written, he had not yet published a single word. Had it not been for that letter, the many volumes compiled after his death from his talks and essays would never have been printed and his illumination would have been lost to posterity.

And if he had passed away prior to receipt of the letter, he would be unknown today. His influence until then had been almost exclusively limited to a small circle of private students in London.

The recipient of the aforementioned letter was Rabbi Eliyahu Eliezer Dessler; the author was Rabbi Dovid Dryan, the *shochet* of Gateshead. A decade earlier, Reb Dovid had founded a yeshiva in Gateshead, a nondescript working-class town in the north of England, and he now proposed to establish there a kollel of outstanding young scholars. In his letter, he sought a partner for this undertaking.

Twenty-one other rabbis received the same letter. Of those, 18 apparently considered Reb Dovid's proposal too implausible to merit a response of any kind. The other three either claimed the time was not propitious or that their personal circumstances did not then permit them to consider the proposal.

Only Rabbi Dessler was interested in joining Reb Dovid in his undertaking. Though he could not have known it at the time, with that response he had catapulted himself to the forefront of a major transformation of the Torah life in Western Europe. He had stepped out of the shadows into the limelight, and would remain on the public stage for the rest of his life.

Within a few months, the Gateshead Kollel, with Rabbi Dessler at its head, was a reality. The face of English — indeed all Western European — Jewry would never be the same. Just as Rabbi Aharon Kotler was doing in America, Rabbi Dessler would bring the ideal of Torah *lishmah* — of Torah learning unrelated to any thought of future position — to England.

A biographer of Rabbi Dessler confronts at the outset one very basic question: Why do we need a biography of Rabbi Dessler? That question, it must be stressed, does not reflect any doubts about Rabbi Dessler's historical significance. Just the opposite.

The questioner takes for granted Rabbi Dessler's status as one of the most profound Torah thinkers of the twentieth century. His question is: Given Rabbi Dessler's greatness as a thinker, why bother with the details of his biography? We have his five-volume *Michtav M'Eliyahu*. Let us study that without becoming bogged down in the details of the author's life.

And indeed there can be no doubt about the seminal quality of Rabbi Dessler's thought. It would be hard to name another modern Torah thinker who has done so much to shape the way we view the world.

His ideas and the imagery he used to express them have so thoroughly entered our discourse that we often forget that they were first published just over forty years ago. What yeshiva or seminary student, for instance, has not heard numerous times that, contrary to what the world thinks, it is not love that leads to giving but giving that leads to love? Yet many may not even know that the source of that insight is Rabbi Dessler's "*Kuntras HaChessed* — Essay on Lovingkindness."

Or consider the battlefield imagery with which Rabbi Dessler describes the *nekudas habechirah* (the point of free will) in his *Kuntras HaBechirah* — "Essay on Free Will." Each person has those areas that no longer represent a challenge for him, and in which he can be reasonably confident that his *yetzer hara* will not prevail. Those areas are conquered territory far behind the front lines and removed from the battlefield. At the same time, each person has those areas which are beyond his capacity to exercise his free will. They can be viewed as deep in enemy territory.

Meanwhile the battlefront is constantly shifting, and it is along the constantly moving battlefront that one truly exercises free will, for there the apprehension of the truth is in delicately balanced equipoise with the siren call of the *yetzer*. Having read Rabbi Dessler's description, one can never again visualize the exercise of free will in the same way.

Rabbi Dessler's influence extended far beyond particular ideas or means of conceptualizing those ideas. He introduced the *Maharal's* in-depth approach to *Aggadata*, which finds meaning in precise analysis of every word of *Chazal*, into the world of the yeshivos, and thereby shaped the method of learning *Aggadata* in the yeshivos.

Among his rules for learning *Aggadata* was that whenever we find an apparent argument between two Sages in a matter of *Aggadata* we are really being presented with the same truth from two vantage points. Rather than contradicting one another, the two views complement each other, and must be understood in conjunction with one another. After Rabbi Dessler, this approach has come to dominate all subsequent discussions of *Aggadata*.

But Rabbi Dessler was not just a thinker. He was one of the leading builders of Torah institutions in our time. Just as it is said of the Chofetz Chaim that his *tzidkus* (righteousness) obscured his greatness as a *talmid chacham*, so has Rabbi Dessler's greatness as a thinker caused us to lose sight of his concrete achievements as a builder of institutions.

The Gateshead Kollel, which became the training ground for almost every great Western European *talmid chacham*, was his creation, forged out of his willingness to undertake a superhuman schedule. That schedule required him to be at once the sole fundraiser for the Kollel and its spiritual guide.

A few years after the establishment of the Kollel, Rabbi Dessler played a crucial role in the founding of the Gateshead Teachers Seminary, through whose portals thousands of girls have passed under the direction of those hand-picked by Rabbi Dessler.

Having done so much to alter the status of Torah learning in England, Rabbi Dessler did the same as *Mashgiach* of Ponevezh Yeshiva in Bnei Brak. When he arrived in *Eretz Yisrael* in 1949, yeshiva students in the country numbered in the hundreds, not in the tens of thousands as today. As *Mashgiach* of *Eretz Yisrael's* largest and most prominent yeshiva, the vision of Torah learning that he introduced into the Ponevezh *beis medrash* inevitably had a major impact on the entire Torah world of *Eretz Yisrael*. His *talmidim* from that period were the first generation of the modern yeshiva world in *Eretz Yisrael* — Israeli-born sons of largely European parents.

The ultimate reason for a biography of Rabbi Dessler, however, is not his greatness as a thinker alone nor his historical impact alone. But rather the way thought and life illuminate one another. He himself was an exemplar of the *mussar* ideals of Kelm in which he was raised and which continued to exercise a powerful hold on him the rest of his life.

Rabbi Dessler's unremitting efforts to lay the foundations for today's yeshiva world in England and *Eretz Yisrael* and his own willingness to travel anywhere to spread knowledge of Torah were not unrelated to his thought. They were a direct outgrowth of his teachings on the relationship of the individual and the *klal* (community), and the need of the individual to submit himself to the needs of the *klal*. In the wake of the Holocaust, he burned with the feeling that individual life no longer existed. For him, the question confronting every Jew who escaped the fires was: For what purpose did Hashem spare me?

Many of the crucial categories of Rabbi Dessler's thought found their most concrete realization in his own person. He divided mankind, for instance, into "givers" and "takers," And his own life — his letters, the way he related to *talmidim*, his service to strangers, his dedication to the *klal* — provides a clear example of all that was implied, for him, in being a "giver."

The mark of a *sefer kodesh*, a holy book, writes Rabbi Tzadok HaKohen of Lublin, is that it and its author are one. The work represents not just the ideas of the author or the fruits of his research; it is him. If we are to fully understand the *kedushah* (holiness) of *Michtav M'Eliyahu* and why it has had such an enduring impact on our generation, we must know its author.

Chapter 1

Childhood

SOME HAVE TO CLIMB THE MOUNTAIN; SOME ARE BORN on the summit.¹ Rabbi Eliyahu Eliezer Dessler was born on the top of the mountain.

He was both a biological and spiritual great-grandson of Rabbi Yisrael Salanter, founder of the 19th-century movement of ethical and spiritual revival known as the Mussar movement. His mother, Henne Freidel, was the daughter of Reb Yisrael's daughter Malke Hinde and Rabbi Eliyahu Eliezer Grodnensky, one of the leading *dayanim* of Vilna.²

On his paternal side, Rabbi Dessler was a direct spiritual descendant of Reb Yisrael. His father, Rabbi Reuven Dov Dessler, was one

---

1. The *Chiddushei HaRim*, the first Gerrer Rebbe, is said to have used this metaphor to describe the position of his grandson and successor, the *Sefas Emes*, when the latter was a young boy.

2. Rabbi Grodnensky was appointed as a *dayan* in Vilna at the tender age of 25. He commanded the respect of leaders of his generation, as evidenced by his inclusion in a delegation of leading rabbis sent to defend the *cheder* system before the Czar in 1870. Upon his death in 1887, he was succeeded on the Vilna *beis din* by his son-in-law Rabbi Chaim Ozer Grodzenski. *Rabbi Nachum Velvel Dessler, Ilana D'Chaye (Hebrew)*, p. 79.

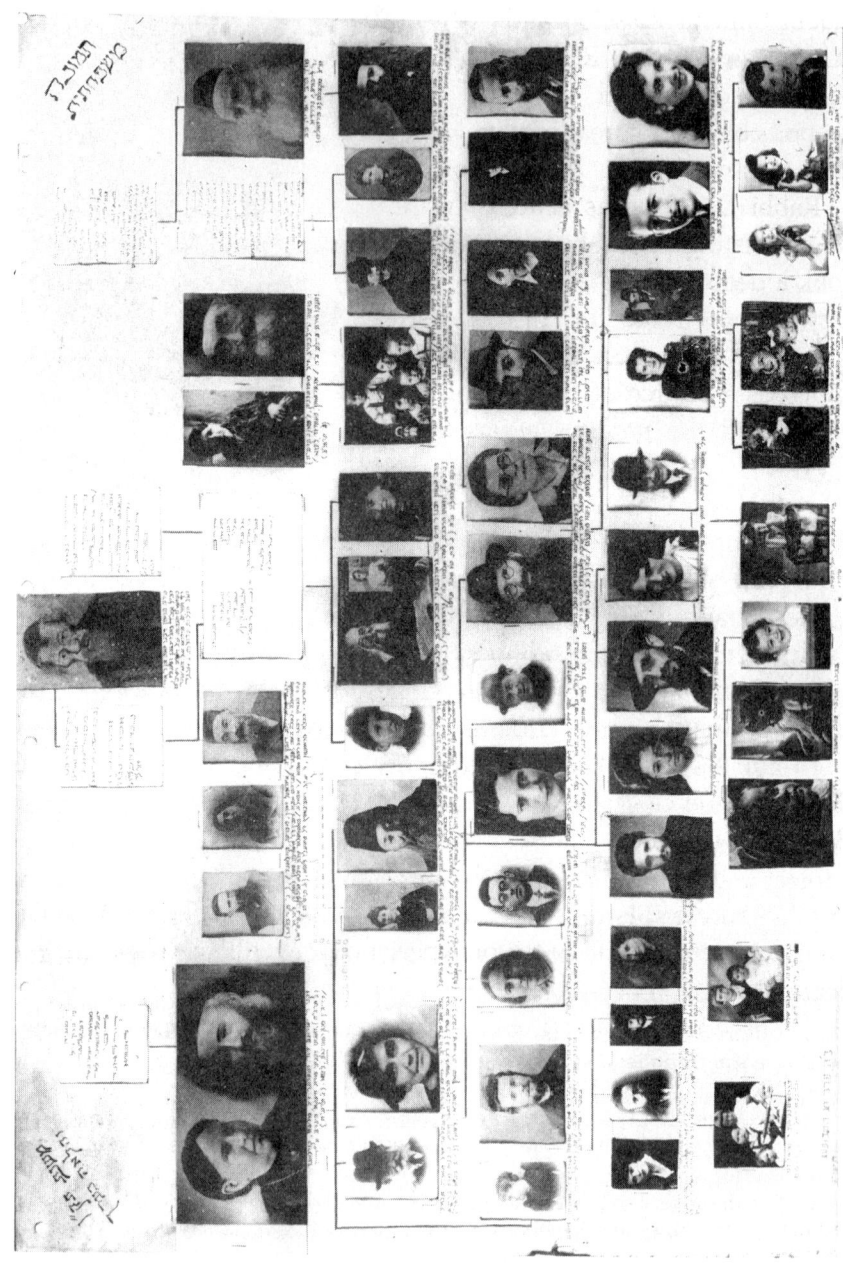

The Dessler family tree

of the closest *talmidim* of the Alter of Kelm, Rabbi Simcha Zissel Braude (Ziv). The Alter was, in turn, Reb Yisrael's foremost disciple and the one most responsible for spreading his master's *mussar* ideals.

Rabbi Dessler was acutely aware of his distinguished lineage, and he took a deep interest in family genealogy.[3] Knowledge of his ancestry, however, was not a point of pride so much as a source of obligation. Thus he mentioned the family's *yichus* (ancestry) to his children with some frequency as a prod to spiritual striving, but only rarely referred to it outside the family.[4] All his life, Rabbi Dessler guarded himself vigilantly against any feeling of pride at having been born on the spiritual mountain peak and the complacency that might follow from such pride. In both in his public teaching and in his private correspondence, he stressed that anything that a person does as a matter of course because he was born into a spiritually elevated family confers no merit upon him. To one of the closest of his students in London, Solomon (Sliman) Sassoon, he wrote:

R' Zev Wolf Lipkin, father of R' Yisrael Salanter

> And if it is true [that a person is not punished for actions over which he does not experience free will], is it not equally

---

3. Rabbi Dessler himself did much of the extensive genealogical research found in *Ilana D'Chaye*, a genealogy of the Dessler family published by his son, Rabbi Nachum Velvel Dessler, Founder and Dean of the Hebrew Academy of Cleveland.

4. Rabbi Nachum Velvel Dessler.
The portraits of five people hung in Rabbi Dessler's home in London: Rabbi Zev Wolf Lipkin, father of Rabbi Yisrael Salanter and *av beis din* of Goldingen and Telshe; Rabbi Tzvi Hirsch Braude, the Alter of Kelm's son-in-law and successor; Rabbi Nachum Velvel Ziv, the Alter's son and father of Rebbetzin Dessler; Rabbi Reuven Dov Dessler, Rabbi Dessler's father; and Rabbi Chaim Ozer Grodzenski, the *gadol hador* until his passing in 1940. (Reb Chaim Ozer's first wife, Leah Alte, was the older sister of Rabbi Dessler's mother.) Even when his students asked about the pictures, Rabbi Dessler never mentioned that he was closely related to all of them. *Rabbi Mordechai Miller.*

Chapter One: Childhood / 13

true of the reward for *mitzvos?* Why should there be reward for that which comes without effort? ... Therefore one who is trained to a certain level of observance and did not struggle to reach it has no reward coming to him.

Accordingly, a person may think to himself confidently that he is coming to the Day of Judgment with a large store of *mitzvos* to his credit, and find that they are not to his credit but to the credit of his parents who trained him that way.[5]

Nothing posed a greater threat to true spiritual growth, in his mind, than satisfaction with a spiritual level that one had not attained through one's own efforts. "The *yetzer* allows a person to do many *mitzvos,*" he wrote to students in Gateshead Seminary, "as long as they do not rise above the level of *mitzvos anoshim mlumoda* (rote actions), for such acts do not involve anything of truth."

The Dessler Family

THE DESSLERS WERE FOR MANY GENERATIONS WELL-TO-DO merchants. The family name derived from an ancestor who owned a large tract of land in Dessel, a village not far from the Baltic port of Libau. Known in Libau as *"der Desseler,"* he adopted the name when the Czar required Jews to choose last names.[6]

Rabbi Dessler's grandfather Rabbi Yisrael David Dessler and great-uncle Reb Eliezer were successful businessmen and well-known philanthropists in Libau. Both personified the type of *"baalebatim"* that it was the purpose of the Mussar movement to create — men widely conversant in Torah and imbued with a deep *yiras Shamayim* (Fear of Heaven), who nevertheless supported themselves from their own labor.[7]

Near the end of his life, Rabbi Dessler's father, Reb Reuven Dov,

---

5. *Michtav Me'Eliyahu,* Vol. IV, p. 322.
6. Rabbi Nachum Velvel Dessler, *Ilana D'Chaye,* p. 79.
7. Rabbi Yisrael Salanter knew that Eastern European Jewry would continue to produce great rabbinic leaders. What he feared was the disappearance of learned *baalebatim,* steeped in *mussar.* The *mussar kloizen* (houses of *mussar*) he established were designed to produce such *baalebatim.* Rabbi Dov Katz, *Tenuas HaMussar,* Vol. II, pp. 22-23; Katz, Vol. V. p. 125.

Yisrael David and Chinka Hinde Dessler

wrote a letter to his brother Reb Chaim Gedaliah in which he described their father Yisrael David and mother Chinka Hinde as "spiritually elevated, lovers of *chesed*, and G-d-fearing."[8]

When the Alter of Kelm opened up his Talmud Torah in 1875 in Grubin, a small town not far from Libau, the Dessler brothers were among his leading supporters. Reb Eliezer purchased the fine building housing the Talmud Torah and its extensive grounds for 11,000 rubles.[9] Rabbi Yisrael David Dessler was also close to the Alter. When a life-threatening heart condition forced the Alter to return to Kelm in 1881, he entrusted Reb Yisrael David with the mission of going to Rabbi Yisrael Salanter for guidance as to the future of the Talmud Torah. Previously, Reb Yisrael had told his leading disciple that the Talmud Torah, with its combination of *limudei kodesh* and general studies, could only exist under the Alter's direct supervision. Without the Alter's emphasis on *mussar* and *yiras Shamayim* (Fear of Heaven), Reb Yisrael warned, the Talmud Torah might pro-

---

8. Rabbi Eliyahu Eliezer Dessler, ed., *Kisvei HaSaba Mi'Kelm* (Hebrew), Vol. II, p. 576; Katz, Vol. V, p. 125.

9. Katz, Vol. II, p. 56.
 The Alter refused to take the building and its surrounding grounds as an outright gift, and accepted it only on the condition that it revert to the donor if the Talmud Torah closed down, as it eventually did in 1886.

Chapter One: Childhood

R' Yisrael David and Chinka Hinde (L) with R' Reuven Dov and Henne holding young Elya Lazer Dessler

duce a Golden Calf. Nevertheless, Reb Yisrael urged the Alter to continue to supervise the Talmud Torah from afar rather than close it completely. The closure, he said, would be a disaster comparable to the destruction of the *Beis HaMikdash*.[10]

The Talmud Torah in Grubin was expressly designed to produce *baalebatim* in the mold envisioned by Rabbi Yisrael Salanter, and most of the students were drawn from wealthy families like the Desslers. It was thus natural for Rabbi Yisrael David Dessler to not only support the Talmud Torah, but to entrust his sons' education to the Alter. Reuven Dov Dessler attended the Talmud Torah from its opening in 1875, when he was 12, until its closing in 1886. His younger brother Chaim Gedaliah, ten years his junior, joined him later.[11]

Though Grubin produced a number of outstanding *talmidim*, none was closer to the Alter than Rabbi Reuven Dov Dessler. The Alter of Kelm described him as the greatest of his *talmidim* in *yiras Shamayim*, and said that all his efforts in Grubin were worthwhile to have produced one Reuven Dov Dessler.[12] Towards the end of Grubin's existence, Reb Reuven Dov was already playing an administrative role in the institution.

---

10. Ibid., pp. 57-58; Ibid., Vol. V, p. 126.
11. Ibid., p. 126.
12. Ibid., p. 129.

Reb Reuven Dov was one of a secret group of veteran *talmidim* organized by the Alter known as הד״ט — הדבק טוב (tightly bound). The group included Rabbi Tzvi Hirsch Braude, the Alter's son-in-law and successor, Rabbi Nachum Velvel Ziv, the Alter's son, and Rabbi Sender Lipkin, a nephew of Rabbi Yisrael Salanter. The members pledged to strengthen one another in learning Torah in depth and the study of *mussar*.[13] Each undertook to learn at least half an hour of *mussar* a day and to have fixed learning times for *Orach Chaim*[14] and *Tomer Devorah*.[15] Every tenth day after Yom Kippur *(Yom Asiri Kodesh)* was to be devoted exclusively to holy pursuits. The Alter promulgated a series of requirements to ensure that this purpose was fulfilled.[16]

In addition, the members agreed to gather at least once a year "to rejoice in the gathering of brothers together" and to send written self-critiques dealing with how well they had fulfilled their common undertakings to a central headquarters at least once a month.

After the closing of Grubin in 1886, Reb Reuven Dov followed his master to Kelm where he continued to study under the Alter until marrying in 1891. By the time his only child Eliyahu Eliezer (named after his maternal grandfather) was born 16 *Sivan*, 5652 (1892), Reb Reuven Dov had already embarked upon a business career, in accord with the cardinal Kelm principle that one should not be dependent on Torah study for one's livelihood.

The Dessler Home

CONCRETE FACTS ABOUT THE EARLY YEARS OF ELYA LAZER, as he was known in the family, are almost totally lacking. Like his father before him, he was born in Libau. His mother passed away when he was only two and a half years old, and he had few, if any, memories of her.

---

13. Ibid., Vol. II, pp. 63-64.

14. The section of *Shulchan Aruch* dealing with the daily obligations of a Jew.

15. *Tomer Devorah* was written by the great Kabbalist Rabbi Moshe Cordevero of Tzefat, and delineates thirteen aspects of Hashem's *chesed* with mankind. The Alter particularly loved *Tomer Devorah* for its detailed description of the ways in which Jews are called upon to emulate the *chesed* of *HaKadosh Baruch Hu*, and he learned it every day. Katz, Vol. II, p. 110.

16. Ibid., p. 31.

Young Elya Lazer being held by his mother

Fortunately for him, his father married again while he was still young. His stepmother Fruma Rachel was the daughter of Rabbi Yaakov Rabinowitz, one of the leading citizens of Telshe. She never had children of her own and raised Elya Lazer as if he were her own son. Rabbi Dessler always referred to her lovingly as "my mother and teacher, who raised me with the love of a real mother"[17] or simply as "mother, the *tzadekas* (righteous woman)."[18]

When Elya Lazer was 7 or 8, the Dessler family moved to Homel (or Gomel in Russian) on the border between the Ukraine and White Russia. There Reb Reuven Dov entered into a very successful partnership with his brother Reb Chaim Gedaliah — first as timber merchants and later in the export-import of precious metals.

To the outside world, the Dessler brothers' appeared as prosperous businessmen, mixing easily with other businessmen, both Jewish and gentile. Yet even their business was run in a way that reflected the highest ethical aspirations of the Mussar movement. Each brother took from the business only what he needed for his living expenses. Thus Reb Reuven Dov, who had only one child, took less from the business than Reb Gedaliah, who had five children. The leftover business profits were then devoted primarily to communal *tzedakah* needs.

Fruma Rachel Dessler

The Dessler brothers' *tzedakah* activities were extensive. In addition to their support

---

17. *Michtav Me'Eliyahu*, Vol. V, p. 534.
18. Ibid., Vol. I, p. 25.

for the Kelm Talmud Torah, they themselves founded a part-time yeshiva in Homel for working boys called *Tiferes Bachurim* and supplied kosher food to Jewish soldiers stationed near Homel. During World War I, both brothers and their wives went to great efforts to aid the refugees who poured into Homel. Rabbi Gedaliah Dessler's wife Bertha spent her days tending to typhus victims. Neighbors were shocked when she took the family of Rabbi Yaakov Katz into her home after Rebbetzin Katz died of typhus.

Meanwhile, Reb Reuven Dov housed Rabbi Katz's entire yeshiva from Klikel, Latvia in his home. Rabbi Chaim Ozer Grodzenski and Rabbi Elchonon Wasserman were among the luminaries who stayed with the Dessler brothers for extended periods of time during the war.

Reb Reuven Dov and Reb Gedaliah also established an armaments factory in Tula, in which they employed yeshiva students, who were thereby able to obtain draft deferments because they were working in the defense industry.[19]

The two brothers were extremely close. They lived in adjacent homes, married half sisters, and learned together for hours every day. Towards the end of his life, Reb Reuven Dov sent Reb Gedaliah a letter summarizing their joint activities over a period of forty years. In that letter, he expressed his joy that "there was almost never any separation between us in thought, ... and we helped one another to realize our goals." He also celebrated the fact that their Talmud learning had never become something matter of fact.[20]

In one of his few reminiscences from his childhood, Rabbi Dessler describes the devotion to learning of his father and uncle:

> I remember how, when I was a boy of nine, my revered father and my uncle Gedaliah (may the memory of both those *tzaddikim* be blessed) used to get up around midnight on those long winter Friday nights, and learn Torah together for

---

19. Devora Dessler Olshtein, "A Baal Mussar from Kelm, a Businessman in Pre-war Europe," in *Torah Lives*, Rabbi Nisson Wolpin ed., [N.Y., Mesorah Publications], pp. 123-24; see also Olshtein, *Zichronos Chayai*, pp. 8-11.
20. *Kisvei HaSaba Mi'Kelem*, Vol. II, p. 576.

about nine hours at a stretch, until the morning service. And I used to get up early and learn with my rebbi for a few hours. Mother (that *tzadekes* of blessed memory) used to get up too, and she would study *Midrash, Ramban,* and *Malbim* on the weekly *Sidra*. When she came down it was like a *Yom Tov* for me, for she used to serve us cups of steaming hot coffee accompanied by some very hot and delicious latkes.[21]

Except for that one brief reminiscence, Rabbi Dessler provided few glimpses of his early childhood.[22] Beyond the bare facts already recorded, we have only surmise, conjecture, and extrapolation based on our knowledge of the Dessler family and the *mussar* tradition in which it was steeped.

Though Rabbi Dessler left no account of his childhood, his younger cousin Devora Dessler Olshtein has written at length of her childhood growing up in the house of Rabbi Gedaliah Dessler. Given the exceptional closeness of Reb Reuven Dov and Reb Gedaliah, it is reasonable to assume that Mrs. Olshtein's description of her home largely accords with that in which Elya Lazer grew up.

Despite their wealth and large homes, the Dessler brothers did not live luxuriously. Money meant little to them, as they both proved later in life when reduced to poverty and forced to live with crushing debts.[23]

---

21. *Michtav Me'Eliyahu,* Vol. I, p. 25; Rabbi Aryeh Carmell, *Strive for Truth,* Vol. I, pp. 97-98. [*Strive for Truth* is Rabbi Carmell's adaption into English of Rabbi Dessler's *Michtav Me'Eliyahu.*]

22. Rabbi Dessler himself rarely spoke about his personal life. If he told stories at all, he preferred to speak about the Alter of Kelm or of great figures he had known.
See Katz, Vol. II, pp. 27, 37, 57, 58, and 60, for examples of stories about the Alter that Rabbi Dessler heard from his father. For stories Rabbi Dessler told about his father-in-law, Rabbi Nachum Velvel Ziv, see ibid., pp. 78, 84.

23. The strength of character of both brothers was severely tested from the Bolshevik Revolution until the end of their lives. Poverty, imprisonment, illness, and the loss of spouses in tragic circumstances were just some of the trials they endured.
During his year of imprisonment by the Bolshevik regime, Reb Gedaliah lived on the most meager diet. Yet when he was transferred from one prison to another on Shabbos, he used a food package that had just arrived from his family to bribe a non-Jewish guard to carry his *tefillin, tallis,* and *siddur* to the new prison. Devorah Dessler Olshtein, "A Baal Mussar from Kelm, a Businessman in Pre-War Europe," in *Torah Lives,* Rabbi Nisson Wolpin, ed., p. 126-27. [The article in *Torah Lives* is adapted from Mrs. Olshtein's Hebrew language memoir *Zichronos Chayai.*]

The food was simple and children were expected to eat what they were served. If they did not, they knew they would have to wait until the next meal.[24]

The first sound Devora Dessler heard when she woke in the morning was that of her father's *Gemara niggun,* and it was the last sound that accompanied her to sleep as well. Reb Gedaliah *davened* every morning at 6:30 a.m., and learned after the minyan until 12:30 p.m. He never ate until the end of his morning learning, and every Monday and Thursday he fasted the entire day.[25]

Reb Gedaliah's children saw him primarily at the family dinner at 1 p.m. and over long Shabbos meals. Even during the week, the dinner-table conversation centered on the weekly Torah reading, various *mitzvos,* or something that Reb Gedaliah had learned that morning. Neither business or politics were ever discussed at the table. Reb Gedaliah did not even mention his *chesed* activities, most of which the children only learned about from others after he had passed away.[26]

Discipline in the house was strict, but enforcement was rarely required. A look from Reb Gedaliah was enough to cause his children to cease and desist from any untoward behavior. If punishment was necessary, Reb Gedaliah waited a full day before meting it out so that the anticipation was worse than the punishment itself. Once one of Reb Gedaliah's sons hit his brother, and the result was a two-hour lecture from their father.

Reb Gedaliah's children led a sheltered existence in Homel. There were few religious children to play with so they were limited to playing with one another.[27] Elya Lazer did not even have siblings to play with and was considerably older than his cousins. His childhood, one suspects, was spent almost entirely in the company of adults.

---

24. *Zichronos Chayai,* p. 13.
25. "A Baal Mussar from Kelm, a Businessman in Pre-War Europe," in *Torah Lives,* op. cit., pp. 127-28.
26. *Zichronos Chayai,* pp. 12-13.
27. Ibid., p. 7.

THE TOWERING *MUSSAR* PERSONALITY OF HIS FATHER WAS undoubtedly the primary influence of Elya Lazer's early years. Though we do not possess Rabbi Dessler's letters to his father after leaving Homel for Kelm, even the many letters of his middle age, written from England, reveal his exceptional respect for his father and the closeness between the two. A typical letter to his father might begin with ten expressions of honor.[28] Yet the simple phrase "who has showered upon me goodness beyond measure from my birth until today," contained in one salutation,[29] by itself summed up Rabbi Dessler's deep sense of indebtedness to his father.

His Father's Influence

R' Reuven Dov Dessler

Rabbi Dessler's letters to his father are full of praise for the words of *mussar* contained in his father's epistles, and he beseeches his father to write frequently — at least twice a week.[30] The "discoveries" in *hashkafah* that gave Rabbi Dessler such pleasure during the early years of solitude in London were inevitably conveyed to his father.

The Alter of Kelm stressed that proper *chinuch* (training) begins from a very early age,[31] and we can be sure that his disciple Reb Reuven Dov closely supervised his son's education and spared neither expense nor effort on his son's education. In a 1929 letter from London to his father in Kelm, Rabbi Dessler protested his father's refusal to accept money that he had sent him: "Are the treasure chests of money that you spent so freely on my behalf from youth nothing? Is it written anywhere in *Shas* (the Talmud) that a father is

---

28. A typical example: אל הוד הדרת כבוד אדוני אבי מורי ורבי, מטיבי טובות נצח, מזה שנאמר בו דא קנית כולא קנית. *Michtav Me'Eliyahu*, Vol. III, p. 328.

29. Ibid., p. 309.

30. Ibid., Vol. V, p. 504.

31. The Alter claimed to have once noticed an improper love of money in one of his young children, and immediately set out to uproot this trait. Katz, Vol. II, p. 75.

required to spend fortunes on the education of his son?"³²

The Desslers *davened* in the Chabad *shtibel* in Homel because the *nusach Ashkenazi shuls* were subject to frequent disturbances by the socialist Bund.³³

During his formative years in Homel, Rabbi Dessler studied with Reb Mordechai Yoel, one of the best-known authorities on the writings of Reb Shneur Zalman of Liadi.³⁴

R' Gedaliah Dessler

It is probable that his vast knowledge in the books of Chassidic Masters has its origin in this studies relationship.

While Elya Lazer's spiritual growth remained in his father's hands, his formal studies were largely under the supervision of tutors. Those studies were patterned on the curriculum of Grubin — intense *limudei kodesh* combined with an exposure to mathematics,

---

32. *Michtav Me'Eliyahu*, Vol. V, p. 503.

Rabbi Dessler did not content himself with protesting his indebtedness to his father, but argued on halachic grounds that he was obligated to return monies his father had spent on his education when he was wealthy now that he was living in poverty. Both the *Rosh* and *Rashba* rule that if a rich man gives money to *tzedakah* (communal charity) and then loses his money, *tzedakah* must provide him with enough money to live, because there is an implied condition in the original gift. There is even more reason for implying such a condition in the case of money spent by a father on a son, Rabbi Dessler argued, since the son's obligation to his father is a natural one felt by all human beings.

33. Rabbi Aharon Sorasky, *Marbitzei Torah U'Mussar*, Vol. III, p. 53.

34. Heard from Rabbi Dessler by Rabbi Dovid Tzvi Hillman, one of his *talmidim* in Ponevezh Yeshiva.

35. Rabbi Dessler told Professor Zev Lev that he had once found himself together in a train cabin with a Turkish Jew. Between them they spoke 13 languages, but could not find one in common.

Rabbi Dessler was fluent in written and spoken Yiddish, Hebrew, and English. He also knew Russian and German, both of which were included in the curriculum of Grubin, and which would have proven useful for one being groomed to follow in his father's footsteps in international commerce.

R' Chaim Ozer Grodzenski as a young man

languages (of which Rabbi Dessler spoke many fluently[35]), and some of the classics of world literature.[36] Eventually private tutors proved inadequate to provide the young boy what he needed in his studies. Early in life, he already demonstrated remarkable powers of concentration and an unusual depth of thought. His uncle Rabbi Chaim Ozer Grodzenski pronounced him a wonder child, and attempted to send him suitable tutors from Vilna. When Rabbi Reuven Dov Dessler found heretical books in the possession of one of those tutors, he realized that the time had come to part with his beloved son and send him to yeshiva.[37] Reb Reuven Dov was far too rooted in Kelm to consider any other yeshiva for Elya Lazer. Thus it was that Elya Lazer found himself bound for Kelm and the company of mature scholars shortly after his *bar mitzvah*.

---

36. Rabbi Aryeh Carmell.
   Rabbi Dessler's early general education served him well later in life. Almost all the young men he taught in London were headed toward university or other advanced secular training, and his own familiarity with some of the subject matter they were studying made it easier for him to answer the issues raised by their secular educations. Throughout his life, Rabbi Dessler's deeply philosophical approach drew many intellectuals to his lectures. Part of his attraction surely lay in the fact that he could speak their language with ease.

37. *Marbitzei Torah U'Mussar*, Vol. III, pp. 54-55.

Chapter 2
Arrival in Kelm

ELYA LAZER ARRIVED IN KELM, TOGETHER WITH HIS father, two days before *Rosh Chodesh Shevat* 5666 (1906). He had likely been in Kelm several times previously. Reb Reuven Dov returned to Kelm every *Elul*, and it would have been natural for him to take his only child with him on those visits. But there was obviously a world of difference between coming to Kelm together with one's father and as a *talmid* of the Talmud Torah.

Just past the age of *bar mitzvah* and never having learned a single day in a yeshiva, Elya Lazer found himself suddenly thrust into a world of mature scholars. From the closing of Grubin in 1886, the Kelm Talmud Torah served as a finishing school for the perfection of *middos*. Though most of the day was spent learning *Gemara*, there were no regular *shiurim*, as in other yeshivos. Kelm was designed for those who had already attained an advanced level in learning. Of the 25 to 35 scholars learning full time in the *Beis HaTalmud*, many, and perhaps most, were already married, and a man of 28 was not yet considered an *alter bachur* (an older unmarried student).[1] To appear older than his years, Elya Lazer tried wearing clothes usually worn by older *bachurim*. But his suit and wide-brimmed hat were a poor fit for his diminutive frame and did little to conceal his youth.[2]

Whatever he had heard of Kelm from his father, Elya Lazer still had a lot to learn. Shortly after he arrived, he found a room, which he proceeded to decorate to his satisfaction. Apparently his actions did not meet with approval — likely he had shown too much concern with his physical surroundings for the austere tastes of Kelm — and he received a long lecture.[3] Elya Lazer was used to learning alone in a loud voice. Rabbi Isaac Sher, the future Slabodka Rosh Yeshiva, put a stop to that, and told him to learn quietly so as not to disturb others.[4]

Reb Reuven Dov had arranged for Elya Lazer to take his meals with Rebbetzin Nechama Liba Braude, the Alter's daughter and wife of the Rosh Yeshiva Rabbi Tzvi Hirsch Braude. The first day she served him a tasteless porridge, and she continued to do so every day for years. That was his introduction to the Kelm practice of *shviras haratzon*, breaking one's desires. Years later, Rabbi Dessler would remark that she had certainly succeeded in one respect: Thereafter any food he ate always tasted wonderful.[5]

---

1. Rabbi Mordechai Zuckerman.

   No precise information exists on the number of *talmidim*, their age, or marital status at the time of Rabbi Dessler's arrival in Kelm. What information we possess is from the few remaining survivors of pre-Holocaust Kelm. Nevertheless it is clear that Kelm was always designed for mature scholars.

   Though the original Talmud Torah in Kelm, and later that in Grubin (see Chap. 3), were primarily for teenage students, from the time of the Alter's return to Kelm in 1886, he accepted only more mature students. In one of his lectures, he stated:

   > I do not accept very young people into the yeshiva any more. They cling too much to the concepts of their childhood and can never quite relinquish them. Even if a younger student were to learn more profound matters in the yeshiva, he would always reduce them to the concepts with which he came to us.

   Rabbi Elchonon Blumenthal, Trials and Challenges, p. 319. Rabbi Blumenthal learned in Kelm for a year in the late '30s.

2. Rabbi Aharon Sorasky, *Marbitzei Torah U'Mussar*, Vol. III, p. 55.

3. Heard from Rabbi Dessler by Rabbi Betzalel Rakov, *rav* of Gateshead, England. Rabbi Rakov recalls that the lecture was delivered by Rabbi Nachum Velvel Ziv, Rabbi Dessler's future father-in-law.

4. Ibid.

5. Rabbi Aryeh Carmell.

However difficult the initial adjustment, Elya Lazer soon found his way. In Kelm, his very soul was forged. As he wrote to his daughter on the eve of World War II, "I had the great privilege of sitting in the House of Hashem for eighteen years. Anything I have within me is from there ... Every hair, every fibre is connected to that place."[6]

Kelm — The Town

KELM WAS TYPICAL OF THE SMALL JEWISH TOWNS THAT DOTTED northwest Lithuania. An 1897 census put the town's population at 3,914, including 2,710 Jews.[7] The center of town, except for the public buildings, was almost exclusively Jewish, with Lithuanians living on the periphery and in the surrounding countryside. Most contact between Jews and non-Jews came on Thursday market day when Lithuanian peasants from the surrounding rural areas came to town to sell their cows, milk, vegetables, chickens, eggs, and grain and to buy whatever they needed from local Jewish shopkeepers.[8]

Life was primitive and rough — probably not so different from what it had been a hundred years earlier. Most Jews lived in simple log cabins with either straw or tin roofs and without any indoor plumbing. One either drew water from the well oneself or paid water-carriers to bring it. Not until the mid-1920s would the homes in Kelm be electrified.[9] A large stove in the middle of each house was used both for cooking and for heating during the bitter cold Lithuanian winters. All family members had to sleep with their bedroom doors open to benefit from the heat of the stove, which had generally burned out by midnight and remained that way until the first intrepid family member got out of bed early in the morning to fuel and light the stove again.[10]

---

6. Letter to his daughter Hennie, who was visiting relatives in Kelm in 1939. *Michtav Me'Eliyahu*, Vol. IV, p. 330.

7. Ida Marcus-Karbolnik and Bat-Sheva Levitan-Karbolnik, *Kelm — Eitz Karus* (Hebrew), p. 1.

8. "Reminiscences of Rebbetzin Zlata Levenstein Ginsburg" in *The World That Was: Lithuania*, Rabbi Yitzchak Kasnett ed., p. 65.

9. Ibid., pp. 66-8.
    Even then, the electricity was turned off every night at midnight. *Rabbi Nachum Velvel Dessler.*

10. "Reminiscences of Rebbetzin Zlata Levenstein Ginsburg," op. cit., p. 67.

Chapter Two: Arrival in Kelm

Except for the main highway that passed through Kelm and joined Shavel to the east and Tavrig (near the German border) to the west, the streets were unpaved. Sidewalks typically consisted of two wooden planks placed side by side. Much of the year, descent from the sidewalk meant stepping into mud.[11]

Economically, Kelm Jewry may have been slightly more secure than Jews in many similar small towns, but poverty was widespread. There were many families in which chicken and meat were unknown even for Shabbos, and there were even families in which sisters might share one pair of shoes.[12] Most Jews made their living selling clothing, footwear, or small household items to the surrounding peasantry and to their fellow Jews. Butchers, bakers, carpenters, glass-cutters, hat-makers, house-painters, tailors, and small foodstores primarily serviced the Jewish community.[13]

By the '20s, there were a handful of small Jewish-owned factories producing tin products and the like. Perhaps an equal number of Jews had acquired agricultural land for farming. By that time, Jews also controlled much of the transport industry, including buses travelling between Germany and Latvia and trucks to transport goods.[14]

Undistinguished as it was physically or economically from dozens of other small Lithuanian villages, Kelm was known for its Torah learning and piety. To be the *rav* of Kelm was considered a mark of distinction in the world of Lithuanian *rabbanus*. In his memoirs of life in Kelm from 1858 to 1906, Eliezer Eliyahu Friedman wrote that there was not one true *am ha'aretz* in the entire town in his day.[15]

Most of the more financially secure Jews were steeped in Talmudic learning. Even among those engaged in demanding physical labor, there were many who went to shul after work to learn

---

11. "Reminiscences of Rabbi Nachum Velvel Dessler," in *The World That Was: Lithuania*, Rabbi Yitzchak Kasnett, ed., p. 58.
12. Olshtein, *Zichronos Chayai*, p. 25.
13. *Kelm — Eitz Karus*, pp. 25-26.
14. Ibid., pp. 21, 25-6.
15. Ibid., p. 26.

Talmud. Those who did not learn Talmud were likely to attend one of the daily *shiurim* in *Mishnayos, Ein Yaakov, Chayei Adam*, or *Menoras HaMeor*.[16]

During the lifetime of the Alter, men and women did not walk on the same side of the street, and that custom may still have been in effect when Elya Lazer arrived in 1906.[17] Even in the '20s, every man in town still wore a head covering of some kind, and on Shabbos many wore top hats.[18]

The Beis Haknesses in Kelm

Kelm is, of course, best known as the home of the Alter of Kelm and his Talmud Torah. Yet Kelm's reputation as a town of Torah study and piety was well established prior to the Talmud Torah, and the town continued to produce outstanding religious personalities not directly associated with the Talmud Torah. The Kelmer Maggid, Rabbi Moshe Yitzchak Darshan, was perhaps the most famous *maggid* of his time. A *talmid* of Rabbi Yisrael Salanter, he traveled from town to town giving ecstatic sermons, filled with vivid, poetic imagery, and frequently biting wit.[19]

The Alter himself said of another contemporary, Reb Leib Chassid, "the title *tzaddik* befits him." Shortly before his death in Koenigsberg, Rabbi Yisrael Salanter came to Kelm, and he made a special point of going to visit Reb Leib Chassid, about whom he had heard a great deal. Reb Leib Chassid did not recognize his guest, and after a while excused himself on the grounds that the

---

16. Ibid., pp. 26-27; "Reminiscences of Rabbi Nachum Velvel Dessler," op. cit., p. 58.
17. Ibid., p. 57.
18. *Kelm — Eitz Karus* p. 6.
19. Ibid., p. 45.

Chapter Two: Arrival in Kelm

great *gaon* and *tzaddik* Rabbi Yisrael Salanter was coming to town and he wanted to greet him. Reb Yisrael replied, "He's neither such a *gaon* or *tzaddik*." Horrified, Reb Leib Chassid told him, "I don't know who you are. But you must not talk that way."[20] Rabbi Ber Hirsch Heller, the *Mashgiach* in Slabodka Yeshiva, once passed through Kelm and decided to avail himself of the opportunity to visit Reb Leib Chassid. He was greeted with such an effusion of joy that it was obvious to him that he had been mistaken for an old acquaintance. Only later did he learn that Reb Leib Chassid greeted everyone in this fashion. The next time he planned to be in Kelm, Reb Ber Hirsch gave advance notice of his intention to visit, and this time he found Reb Leib dressed in Shabbos clothing, new sand spread on the earth floor, and candles lit on the table. "Greeting a guest is greater than greeting the *Shechinah*," Reb Leib explained. "Whatever we do for Shabbos we should certainly do for a guest."[21]

R' Zelig Tarshish

Both the Kelmer Maggid and Reb Leib Chassid passed away before Elya Lazer arrived in Kelm, but one famous *tzaddik* whom he certainly knew was Rabbi Zelig Tarshish. Reb Zelig spent the entire day in *tallis* and *tefillin*. The local Lithuanians recognized him as a holy man. They would kiss the ends of his *tallis* when he passed. When he walked through the market square, the peasants cleared a path for him in the hope that he would pass by their stall. Having Reb Zelig step through one's area was considered a guarantee of

---

20. Rabbi Nosson Kamenetsky.
   Another version of this story names Reb Leib Chassid's visitor as the Ohr Somayach, Rabbi Meir Simcha of Dvinsk.
21. Yonason Rosenblum, *Reb Yaakov*, p. 87.

a successful day. The local bullies, who often cursed and insulted Jews, feared Reb Zelig.[22]

Even those Jews who were not strict in their personal observance treated Reb Zelig with great respect. When he walked in the woods on Shabbos, boys who were playing ball stopped as soon as they saw him.[23] A group of Jews from nearby Shavel, a larger city in which non-observance was far more common than in Kelm, once came to a wedding in Kelm with the intention of introducing mixed dancing. Reb Zelig heard of their plan, and began to *daven Ma'ariv* in the place of the intended dancing. The would-be dancers quickly dispersed.[24]

The Talmud Torah, surrounded by a high fence, stood somewhat apart from the rest of Kelm life. Only on Simchas Torah and other holidays was the Talmud Torah open to the public.[25] On Simchas Torah, the singing and dancing did not stop all day. Cakes, apples, wine, and other drinks were set out on tables for all the Jews of Kelm who came to join in the celebrations, and the Talmud Torah was soon overflowing. At the end of the day, the rabbis of the Talmud Torah would lead the crowd in dancing from the Talmud Torah to the center of town.[26]

The separation between the Talmud Torah and the rest of Kelm Jewry was, of course, only partial, and the Talmud Torah inevitably had an impact on the spiritual life of Kelm. Some of those who learned in the Talmud Torah were already married and owned stores in town, in which they would spend two or three hours a day. In addition, a group of local *baalebatim davened* in the Talmud Torah and learned part of the day there.

During *Elul*, Kelm filled with former *talmidim* of the Talmud Torah, who returned for a month of intense spiritual preparation in

---

22. *Kelm — Eitz Karus*, pp. 45-46.
23. "Reminiscences of Rebbetzin Zlata Levenstein Ginsburg," op. cit., p. 76.
24. *Zichronos Chayai*, pp. 24-5.
25. Ibid., p. 28.
26. Rabbi Zalman Sender Kremerman. Rabbi Kremerman is the son of Rabbi Elya Kremerman, who was *rosh yeshiva* of the *yeshiva ketana* established by his brother-in-law Rabbi Eliyahu Lopian.

anticipation of the *Yamim Noraim*. Normally, no more than thirty to thirty-five men learned in the *beis medrash* of the Talmud Torah. But for the *Yamim Noraim* the room somehow accommodated many more.[27]

In Kelm, as everywhere throughout Lithuania, there was a decline in religious observance in Rabbi Dessler's day. Zionist organizations made significant inroads, particularly among the young people. To combat religious apathy among the youth, Rabbi Elya Lopian and Rabbi Yisrael Stamm established the *Shulamis* school for girls and a *Zeirei Yisrael* society.[28] Yet even those furthest removed from religion still showed deference for Torah scholars. Public *chilul Shabbos* in the streets of Kelm was unknown.[29]

Despite the decline in religious observance, the religious life of Kelm Jewry remained a rich one up until the extermination of the town's Jews by the Germans and Lithuanians. Kelm's 400-500 Jewish

The Shulamis School in Kelm

---

27. "Reminiscences of Rabbi Nachum Velvel Dessler," op. cit., pp. 56-7.
   Rebbetzin Zlata Ginsburg puts the number of those learning full time in the Talmud Torah in the early '20s at twenty-two "and sometimes as many as thirty." "Reminiscences of Rebbetzin Zlata Levenstein Ginsburg," op. cit., p. 69.
28. *Lev Eliyahu* (Hebrew), Vol. I, p. 16; *Kelm — Eitz Karus*, p. 27.
29. Ibid., p. 6; "Reminiscences of Rebbetzin Zlata Levenstein Ginsburg," p. 69.

families supported a wide array of *chesed* organizations: *Hachnasas Kallah* for poor brides, *Linas HaTzedek*, whose members remained by bedsides of sick people at night; *Matan B'Seser* to provide for families in need; *Bikur Cholim* to visit the sick; and *Malbish Arumim* to provide clothing to poor families.[30]

A preschool group in Kelm

Rabbi Dessler's oldest child, Rabbi Nachum Velvel Dessler, who was born in 1921, still remembers the atmosphere in the Kelm of his childhood as one of pure Torah. He recalls a *din Torah* in which the seller insisted that he had intended to sell an item for less and the buyer claimed, no less forcefully, that he had intended to pay more.[31]

His playmates (who were mostly drawn from families associated with the Talmud Torah) had no games or toys, and the games they made up among themselves revolved around Torah. Young children would run to the brook, for instance, and place their ears on the ground to see whether they could hear the sound of running water. When they heard the sound of the water, they would cry out that they heard Korach crying.[32]

From *Tishah B'Av* through the *Yamim Noraim* a change was felt in the air, and fear of the impending judgment could be seen on the faces of the adults. Even young children spoke quietly, and if a child was misbehaving or making too much noise, it was enough to remind him of *Elul* to silence him.[33]

One of Kelm's richest families was the Udvin family, owners of a flour mill and the electricity concession. Mrs. Udvin gave birth to 18

---

30. *Orchos Chesed* (Hebrew), a private pamphlet published in honor of Rabbi Chaim Dov Silver, p. 23.

31. "Reminiscences of Rabbi Nachum Velvel Dessler," op. cit., p. 58.

32. Ibid., p. 57.

33. Rabbi Zalman Sender Kremerman.

children of whom 12 survived infancy. She was always the first to arrive at the wedding of any poor bride, and she would invariably come to the affair nicely dressed and bearing an expensive present.[34] When Mrs. Udvin heard of a recently orphaned girl in a nearby town, she immediately took the young girl in and raised her as a daughter.[35]

The Udvin children were often sent to put food packages outside the door of Rabbi Zelig Tarshish and other Torah scholars. Mrs. Udvin did not say, "Please take some food to so-and-so, who, *nebech*, has nothing to eat." Rather the children were told that they were bringing food to a great Torah scholar "who spends his entire day learning." They were instructed to run away quickly so that the beneficiary never knew from where the food came.[36]

The respect the Udvin children showed their parents was extraordinary even in Kelm, but it hints to the relations between parents and children that prevailed. Binyamin, one of the Udvin sons, sometimes stood for hours at a time on the street outside the family's home asking wagon drivers to drive slower so that they would not disturb his father's sleep.[37] On *Erev Yom Kippur*, the Udvin children would line up outside their parents' door for a blessing. As each one entered in turn, he or she would start crying, "Abba and Ima, perhaps I have offended you in some way."[38]

The Legacy of Kelm

EXCEPT FOR THE FOUR YEARS OF WORLD WAR I, RABBI DESSLER remained in Kelm almost continuously from his entry into the Talmud Torah in 1906 until forced to leave Lithuania for England in 1928. In a very real sense, he never left Kelm. Though he would, in time, blend the pure Kelm *mussar* in which he was raised with many other strands of Jewish thought, he always remained the Kelm product *par excellence.*

Everything about him cried out Kelm. The qualities for which Kelm was famed — self-control, humility, unflinching pursuit of

---

34. *Zichronos Chayai*, p. 25.
35. *Orchos Chesed*, p. 24.
36. Mrs. Channah Gisa Silver, one of the Udvin daughters.
37. *Zichronos Chayai*, p. 25.
38. Mrs. Channah Gisa Silver.

truth, the ability to plumb a topic to the depths, love of one's fellow man, abhorrence of honor, and *menuchas hanefesh* — were precisely the qualities that struck everyone who met Rabbi Dessler.

He never lost his awe for Kelm. More than twenty years after he last set foot in the Talmud Torah, he was introduced before a speech in Haifa as one of the few survivors of the Talmud Torah of Kelm. He rose to speak in a trembling voice and protested, "*Chas v'shalom*, I was not a *talmid* of the *Beis HaTalmud* of Kelm. I was never inside. At most, I touched the door handle, but the *bais medrash* itself no eye has ever seen…"

Upon hearing the news of the destruction of Kelm by the Nazis, Rabbi Dessler eulogized the Talmud Torah as a unique refuge of holiness:

> There was one little place of *HaKadosh Baruch Hu* in the world, the Sanctuary of Truth in our generation. A place of modesty, of humility, of walking humbly with G-d.
>
> Many passed by and saw nothing there. They saw nothing, for most people cannot apprehend truth that does not proclaim itself … "Not in the whirlwind is Hashem found, but rather in the still, small voice."
>
> In [the men of the Talmud Torah], truth was found without any admixture of falsehood … In truth, they succeeded in hiding their greatness. No one knew of their great value. Truth was a secret to be revealed only to its adherents.
>
> There was a small town, and Kelm was its name. Who remembers this town, who remembers the glory of the light of truth? A few men of merit, small in number…
>
> There was a small house in the town known as the *Bais HaTalmud*. Is there anyone who knows the awesome holiness that was contained within, its every corner filled with truth?[39]

What was this sanctuary of *HaKadosh Baruch Hu* in the world? Who was its founder?

---

39. Letter to his son Rabbi Nachum Velvel Dessler upon hearing of the destruction of Kelm. *Michtav Me'Eliyahu*, Vol. III, p. 346.

Chapter 3

The Alter

ELYA LAZER ARRIVED IN KELM ALMOST EIGHT YEARS AFTER the passing of the Alter of Kelm, Rabbi Simcha Zissel Braude, on 8 Av, 5658 (1898). But the Alter's presence still hovered over the Talmud Torah. The Alter's successors — his brother Rabbi Leib Braude; Reb Leib's son and the Alter's son-in-law, Rabbi Zvi Hirsch Braude; and the Alter's son Rabbi Nachum Velvel Ziv — took care to ensure that nothing changed from the Alter's lifetime.

The Alter was a revolutionary; not so his successors. They concerned themselves with preserving the Kelm revolution as the Alter had left it. His approach was viewed as sancrosanct. When Rabbi Reuven Dov Dessler served as *mashgiach* in a yeshiva that had taken refuge in Homel during World War I, he often repeated *shmuessen* of the Alter exactly as he had heard them, down to the facial movements and intonations.[1] It is symbolic that the small attic in the Talmud Torah, which served as the Alter's private retreat, and in

---
1. Katz, *Tenuas HaMussar,* Vol. V, p. 134.

which he pursued his trade as a bookbinder, remained untouched from the time of his death until the destruction of Kelm by the Nazis and their Lithuanian henchmen.[2]

The Alter was one of the three main disciples of Rabbi Yisrael Salanter, founder of the Mussar movement. (The other two were Rabbi Yitzchak Blazer, known as Rabbi Itzele Peterburger, and Rabbi Naftali Amsterdam.) Rabbi Simcha Zissel was the oldest of these, and, it appears, the one closest to Reb Yisrael. Reb Yisrael used to say of him, "You are beautiful, my beloved, in every respect, and no blemish is found in you" (*Shir HaShirim* 4:7).[3] Even during the periods in which Reb Yisrael distanced himself from his *talmid* as part of the special educational regimen designed for him, he would tell the other disciples, "Do you dare to compare yourselves to my Simcha Zissel?"[4]

Reb Simcha Zissel was born in 1824 in Kelm into a line of thirteen generations of rabbis. Among his distinguished ancestors were the Maharal of Prague and the Chacham Tzvi.[5]

Reb Simcha Zissel's father, Rabbi Yisrael Braude, knew every page of the Talmud, with *Tosafos* and the *Maharsha's* commentary, as if he had just learned it. After some early, but short-lived, successes in business, he served for the rest of his life as a *dayan* in Kelm. The Alter himself testified that his mother, Chaya, never walked more than four *amos* (cubits) without thinking Torah thoughts. She made a practice of collecting money for poor families at local funerals, a practice from which she did not deviate even at the funeral of her only daughter. When others remonstrated with her, she replied, "Must the poor suffer just because I'm in *aveilus* (mourning)?"[6]

From an early age, young Simcha Zissel stood out from his contemporaries. As a young boy, he was invariably the leader of all youthful escapades. Yet even then he would often disappear for

---

2. Rabbi Nachum Velvel Dessler.
3. Katz, Vol. II, pp. 25-26.
4. Ibid.
5. Ibid.
6. Ibid., pp. 26-27.

hours to read *Chovos Halevavos*. At around 9 years old, he presented all his young playmates with treats and announced to them that he was henceforth severing all contact.[7] By his *bar mitzvah*, he had already completed all of *Seder Nezikin* in Talmud.

After marriage at a young age to Soroh Leah, who came from Vidz, a smaller village near Kelm, the Alter left Kelm for a number of years of concentrated study, much of it under the tutelage of Rabbi Mordechai Gimpel of Rasanova, one of the greatest scholars of the generation. In 1849, Rabbi Yisrael Salanter established a small *mussar kloiz* (house of study) in Kovno. Reb Simcha Zissel traveled to Kovno, initially with the intention of challenging Reb Yisrael's new path. But after hearing Reb Yisrael's first *shmuess*, he was won over and decided to stay and learn *mussar* under Reb Yisrael. Reb Yisrael instructed him to devote himself to *mussar* texts and dissecting the various *middos* (traits) that comprise the human personality. That study became the exclusive focus of Reb Simcha Zissel's first year in Kovno, as well as his life's work.[8]

During the Kovna period, Reb Simcha Zissel learned the classic *mussar* texts over and over again. For six consecutive years, he studied the third chapter of Rabbeinu Yonah's *Sha'arei Teshuvah*. At one point, Reb Yisrael told him that he no longer needed to learn so much *mussar*. Reb Simcha Zissel debated whether to listen to his *rebbi* until Reb Yisrael clarified that he meant that three hours a day of *mussar* would be enough.[9]

For many years, Reb Simcha Zissel maintained the Vilna Gaon's regimen of sleeping only two and a half hours a day, and not at all from *Ma'ariv* until sunrise. Rabbi Eliezer Gordon, the *rav* of Kelm and later the first Telshe Rosh Yeshiva, testified that Reb Simcha Zissel knew all *Moed, Nashim,* and *Nezikin* by heart, and that he

---

7. Ibid., p. 27.
  Rabbi Dessler used to relate this story in the name of his father. When he did so, he would point out a *mussar* lesson from Reb Simcha Zissel's conduct. Recognizing that his spiritual growth should not be at the expense of others, the young Simcha Zissel sought the agreement of his playmates to his separation from them before cutting off contact. The treats were the inducement for their consent. *Rabbi Aryeh Carmell.*
8. Katz, Vol. II, p. 27.
9. Ibid., pp. 30-31.

could identify every halachah in *Shulchan Aruch*, as well as every comment of a major commentator, by *sif kattan* (footnote reference). When Rabbi Gordon was *rav* of Kelm, he and Reb Simcha Zissel used to learn together for hours every Shabbos. Rabbi Gordon particularly enjoyed seeing whether his *chiddushim* of the week would withstand the scrutiny of Reb Simcha Zissel's thorough and critical mind.[10]

The personality that emerged from the years studying under Reb Yisrael was one of uncommon beauty. All who came into contact with him felt the attraction of his personality. He was aristocratic in bearing — each movement deliberate and precise. His eyes, according to Kelm resident E.E. Friedman, pierced through one's heart.[11] And his clothes were so neat and ironed that people often complimented him on his new purchase for garments that were twenty years old.[12]

Reb Simcha Zissel never acted without a clear vision of his goal, and once that vision was in place he never deviated from his course. His self-control was nearly absolute. Nothing could cause him to lose his composure, and his external demeanor remained unchanged no matter what the circumstances in which he found himself. His mental processes were so orderly and disciplined that he could review at the end of the day every thing he had thought about that day.[13]

He and his family lived in the most abject poverty. There were times that they lacked money for food and firewood, or that he was unable to send his *shmuessen* to *talmidim* for want of postage. Yet he would never take a penny from the Talmud Torah or any other institution with which he was associated.[14]

---

10. Ibid., pp. 29-30.

11. Ibid., p. 38.

12. Ibid.

13. Rabbi Dessler reported this statement in the name of his father. Ibid., p. 37.

14. One time he gave his wife a large sum of money. But she refused to spend it for fear that it came from the Talmud Torah. Only when Reb Simcha Zissel assured her that it was a present from Rabbi Yitzchak Blazer for having secured him the position as *rav* of St. Petersburg did she consent to spend the money.

Rabbi Tzvi Hirsch Braude was once asked to describe his father-in-law. He compared the Alter to a lion tamer. A lion tamer never removes his attention from the lion for a second, for any lapse in attention could prove fatal. So the Alter kept every one of his desires in constant check by never removing his attention for a single second.[15]

Over the course of his life, the Alter developed countless stratagems to increase his self-control. He never expressed anger, for instance, without first putting on a special garment set aside for that purpose. After he once detected within himself a strong physical desire for fruit soup, he never again ate it. He ate only small, bony fish so that he would be forced to eat deliberately and not like a glutton.[16]

Even on his deathbed, he insisted on rising to *daven* out of fear that perhaps he was succumbing to laziness by lying in bed. Before he finished tying his second shoe, his heart gave out.[17]

Educator

AFTER RABBI YISRAEL SALANTER'S DEPARTURE FROM KOVNO FOR Western Europe in 1858, Reb Simcha Zissel embarked on his life's work as an educator. Likely at Reb Yisrael's behest, he began teaching young children in Reb Yisrael's native town of Zager. There he was also responsible for the local *mussar kloiz*. Among those who frequented the *kloiz* was the future tea magnate Rabbi Kalman Zev Wissotsky, who had studied under Reb Yisrael in Kovno. When Wissotsky moved from Zager to Moscow in 1860, Reb Simcha Zissel went with him as a private *rebbi* of sorts. After nearly two years in Moscow, he again returned to Kelm.[18]

In Kelm, Reb Simcha Zissel began giving *drashos* (sermons) in the main *shul* on Shabbos, but his highly philosophical talks proved unsuited to a large audience. He did, however, attract a group of devoted followers among the local *baalebatim*. By 1866, he had formulated his educational philosophy and marshaled sufficient financial backing to open up his own institution: the Talmud Torah of Kelm. His local supporters shouldered much of the administrative burden for the new institution, and most of the large annual

---
15. Ibid., p. 36.
16. Ibid., p. 39.
17. Ibid., pp. 71-73.
18. Ibid., pp. 51-52.

budget was covered by wealthy patrons, such as Wissotsky. In 1872, Reb Simcha Zissel purchased the building and grounds where the Talmud Torah remained until the Nazi invasion.[19]

From 1866 to 1876, the Talmud Torah served boys only up to the age of 16 or 17. (Even after the Talmud Torah was transformed into a *beis medrash* for mature scholars, many of them already married, it continued to be known as the Kelmer Talmud Torah.) Many of the students were drawn from the merchant class, and, in addition to Talmud and *TaNaCh*, the curriculum included grammar, mathematics, Russian, and Russian composition.[20] The Talmud Torah was based on a foundation of Torah, *yiras Shamayim*, and *derech eretz*. It was crucial, in Reb Simcha Zissel's view, for the students to understand the way that people act and speak, including their various forms of trickery. External decorum — e.g., combing one's hair everyday — was much emphasized.[21]

The day was tightly organized. Before breakfast, there was a half an hour of learning *Orach Chaim* and a brief *shiur*. The morning was devoted to *Gemara* learning, with the most advanced students hearing a *shiur* from Rabbi Eliezer Gordon three times a week.[22] Each day concluded with half an hour of *mussar* study.

The Alter's stress on order and discipline was unprecedented in Eastern Europe at the time, and the Talmud Torah began to attract a select student body. One visiting *rav* exclaimed, "I do not have enough words to describe *Beis HaTalmud* in detail. I can only say, 'That which I hoped for I have seen.'"[23]

In 1876, however, someone denounced Reb Simcha Zissel to the Czarist authorities for fomenting revolution, and he was forced to flee Kelm and close the Talmud Torah. (In connection with his flight, he

---

19. Ibid., pp. 52-3.
   The original deed listed the Alter and Reb Leib Chassid as joint owners of the property, but title was eventually transferred to the Alter alone.

20. Ibid. pp. 53, 159, and 161.

21. Ibid., pp. 158-9.

22. Rabbi Gordon only became *rav* of Kelm in 1874 so those lectures could only have taken place over a two-year span. Katz, Vol. II, p. 161, fn. 9.

23. Ibid., p. 160.

changed his family name from Braude to Ziv.[24]) That same year he reopened the Talmud Torah in Grubin, Latvia. Though the new Talmud Torah also opened its doors to boys 12 to 13 years old, *talmidim* remained to a much older age than had been the case in Kelm.

The Alter viewed Grubin as the high point of his educational efforts. By taking students from around *bar mitzvah* age, he was able to mold them to a degree seldom possible with older students. To be considered for admission, a student had to commit himself to remaining in the Talmud Torah for a minimum of five years and to return home only for a limited number of vacation days a year.

Every moment of the day was governed by a detailed schedule. Adherence to that schedule was expected and lateness punished. A number of special short periods for *mussar* were scheduled into the day to teach the students to value every minute. Before Minchah, for instance, there was a five-minute period during which the *talmidim* were expected to think deeply on one particular subject that they had chosen in advance.

As in Kelm, several hours in the afternoon in Grubin were devoted to the types of general studies that most of the students would one day need in business. The school was even accredited by the Russian government, and Reb Simcha Zissel encouraged the students to excel in their exams. If asked a question by the government inspectors outside of the curriculum they had studied, they were to think carefully before responding and to answer in such a way as to reflect well on the Jewish people.[25]

If the general studies in Grubin were unique for the time, so too was the amount of time devoted to *mussar*. In addition to the regular times set aside for the study of *mussar* during the day, every day ended with a long *shmuess* by the Alter.

Despite the criticisms directed at his institution for introducing general studies, the Alter remained convinced that Grubin provided a model for the study of Torah, *yirah*, and the *kochos hanefesh* (literally, the powers of the soul, but perhaps best understood as depth psychology) all together. Without knowledge of the human person-

---

24. Ibid., p. 55.
25. Ibid., pp. 170-1.

ality in general and oneself in particular, said the Alter, a person remains nothing more than an animal pursuing his desires. "One who knows himself," he would quote *Chovos Halevavos*, "knows his G-d, and one who does not know himself does not know G-d."[26]

Grubin was, in Reb Simcha Zissel's view, a gift to the Jewish people, and just as one is obligated to tell a friend if he has benefited him in some way, so, he said, was it a *mitzvah* to publicize the achievements of Grubin. In letter after letter, he described the *talmidim* "as if reborn a second time and a new spirit born within them."[27] The Alter charged his critics with having no knowledge of *Beis HaTalmud* or its products. He compared them to the critics of the *Rambam's Moreh Nevuchim*, and clearly identified with the *Rambam's* retort to his critics: "Let a thousand fools perish if one who fulfills the true *tzuras ha'adam* is produced."[28]

Besides the Dessler brothers, Grubin produced a number of other outstanding *talmidim*, including: Rabbi Eliezer Shulowitz, the founder of the Lomza Yeshiva; Rabbi Ben Zion Zev Nekritz, the first *Mashgiach* in Telshe; Rabbi Dov Tzvi Heller, *Mashgiach* in Slabodka and the father-in-law of Rabbi Avraham Grodzinski and Rabbi Yaakov Kaminetsky; Rabbis Sender and Dovid Lipkin, the nephews of Rabbi Yisrael Salanter.[29]

In 1881, a severe heart condition forced the Alter to return to Kelm. Rather than close Grubin, as he initially intended to do, he continued to supervise it from afar, while the day-to-day administration fell to his son Rabbi Nachum Velvel Ziv, assisted by Rabbi Reuven Dov Dessler.[30] At the same time, a small group of ten or so students gathered around Reb Simcha Zissel in the Kelm Talmud Torah.[31]

By 1886, the Alter's health had further deteriorated to the point

---

26. Ibid., pp. 172, 175-6.
27. Ibid., p. 173.
28. Ibid., p. 178.
  While this statement is often quoted in the name of the *Rambam*, what the *Rambam* actually wrote is: "Bear the insults of 10,000 fools, if you can thereby benefit one wise man."
29. Ibid., p. 57.
30. Ibid., p. 57.
31. Ibid., p. 58.

that he felt compelled to close Grubin. He could no longer exercise the degree of supervision that Rabbi Yisrael Salanter had told him was necessary for such a bold experiment in combining *limudei kodesh* and general studies.

Rather than marking the end of the Alter's endeavors, the closing of Grubin ushered in the most productive period of his life. A steady stream of advanced students and married men started flowing into Kelm from other yeshivos, and the Talmud Torah known to posterity took form.

The Alter of Slabodka, Rabbi Nosson Tzvi Finkel, who had been one of the Alter's first followers and his assistant in Grubin,[32] began sending to Kelm outstanding *talmidei chachamim* about to embark on public careers as *roshei yeshiva* or *rabbanim*. Among the greatest of these *talmidei chachamim* were: Rabbi Isser Zalman Meltzer, Rosh Yeshiva in Slutsk and later of Eitz Chaim in Jerusalem; Rabbi Moshe Mordechai Epstein, Rosh Yeshiva in Slabodka and Chevron; Rabbi Naftali Trop, Rosh Yeshiva in Radin; Rabbi Aharon Bakst, *rav* of Suwalk, Lomza, and Shavel; Rabbi Dovid Tevil Dinovsky, *rav* of Maltz; and Rabbi Boruch Horowitz, a *maggid shiur* in Slabodka.[33]

During his last thirteen years, the Alter also shaped most of the leading European *mashgichim* of the period: Rabbi Eliezer Lopat, *Mashgiach* in Telshe and Radin; Rabbi Avraham Drushkowitz, *Mashgiach* in Volozhin; Rabbi Zalman HaKohen Dolinsky, *Mashgiach* in Slabodka and Radin; Rabbi Yaakov Katz, *Mashgiach* in Telshe; Rabbi Leib Chasman, *Mashgiach* in Telshe and Chevron; Rabbi Shmuel Fondiler, *Mashgiach* in Telshe and later *rav* of Riteve; and Rabbi Sheftel Kramer, *Mashgiach* in Slutsk. One of the Alter's last *talmidim* was Rabbi Yerucham Levovitz,[34] the great pre-War *Mashgiach* of the Mirrer Yeshiva and one of the dominant

---

32. Two other early *talmidim* whose impact on the Eastern European yeshiva world was immense were: Rabbi Yosef Yoizel Hurwitz, later famed as the Alter of Novordhok, and Rabbi Yosef Leib Bloch, who subsequently became the Telshe Rosh Yeshiva and whose *Shiurei Daas* is the classic statement of Telshe *mussar*. Katz, Vol. II, p. 61. A great-granddaughter of Rabbi Dessler, Basya Brudny, married Velvel Busel, a great-grandson of Rabbi Yosef Leib Bloch.
33. Ibid.
34. Two of Rabbi Dessler's great-granddaughters married great-grandsons of Reb

mussar personalities in the pre-War European yeshiva world.

The Alter's doctors expected that his heart would give out any moment. One professor told him that his survival defied medical explanation and could only be attributed to his own spiritual powers. He was so weak that he had to eat sometimes even in the middle of *Shemoneh Esrei* and was absolutely forbidden to fast on Yom Kippur.[35]

Yet as weak as he was, he often spoke for over two hours at a time. Once in the middle of a *shmuess*, he started hemorrhaging and coughing up blood, but after a short rest he insisted on continuing. Missing the *shmuess*, he explained, posed a certain mortal danger to the souls of his listeners, whereas continuing was only a possible danger to his life.[36]

Despite his failing health, the Alter not only guided every aspect of the Talmud Torah until his death in the summer of 1898, but created an institution that remained much as he left it until destroyed by the Nazis. After his passing, Kelm continued to be the training school for virtually every European *mashgiach*. Rabbi Yitzchak Isaac Sher[37] and Rabbi Avraham Grodzinski of Slabodka, Rabbi Moshe Rosenstein of Lomza, Rabbi Abba Grosbard of Ponevezh, Rabbi Yosef Leib Nenedik of Kletzk, and Rabbi Yechezkel Levenstein of Mir and later Rabbi Dessler's successor in Ponevezh in *Eretz Yisrael* were all *talmidim* of Kelm during the period that Rabbi Dessler learned there. Rabbi Elya Lopian[38] was an older contemporary of Rabbi Dessler's in Kelm, where he was head of the *yeshiva ketana* for younger boys before preceding Rabbi Dessler to England.

The question that confronts us is: What was so special about the approach of Kelm that the influence of a small group of scholars molded within its walls infiltrated every major European yeshiva?

Yerucham — Malka Frieda Schiff married Zev Zeilberger and Gila Dessler married Nosson Yaakov Levovitz.

35. Ibid., pp. 71-72.
36. Ibid., p. 72.
37. Rabbi Sher was the Rosh Yeshiva, not the *Mashgiach*, in Slabodka Yeshiva, but he remained closely identified with the Mussar movement as the author of the two-volume *Leket Sichos Mussar*.
38. His granddaughter Nechama Lopian later married a great-grandson of Rabbi Dessler, Tzvi Yoel Dessler.

Chapter 4

Chochmah U'Mussar

KLAL YISRAEL IS BUILT UPON TWO *BATEI MEDRASH:* THE *Beis Medrash* of *Avraham Avinu* and the *Beis Medrash* of *Moshe Rabbeinu*. They are respectively the *beis medrash* of *emunah* and the *beis medrash* of Torah.[1]

The Beis Medrash of Avraham Avinu

The *Rambam*, at the beginning of the Laws Concerning Idolatry, describes how all the peoples of the world degenerated into idol worship "until the pillar of the world, *Avraham Avinu*, was born." And Avraham "began to think day and night ... until he comprehended the true path ... through his proper understanding." Eventually Avraham planted in the hearts of tens of thousands the fundamental principle that there is one G-d in the world and that He alone is worthy of being worshipped. And he wrote books on

---

1. The following discussion of the concept of a *Beis Medrash* of *Avraham Avinu*, and its application to Kelm, is based on a eulogy given by Rabbi Moshe Shapiro for his father Rabbi Meir Shapiro, who was a grandson of the Alter's younger brother and raised, in part, by the Alter's daughter Nechama Liba Braude.

this subject, which he passed on to his son Yitzchak and which Yitzchak then passed on to his son Yaakov.[2]

With the passage of time and the long Egyptian exile, the teachings of *Avraham Avinu* were almost lost to his descendants, as they began to learn from their neighbors and worship the stars once again. At that point, *HaKadosh Baruch Hu*, in fulfillment of his promise to Avraham, sent *Moshe Rabbeinu* "through whom the Torah was completed."[3]

Moshe Rabbeinu completed the Torah, but the foundation upon which it was built was the belief in Hashem first implanted by the *Avos*. Without that prior belief, the Torah cannot be received.

In our time, the subject of study in all the great yeshivos is the Torah of *Moshe Rabbeinu*. But the Talmud Torah of Kelm was different. Kelm was a unique continuation of the *Beis Medrash* of *Avraham Avinu*; its subject was *emunah*.

In Kelm, too, the *talmidim* studied Talmud ten to twelve hours a day, but the focus of their efforts lay in clarifying the basics of *emunah* and making those concepts part of themselves until they no longer existed as ideas in the mind but as knowledge of the heart.

The Talmud (*Bava Metzia* 12b) describes anyone who depends on his father for his food as a minor (*katan*). And similarly one whose *emunah* is dependent on others and derivative might be described as one of the *"ketanei emunah"* (people of little faith). Kelm produced men of great faith, men who devoted their lives to strengthening their *emunah* and transmitting it to others.

The Alter was the model for this effort. He spent three to four hours every day working on his own *emunah*. He was, for instance, constantly searching for examples of Hashem acting *middah keneged middah* (measure for measure) in order to fortify his faith. He avoided doctors as much as possible so as not to fall into the trap of treating them as if they were infallible by virtue of their medical expertise.[4]

Those efforts bore fruit. Rabbi Yitzchak Blazer used to say, "If a

---

2. Rambam, *Mishneh Torah, Hilchos Avodas Kochavim* 1:1-3.
3. Ibid., *Hilchos Melachim* 9:1.
4. Katz, *Tenuas HaMussar*, Vol. II, pp. 32-3.

person wants to learn *emunah,* let him go to Reb Simcha Zissel."⁵ It was good advice. Reb Simcha Zissel and his successors trained the *menahel ruchani* in virtually every major Lithuanian yeshiva, and through them the *emunah* of Kelm penetrated into every yeshiva.

THE ALTER PICTURED A WORLD IN WHICH MAN'S DIVINE INTELlect is constantly pitted against his immediate desires. He divided those desires into two groups: the physical desires and the more spiritual desires, such as that for *kavod* (honor). Both types of desire cause a person to lose perspective by forcing him to focus on the immediate satisfaction of those desires.

Chochmah

In most people, the world of the senses is much stronger than the concepts of the mind. As children, the physical desires completely dominate, and once habits based on the dominance of those desires have become entrenched, it is extremely difficult to supplant them.⁶ Few succeed, and for those who do not, the intelligence remains in the service of the physical desires and the pursuit of honor.

Love of oneself is the common element linking physical desires and the pursuit of honor. For the Alter, then, self-love was the root of all evil and incompatible with the love of G-d. "The primary form of idol worship that lurks in the heart of man and which must be uprooted is love of self," he wrote. "That self-love is a violation of the prohibition, 'You shall not have any foreign gods.'"⁷

Having identified self-love as the root of all bad *middos,* the Alter opposed it with another love — love of one's fellow man, *ahavos habrios.* The Alter further identified *ahavas habrios* as a necessary condition for true *ahavas haBorei* (love of G-d) as well. Only when all the servants of the King live in peace and harmony with one another are they fully capable of accepting *ol malchus Shamayim* (the

---

5. Ibid., p. 31.

6. The Alter used to quote Aristotle's explanation of why youth is denied wisdom: Because in youth the intelligence is subjugated to the senses. *Katz, Vol. II, p. 111.*

7. Ibid., p. 110.

Kingdom of Heaven). If the servants of the King are not united, then it is clear that they have not dedicated themselves completely to service of the King.[8]

Hashem created the world in such a way, the Alter noted, that each person is dependent on others. For the world to function properly, then, each person must become both a recipient of *chesed* and the doer of *chesed*. None of Hashem's attributes cry out from the Creation so loudly as His love for His creatures, and when a person emulates Hashem's *chesed* he thereby becomes a partner in Creation.[9]

The Alter's great achievement, however, lay not in his description of the spiritual struggle confronting every Jew: the battle between desire and one's Divine intelligence, between love of self and love of the Creator and one's fellow man. Rather his originality lay in the antidote he proposed — clarity of thought — and the discovery of a methodology to develop that clarity. Without such clarity, said the Alter, man is nothing more than a horse.

The entire basis of the Alter's training, according to Rabbi Yerucham Levovitz, consisted of instilling in his followers a burning desire to acquire *chochmah* (wisdom) and a love of truth.[10] No power is more underutilized, the Alter taught, than that of clear thought. Most people have never employed their minds other than in service of their desires, and their thoughts are invariably tainted with self-interest and fatally superficiality.[11] Whatever intellectual conceptions they possess remain those from childhood.

Any genuine understanding, the Alter taught, must be continually refined. In the second paragraph of *Shema*, the *mitzvos* are described as those which "I command you today." Rashi comments on the word "today" that the *mitzvos* should be in our eyes something new as if given today. That does not mean, said the Alter, merely that we must view the *mitzvos* as a gift given anew every

---

8. Ibid., p. 134.
9. Ibid., pp. 132-34.
10. Ibid.
11. Ibid., p. 109.

day. Rather they must be understood as if for the first time each day.[12] For the *mitzvos* to be in our eyes as if they were commanded today requires that one never rest content with his previous understanding. If one's relationship to Hashem is not being constantly deepened, then he has not truly accepted the yoke of *mitzvos* and of G-d's rule.[13]

Rabbi Dessler's discussion of the acquisition of *emunah* as a process of ever-deepening recognition of truth, based on unrelenting effort, conforms to the process the Alter described. *Emunah*, Rabbi Dessler writes, is the recognition of truth. If a person reflects sufficiently on that truth, it takes on the undeniability of a mathematical proposition and eventually the immediacy of sensory perceptions.[14]

Since most people have little experience thinking in depth, that power must be developed incrementally over time. In the various educational institutions he founded, the Alter instituted a number of five-minute periods during the day to be set aside for reflecting on one particular subject only. Working in small blocks of time, the students learned how to think in a disciplined fashion about a particular topic.

He also enunciated specific rules to transform intellectual insights into sources of genuine enlightenment. He instructed his students to continually ask themselves, "What new insight have I achieved, and what are the sources of my knowledge?" Once that insight was firmly grounded, Kelmer learned to extrapolate from the general principle derived to all its specific applications and to ask: What consequences follow from this principle for my life?[15]

Kelm stressed the ability to remove from one's mind anything that might distract one from the topic at hand. The *menuchas hane-*

---

12. Rabbi Elchonon Blumenthal, *Trials and Challenges*, p. 319.
    The greatness of Rabbi Yisrael Salanter, according to the Alter, was that he took nothing for granted and continually learned everything as if for the first time. Ibid., p. 320.

13. Katz, Vol. II, pp. 108-9.

14. *Michtav Me'Eliyahu*, Vol. I, p. 171; Carmell, *Strive for Truth*, Vol. II, p. 222.

15. Katz, Vol. II, p. 105.

fesh (calm) so prized by Kelmer described, above all, an obliviousness to anything but the subject of one's current intellectual exertions.[16]

The *kabbalos* (resolutions) of Rabbi Dessler's father, Reb Reuven Dov, reflect Kelm's emphasis on disciplined thought. He admonishes himself that "becom[ing] accustomed to thinking in an orderly fashion is the fundamental necessity to avoid hopeless confusion of thought." Resolutions to "avoid mixing different thoughts in a manner likely to confuse" and "to fix times to think about a particular matter without confusion of one matter and another" recur frequently in Reb Reuven Dov's personal *kabbalos*.[17]

Kelm *davening* reflected the emphasis on intense concentration and ever-deepening understanding. The Alter once spoke for two straight years in Grubin on the meaning of the prayers and how to attach particular thoughts to different verses in the *davening*. "Better a little bit with *kavannah* (concentration)" was the watchword in Kelm, and additions to the *davening* were kept to a minimum. In *Selichos*, for instance, the repetitions of the Thirteen Attributes of Hashem were reduced in favor of concentrating on the desire to emulate those Attributes.[18]

The prayers were extremely slow — *pesukei d'zimra* alone lasted fifty minutes.[19] The Alter's *Shemoneh Esrei* could take up to an hour, and sometimes at the end, he would collapse into a chair.[20] *Kaddish* was enunciated with great care by the *shaliach tzibbur*, with a slight pause between every word, to afford everyone an opportunity to reflect on the meaning of the words.

Poor people were not allowed to solicit money during the prayers. Instead a plate was placed just inside the door into which

---

16. Ibid., pp. 103-04.
17. Ibid., pp. 146-47.
18. Ibid., pp. 34, 145.
19. Interestingly, the longer *pesukei d'zimra* of Shabbos also took exactly 50 minutes in order to teach one how to *daven* "quickly" if need be. *Reb Yaakov*, p. 89.
20. Ibid., p. 34.

contributions were dropped after the *davening*.[21] Everyone rose and sat in unison upon signals given by the *gabbai*.[22]

The result of everyone *davening* together with deep concentration was an extremely elevated *davening*. In Kelm, recalls Rabbi Mordechai Zuckerman, a *talmid* from the last period, anyone who wanted to *daven* was assured of success because so much effort had been invested in creating a conducive framework. The experience of everyone *davening* together made it impossible to recite *Hallel*, for instance, without being brought to tears.

The intensity of the *davening*, however, was entirely inward: Absolute silence reigned in the *beis medrash*, unpunctuated by outbursts of any type or dramatic external actions.[23] One of the *gabbai's* tasks was to give a bang if anyone raised his voice above the norm and thereby distracted others.

Mussar

AS HIGHLY AS KELM VALUED PURE THOUGHT, HOWEVER, THE Alter never imagined that intellectual insight by itself possessed the power to contravene the pull of the senses. Unless wisdom was internalized and made part of oneself, it remained of little value. The ultimate test of the quality of one's thought was the degree to which it was reflected in one's actions and feelings of closeness to Hashem.[24]

In the Alter's terminology, intellectual insight — the ability to determine what actions and thoughts are an expression of God's will — is *chochmah*. The process by which those insights are integrated into the depths of one's being and translated into action is *mussar*.[25] The two are interdependent; either one without the other is of little worth. (The Alter's posthumously published writings were appropriately entitled *Chochmah U'Mussar*.)

The ideas of the Torah are not absorbed automatically. That absorption requires *hispa'alus*, an arousal of one's inner spiritual

---

21. Rabbi Zalman Sender Kremerman.
22. Ibid., pp. 151-52.
23. Ibid.
24. Ibid., p. 110.
25. See Rabbi Zev Leff, *Outlooks and Insights*, p. 220.

forces.[26] *Mussar*, in the Alter's view, was the specific discipline for integration of thought and self. In the Alter's pithy formulation: "Mussar is the dynamite of the soul."[27]

In the polemical battle between the supporters of the Mussar movement and its opponents, the Alter was the movement's most outspoken proponent. He dismissed its opponents as "fools," whose opinions could be ignored with impunity, for their failure to recognize the need for a concrete regimen for making the Torah part of oneself.[28]

The Alter cited numerous statements from *Chazal* to prove that Torah study requires prior refining of one's *middos* (character traits). He viewed, for example, *Chazal's* statement, "For one who purifies himself, Torah is the spice of life, and poison for one who does not merit it" (*Yoma* 72b), as proof of the theory of the Mussar movement. The pure ones, according to him, are those who have prepared themselves to receive Torah through character refinement.[29]

Similarly he interpreted the verse, "The *tzaddikim* will go in the [ways of Hashem], while the wicked will fall in them" (*Hoshea* 14:10), to mean that one who has worked to perfect his *middos* (character traits) will naturally comprehend the truth of the Torah and grow rapidly in Torah learning, while everyone else will stumble in their learning.[30]

Every new insight in Torah learning or into one's own personality, the Alter counseled, must be accompanied by some form of emotional arousal. But emotional arousal was not a goal in itself. Rather it served as a spur to yet deeper thought. As Rabbi Dessler writes with respect to *teshuvah* (repentance): "[T]he emotions are notoriously changeable and thus *teshuvah* [based on emotional arousal] will not last." Emotions can open up the heart, but something more is required to penetrate within.[31]

---

26. Blumenthal, p. 40.
27. Ibid., p. 318.
28. Katz, Vol. II, p. 65.
29. Ibid., p. 66.
30. Ibid., p. 67.
31. *Michtav Me'Eliyahu*, Vol. II, p. 78; Rabbi Aryeh Carmell, *Sanctuaries in Time* (Vol. IV in the *Strive for Truth* series), pp. 111-12.

Following his teacher Rabbi Yisrael Salanter, the Alter stressed a wide variety of techniques designed to help Torah ideas penetrate into the heart. One such technique was repeating a verse or a statement of *Chazal* over and over again in a special melody. The Alter once sat in his *sukkah* chanting the same verse in his own haunting melody for six straight hours.[32]

Another time Rabbi Naftoli Amsterdam shared a room with the Alter in an inn. "I slept," testified Reb Naftoli, "but he spent the night learning *mussar* based on the verse, פתחו לי שערי צדק אבוא בם אודה י-ה — Open for me the gates of righteousness that I may enter therein and give thanks to Hashem (*Tehillim* 118:19-20)." A student once hid himself in the Alter's private attic in the Talmud Torah and saw him sing and dance for a half an hour to the words, שש אנוכי על אמרתך — How I rejoice over Your words ... (*Tehillim* 119:162).[33]

Meshalim drawn from everyday life were another means of opening up the heart. Kelm taught how to look at the world with wide-open and alert eyes and to use everything one observed as grist for the mill of *mussar*.

In *Michtav Me'Eliyahu*, Rabbi Dessler provides a classic example of a Kelm *mashal*. *Chazal* say, "Better one hour of spiritual bliss in the world to come than the entire life in this world" (*Pirkei Avos* 4:17). To comprehend what this means, Rabbi Tzvi Hirsch Braude recommended that one first imagine every moment of pleasure and happiness he had ever experienced concentrated into a short period of time. Then multiply that by all the pleasures experienced by everyone currently living, for that pleasure too is included in "the entire life in this world." Finally, add together all the pleasures of everyone who has ever lived since the beginning of time. And all that concentrated pleasure is nothing compared to a brief moment — literally the time required for the cooling of the spirit — in the World to Come.

And the pleasure of the World to Come referred to here is only a "whiff" of the real spiritual pleasure to come — the spiritual analogue

---

32. Katz, Vol. II, p. 34.
33. Ibid., p. 134.

to the physical pleasure aroused by the aromas wafting out of a bakery shop.[34]

Knowledge of the *kochos hanefesh* (all one's internal spiritual potential) and one's own unique nature constituted one of the foundations of Kelm *mussar*. That knowledge, according to the Alter, held the key to the integration of thought and action, for without it one was helpless in the face of his *yetzer hara*. The goal of the *yetzer hara* is to prevent intellectual apprehension from being translated into action, and to thwart it one must know its strategies.

Rabbi Reuven Dov Dessler nicely captured Kelm's stress on a clear understanding of the various means employed by the *yetzer hara* to deflect a person from the service of G-d:

> Just as in diseases of the body…, doctors struggle generation after generation … to grasp the workings of the body — how it becomes sick and how it is healed — [so it is with the workings of] the soul and the *middos*, which are even more sensitive, and whose treatment requires even more sensitivity and breadth of outlook, for evil is always at hand eager to overcome good.[35]

In addition to the general understanding of the workings of the soul, each individual must understand his own unique constitution, including those areas in which he is particularly vulnerable. Every person, said the Alter, has some particular strength that if developed properly will bring him close to Hashem and a corresponding weakness that if left unattended can cause him to fall to the depths of depravity.[36]

Reb Reuven Dov again expressed the classic Kelm approach towards self-knowledge:

---

34. *Michtav Me'Eliyahu*, Vol. V, p. 4; Rabbi Aryeh Carmell, *Strive for Truth*, Vol. I., pp. 31-33.
35. Katz, Vol. V, p. 127.
36. Rabbi Dessler in the name of his father.

> The first thing is for a person to know himself and all his natural characteristics and their workings... Even the most depraved person has a pattern to his depravity, ... and every individual is different.
>
> The beginning of the art of improving one's *middos* is understanding the subconscious workings of one's heart and soul. And that requires constant work and deep contemplation. On this knowledge was built the Talmud Torah of Kelm, and that is its glory.[37]

Reb Reuven Dov portrayed a person without that knowledge as comparable to an heir to a great fortune without any idea of how to employ his money. Eventually all his money will be lost. Similarly, no matter how great a person's potential, if he lacks self-understanding, his potential will eventually be dissipated.[38]

The highest praise in Kelm was to describe someone as *erlich* (honest). Above all, *erlichkeit* (honesty) referred to honesty with oneself — the refusal to fool oneself and the willingness to submit one's actions to minute dissection in search of traces of impure motivations.[39]

The same continuous self-scrutiny that Kelm *erlichkeit* required with regard to one's character also applied to one's *emunah*. In a very interesting letter to his father, Rabbi Dessler demonstrated how scrupulously honest one must be in his professions of faith. We are forbidden, he noted, to pronounce the *Shem Havayah* — י-ה-ו-ה — because we are not yet capable of affirming it with complete *emunah*.

---

37. Katz, Vol. V, p. 128.

38. Ibid., p. 128.

39. Rabbi Shalom Schwadron once witnessed a dispute in learning between two Kelm products, Rabbi Yehudah Leib Chasman and Rabbi Zemach Shlomovitz, that captures the meaning of *erlichkeit* in the Kelm lexicon. After an extended discussion, Reb Zemach admitted that Rabbi Chasman's interpretation was right. But Rabbi Chasman was not quite satisfied. "You still haven't said that you were wrong," he pointed out.

"Obviously if you are right, I am wrong," the Reb Zemach replied.

"No," Reb Leib insisted, "You must say, I was wrong.'"

Kelm *erlichkeit* could tolerate no evasion no matter how subtle.

For human beings, bound by time, the full revelation of Hashem's glory still lies in the future. But for Hashem Himself, Who is above time, past, present and future are simultaneous. From His perspective, He is not awaiting some future event to be fully revealed; His perfection is now. That is why the Divine Name does not describe Hashem just in terms of the future, i.e., י-ה-ו-ה (even though Hashem Himself refers to Himself in the future as א-ה-ו-ה), but as a combination of past, present and future: י-ה-ו-ה.

Yet from our human perspective, we can not yet perceive Hashem's ultimate perfection. We are thereby forbidden to pronounce His Name. Until our faith is as clear as something perceived with our senses, we are forbidden to proclaim Hashem's essence above time, just as Daniel and Yirmiyahu refused to describe Hashem as Great, Powerful, and Awesome at a time when all these qualities were not manifest to them. To pronounce the *Shem Havayah*, then, is forbidden to us because it is a lie from our limited, human perspective.

This discussion of the severe penalty for pronouncing G-d's Name, when we cannot yet affirm wholeheartedly all that is implied by that Name, led Rabbi Dessler to a truly frightening proposition. Any time we profess a greater degree of *emunah* than we actually possess, we are liable for lying. From this, we see how great is our obligation to continually strengthen our *emunah* so that we do not give expression to a false faith in either word or thought.[40]

So they taught in the *Beis Medrash* of *Avraham Avinu*.

---

40. *Michtav Me'Eliyahu*, Vol. III, pp. 314-316.

Chapter 5

Kelmer Chinuch

RABBI YISRAEL SALANTER ONCE DETAILED THE PRAISES of his leading disciples: Rabbi Yitzchak Blazer was the *Lamdan*, Rabbi Naftali Amsterdam the *Tzaddik*, and Rabbi Simcha Zissel Braude the *Chacham*. The Alter's *chochmah* (wisdom) referred above all to his genius as an educator. The *ba'alei mussar* used to say that the Alter could take a student apart screw by screw and then refashion him anew.[1] Above all, he succeeded in transmitting to a select group of *talmidim* his vision of *mussar* in a form they could then pass on to their *talmidim*.

A Spiritual Elite

Though the number of *talmidim* in the Talmud Torah never numbered more than 30 to 35, the influence of that small group was, in time, felt in almost every major European yeshiva. Word of Kelm eventually reached even the outside world. It is related that at a gathering of rectors of German universities, convened to divide the

---
1. Katz, *Tenuas HaMussar*, Vol. II, p. 150.

academic faculties between the various universities, one professor stood up and said: There is a subject that is taught only one place in the world. The place — the small Russian town of Kelm; the subject — the perfection of the character.[2]

The learning *sedarim* in Kelm paralleled those in other yeshivos, except for the hour-long nightly *mussar seder*.[3] But only those questing for self-perfection came to Kelm. In Slabodka it was possible to speak of students who were *"ba'alei mussar"* and those who were not. The distinction would have been meaningless in Kelm where every *talmid* was a *"ba'al mussar."*

The Alter had no interest in attracting many *talmidim* to Kelm. Quite the contrary. Entry into the Talmud Torah was deliberately restricted to a select few." I am far from any desire to increase the numbers," the Alter wrote. "I seek only to increase the quality. Just the opposite from the goal of others."[4]

Kelm was exclusively for the training of a small number of exceptional individuals of great spiritual potential. The comment of *Chovos Halevavos* — "a little bit of purity is a great deal" — served as the Alter's motto.[5] Even Rabbi Yerucham Levovitz had to wait many months before gaining official admission. Reb Yerucham first came to Kelm in 1897 for *Elul zman*. Not until the following Pesach, however, did the Alter motion to him that he could remain in the *beis medrash* for the Alter's *shmuess*. That gesture constituted his official acceptance into the Talmud Torah.[6]

The Alter knew exactly what he was looking for in *talmidim:* "those who will bear the yoke together with friends without any thought of personal benefit or *kavod*… [and] will commit themselves to conduct themselves according to my words and advice." Every *talmid* had to pass the rigorous scrutiny of the Alter to be admitted.

---

2. Ibid., p. 141.
3. Ibid., p. 132.
4. Ibid., p. 59.
5. Ibid., pp. 58-9.
   On the ways in which Rabbi Dessler emulated the Alter in his exclusive focus on producing individuals who would in turn influence others see Chap. 16 below.
6. Rabbi Dovid Povarsky, a *talmid* of Reb Yerucham's in Mirrer Yeshiva and subsequently Rosh Yeshiva of Ponevezh Yeshiva.

Only those possessing a refined manner, some worldly knowledge, a thirst for spiritual elevation, and, in most cases, an effusive letter of recommendation from their *mashgiach* could hope to gain entry. To such people, and such people alone, was the Alter prepared to draw close and dedicate himself.[7]

Brilliance was neither a necessary or sufficient condition for entry into the Beis HaTalmud HaGadol of Kelm, and those seeking entry took no exams. Absolute self-control, however, was required, and without character references aspiring candidates had little or no chance of gaining entry.[8]

Rabbi Tzvi Hirsch Braude once gave the following *mashal* to describe the kind of students for whom Kelm was built. When he was a young boy, a train carrying the Czar passed through Reb Tzvi Hirsch's hometown in the middle of the night. A large group of peasants came to pay their respects, and as soon as the train arrived, they began whooping and cheering wildly. After a few minutes, one of the Czar's ministers emerged to thank the crowd for coming. He requested them, however, to refrain from further cheering because the Czar was sleeping. As soon as he reentered the train coach, the whooping started anew. After a few minutes the minister came out again to deliver the same message, and once again the peasants failed to pay the slightest attention.

Finally, the commander of the Czar's personal guard came out to speak to the crowd. His message was blunt: Any more noise and you will all be shot on the spot. With that the crowd fell silent.

In Kelm, Reb Tzvi Hirsch concluded, we seek *talmidim* who respond to refined speech and do not have to be talked to like rough peasants.[9]

A Framework for Perfection

THE ALTER SOUGHT TO CREATE A SELF-ENCLOSED ENVIRONMENT dedicated to the quest for perfection. A high fence surrounding the grounds separated the Talmud Torah from the outside world. The Alter traveled all the way to Libau to select the wood for that fence. In

---

7. Ibid., pp. 51, 58, 142.
8. Rabbi Mordechai Zuckerman.
9. Rabbi Eliyahu Lopian.

addition, the curtains of the *beis medrash* were half-drawn at all times to lessen the temptation to peer outside.[10] Upon entering the precincts of the Talmud Torah, a person immediately felt that he had entered a world apart. Not a word of *divrei chullin* (everyday conversation) could be heard in the Talmud Torah, and the order and calmness all around was palpable. Once, as the *sefer Torah* was being returned to the *Aron Kodesh*, one *talmid* turned to another and whispered something. In an instant, the whole room turned towards him as if he had been caught stealing.[11]

A rear view of the Kelm Talmud Torah; note the wood fence

The Alter created a minutely planned environment — a framework for spiritual *aliyah*. If a person wanted to learn five hours without lifting his head, everything in Kelm was designed to facilitate that desire; if he wanted to improve his *davening*, Kelm would also facilitate that.[12] Nowhere else was perfection of *middos* so explicitly the focus. Every minute of the day was planned and assigned a definite purpose.

Both the younger students in Grubin and the more mature students in Kelm were divided into *vaadim* in which the members gathered several times a week to assess one another's spiritual progress and to devise means for their mutual spiritual elevation. Especially in Grubin, the *vaadim* were usually headed by an older student, who spoke on a previously announced topic.

The *vaadim* typically imposed a strict discipline on their members. In the *vaadim*, *talmidim* learned to weigh each word before they spoke.

---

10. Ibid., p. 152.
11. Rabbi Mordechai Zuckerman.
12. Rabbi Mordechai Zuckerman.

The Kelm Talmud Torah

"Let it be as difficult to speak a word as to take a coin out of one's pocket," was a typical *kabbalah* (resolution).[13] Composing such *kabbalos* as a means of mutual reinforcement was one of the principal activities of the *vaadim*, and these *kabbalos* were often enforced by a system of fines.[14]

Kabbalos were treated as nothing less than vows. Once in the middle of *davening*, the Alter suddenly got up from his place, went to the back of the *beis medrash* to look into a *siddur* (prayerbook), and then returned to his place. Only later did his *talmidim* realize what had happened. One of the Alter's *kabbalos* that year was to *daven* out of a *siddur*. A word had become torn in his own *siddur*, and rather than recite that word by heart, he had picked up another *siddur* to read the missing word.[15]

In addition to the *vaadim*, the *talmidim* in Kelm made a practice of choosing a friend to regularly evaluate their conduct and *middos* on the theory that a person is not fully capable of noticing his own failings. Once a grandson of the *Chofetz Chaim* came to study in Kelm, and someone asked him why, with such an illustrious grandfather, he felt the need for Kelm. He replied, "From my grandfather, I learn what I have to become. In Kelm, I learn what I am now."[16]

Discipline and Order

THE ALTER BASED HIS EDUCATIONAL PHILOSOPHY ON THE complex interplay of thought and action. Improper actions, in his view, both reflected bad *middos* and could cause a further decline in *middos*. Once a group of students found the gate to the Talmud Torah locked. One

---

13. Ibid., p. 149.
14. Ibid., Vol. V, p. 143.
15. Ibid., Vol. II, p. 40.
16. Rabbi Dovid Povarsky.

of them climbed over the gate and succeeded in letting his friends in from the inside. When the Alter learned of what had happened, he gave a *shmuess* that began with the words, "One who breaks down the fence will be bitten by a snake"(*Koheles* 10:8). Someone who could climb over one fence — the action of a thief — might, in the Alter's opinion, come to break every spiritual and physical fence in the world.

Middos, the Alter believed, were inculcated by constant repetition and attention to the smallest detail. Discipline and order were the watchwords of Kelm education. Any sloppy or careless action reflected a lack of the constancy of thought and unremitting attention Kelm demanded. The smallest action — e.g., making sure to close the door behind oneself — was its own *avodah*.

The wastebaskets in Kelm were specially designed with a narrow bottom so that if one did not place the refuse into the wastebasket with care it would tip over spilling all its contents.[17] In such little ways did Kelm instill the importance of taking care with every single movement.

Middos, in the Alter's view, have both an external and internal expression. Physical laziness parallels a certain mental sloth as well, and by uprooting the former, one can also uproot the latter as well. The Alter considered laziness one of the most dangerous of all *middos*, leading to a loss of all ambition and all striving for perfection. He imposed on his students many exercises to uproot it. They were forbidden to lean on their hands while learning or to learn lying down. No more than ten minutes was permitted from the time of being awakened to appearing fully dressed in the *beis medrash*.[18]

Seder (orderliness) was another characteristic where the external and internal expressions were inextricably linked. By stressing external order, the Alter believed, one could, over time, give structure and order to the internal thought processes as well. A lack of external order, he felt, inevitably revealed a lack of structure and methodology in one's thoughts. When he visited his son Nachum

---

17. Rabbi Dovid Povarsky.
18. Ibid., p. 128.

Velvel in yeshiva, he would first inspect his son's room to make sure that it was neat and organized before greeting him.[19]

Each student in Kelm had a specific place for his possessions, and anyone whose possessions were not neatly arranged or in the wrong place could count on incurring the Alter's displeasure. A visitor to the Kelm *beis medrash* once entered during one of the Alter's *shmuessen*. From the somber tone, he assumed that the Alter was delivering a *hesped*. Only midway through the *shmuess* did the visitor realize that the subject was a pair of galoshes that one of the *talmidim* had placed upside down in its compartment. The visitor later reported that the Alter had delivered a eulogy over an incorrectly placed pair of galoshes.[20]

The Alter succeeded to a remarkable degree in inculcating a sense of external order in his *talmidim*. In Grubin, for instance, the outside restrooms were always locked and the key placed in a specially designated place. In the decade of Grubin's existence, no one could recall someone forgetting to lock the door or return the key to its proper place.[21]

At the bar mitzvah of Nachum Velvel Dessler, a relative, who was visiting Kelm for the first time in 13 years, mentioned how he had found his cane hanging in the vestibule in the exact place he had left it 13 years earlier. Apparently the cane had been taken down and cleaned periodically and then put back in its place, for not a trace of dust could be found on it.[22] Similarly, a small coin left on the windowsill would remain there for decades. Every *Erev Shabbos*, the *talmid* who had purchased the right to clean the *beis medrash* would lift the coin, dust underneath and return it to its place.[23]

One Shavuos night, Reb Yaakov Kamenetsky was learning in the

---

19. Ibid., pp. 155-56.
20. Ibid., p. 154.
   Rabbi Zelik Epstein heard from his father, who was a student in Kelm at the time, that from then on the Alter never permitted a stranger into the *beis medrash* during one of his *shmuessen*. If a stranger entered, he would stop in midsentence until he had left.
21. Ibid., p. 169.
22. "Reminiscences of Rabbi Nachum Velvel Dessler," op. cit., p. 59.
23. Katz, Vol. II, p. 153.

Talmud Torah. The custom in Kelm was to wear a hat for *davening*. To put on his hat, Reb Yaakov removed his rabbinical *yarmulke*, and due to the long night absentmindedly placed it in the *Gemara* he had been learning. Years later, on one of his periodic visits to Kelm, from nearby Tzitevian where he was *rav*, he entered into a Talmudic discussion with Rabbi Doniel Movshovitz. In the course of the conversation, Reb Yaakov went to consult the same tractate he had been learning that Shavuos night years earlier.

He pulled down the volume from the bookcase and it opened automatically to the page he had been learning due to the *yarmulke* that remained right where he had left it. Despite the hundreds of times that volume had been used in the intervening years, each student had been careful to replace the *yarmulke* precisely where he had found it.[24]

Menuchas HaNefesh

KELM CULTIVATED *MENUCHAS HANEFESH,* CALMNESS OF SPIRIT, as the most prized of spiritual attainments. That *menuchas hanefesh* was reflected in the refinement of both speech and deed — every action and word preceded by thought.[25] Pause before acting — make sure the door is fully closed; check the bench before sitting down; do nothing without a clearly defined purpose in mind. Pause before speaking — when asked for advice, never answer immediately; before sharing a *chiddush,* think about it for a quarter of an hour.

Always remain calm, unhurried, and reflective, Kelm taught, for without those qualities one's thinking will inevitably become confused. Concentrate on every word in the first *berachah* of *Shemoneh Esrei.*[26]

Avoid anything that can lead to confusion. And when the inevitable distractions appear, train oneself to overcome them. Yom Kippur, the day of the year requiring the most intense concentration, falls right in the middle of the harvest season, said the Alter, to teach the importance of retaining one's composure no matter what else is happening.[27]

---

24. Rosenblum, *Reb Yaakov,* pp. 88-89.
25. Rabbi Nachum Velvel Dessler.
26. Katz, Vol. II, pp. 125-26.

No emotion posed so much danger to one's self-control as anger, and Kelm *talmidim* worked very hard at controlling any expression of anger. For example, Reb Reuven Dov Dessler resolved that he if ever felt aggrieved by another's actions or words to immediately concentrate on all that person's good qualities.[28]

Even mitzvos had to be performed with calm. Kelm had a term for it: *z'rizus b'menuchah*, showing eagerness to do a mitzvah while remaining calm. *Z'rizus*, explained Rabbi Avraham Grodzinski, is a matter of the head not the feet.[29]

In Kelm, *talmidim* learned to account for every single action. In particular, they trained themselves never to turn their heads — and thus divert their attention — while learning or *davening*. In the terminology of Kelm *mussar*, that discipline was called "fixing one's head on one's shoulders." To turn one's head betrayed a lack of concentration and a tendency to be distracted in one's thinking.

During his six-month sojourn in Kelm just after his marriage, Rabbi Yaakov Kamenetsky was criticized for having failed in this regard. Hearing a *yisrael* called for the first *aliyah*, he alerted the *gabbai* that a *kohen* had just entered the *beis medrash*. Rather than being complimented for his attentiveness, Reb Yaakov was reprimanded for having looked around.[30] At least no one said of him what the Alter had once said of a *talmid* who peeked out the window when the firefighters clanged by: "Nothing will ever come of him."[31]

In his later years, Rabbi Eliyahu Lopian, one of the great products of Kelm, once found himself waiting for a bus to take him to a doctor's appointment. The bus was very late, and at one point, Reb Elya turned his head to see whether it was coming. As soon as he did so, he exclaimed, "Oy, I would have received a strong rebuke for that in Kelm."[32] Since turning the head could not make the bus arrive sooner, it was a useless action and reflected a lack of *menuchas hanefesh*.

---

27. Ibid., p. 126.
28. Ibid., Vol. V, p. 147.
29. Rosenblum, *Reb Yaakov*, p. 88; Rabbi Shlomo Wolbe, *Alei Shur* (Hebrew), Vol. II, p. 255.
30. Rosenblum, ibid.
31. Katz, Vol. II, p. 153.
32. Rabbi Aryeh Carmell.

The Alter succeeded in instilling even younger boys with an ability to ignore any distractions. The entire town of Grubin lay within the domain of one Russian nobleman. Once, after a day of feasting and drinking, the nobleman boasted to his friends of the remarkable educational institution within his realm and insisted that his fellow nobles accompany him forthwith to view the Talmud Torah with their own eyes. The drunken party pulled into the courtyard in their carriages, with a tremendous racket. Yet not one of the boys — and some were as young as 12 or 13 — even lifted his head to see what was happening.[33]

Combating Self-Love

AS WE HAVE MENTIONED (CHAPTER 4), THE ALTER IDENTIFIED self-love as the source of all evil. To combat self-love, he developed a two-tiered strategy. The first level was to substitute *ahavas habrios* (love for others). The second was to directly confront its most destructive manifestations — the desire for physical pleasure and the pursuit of honor.

The Alter imbued his *talmidim* with an intense love for one another as an antidote to the natural human selfishness. Among Kelm *talmidim*, the yeshiva was universally known as the *Bais* (the house), and the relatively small number of those attached to the *Bais* at any given time constituted a spiritual family.

The intensity of a small group, each member focused on a common spiritual task, fostered a deep sense of brotherhood between Kelm *talmidim*. When Moshe Rosenstein, later the *mashgiach* in Lomza, first arrived in Kelm he was puzzled by the effusive greeting of the first student he met. Assuming from the warmth with which he was received that the *talmid* must be a long-lost friend, he racked his brain to recall his name. Only when he was greeted with equal warmth by a second and then a third *talmid* did he realize that everyone was greeted in this fashion.[34]

The Alter taught his students to rejoice in discovering the good points of their colleagues. He himself set aside specific times to reflect upon the virtues of others, and his *talmidim* followed suit. One

---

33. Ibid., pp. 168-9.
34. Ibid., p. 148.

of Reb Reuven's *kabbalos* was "to think about the strengths of others ... from the point of view of one who loves them ... [and] rejoices in their virtues." He also resolved "not to go a single day without doing something for someone else, whether great or small, whether directly or with money or speech."[35]

Every *Elul*, a yellow poster hung in the Kelm *beis medrash* on which the Alter had inscribed his principal reminder for Rosh Hashanah:

> All the Rosh Hashanah prayers are designed to glorify the Kingdom of Heaven, and we, for our part, are called upon to crown the Lord as King of Kings. With what shall we crown Him? With love for others and charitable acts, as Moshe said in his parting blessing: "There will be a king in Yeshurun when the leaders of the people gather together, with the tribes of Israel as one." In other words, only if we are united and act out of a sense of unity and brotherly love will we be worthy of crowning the King, *HaKadosh Baruch Hu*.[36]

The Alter developed a particular regimen to encourage feelings of closeness between the students and concern for others. The Talmud Torah employed no servants. Even the most menial tasks were performed by the *talmidim*. Those tasks encouraged a sense of mutual responsibility on the physical plane, just as the *vaadim* encouraged a feeling of mutual responsibility on the spiritual plane.

The more menial the task, the more highly sought after it was. As the youngest student when he arrived, Elya Lazer had no hope of securing a difficult task, like cleaning the floors of the *beis medrash*, and had to content himself with being sent to purchase the stamps for the yeshiva.[37]

So highly prized were the various chores that no one would have ever considered performing another's task and thus robbing him of the opportunity. To watch great Torah scholars sweeping the floor

---
35. Ibid., Vol. V, p. 147.
36. Rabbi Elchonon Blumenthal, *Trials and Challenges*, p. 34.
37. Rabbi Aryeh Carmell.

of the *beis medrash* with great care, said Rabbi Yerucham Levovitz, was a living picture of the absolute dedication to their task that each of the functionaries, even the doorkeepers, showed in the Temple.[38]

A wealthy woman from Koenigsberg once came to the yeshiva and found her son sweeping the stairwell. She approached the Alter and accused him of having turned her son into a cleaning man. The Alter replied calmly with a pun on the Yiddish verb *kert*, meaning both to sweep and to overturn: "*Ver es kert do kert die velt* — Whoever sweeps here overturns the world."[39]

Kelm stressed the importance of using one's imagination in order to empathize with others. The ultimate goal — never capable of being fully attained — was to reach such a degree of identification with others that doing *chesed* for them became, not just the performance of a mitzvah, but something as natural as acting on behalf of oneself.

The Alter's own powers of identification with others were honed over a lifetime. When he saw chain gangs of prisoners repairing the roads or building new ones in the vicinity of Kelm, he wondered, "How can anyone just walk casually on roads which have been built at such a cost in the suffering of others?"[40] Even on his deathbed, his thoughts were still on the welfare of others. One of his last instructions to his family was to be sure to wash all his clothes before distributing them to the poor after his death.[41]

The Alter not only sought to extirpate selfishness at its source, he attacked the consequences of self-love: the pursuit of *kavod* and sensual pleasure. Kelm anathematized *kavod* (honor). Humility and hiddenness marked the true Kelm product. Anything that called attention to self of necessity reflected the intrusion of some value other than the rigorous pursuit of truth.

---

38. Rabbi Yerucham Levovitz, *Daas Chochmah U'Mussar* (Hebrew), Vol. I, p. 183; Rabbi Shlomo Wolbe, *HaAdam Bi'kar*, p. 9.
39. Katz, Vol. II, p. 155.
40. Ibid., p. 42.
41. Ibid.

Inside the Kelm Talmud Torah

In Kelm, no one stood in the place of honor in the first row of the *beis hamedrash*. There were no titles and *talmidim* did not even stand out of respect for their *rebbei'im*, much less one another. The Alter showed extreme distaste when anyone stood for him, and did not allow himself to be addressed with any honorific titles.

To the *talmidim* in Grubin he wrote, "Honor destroys both the body and the soul. It is a disgrace for me to be addressed as 'our master and teacher,' since I am neither. For the good of the House, I did not protest this great humiliation. But now I must ask that no one address me in this fashion again. I should be addressed only as 'the one who loves us and seeks our good.' I think that might be the truth."[42]

Any show of honor was considered tantamount to administering poison to the one so honored. Men were called to the Torah only by their names with no titles of any kind.[43] The Alter too was called up without any title. Even Rabbi Elchonon Wasserman was simply called

---

42. Ibid., p. 47.
43. Ibid., p. 150.

up as Elchonon Bunim ben Naftoli.[44] The only exception made to this rule in the Alter's lifetime was for the *Chofetz Chaim,* whom the Alter instructed the *gabbai* to call as "*Moreinu* (our teacher)."[45]

The Alter permitted no distinctions between *talmidim* on the basis of wealth lest wealth become a badge of pride. In Grubin, *talmidim* were strictly limited to eating what was served and no one was allowed to purchase any extra food.

Since the pursuit of physical pleasure is an expression of self-love, the Alter taught, any involvement in physicality removes one from G-d. Kelm developed a regimen for fighting against desire known as "*shviras haratzon* — breaking the will." Kelm *talmidim* made a practice, for instance, of never opening a letter on the day it was received no matter how intensely anticipated it was.[46]

Nothing so strengthened a person, the Alter said, as succeeding in removing from his mind the desire for something sinful. Every such victory was like pouring coals on the head of the *yetzer,* in the words of Reb Reuven Dov, and thus "more precious than pearls."[47] As such, even the smallest of victories over the *yetzer* deserved to be savored and guarded. Ultimately, however, the most effective way to diminish the power of the *yetzer,* said the Alter, is to experience an intellectual pleasure so intense that it overwhelms any pleasure the physical world can offer.[48]

The Quest for Perfection

PERFECTION WAS THE GOAL OF KELM *CHINUCH.* THE ALTER AND his successors hand-picked a small number of students who they felt were suited to the specific discipline of Kelm. The Alter had a clear vision of an *adam hashalem,* a harmonious whole, that he wished to create, and each Kelm product bore the unmistakable stamp of Kelm.[49]

---

44. *Orchos Chesed,* op. cit., p. 20.
45. *Me'ir Einei Yisrael,* Vol. II, p. 274.
46. Rabbi Shlomo Wolbe, *HaAdam Bi'kar* (Hebrew), p. 9.
47. Katz, Vol. V, p. 142.
48. Ibid., p. 131.
49. The Alter, of course, was too great an educator to produce *talmidim* cut from a single mold. Among those who fell under his early influence were such radically

To understand what was unique about Kelm it would be useful to contrast it to the much larger Slabodka Yeshiva. Though the Alter of Slabodka was a student of the Alter of Kelm, his approach emphasized *gadlus ha'adam* (the greatness of man) over perfection. He sought to develop the outstanding traits of each individual to the maximum. As a consequence, no two Slabodka *talmidim* were alike.[50]

The perfection sought in Kelm was not limited by time or space. Where the *maskilim* had taught, "Be a Jew at home and a man abroad," the Alter taught, "Be a Jew and a man in your house and a Jew and a man abroad."

To do so required knowledge of both the Torah and of the world — *mili d'Shamaya* and *mili d'alma*. "The whole world is a house of *mussar* and every human being is a book of *mussar*," the Alter taught. Otherwordly was, in his parlance, not a term of praise, but rather a shortcoming that limited the stage upon which a Jew could fulfill the duties of the heart incumbent upon him.[51]

To maintain one's *bitachon* (trust in Hashem), for instance, one must first know the pitfalls that the world poses to *bitachon*; he must know those circumstances that should be avoided and those that should be embraced. Rabbi Hillel Goldberg has summarized the Kelm approach well:

---

different personalities as Rabbi Yosef Leib Bloch, the Telzer Rosh Yeshiva, the Alter of Novordhok, and the Alter of Slobodka. Moreover, Kelm *talmidim* were mature scholars who came to Kelm from a wide diversity of yeshivos. Yet, over time, Kelm tended to attract a particular type, and its products had certain traits that marked them as Kelmers...

50. Rabbi Mordechai Zuckerman. Rabbi Zuckerman learned in Kelm for several years. During World War II, he was together with Rabbi Avraham Grodzinski, the Slabodka *Mashgiach*, in the Kovno ghetto. The two became very close, and Rabbi Zuckerman was exposed to the approach of Slabodka as well.

The differing approaches of the two yeshivos can be seen in the remarks of two of their outstanding products. Rabbi Yerucham Levovitz, the quintessential Kelm product, once commented on the *Mishnah* in *Eruvin* (80a), in which Rabbi Yehoshua *paskens* that a loaf of bread, no matter how small, is suitable for *eruv chatzeros*, but a piece of bread, no matter how large, is not: "One sees from here that *shleimus* is preferable to *gadlus*."

Rabbi Meir Chodosh, *Mashgiach* of Hebron Yeshiva and a product of Slabodka, however, once observed that a person can have every limb perfectly formed and still be a midget.

51. Ibid., pp. 104, 172.

As the whole world is the arena in which Hashem's *mitzvos* are performed, each person must know how the world can help and hurt *mitzvah* performance. As the individual psyche is the arena in which each person must give his whole being to *avodas Hashem*, he must understand his psyche to purify it in relation to itself — to rid it of self-deception — and in relation to others — to rid it of selfishness and manipulation.[52]

---

52. Hillel Goldberg, *The Fire Within*, pp. 74-5.

Chapter 6

Budding Torah Scholar

ELYA LAZER WAS NOT ONLY BY FAR THE YOUNGEST MEMBER of the Talmud Torah in his early days in Kelm, he was also the only one never to have learned in one of the premier Eastern European yeshivos. Prior to his arrival in Kelm, he had learned only with private tutors.

There were no fixed *shiurim* in Talmud in Kelm precisely because every *talmid* was assumed to already be an advanced scholar in his own right. Though the *roshei yeshiva* — in particular, Rabbi Doniel Movshovitz, the last *rosh yeshiva* — were among the greatest scholars of Lithuania, no one came to Kelm for the purpose of gaining a new approach to learning. What drew *talmidim* to Kelm was the desire to reach the highest possible level of perfection in *middos*.

Despite the fact that Kelm was not designed to train *talmidei chachamim* but to polish those who were already scholars, Rabbi Dessler did develop into a Torah scholar of stature in Kelm. That side of him, however, is not generally known. In the last decade and a half of his life, when he first came to public prominence, it was as the preeminent explicator of *Aggadata*. During most of that period, he steadfastly refrained from "talking in learning" in halachic subjects, on the grounds that he had been chosen for another role in each of the institutions with which he was associated.

Not until more than thirty years after his passing were the first of his *chiddushei Torah* published as *Chiddushei HaGaon Rabbi Eliyahu Eliezer on Shas*.[1] In his *haskamah* to that volume, Rabbi Eliezer Menachem Man Schach states that publicizing Rabbi Dessler's genius in Talmudic learning is a great and worthwhile undertaking.

In Kelm, Rabbi Dessler's *hasmadah* (diligence) was soon noted, and he gained the nickname Elinka the *Masmid*. He used to barricade himself in a corner with *shtenders* all around him. It became a favorite game among the local *cheder* boys to see whether they could disturb the concentration of Elinka the *Masmid*.[2]

In addition to his *hasmadah* (diligence), young Elya Lazer must have revealed a depth of thought far beyond his years. When he was only 17, Rabbi Shlomo Elyashiv, author of *Leshem Shevo V'Achlama* and the greatest Lithuanian Kabbalist of his time, offered to study Kabbalah privately with him. Rabbi Dessler's father, however, strongly opposed the idea, and his son complied with his wishes. Years later, Rabbi Dessler expressed his gratitude to his father for his advice. As he told his cousin Rabbi Simcha Zissel Dessler, he had the satisfaction of having acquired any knowledge he had of the esoteric Torah through his own strenuous efforts.

Between the age of 14 when he came to Kelm and his marriage fourteen years later, Rabbi Dessler completed the entire Talmud four times.[3] On one of the few occasions in his later years when he revealed anything of his stature in learning, he invited a group of his students in Ponevezh to his house to drink a *"l'chaim"* with him. He

---

1. Rabbi Dessler's Torah novellae were published posthumously by Reb David Solomon Sassoon.
2. Rabbi Aryeh Carmell.
3. Rabbi Mordecai Miller.

explained that he was celebrating having completed *Shulchan Aruch, Yoreh Deah* for the sixtieth time.[4]

As to the quality of Rabbi Dessler's learning, we have the testimony of no less an authority that his uncle Rabbi Chaim Ozer Grozensky, the undisputed *gadol hador*. In the early 1920s, Reb Chaim Ozer offered Rabbi Dessler a position on his *beis din* in Vilna. Over the years, Rabbi Dessler frequently sent his *chiddushei Torah* to Reb Chaim Ozer, who even cites one of them approvingly in his three-volume collection of responsa *Achiezer*.[5] In one of his many letters to Rabbi Dessler, Reb Chaim Ozer addresses him as one destined for genius and glory. Reb Chaim Ozer mentions that he has received Rabbi Dessler's *chiddushei Torah* (Torah novellae) and that he found those he looked into solidly based.[6]

Though Reb Chaim Ozer refused all his life to give *semichah*,[7] he did so on behalf of Rabbi Dessler. In 1929, he wrote:

> From his childhood, I already recognized his outstanding abilities, and that he had the potential to be one of the *gedolei hador* of our times. Afterwards he added to his knowledge of the Torah. Besides his greatness in learning, his fear of Heaven precedes his wisdom, and he is a new vessel filled with old wine in breadth of knowledge, and sharpness, and his depth of understanding.
>
> Many times we have discussed halachic matters, and I have seen a number of his writings on different topics that reveal the depth of his understanding. One who possesses all these qualities is certainly fitting to hold up the banner of Torah and render halachic rulings in a major city. And we grant him *semichah* in every matter — both in *Yoreh Deah* and *Choshen Mishpat*.

---

4. Rabbi Moshe Turk.

5. See *Achiezer, Yoreh Deah* 1:4.

6. Rabbi Aharon Sorasky, *Achiezer: Collected Letters* (Hebrew), Vol. II, Letter 375.

7. The only other exceptions he made were on behalf of the *Chofetz Chaim* and Rabbi Shimon Shkop when they needed *semichah* in connection with dealings with the Russian government. See *Achiezer: Collected Letters*, Vol. II, Letter 382 (editor's note).

Happy is the community that chooses him and places the crown of *rabbanus* on his head, and they will have pleasure from him in every respect.[8]

WITH THE EXCEPTION OF HIS FATHER, NO ONE INFLUENCED Rabbi Dessler's development more that Rabbi Tzvi Hirsch Braude, **Rabbi Tzvi Hirsch Braude** the Alter's son-in-law and successor. Rabbi Dessler was the youngest member of a group of eminent Kelm products who knew the Alter only through Reb Tzvi Hirsch. That group included Rabbi Doniel Movshowitz and Rabbi Gershon Miadnik, the last heads of the Talmud Torah, Rabbi Moshe Rosenstein, Rabbi Yechezkel Levenstein, and Rabbi Abba Grossbard. Even Rabbi Yerucham Levovitz spent less than a year in the Alter's presence. The rest of his eight years in Kelm were spent learning under Rabbi Leib Braude, the Alter's brother and immediate successor, and Reb Leib's son, Reb Tzvi Hirsch, who succeeded his father when the former moved to *Eretz Yisrael* in 1901.

No further proof of Reb Tzvi Hirsch's greatness is needed beyond his role in shaping the two of the most influential *ba'alei hashkafah* of our century: Rabbi Yerucham Levovitz and Rabbi Dessler. But there is more, including the exceptional devotion of his *talmidim*.

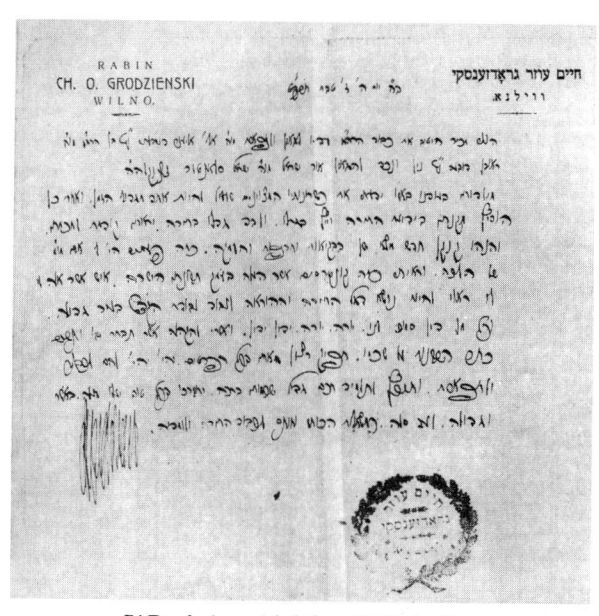

R' Dessler's semichah from R' Chaim Ozer

---

8. *Achiezer: Collected Letters* (Hebrew), Vol. II, Letter 333.

In 1907, Reb Tzvi Hirsch left Kelm to visit his father in *Eretz Yisrael*. When he had still not returned after several months, his *talmidim* feared that he might be planning to stay permanently. They wrote to his father of the great loss to the Talmud Torah caused by Reb Tzvi Hirsch's prolonged absence and urged him to send Reb Tzvi Hirsch back immediately. At the same time, they wrote Rabbi Yitzchak Blazer, who was then living in Jerusalem, requesting him to prevail upon Reb Tzvi Hirsch to return. Among the signatories to these letters were Rabbi Doniel Movshovitz, Rabbi Yitzchak Isaac Sher, Rabbi Yosef Aryeh Nenedik, and Rabbi Eliyahu Lopian. Once he realized how dependent the *talmidim* were on his son, Reb Leib sent Reb Tzvi Hirsch back to Kelm.[9]

In the eyes of his *talmidim*, Reb Tzvi Hirsch represented continuity from the Alter to the present. Reb Yerucham spoke for the entire Talmud Torah when he said, "We do not lie to ourselves if we say that the Alter did not die and that his spirit is still with us. Who protected him from death? ... His son Rabbi Tzvi Hirsch Braude."[10]

"Son" is not too strong a term to describe the relationship between the Alter and Reb Tzvi Hirsch. The Alter's indirect influence on Reb Tzvi Hirsch reached back to the cradle. Reb Tzvi Hirsch's father, Reb Leib Braude, was not only the Alter's younger brother but one of his closest *talmidim*. The Alter, who was much older, played a large role in Reb Leib's upbringing and described his brother as one of the few who really understood *mussar*.[11]

From the age of 11, Reb Tzvi Hirsch's entire *chinuch* was under the Alter's direct supervision — first in Grubin and later in Kelm. The Alter viewed Reb Tzvi Hirsch as his spiritual heir, and used to spend much time alone with him, including long walks together on Shabbos afternoon.

As the Alter's spiritual heir, it was natural that Reb Tzvi Hirsch marry the Alter's younger daughter Nechama Liba. Nechama Liba was a major *mussar* personality in her own right. Rabbi Yerucham Levovitz, Rabbi Elya Lopian, and Rabbi Moshe Rosenstein visited her

---

9. Katz, *Tenuas HaMussar,* Vol. II, pp. 97-8.
10. Ibid., p. 96.
11. Ibid., pp. 98-9.

regularly once a week to hear words of *emunah* and *bitachon*.[12] In the introduction to his work *Yesodei HaDaas*, Rabbi Rosenstein, the Lomza *Mashgiach*, lists her as the fourth of his teachers and writes, "As a guest in her house over a span of years, I had the opportunity to observe her conduct, …, and I learned a very great deal from her."[13]

The Alter, who could be highly critical of his children, called her "my wise daughter from whom I receive such *nachas*," and said that she understood his *shmuessen*, as well as anyone. He termed her "a wonder" for having succeeded in changing her basic nature through *mussar*. After the Alter's death, many *ba'alei mussar* visited Nechama Liba to hear her memories of Kelm and her father.[14]

Even when she sat in the boots and galoshes store from which she and Reb Tzvi Hirsch earned their living, Nechama Liba could be found reading a *mussar* work. As a teenager, Rabbi Nachum Velvel Dessler spent a summer vacation in Kelm helping his great-aunt in her store. His job was to translate the prices on each pair of boots from what it had been in 1913, when Reb Tzvi Hirsch passed away, into the currency of the 1930s. Nechama Liba instructed him to be careful that the new price represented no more than a ten percent profit on what Reb Tzvi Hirsch had paid for the boots twenty years earlier, despite the fact that prices had risen substantially in the interim. Periodically, she would ask Reb Nochum Velvel how much they had earned that week. As soon as she reached a predetermined sum, she would immediately close the store, telling the surprised teenager, "The other store owners also have to earn a living."[15]

R' Tzvi Hirsch Braude

---

12. Rabbi Moshe Shapiro in a *hesped* for his father Rabbi Meir Yitzchak Shapiro in Ponevezh Yeshiva. Rabbi Meir Yitzchak Shapiro, a grandson of the Alter's brother, was partly raised by Rebbetzin Nechama Liba.

13. Ibid., pp. 89-90.

14. Ibid., p. 89.

15. "Reminiscences of Rabbi Nachum Velvel Dessler," op. cit., p. 59.

Chapter Six: Budding Torah Scholar

Reb Tzvi Hirsch exemplified the Kelm ideal of perfection. Asked once why he had returned to Kelm after almost twenty years as a successful merchant in the Prussian city of Koenigsberg, Reb Nachum Velvel Ziv replied that he had come to be near his brother-in-law Reb Tzvi Hirsch. Reb Tzvi Hirsch, he said, was the clearest possible proof that Torah is *min haShamayim* (from Heaven), for if Torah were not Divine it would have been impossible to produce a person of such perfection.[16]

A list of *kabbalos* found in Reb Tzvi Hirsch's papers reflects the goals of Kelm *chinuch:* (1) Pay attention to speak truthfully and to avoid falsehood in all one's dealings; (2) *Ahavas habrios* — to do acts of *chesed* with every Jew, especially the poor, sick, and broken spirited; (6) to minimize all physical pleasure in order to break the will; (9) to do nothing suddenly, but rather to reflect what to do according to the halachah and the demands of *mussar;* (11) to learn an hour of *mussar* daily with a group for the purpose of reflecting on one's actions both past and future.[17]

The perfection for which they strove in Kelm meant living according to an internal compass that did not vary according to external circumstances. Reb Tzvi Hirsch personified that consistency. He was exactly the same person whether in his store or in the *beis medrash*, and in both places the beauty of his *middos* struck all with whom he came into contact. Rabbi Yerucham Levovitz said of his teacher that he was no different in his shop or learning at his *shtender* in the yeshiva. He brought the same qualities — alertness, precision, order, and honesty — to both. Moreover, just being in his presence was sufficient to convey these qualities to others.[18]

Though Reb Tzvi Hirsch's thoughts were on an extremely elevated plane, they did not cause him to forget those around him. In his home, he could often be found helping the servant girls with their tasks, and he showed a warm, kindly countenance to all. The local peasants bowed down to him and would attempt to kiss his hand as he passed.[19]

---

16. Wolbe, *HaAdam Bi'kar*, p. 10.
17. Katz, Vol. II, pp. 94-5.
18. Rabbi Elchonon Blumenthal, *Trials and Challenges*, p. 329.
19. Katz, Vol. II, pp. 93-4.

Nearly every Jew in Kelm attended his funeral and all the local stores were closed as a sign of affection as well as respect.

Reb Tzvi Hirsch used to say that if a person cannot control even his outer movements, he has no hope of controlling his heart or mind. And it was said of him that even the movement of his eyebrows was purposive.[20]

Most of his life, Reb Tzvi Hirsch suffered from excruciating migraine headaches, yet he always wore the same calm smile. Once a visitor came to visit him while he was in the throes of one of his migraines. Reb Tzvi Hirsch removed the compresses that he used to relieve the throbbing in his head so that his visitor would not cut short his visit out of concern for his well-being. He only replaced the compresses when his visitor had left. Asked how he could show such an untroubled appearance while in such agony, he replied with the words of *Mishlei* (18:14): "A man's spirit lightens his disease."[21]

The excuse of being compelled by circumstances beyond one's control was almost unknown in Kelm, and particularly to Reb Tzvi Hirsch. Even when he could no longer walk alone in the streets for fear that he might collapse, his schedule remained unchanged and he rarely missed a *seder* in the *beis medrash*. Three days before he died, he closed his eyes as if he was about to faint while giving a *shmuess* sitting on a bench at the back of the *beis medrash*. As soon as he recovered, however, he continued as if nothing had happened.[22]

Reb Tzvi Hirsch passed away in 1913 at the age of 48 after thirteen years at the helm of the Talmud Torah. Months after his passing, Rabbi Eliyahu Lopian returned to Kelm and was surprised to find Rabbi Nachum Velvel Ziv still in intense mourning for his brother-in-law. The Talmud describes the first days of mourning as days of crying, and Rabbi Lopian could not understand how Reb Nachum Velvel, who was extremely meticulous to fulfill every word of *Chazal*, could still give external vent to his mourning. Reb Nachum Velvel explained that the three days of mourning referred

---

20. Ibid., p. 93.
21. Ibid., pp. 93-4.
22. Ibid., p. 98.

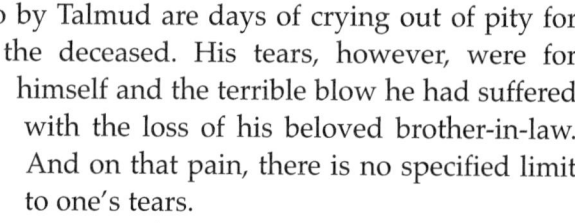

Rebbetzin Nechama Liba

to by Talmud are days of crying out of pity for the deceased. His tears, however, were for himself and the terrible blow he had suffered with the loss of his beloved brother-in-law. And on that pain, there is no specified limit to one's tears.

Reb Nachum Velvel's feelings were shared by the entire Talmud Torah. Nearly a year after Reb Tzvi Hirsch's passing, his widow Nechama Liba entered the Talmud Torah on Purim and sensed that the joy of years past was missing. She realized that the *talmidim* were melachcholy from contemplating the absence of their beloved *rebbe*. Nechama Liba announced that Reb Tzvi Hirsch would have been very disturbed to find that his passing had lessened the rejoicing of Purim and insisted that the celebrations should take place with all the enthusiasm of years past.[23]

Rabbi Dessler learned seven years under Reb Tzvi Hirsch. Even a cursory glance at *Michtav Me'Eliyahu* reveals how profound the impact of Reb Tzvi Hirsch was on him. A number of the *meshalim* and concepts that Rabbi Dessler made famous actually originated with Reb Tzvi Hirsch, whom he always describes as "my saintly rebbi" or "my revered rebbi."

Perhaps the best known of Reb Tzvi Hirsch's *meshalim* is that of a Jew moving through time in a yearly cycle. Most people think of time as something that passes. Reb Tzvi Hirsch, however, described a Jew as passing through time. Each year he arrives back at the same place in time as the previous year. Each festival is a "stop" on the journey with its own particular spiritual influences. When we "arrive" back at Pesach, for instance, we are imbued by the day with the potential to experience freedom just as our ancestors did upon leaving Egypt.[24]

In Kelm, they worked hard on piercing the veil of "nature" to see

---

23. Ibid., p. 90.
24. *Michtav Me'Eliyahu*, Vol. I, p. 103; *Strive for Truth*, Vol. II, p. 21.

the hand of G-d behind every event in the world. Reb Tzvi Hirsch used to compare those who attribute an independent existence to "the natural order" to someone who peers through a keyhole and sees a pen moving across a piece of paper and concludes that the pen is moving on its own. Rabbi Dessler made that metaphor the centerpiece of a major series of articles on "nature."[25]

Reb Tzvi Hirsch represented for Rabbi Dessler what it meant to internalize the ideas of the Torah. In an essay on Chanukah, Rabbi Dessler discusses the argument between Beis Shammai and Beis Hillel over whether we light an additional candle every night or one less candle every night. Beis Shammai held that we should light the candles in descending order — i.e., eight on the first night, seven on the second, and so on.

According to Beis Shammai, the performance of the *mitzvah* should reflect the spiritual level of the one performing the *mitzvah*. Most people's performance of the *mitzvos* never rises beyond the external level, and for them the joy of the holiday therefore fades with each passing day. To reflect that reality, Beis Shammai argued, the Chanukah lights should be lit in descending order.

Beis Hillel, however, held that the candles should be lit in ascending order — one on the first night, two on the second night, etc. According to Bais Hillel the performance of the *mitzvah* should be modeled after the ideal, as represented by the great *tzaddikim*. Such *tzaddikim* reflect deeply upon the meaning of the holiday, internalizing its message in the process. Their joy increases with each passing day, because "each day adds to their understanding of the Festival and its laws and their appreciation of the divine gift it represents."[26]

Rabbi Tzvi Hirsch epitomized such a *tzaddik*. As Rabbi Dessler describes him: "As the Yom Tov came in, his face was wondrous to behold; one saw in him the veritable joy of a higher world. The saintly joy of his visage and his whole bearing grew in angelic intensity with each passing day."[27]

---
25. See *Michtav Me'Eliyahu*, Vol. I, p. 181; *Strive for Truth*, Vol. II, p. 247.
26. *Michtav Me'Eliyahu*, Vol. II, p. 121; Rabbi Aryeh Carmell, *Sanctuaries in Time*, p. 145.
27. *Michtav Me'Eliyahu*, ibid.; *Sanctuaries in Time*, p. 146.

Rabbi Nachum Velvel Ziv

RABBI NACHUM VELVEL ZIV, THE ALTER'S SON AND FATHER OF Rabbi Dessler's future wife, succeeded Reb Tzvi Hirsch as head of the Talmud Torah in 1913. Three years earlier, he had returned to Kelm, after twenty years in Koenigsberg, to assist his brother-in-law in running the Talmud Torah.

From his external appearance in Koenigsberg, no one would have guessed that Reb Nachum Velvel was someone of whom Rabbi Yerucham Levovitz said, "He had the power to attract the entire world to *mussar*, but out of his modesty did not recognize his own capabilities."[28] His attire gave no hint of his Eastern European background. He dressed like any other well-to-do German-Jewish businessman.

One time he invited an important Eastern European *rav*, who was in Koenigsberg for medical treatments, to his home. A quick glance at Reb Nachum Velvel's elegantly appointed house convinced the *rav* that this was not a place in which he could eat. Pleading a lack of appetite, he refused to drink anything more than a cup of tea.

R' Nachum Velvel Ziv as a young man

In the middle of the night, the *rav* was awakened from his sleep by the sound of someone crying. His curiosity aroused, he left his bed and peeked into the room from which the crying was coming. There he saw Reb Nachum Velvel repeating over and over the words of *Ecclesiates* (9:10): "For there is neither doing nor reckoning nor knowledge nor wisdom in the grave where you are going." Afterwards Reb Nachum Velvel opened up his *Gemara* and began to learn.[29]

His learning *seder* during the years in Koenigsberg began at 3 a.m.

---

28. Katz, Vol. II, p. 87.
29. Ibid., pp. 83-4.
    Rabbi Dessler was the source of this story.

and lasted until *Shacharis*. After *Shacharis*, he conducted business until 2 p.m. The rest of the day was devoted to learning and communal projects. Customers knew that Reb Nachum Velvel's closing time was inviolable and that any deal that was not concluded by 2 p.m. would have to wait until the next day.[30]

Reb Nachum Velvel's refusal to extend the working day reflected his deep *emunah*, a quality for which the Alter himself praised him. That we have to work or engage in commercial activity at all, explained Reb Nachum Velvel, is nothing less than a Divine decree, but we should never make the mistake of attributing our financial success or failures to our own efforts. Once he noticed that a family member was putting what he considered undue pressure on a customer to conclude a deal, and he motioned to him that he should stop at once. Any such extraordinary exertions in business betrayed, in his view, a lack of *emunah* and a faith in the power of one's own hands.[31]

Whenever he traveled, Reb Nachum Velvel took advantage of the opportunity to increase his hours of learning. If he took a train, he always secured a private chamber so that his learning would not be disturbed. And if the train had a layover at a particular stop, he would rent a carriage to take him to the local *beis medrash* so that he could continue his learning there. One time, Rabbi Dessler accompanied him from Kelm to Vilna. Before they embarked, Reb Nachum Velvel asked Rabbi Dessler not to speak to him during the course of the journey. When they arrived in Vilna, Reb Nachum Velvel apologized to Rabbi Dessler, but explained that the opportunity for uninterrupted thought had been too precious to waste.[32]

Learning to identify with others, particularly with their suffering, was one of the fundamentals of Kelm. Reb Nachum Velvel excelled in this ability. Koenigsberg was a major medical center, and there were always Eastern European Jews, far from home, in the hospital.

---

30. Ibid., p. 78.
31. Ibid., p. 81.
32. Ibid., p. 78.
 Rabbi Dessler himself recounted this incident.

Every Sunday, Reb Nachum Velvel would visit the hospital and bring with him entire suitcases neatly packed for any *talmidei chachamim* who were patients and might not have access to food meeting their standards of *kashrus*. Over the years, Reb Nachum Velvel acquired a considerable expertise in medical matters, and that knowledge was placed at the disposal of any Jew who came to Koenigsberg for treatment.[33]

One time a neighbor of Reb Nachum Velvel was arrested and charged with a serious crime. For the duration of the neighbor's imprisonment, Reb Nachum Velvel would not permit any laughter in his house. "How can you laugh when our neighbor is languishing in prison?" he demanded to know.[34]

Reb Nachum Velvel inherited his father's power of speech, especially his power of vivid description. Once he was asked to speak at a *simchah* after a distinguished *talmid chacham* from Vilna. The preceding speaker had spoken very poorly, and Reb Nachum Velvel absolutely refused to speak after him, despite numerous entreaties. He later explained to his family that he feared that he would embarrass the previous speaker.[35]

For Kelmers, death was the final test of whether they had truly attained *menuchas hanefesh*, the ability to confront any situation without becoming confused. The final passage from this world of all the great figures of Kelm was exemplary, but none more so than that of Reb Nachum Velvel.

The night before his passing, he suffered sharp pains, which he described as akin to having needles jabbed into him. Nevertheless his demeanor remained unchanged, and he even came to the Talmud Torah and delivered a *shmuess* on the topic: Better the day of death than the day of birth. He had previously given the same *drashah* in the *beis medrash*, but felt it important now that the time

---

33. Ibid., p. 85.
34. Ibid., p. 84.
   Reb Nachum Velvel's daughter Rebbetzin Dessler exhibited the same extraordinary sensitivity to the suffering of others. See Chap. 13, p. 184
35. Ibid., p. 84.
   Rabbi Dessler was the source of this particular story.

had actually arrived to express publicly the "joy one experiences who truly feels this way as the day of death approaches."[36]

R' Nachum Velvel Ziv

Thursday afternoon, he realized that he would not live to see another Shabbos and expressed the hope that he would pass away on *Erev Shabbos*, which is described as meritorious. Knowing that his *levayah* might be close to the beginning of Shabbos, he worried that his daughter Frieda, who had a bad leg, would be forced to rush home by foot. Rather than rely on someone else to order a carriage for her, he personally ordered one to transport his wife and daughters to the cemetery and back.

On Friday morning, realizing the end was near, Reb Nachum Velvel instructed his family with utter calm in how to conduct themselves at the *levayah*. Fearing that they would be overcome by grief at the Shabbos table, he reminded them to be careful not to swallow fish bones at the Shabbos meal.[37]

Even in *mussar* circles, Reb Nachum Velvel's calm as he approached death excited widespread admiration and was held up as an example.

When the family of Rabbi Nachum Velvel Ziv was sitting *shivah* for him, one of those who came to offer his condolences was the Russian doctor who had attended him in his final illness. The doctor was a giant of a man, and when he walked into Rabbi Nachum Velvel's house he seemed to fill the entire doorway. Coming into the room in which the family was sitting, the doctor noticed the pain on the face of Rabbi Nachum Velvel's sister Nechama Liba. He stopped, pointed at her, and said in Yiddish, "What are you crying about? Would that I were as alive at this moment as he is."[38]

---

36. Ibid., p. 88.

37. Ibid., pp. 87-88.

38. Heard by Rabbi Moshe Shapiro from his father Rabbi Meir Shapiro, who, as a young boy, was a *ben bayis* by Rabbi Nachum Velvel Ziv.

Chapter Six: Budding Torah Scholar / 87

Chapter 7

War and Poverty

WITH THE OUTBREAK OF WORLD WAR I IN AUGUST of 1914, Kelm was directly in the path of the advancing German armies. Only Rabbi Nachum Velvel Ziv's calm prevented the entire Jewish population from fleeing in panic.[1] Until his death in early 1916, Reb Nachum Velvel managed to maintain the *sedarim* in the yeshiva as they had always been, even though there were times that he was nearly alone in the *beis medrash*.[2]

Emunas Chachamim

Eventually most of the unmarried students left Kelm and sought refuge far from the frontlines. One group went to Riga, where Rabbi Yaakov Katz formed a yeshiva of students fleeing the various Lithuanian yeshivos. In 1915, Rabbi Katz, who was a close friend of Reb Reuven Dov from their days together in Kelm, brought his

---

1. Katz, *Tenuas HaMussar*, Vol. II, p. 86.
2. Ibid., p. 87.

yeshiva to Homel, where his family and many of the students found shelter with the Dessler brothers.³

Reb Reuven Dov served as the *Mashgiach* of the yeshiva in Homel. In that role, he made a great impression on the *talmidim*. In *mussar seder*, the walls of the *beis medrash* would shake as he repeated over and over a statement of *Chazal*, such as, "Envy, desire, and honor remove a person from the world." Many of his *shmuessen* were exactly as he remembered them from the Alter, even in the manner of delivery. He was a powerful speaker, who kept his audience mesmerized with his vivid descriptions.⁴

Every *shmuess* concluded with words of rebuke directed at himself — e.g., "If the great ones of the generation could fall, what shall we say for ourselves." Reb Reuven Dov's *shmuessen* had a profound effect on the *bachurim*, who would sit in their places when he had finished, not even lifting their heads to look at one another. A number of his *talmidim* went on to become distinguished Torah personalities in their own right.⁵

A steady stream of refugees poured into Homel during the war, including many students of the Lithuanian yeshivos. The yeshivos attempted to regroup in towns like Kremenchug and Homel far away from the border. Among those who found refuge in Homel for a period of time was Rabbi Yozef Yoizel Horowitz, the Alter of Novordhok. The Alter's whole worldview was predicated on the necessity of choosing between a life of spiritual striving and material pleasures. Recognizing, as he did, Reb Reuven Dov's elevated spiritual level, the Alter of Novordhok was doubly offended by the latter's comfortable lifestyle, which seemed a direct contradiction to the entire philosophy of Novordhok.

On Purim, the Alter of Novordhok visited Reb Reuven Dov and

---

3. Ibid., pp. 74-5.
   One of the students who lived in Reb Reuven Dov's house was Rabbi Mendel Zaks, the future son-in-law of the *Chofetz Chaim*.
4. Ibid., Vol. V, p.134.
5. Ibid., pp. 136-7.
   Rabbi Dov Katz, the author of *Tenuas HaMussar*, was the son of Rabbi Yaakov Katz, and these descriptions are presumably his personal memories of Reb Reuven Dov's *shmuessen*.

dragged him atop one of the elegant sofas, where the two danced together. Reb Reuven Dov understood well the point the Alter was trying to make and reacted good-naturedly, but remained unshaken in his conviction that spiritual growth did not necessitate a life of poverty.[6]

Another refugee in Homel would have a much more long-lasting impact on Rabbi Dessler. In late summer of 1915, Rabbi Chaim Ozer Grodzenski, *rav* of Vilna and already one of the leaders of the generation, learned of an order for his arrest and exile to Siberia by the Czarist regime. (The Russian government had made Lithuanian Jewry the scapegoat for its early military reversals at the hands of the Germans.) Rabbi Chaim Ozer fled to Homel to the home of his brother-in-law Reb Reuven Dov Dessler and remained there for a full year.[7]

By that time, Rabbi Dessler had returned to his father's house from Kelm, and Reb Chaim Ozer's presence gave him an opportunity to spend long hours with his uncle. While Reb Chaim Ozer had known his nephew since he was a child, the latter was no longer a promising youngster in his uncle's eyes, but a mature scholar of 23. The extraordinary closeness between uncle and nephew reflected in their extensive correspondence in later years is no doubt an outgrowth of the year together in Homel.

By virtue of Reb Chaim Ozer's presence, Reb Reuven Dov's home became a meeting place for *chachamim*. Many other great Lithuanian *rabbanim* and *roshei yeshiva* had found sanctuary deeper into Russia, and they too came to Homel to consult with Reb Chaim Ozer. Reb Reuven Dov took an active part in the rabbinic deliberations during this period, and Rabbi Dessler too seems to have been present, at least as an observer, at many meetings.

Rabbi Dessler recorded his memory of at least one rabbinical meeting led by Reb Chaim Ozer. One rabbi argued that the yeshivos were doomed by the lack of any natural means of support. Reb

---

6. "Reminiscences of Rabbi Nachum Velvel Dessler," op. cit., p. 62.
   A slightly different version of the same story is told in Katz, Vol. V, pp. 138-9.
7. Sorasky, *Achiezer: Collected Letters*, Vol. II, p. 637.

Chaim Ozer replied, "Don't worry, the Torah always exists on miracles; it will never have a natural basis."[8]

Rabbi Dessler's deep *emunas chachamim* likely had its origins in this period. In later years, he often spoke of the necessity for faith in the judgment of the Torah leaders of the generation. He himself frequently sought the guidance of Reb Chaim Ozer and Rabbi Elchonon Wasserman, and, in later years, the *Chazon Ish*.[9]

In a letter to a young follower written after the Holocaust, Rabbi Dessler gave full expression to the impact on him of Reb Chaim Ozer and the other *gedolim* whom he met. The student had apparently questioned whether the leaders of European Jewry had not erred by not encouraging emigration to *Eretz Yisrael*. Rabbi Dessler, in response, came as close to showing anger as he ever did. "Were it not that I understand that you must have picked up these ideas from other people who call themselves *bnei Torah*, but reject their teachers and desecrate G-d's name, I would not have replied to you at all," he wrote back with uncharacteristic sharpness.

He continued with a description of what it was like to be in the presence of such giants as they deliberated on matters of concern to all of *Klal Yisrael*:

> I had the merit to know several of these great men personally... — such as the *Chofetz Chaim* of sainted memory, Reb Chaim of Brisk of sainted memory, and Reb Chaim Ozer of sainted mem-

---

8. *Michtav Me'Eliyahu*, Vol. I, p. 186; *Strive for Truth*, Vol. II, p. 260.

In the same essay, Rabbi Dessler records the opinion of the *Chofetz Chaim* that it is wrong to create large endowment funds for yeshivos. Such monies should rather be used to build new yeshivos. And if someone asks, where will the support for those yeshivos come from, said the *Chofetz Chaim*, "That is Hashem's business." Ibid. p. 261.

9. Rabbi Zusia Waltner, one of the founding members of the Gateshead Kollel.

During this period or perhaps earlier, Rabbi Dessler established a personal relationship with the *Chofetz Chaim*. Reb Reuven Dov always consulted the *Chofetz Chaim* before any major new step in his life, and it is likely that his son accompanied him on some of these visits. "Reminiscences of Rabbi Nachum Velvel Dessler," op. cit., p. 55.

Years later, Rabbi Dessler told his cousin Rabbi Simcha Zissel Dessler that he had learned how to cast the *Goral HaGra* from the *Chofetz Chaim*. In the *Chofetz Chaim's* letters to Dayan Shmuel Yitzchak Hillman in London in the late '20s, he would often add a postscript inquiring about the well-being of "Reb Reuven Dov's son," Reb Eliyahu Dessler.

ory — and I have observed them at meetings on matters concerning *Klal Yisrael*. And I can tell you with all sincerity that the amazing agility of their minds could be perceived even by puny intellects such as ours ... [though] there was not the slightest chance that anyone like you or me could follow completely the crystal-like clarity of their understanding.

And more: Whoever was present at their meetings could see with their own eyes the extent and depth of the sense of responsibility with which they approached these matters; it could be seen on their faces when they deliberated for the sake of Heaven and devoted their minds to considering the problems of *Klal Yisrael*.

Anyone who did not see this has never seen feelings of responsibility in his life. Whoever had the merit to stand before them on such an occasion could have no doubt that he could see the *Shechinah* resting on the work of their hands and that the Holy Spirit was present in their assembly.[10]

Rabbi Dessler concluded his response by characterizing "lack of self-effacement towards our Rabbis [as] the root of all sin and the beginning of all destruction" and faith in the Sages as the "root of spiritual progress."[11]

WORLD WAR I AND ITS AFTERMATH ALSO BROUGHT ABOUT A dramatic reversal in the Dessler family's economic fortunes. Shortly after the Bolshevik seizure of power in 1918, the old currency, the ruble, was declared invalid. As a result, Reb Reuven Dov went instantaneously from being an extremely wealthy man to a pauper, without the means to buy food for Shabbos. Rabbi Dessler said of that experience, "Had my father not been a *ba'al mussar*, he could never have survived the shock."[12] Far from being broken by becoming a pauper overnight, Reb Reuven Dov kept two suitcases of worthless rubles for the rest

Reversal of Fortune

---

10. *Michtav Me'Eliyahu*, Vol. I, p. 75; *Strive for Truth*, Vol. I, pp. 217-8.
11. *Michtav Me'Eliyahu*, Vol. I, p. 77; *Strive for Truth*, Vol I, p. 223.
12. Rabbi Moshe Turk.

The money R' Reuven Dov gave Nachum Velvel

of his life. As a young boy, Rabbi Nachum Velvel Dessler discovered the suitcases in his grandfather's attic. Reb Reuven Dov told him how when the tides of war turned against the Germans, he had converted all his German marks into Russian rubles, which appeared to be the more stable currency. Now he kept the money, he explained to his grandson, to remind himself of the worthlessness of money. Reb Reuven Dov urged his grandson to take some of the rubles as a tangible reminder that "many are the thoughts in the heart of man, but only the counsel of Hashem endures" (*Mishlei* 19:21).[13]

The family's instantaneous poverty seems to have confirmed in Rabbi Dessler the belief that material plenty can contribute absolutely nothing to one's happiness. The insistence that happiness in life can only be achieved through spiritual achievement is at the center of his teaching. In a 1935 letter to his son Nachum Velvel, Rabbi Dessler stated his view as clearly as possible:

> There is no happiness in the world in material things; there is only happiness in spiritual concerns. The one who enjoys a rich spiritual life is happy. There is no other kind of happiness in existence.[14]

---

13. "Reminiscences of Rabbi Nachum Velvel Dessler," op. cit., p. 60.
14. *Michtav Me'Eliyahu*, Vol. I, p. 3; *Strive for Truth*, Vol. I, p. 29.

R' Gedaliah after his year in prison

In typical Kelm style, Rabbi Dessler also used the Bolshevik's invalidation of the old ruble as a *mashal*. Just as his father discovered that all his money was not worth the paper it was printed on, so might we discover when we come to the World of Truth that all our *"mitzvos,"* in which we have placed so much trust, are invalid currency. Far from being *mitzvos* at all, they may turn out to be empty acts learned by rote for which there is no reward at all.

The Bolshevik Revolution not only deprived the Desslers of all their wealth. It also placed their lives in grave danger. When the Bolsheviks captured Homel in 1920, they arrested Reb Gedaliah Dessler. After depriving him of food and sleep for days, the Bolsheviks extracted a "confession" from him by telling him that the hideous screams of a woman in the next cell were his wife's. He told his inquisitors that he had been entrusted with valuables by someone else. When the chest of valuables was discovered, Reb Gedaliah was charged with being a member of the bourgeoisie for allowing his family to starve while valuables were still in his possession, and the prosecutor asked for the death penalty.

One of the judges had previously worked for Reb Gedaliah, and he testified that if he had not touched the valuables, it was only because he would never touch money that was not his. As a consequence, Reb Gedaliah was sentenced only to life imprisonment. Eventually his wife Bertha succeeded in securing his release, but when he returned home after a year in prison, he was so devastated by the experience that his family did not recognize him.[15]

---

15. Bertha traveled all the way to Moscow on freight cars to appeal his sentence. En route, she almost lost her leg when it became pinned between two boxcars. Bertha took her case to Lenin himself, and succeeded in securing her husband's release. Devorah Dessler Olshtein, "A Baal Mussar from Kelm, a Businessman in Pre-War Europe," *in Torah Lives*, Rabbi Nisson Wolpin, ed., pp. 125-26.

Reb Reuven Dov was more fortunate than his brother. He was not in Homel at the time of the Bolshevik takeover, having previously taken one of his nephews south to the Crimea, where it was hoped that the mild climate would relief his chronic cough. From there, Reb Reuven Dov eventually made his way back to Kelm, though how he did so is far from clear. One biographer mentions mysteriously that he managed to reach Kelm only after following a circuitous path through the "lands of the East," without elaborating further.[16]

Rabbi Dessler preceded his father back to Kelm, but again we have no idea of the route that he followed in leaving revolution-torn Russia. In *Michtav Me'Eliyahu* he describes a period "wandering in the lands of the North." At some time during that period of wandering, he came across "a pack of ravenous wolves running in search of food."[17] His description of the wolves as they pounced on the carcass of a small animal lying in their path became for him a vivid *mashal* of capitalist competition:

> They were unable to devour the prey because each one attacked his neighbor... They bit and fought one another until all were wounded and bled profusely. And so they fought until all lay exhausted on the snow, and only a few of them, the strongest, at last got their teeth into the carcass. A moment passed and these too began fighting one another, biting, clawing, and wounding until the one who was victorious snatched the carcass in his jaws and ran.
>
> As I reflected on this savage scene, I observed the victor running in the distance, his path over the snow marked by the bloodstains from the many wounds he had sustained. I said to myself: "It has cost him blood, but at least he managed to still his hunger. One could apply to him the verse, 'By his life he obtains his bread.'"

---

16. Katz, Vol. II, p. 140.
17. Rabbi Dessler does not specifically identify this period of wandering in the North or what occasioned it. But from what is known of his life, it is hard to imagine his traveling through the wilderness except in the unsettled conditions in the aftermath of World War I and the Bolshevik Revolution.

Then I took another look at the others.... What had they gained from all their fighting? The shame of the vanguished.... They had nothing but [their wounds]. Their hunger, which had caused them to fight in the first place, was as intense as ever.

Rabbi Dessler used this wolf pack to portray the two possibilities confronting one who is driven in life by the pursuit of material goods. Even the winners emerge "wounded, ill, exhausted." And their victory is hollow because their hunger soon returns even stronger than before. And if that is true of the victors, how much more so the losers in the competitive rat race.[18]

Rabbi Dessler arrived back in Kelm, in newly independent Lithuania, sometime in 1918, but his father did not succeed in reaching Kelm until 1920. As the senior surviving *talmid* of the Alter, Reb Reuven took over responsibility for running the Talmud Torah shortly after his arrival. Soon afterwards, he was joined in this role by Rabbi Nachum Velvel Ziv's son-in-law Rabbi Doniel Movshovitz.

Rabbi Yerucham Levovitz, the most charismatic *mussar* personality then alive, was also in Kelm after World War I. Surveying the destruction the war had wrought on Eastern European Jewry, Reb Yerucham was convinced that the times demanded nothing less than a massive infusion of Kelm *mussar*, and to that end he strongly urged Reb Reuven Dov about the necessity of greatly expanding the Talmud Torah.

Reb Reuven Dov, however, equally forcefully rejected this suggestion. The Alter had always insisted that he could only work with a few select individuals, who would, in turn, effect larger groups of their own *talmidim*. That must continue to be the path of the Kelm Talmud Torah, Reb Reuven Dov argued. Any other course would only result in products bearing no resemblance to Kelm, even in a watered-down version.

Rabbi Avraham Trop, son of Rabbi Naftoli Trop, the Rosh Yeshiva in Radin, once commented that even this *"machlokes leshem*

---

18. *Michtav Me'Eliyahu*, Vol. I, pp. 40-1; *Strive for Truth*, Vol. I, pp. 135-36.

Shamayim" (argument for the sake of Heaven) served to bring out the special nature of Kelm. In any other yeshiva at that time, the *talmidim* themselves would have been active participants. Not so in Kelm. There were absolutely no other participants in the discussions besides Reb Yerucham and Reb Reuven Dov. And there was no hint of personal interest on either side. Throughout, Reb Yerucham and Reb Reuven Dov sat side by side in the *beis medrash*. When Reb Yerucham saw that he would not prevail upon Reb Reuven Dov, he simply returned to Mir to carry on the work he had begun there before World War I.

Rabbi Dessler himself had no involvement in the difference of opinion between his father and Reb Yerucham. But while it continued, he had a dream in which the *Ba'al HaTanya* appeared to him and specifically warned him against any involvement in *machlokes*. (When he told this story, Rabbi Dessler mentioned that he had already been learning *Tanya* for three years.)[19]

The story is interesting in itself for what it reveals about Rabbi Dessler's identification with *Tanya*, which would become an important source of inspiration for him. But it also touches upon a fascinating aspect of Kelm: the store that members of the Talmud Torah placed on dreams. Over the years, Rabbi Dessler was guided at crucial junctures in his life by dreams, and on a number of other occasions relied on the *Goral HaGra*.[20]

The reliance on dreams and the *Goral HaGra* reflect the emphasis in Kelm on removing from one's heart any feelings of "by my strength and the power of my hand." The idea that one controls his own destiny and can accurately project the consequences of his actions was a

---

19. Rabbi Wolf Kaufman, Rosh Kollel in Manchester and a student of Rabbi Dessler in the Gateshead Kollel.
    Rabbi Dessler did not specifically mention what *machlokes* the *Ba'al HaTanya* was referring to, but given the degree to which Kelm adhered to the path set by the Alter and the closeness of the feelings between Kelm *talmidim*, it is hard to conceive of another difference of opinion concerning the running of the Talmud Torah.

20. In a newspaper article written shortly after Rabbi Dessler's passing, his cousin Rabbi Simcha Zissel Dessler mentioned that he personally knew of several remarkable instances in which Rabbi Dessler relied on dreams, but that he was not at liberty to reveal them.

dangerous illusion, as far as the products of the Talmud Torah were concerned. In a letter to Rabbi Dessler, Rabbi Doniel Movshovitz describes the practice of Kelm when confronted with a major decision concerning one's material affairs: one weighs the alternatives briefly, makes a decision, and then does not veer from the decision. Thought helps for *divrei Torah*, Reb Doniel continues, quoting *Gemara Sanhedrin* (26b), but it is foolish pride for a person to think that the results of his actions are determined by the acuity of his calculations.[21]

Rabbi Dessler himself writes in the same vein: "It is a great mistake to think that one can achieve one's goals by going into the fine details of factors and causes whose effect we imagine we can forecast."[22] Even one's Torah *chiddushim*, he writes, are in reality gifts from Hashem, not the products of one's unaided wisdom. In an essay entitled, "Nature as Concealment," he describes novel thoughts as the result of the "thinker concentrating his mind to exclude all extraneous thoughts." But the thought itself comes into his mind "unbidden" from Hashem Himself.[23]

In this view, a dream is only a more extreme example of the manner in which our thoughts arise in our mind unbidden, directly from G-d. As long as the recipient of the dream is worthy of such guidance, then the dreams themselves are reliable.

Upon his return to Kelm, Rabbi Dessler was already 26 years old. The time had come to enter the next stage of his life: marriage and family.

---

21. *Kisvei HaSaba Mi'Kelm*, Vol. II, p. 604.
   For Rabbi Dessler's own treatment of these issues see *Michtav Me'Eliyahu*, Vol. I, pp. 178-80; *Strive for Truth*, Vol. II, pp. 242-244.
22. *Michtav Me'Eliyahu*, Vol. I, p. 179; *Strive for Truth*, Vol. II, p. 243.
23. *Michtav Me'Eliyahu*, Vol. I, pp. 182-3; *Strive for Truth*, Vol. II, pp. 250-51.

Chapter 8
Marriage

A year after his return to Kelm, Rabbi Dessler became engaged to Bluma Ziv, the second daughter of Rabbi Nachum Velvel Ziv. They were married a year later, on the second day of *Rosh Chodesh Adar*, תר"פ, 5680 (1920).[1]

The marriage united two families already bound by numerous ties. After the Alter's return to Kelm from Grubin in 1881, Rabbi Dessler's father Reb Reuven Dov served as Rabbi Nachum Velvel Ziv's assistant in the day-to-day running of Grubin. And from 1920 until the late '20s, Reb Reuven Dov ran Beis HaTalmud HaGadol in

---

1. The date is clear from their *kesubah*, but there is an erroneous version of the date, based on a letter written by Rabbi Chaim Ozer Grodzenski to Rabbi Dessler, apparently in the summer of 1919, after Reb Chaim Ozer's return to Vilna. It refers to a rumor that Rabbi Dessler had married on *Lag B'Omer*. Sorasky, *Achiezer — Collected Letters*, Vol. II, Letter 323. That rumor was false, and in a subsequent letter (no. 325), Reb Chaim Ozer refers to a letter from Rabbi Dessler informing him of his intention to marry on the second day of *Rosh Chodesh Adar* 5660 (1920).

It would appear, then, that the young couple was engaged for nearly a year, perhaps because Reb Reuven Dov had still not been able to make his way back to Kelm. (In another letter to Rabbi Dessler (no. 324), written in early 1920, Reb Chaim Ozer mentions having heard that Rabbi Dessler's parents are still in Charkov in White Russia.)

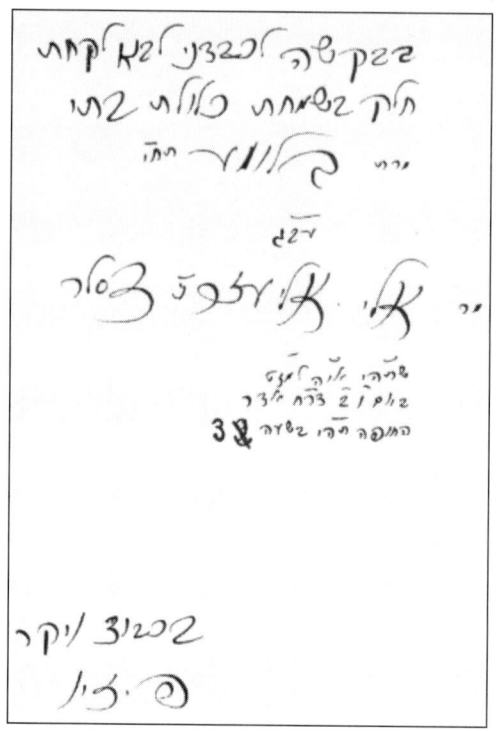
The handwritten invitation to the Dessler-Ziv wedding

conjunction with Rabbi Doniel Movshovitz, the husband of Bluma's older sister Chaya. The marriage also joined together Rabbi Yisrael Salanter's great-grandson with the granddaughter of the Alter of Kelm, Reb Yisrael Salanter's leading disciple.

Reb Chaim Ozer noted the commonality of backgrounds in a letter of *berachah* to Rabbi Dessler. "How fortunate you are to have merited finding a young woman from such a distinguished family, who is so similar to you in firm faith, *mussar* ideals, and *middos*, and how fortunate is the Ziv girl that she found someone so suitable and of such an elevated character," he wrote. "May you find happiness, my dear one, in sharing a life of common aspirations."[2]

Reb Chaim Ozer's blessing of a life together of shared aspirations was more than fulfilled over the next 31 years. Though forced to endure many hardships, including being separated for over two years when Rabbi Dessler first came to England and another six years during World War II, no trace of disharmony ever entered the Desslers' life together.

Rabbi Dessler summarized the philosophy that guided his marriage in the advice that he gave to young couples. In marriage, as in all of life, his first rule was to be a giver and not a taker. Under the

---

2. Sorasky, *Achiezer: Collected Letters*, Vol. II, Letter 323.

chuppah (wedding canopy), his advice was always the same:

> Filling your hearts at this moment is a wondrous desire to give pleasure and happiness to each other. Take care, my dear ones, that you strive to keep this desire always as fresh and strong as it is at the present time. You should know that the moment you find yourselves beginning, instead, to make demands upon each other, your happiness is at an end.[3]

Retaining that desire to give depended, in his view, on separating oneself as far as possible from material desires and the selfishness they inevitably engender. As *mesader kiddushin* for his cousin Rabbi Simcha Zissel Dessler, Rabbi Dessler's blessing for the new couple was that they "should never know the test of wealth."[4]

The happiness of a marriage, in Rabbi Dessler's view, depended primarily on shared spiritual goals. In a letter written to the newly wed Rabbi Zusia Waltner and his bride, in whose apartment he maintained a small attic room during the early years of the

Rabbi Dessler's kesubah

---

3. *Michtav Me'Eliyahu*, Vol. I, p. 39; *Strive for Truth*, Vol. I, p. 132.
4. Mrs. Simcha Zissel Dessler.

Gateshead Kollel, Rabbi Dessler applied one of the Alter's fundamental insights to marriage.

The Alter taught that a person is never satisfied with a borrowed object but only with what he owns. Since all worldly possessions are of necessity only borrowed for an indefinite period of time, any pleasure they provide must pale beside the joy of a *mitzvah*, which brings eternal joy.

Rabbi Dessler then applied the lesson to marriage:

> The unity of marriage is the greatest of life's joys. If so, how much greater will be the joy of those for whom the goal of marriage is spiritual growth and whose cleaving together is a spiritual cleaving as well.[5]

Certainly Rebbetzin Bluma Dessler fully shared her husband's lofty spiritual ambitions. She had been raised in the same intense *mussar* atmosphere as her husband. In the Alter's family, as much was demanded from the girls as the boys. The Alter used to insist that his daughters and wife attend his *shmuessen* in the Talmud Torah.[6] And the Alter's son Reb Nachum Velvel raised his three daughters in the same way.

The servant girls in his house were never asked to do any demeaning tasks. Those were reserved for the Ziv girls themselves.[7] "*A yiddishe tochter vet ton shvere arbit far uns?* — Should a Yiddishe daughter do difficult work for us?" Reb Nachum Velvel would ask.[8] Rebbetzin Dessler once commented that in her father's house children were never served — her parents were too busy attending to the many guests in the house.[9]

Rabbi Nachum Velvel Dessler's childhood memories of his maternal grandmother Rebbetzin Peshe Ziv provide some glimpse of

---

5. *Michtav M'Eliyahu*, Vol. V, pp. 508.
6. Katz, *Tenuas HaMussar*, Vol. II, p. 77.
7. Ibid., p. 84.
8. "Reminiscences of Rabbi Nachum Velvel Dessler," p. 62.
9. Mrs. Naomi Pels, one of the early students in Gateshead Seminary.

the rarefied atmosphere in which his mother was raised. He once refused to eat the food his grandmother offered him, complaining that the plate was *shmutzik* (dirty). His grandmother told him that she would be happy to offer him another plate, but that he must not talk like that. "We do not say the plate is dirty," she said. "We say the plate is not clean."

The young boy could barely comprehend what his grandmother was talking about, and replied, "But everyone speaks like that." His grandmother was unfazed. "That may be," she said, "but you come from a long line of people who do not talk like that."

Rebbetzin Peshe Ziv

Another time, Nachum Velvel was walking with his maternal grandmother in Kelm when she suddenly told him to cross the street. Since they were already on the side of the street of their destination, he could not understand why his grandmother insisted on crossing to the other side of the street. She explained that at that hour of the day they might encounter men coming from the Talmud Torah, who would surely step off the sidewalk into the muddy street to allow them to pass. By continuing on the same side of the street, then, Nachum Velvel and his grandmother might inconvenience *bnei Torah*.[10]

In keeping with the Kelm emphasis on familiarity with *mili d'alma*, Rebbetzin Dessler and her sisters were provided with a fine general education to go with their Torah education. The sisters were regularly consulted by the Jews of Kelm for advice on matters requiring some worldly knowledge.[11] The oldest sister, Rebbetzin Chaya Movshovitz, spoke and wrote German, Russian, French,

---

10. "Reminiscences of Rabbi Nachum Velvel Dessler," p. 58.
   Rebbetzin Dessler's older sister Chaya showed the same kind of sensitivity as her mother when she walked down the street in Kelm. She had very poor eyesight, and to ensure that she did not inadvertently fail to greet properly someone she knew, she always walked with her eyes cast down so she would see no one.

11. Olshtein, *Zichronos Chayai*, p. 23.

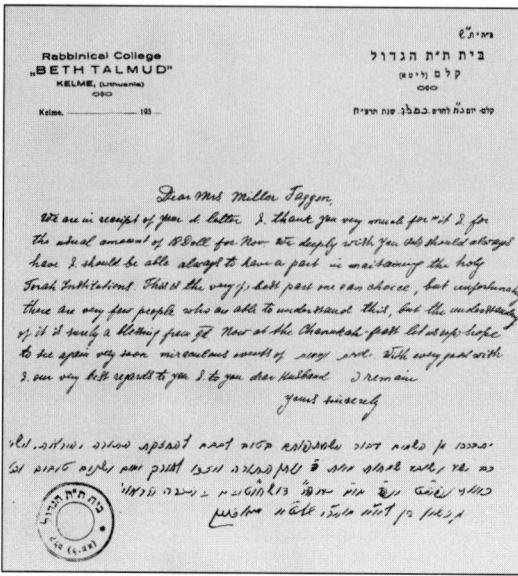

A letter on behalf of the Talmud Torah, in English, written by Rebbetzin Chaya Movshovitz

Hebrew and English fluently. She used to write letters on behalf of the Talmud Torah and to relatives in America in English.[12]

Rebbetzin Dessler's character fully reflected her strenuous *mussar* upbringing. To Mrs. Channah Gisa Silver, who lived together with her in Australia for more than five years, it "was obvious that she was someone special with every step she took." Those who knew her well inevitably describe her in terms reminiscent of her grandfather the Alter: "aristocratic," "an exemplar of *adinut nefesh* (spiritual refinement)."

The resemblance to the Alter was not coincidental. Whenever she prefaced a remark with the words, "In Kelm it was said," the matter was settled for her. She exemplified the *menuchas hanefesh* on which Kelm laid such stress. Even in the most difficult circumstances, she was never heard to complain or to speak in a raised voice. Her *yiras Shamayim* was both deep and hidden. She *davened* three times every day, unless she was entertaining guests, but always in private. In accordance with the tradition of Kelm, in accord with the ruling of the Gra, she never *davened* in a *Beis Knesses*.[13] Even her children were not aware of her prayers.[14]

---

12. Rabbi Nachum Velvel Dessler.

13. Heard by Rabbi Dovid Tzvi Hillman of Bnei Brak during the *shivah* for Rebbetzin Dessler.

14. Heard by Rabbi Meyer Munk from Rabbi Chaim Friedlander, Rabbi Dessler's closest *talmid* in Ponevezh Yeshiva.

BY VIRTUE OF HIS MARRIAGE TO BLUMA ZIV, RABBI DESSLER also became the brother-in-law of Rabbi Doniel Movshovitz and Rabbi Gershon Miadnik, who together guided the Talmud Torah during its final decade.

Rabbi Doniel Movshovitz and Rabbi Gershon Miadnik

Reb Doniel was known throughout Lithuania and beyond for his remarkable mind. The leading *posek* of Lithuania, Rabbi Avraham Dovber Kahane-Shapira of Kovno (the *Dvar Avraham*), said of him, "I don't know another *ba'al kishron* (gifted person) at his level or close to it in all of Lithuania." In addition to his brilliance in Torah, Reb Doniel was known to possess a wide familiarity with general philosophy.[15] Rabbi Dessler himself was in awe of his brother-in-law, whom he described as "the *gadol* of the *gedolim*." His clarity was such, said Rabbi Dessler, that every problem one had with a *sugya* (topic) simply vanished as one talked to him.[16]

Reb Doniel's clarity was matched by his depth and originality. He always went back to the earliest sources on any topic with which he was dealing, whether in Talmud or *hashkafah*. When he said a *shmuess*, he became a *ma'ayan hamisgaber* (an overflowing stream). As soon as he started to speak, he unleashed such powerful emotions that the thoughts just rushed to the surface in a torrent, seemingly beyond his control. After an hour, he would look up at the clock and say, "We haven't even begun to touch upon our intended topic."[17] Yet despite the philosophical depth of his thought, he could speak simple words of *mussar* with excitement.

As great as he was a thinker, Reb Doniel's personality was an even greater wonder. He was like the *Chofetz Chaim* in that a critical word about him was never heard.[18] Indeed, after the passing of the *Chofetz Chaim* in 1933, Rabbi Elchonon Wasserman, who was

---

15. Rabbi Elchonon Blumenthal, *Trials and Challenges*, p. 35.
16. Rabbi Joseph Epstein, a *talmid* of Rabbi Dessler's in London. Rabbi Epstein was one of a handful of European-trained *bachurim* who found their way to Rabbi Dessler in his last years in London.
17. Rabbi Moshe Portman.
18. Rabbi Mordechai Zuckerman.

Chapter Eight: Marriage / 105

older than Reb Doniel, used to come to Kelm every *Elul* just to be with him.

Reb Elchonon applied to Reb Doniel the verse (*Isaiah* 66:1-2), "The Heavens are My throne and the Earth My footstool,...but on *this man* will I look: to the poor and humble person who is zealous regarding My word.... " Reb Elchonon explained himself as follows: All of creation, Hashem says in the words of the prophet, is the Divine footstool. But they derive their entire purpose from the human being of humble spirit who does Hashem's will. Reb Doniel exemplifies those qualities.[19]

That humble spirit manifested itself in everything that he did. When others sought to discuss *mussar* topics with him, he always tried to steer the conversation to Talmudic learning to avoid discussing spiritual levels above his own. He feared falling into the category of one whose understanding exceeds his actions.[20] If he offered a particularly novel understanding of a statement of the Sages, he was always careful to add that his was only one of many possible interpretations. He loathed it when someone limited a *ma'amar Chazal* by prefacing his interpretation, "This is the *pshat*."

Rabbi Doniel Movshovitz

Rebbetzin Chaya Movshovitz

When he saw that his listeners were particularly overwhelmed by one of his insights into the words of the Sages, he hastened to add, "All that I have said until now is only a fraction of their true meaning, and their words are subject to many other interpretatons." Often he would then proceed to give examples of other possible understandings.

The tall, erect Reb Doniel, his deep black eyes set in a pale face, was greatly beloved in Kelm. The Jews of Kelm made a game of try-

---

19. Blumenthal, pp. 35-6.
20. Rabbi Nosson Wachtfogel.

ing to see whether they could greet Reb Doniel before he greeted them, but they rarely succeeded. If someone outside his line of vision surprised him by wishing him good morning first, he would turn and tilt his head in that person's direction, and wish him a clearly enunciated, "Good morning."[21]

His heart overflowed with love for every Jew. In the words of one of his students, "It was as if he sat and learned piles and piles of halachos on every word of the commandment *"v'ahavta l'rayecha kamocha* — love your friend as yourself."[22] After receiving news of the Nazi invasion of Poland, he announced publicly, "Four million of our brothers in Poland are endangered by the accursed evil ones." With that he could not continue so great was his identification with his fellow Jews in Poland.[23]

Reb Doniel placed himself completely at the service of any Jew who came to visit him. After a *shmuess* in the Talmud Torah, a concerned *talmid* once asked him if he was feeling well. He confessed that he had a terrible headache as a result of not having eaten all day. "All day there were visitors," he explained, "and it's impossible to just leave people and go to eat."[24]

Young teenagers received the same effusion of concern. Rabbi Zalman Sender Kremerman, whose father had headed the Kelm *yeshiva ketanah* together with Rabbi Elya Lopian, once passed through Kelm on his way from Telshe. Reb Doniel noticed the 14-year-old boy from his window and invited him into his home. Rebbetzin Movshovitz brought tea and cakes while Reb Doniel plied him with questions about his father and family. All the while, Reb Doniel kept asking him if he wanted more to eat or drink.

The young teenager was so impressed with the honor shown him by one of the *gedolei hador* that he rushed to the Talmud Torah to tell everyone. But no one saw anything remarkable about his story. "Is that something surprising?" they asked. "Reb Doniel stands for every Jewish child."

---

21. Rabbi Moshe Portman.
22. Rabbi Yaakov Meir Kravetz.
23. Rabbi Nosson Wachtfogel.
24. Rabbi Moshe Portman.

Chapter Eight: Marriage / 107

The *bachurim* in the Talmud Torah were the objects of Reb Doniel's special solicitude. He always praised them profusely, and when he sensed that a *bachur* needed to have his confidence built up, he hurried to do so. Nothing that might be of benefit to anyone else escaped his attention. Thus if he met a *talmid* on the way to the post office, he would remind him that the steps to the post office could be very slippery at that time of year.[25]

Rabbi Gershon Miadnik

The unmarried students looked to Reb Doniel for advice on every matter. After the Nazi invasion of Poland, R' Bentzion Leitner was undecided about whether to join an older brother learning in the Mirrer Yeshiva. The lack of a decision gave him no peace until Reb Doniel ordered him to decide. The pain of indecision, he said, is worse than an improper decision. Eventually R' Bentzion elected to join the Mirrer Yeshiva.[26]

Heading the Talmud Torah together with Reb Doniel was his brother-in-law Rabbi Gershon Miadnik, the husband of the youngest of Reb Nachum Velvel Ziv's three daughters, Frieda. The two brother-in-laws lived together in one house adjacent to the yeshiva, and the closeness between them recalled that between an earlier pair of Kelm brothers-in-law: Rabbi Tzvi Hirsch Braude and Rabbi Nachum Velvel Ziv. In the first *Vaad* of the morning, Reb Gershon was always careful to repeat something in the name of Reb Doniel. When he did so, the

Rebbetzin Frieda Miadnik

25. Rabbi Moshe Portman.

26. Before he departed, Reb Doniel asked him how he intended to support himself in Japan, and R' Bentzion replied that the yeshiva would be supported by the Joint Distribution Committee or some similar organization. "Know that there is a great danger in being funded by a committee," Reb Doniel warned him.

awe in which he held his brother-in-law was evident.²⁷

Reb Gershon was responsible for all the Talmud Torah's financial affairs. The Talmud Torah derived a great part of its income from a large building in Kovno that had been donated by a wealthy benefactor, and Reb Gershon traveled to Kovno frequently to supervise the collection of rents from the tenants and the upkeep of the building.

The building in Kovno which provided for the Kelm Torah Torah

In addition to taking care of all the Talmud Torah's financial affairs, Reb Gershon was actively involved in the *beis medrash*. Though there were no formal Talmud *shiurim*, he would occasionally repeat one of the many *shiurim* that he had heard from Rabbi Naftoli Trop when he learned in Radin. Reb Gershon was known to go almost without sleep, yet he always learned with a freshness and zest. Only when eating or engaged in some other mundane task would he doze off. In this he was the exact opposite of most people, who can carry on with their physical activities when exhausted but nod off from the slightest mental exertion while learning.²⁸

Even in Kelm, Reb Gershon was distinguished by his seriousness. Every night before going to sleep, Reb Gershon made a *cheshbon hanefesh* reviewing everything he had done or thought that day. In particular, he reexamined every piece of advice he had given to make sure it still withstood scrutiny.²⁹ He used to explain the verse, "Behold, fear of Hashem is wisdom, and refraining from

---

27. Rabbi Mordecai Zuckerman.
28. Ibid.
29. Ibid.

evil is understanding," (*Job* 28: 28), in a typically Kelm fashion: *yiras Shamayim* is much more than *frumkeit;* it requires the deepest thought.[30]

Yet that seriousness was tempered by a remarkable sweetness of disposition. Reb Gershon used to remind the *gabbai,* whose task it was to give a bang on the *bimah* if anyone's *davening* was disturbing those around him, to show no anger when he gave his *klapp.* The *Ramban's* famous letter to his son in which he warns against any manifestation of anger was a watchword for Reb Gershon. He used to interpolate his own commentary: "Let all your words be gentle" — even words of rebuke; "with every person" — even with a difficult person who can easily cause one to lose his equanimity; "at all times" — even when you are tired or short of patience; "and in this way you will be spared from anger" — your inner anger will be quieted and you will not be easily aroused.[31]

Reb Gershon was actively involved in drawing the local young people to Torah. But his concern extended beyond those with whom he was successful. Once three local Jewish boys were arrested for their involvement in a Communist youth group. Reb Gershon went down to the local police station and succeeded in helping the young men escape while the guard slept. Eventually the three made their way to South Africa.[32]

Failure in Business

NOT LONG AFTER HIS MARRIAGE, RABBI DESSLER WAS OFFERED a position as a *dayan* in Vilna by his uncle Rabbi Chaim Ozer Grodzenski. For reasons that are not entirely clear, he turned down the offer and instead went into business with his father in Riga.

One of the fixed principles of Kelm was the avoidance of earning one's livelihood from Torah learning or from any Torah institution, and perhaps *dayanus* fell into that category in Rabbi Dessler's mind. In addition, he might have felt responsibility to help his father

---

30. Rabbi Yehuda Leib Nekritz.
31. Rabbi Elchonon Hertzman.
32. Olshtein, *Zichronos Chayai,* pp. 23-4.

whose financial fortunes had declined even further and who was no longer young.

With some money they had deposited in an English bank before the war, Reb Reuven Dov and his brother Reb Gedaliah had attempted to reestablish themselves by building a small factory for extracting sunseed oil near Kelm. But before they could even begin large-scale production, the factory burned down. Their insurance agent had failed to send in their policy on the factory, and so the fire cost the Desslers the last of their capital.

The business in Riga proved no more profitable, and Rabbi Dessler and his father were left with huge debts. Those debts weighed heavily on Reb Reuven Dov.[33] One of the principal reasons that Rabbi Dessler left Lithuania for England in the late '20s was to repay them.

Bankruptcy proved to be only the first in a series of trials of Job for Reb Reuven Dov. In 1925, his wife Rachel was killed in a tragic accident. She used to wake up before dawn every morning to light the samovar and prepare tea for Reb Reuven Dov. One morning her dress caught fire from the coals of the samovar. She attempted to run outside to quench the flames by rolling in the snow but fell down a flight of stairs in her panic. A week later she died from the resulting concussion and her burns, in part because there was then no proper medical care available in Kelm.[34]

After his wife's death, Reb Reuven Dov moved in with Rabbi Dessler's family. His health began to decline, and much of Rebbetzin Dessler's time was taken up with preparing him special

---

33. Just how heavily can be inferred from the reaction of Reb Gedaliah to his own heavy indebtedness. After the destruction of the sunseed oil plant, Reb Gedaliah wrote to a German chemical concern with which his father had done business in the hope of becoming their business representative in Lithuania. The firm agreed to extend him credit on the Dessler name.

While he was trying to repay the loans, Reb Gedaliah lived alone in Kovno eating only day-old bread and salty fish. When his family protested that he was destroying his health, he responded, "How can I live on luxuries when I owe people money?" Reb Gedaliah's wife meanwhile opened a flour mill fifteen miles from Kelm which she ran by herself in the Lithuanian countryside. Olshtein, *Zichronos Chayai*, p. 27.

34. Ibid., p. 26.

meals. As Reb Reuven Dov's physical health deteriorated further, Rabbi Dessler decided to take his father to London to consult with medical experts. While in London, Rabbi Dessler made the fateful decision to remain. He hoped to obtain a position that would enable him to repay his creditors.

And so it was that instead of occupying a seat as a *dayan* in the Jerusalem of Lithuania, Rabbi Dessler found himself alone in London, separated from his wife and two children, heavily in debt, and cut off from the spiritual wells from which he had drunk all his life.

Chapter 9

Stranger in a Strange Land

RABBI DESSLER WAS ALREADY 36 YEARS OLD AT THE TIME of his arrival in England. If we ask ourselves what we know about him until that point in his life, the frank reply would have to be: not very much. We know a good deal, of course, about the Talmud Torah of Kelm, in which he grew to maturity, and the ideas of its illustrious founder. We also know a good deal about those who influenced Rabbi Dessler most directly — his father Reb Reuven Dov, his *rebbi* Rabbi Tzvi Hirsch Braude, his father-in-law Rabbi Nachum Velvel Ziv, his brother-in-law Rabbi Doniel Movshovitz, and his uncle, the *gadol hador* Rabbi Chaim Ozer Grodzenski.

But about Rabbi Dessler himself, beyond a few sketchy biographical details, most is conjecture based on knowledge of his family and environment. The primary biographical sources — his letters and the memories of those who knew him — are of no help with respect to the first three fifths of his life. Before he was transplanted from the nurturing environment of Kelm, he had no need to write the hundreds of letters that would one day flow from his pen. And there is no one still alive who knew him well in Kelm. Only with his arrival in England does Rabbi Dessler first begin to emerge from the realm of conjecture.

A Spiritual Wasteland

RABBI DESSLER LEFT US NO RECORD OF HIS THOUGHTS IN HIS early years in London. Only those insights or ideas that could be of benefit to himself or others were committed to writing. And since nothing could possibly be gained by bemoaning his fate, he did not waste his time with complaints. Self-pity, in any event, was completely alien to the Kelm ideal of *menuchas hanefesh*.

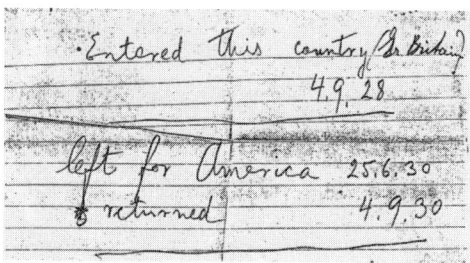

Rabbi Dessler's diary entry upon entering England

Nevertheless there were certainly black moments in those early years in London. The bitterness expressed by Reb Reuven Dov in a letter to his son no doubt reflected Rabbi Dessler's own pain at the situation in which he found himself:

> You have already drained the cup of bitterness upon leaving the [study of] Torah according to your level. You spent the best years of your life in the Jerusalem of Lithuania [Kelm], from whose mountains one quarries precious stone — Fear of Heaven and good *middos*. For our many sins the *yetzer* gained the upper hand. To our disgrace and sorrow ... you are exiled to a land of freedom, ... but one empty of the life-giving sap of *chachmas HaTorah* and Fear of Heaven.[1]

In another letter, written after a summer vacation in nearby Tzitevian,[2] where Rabbi Yaakov Kamenetsky was the *rav*, Reb

---

1. Katz, *Tenuas HaMussar*, Vol. V, p. 150.

2. The leading families of the Kelm Talmud Torah used to spend their summer vacations in the beautiful pine forests surrounding nearby Tzitevian. Though Tzitevian was only a dozen or so kilometers from Kelm, the road was extremely hilly. On the

Reuven Dov again gave vent to his pain at seeing his son torn from a life of Torah study. He remarked that Rabbi Kamenetsky's minimal duties as *rav* of a small village allowed him to devote himself to Torah learning almost all day long and that as a result he had grown remarkably in Tzitevian. Reb Reuven Dov could not restrain himself from expressing the wish that his son were in such a position and not in one in which he was distracted by a wide variety of matters.[3]

Ultimately, Rabbi Dessler's life and the lives of his wife and children would be saved by virtue of his being forced to take up residence in England. But at the time of his arrival in England, he could not possibly have known that. All he knew at that point was that he had been exiled from the only world he had ever known. He had been uprooted from an environment of the most intense spiritual striving imaginable and placed down in a strange land in which the pursuit of money dominated most men's thoughts.

By the standards of Kelm, London of the day was a spiritual wasteland. There were more great *talmidei chachamim* in the small *beis medrash* of the Kelm Talmud Torah than could be found in all of England at the time of Rabbi Dessler's arrival. In Kelm, many *baalebatim* were fluent in *Shas* and *poskim;* in England, many of the spiritual leaders of nominally Orthodox congregations — the so-called English "reverends" — carried in the public domain on Shabbos. Essentials of Jewish life, such as *mikvaos*, were barely known.[4]

Eitz Chaim Yeshiva boasted of two Torah luminaries: Rabbi Eliyahu Lopian and Rabbi Eliezer Grinspan.[5] But the yeshiva itself

---

way up a hill, everybody would get out of the horse-drawn wagons because of the prohibition of *tzar ba'alei chayim* (causing unnecessary suffering to an animal). Nor would they get back in the wagons on the way down the hill for fear that the wagon would hurtle down the steep incline. *Rabbi Nachum Velvel Dessler.*

3. Rosenblum, *Reb Yaakov*, p. 102.

4. Rabbi Aryeh Carmell.

5. After his arrival in England in the mid-'30s, Rabbi Yechezkel Abramsky, the head of the London Beis Din, also began giving a twice-weekly *shiur* in Eitz Chaim.

was controlled by a committee of largely unlearned *baalebatim*.[6] Not until Rabbi Moshe Schneider arrived in London from Frankfurt in 1938 was there a real advanced yeshiva run by the rosh yeshiva.

Rabbi Dessler was almost without anyone on his level to speak to in London. Besides Rabbi Elya Lopian, whom he knew well from Kelm, and Dayan Shmuel Yitzchak Hillman, *av beis din* of London, he had few social contacts in those first years in London.[7] A letter to his father, in which he asks him to write twice a week (instead of once every two weeks), hints to the loneliness he felt in a land not only geographically, but spiritually, distant from Kelm.[8]

Not only was Rabbi Dessler now separated from the rarefied atmosphere of Kelm, he was, in a sense, removed from Jewish society altogether. All his life, he had lived in almost exclusively Jewish communities in which the gentiles existed on the peripheries. Suddenly he was thrust into one of the most populous cities in the world, in which the Jewish neighborhoods were islands in the midst of an overwhelmingly gentile population. His thoughts about this new situation may be deduced from a letter written to his father in 1931 in which he contrasts Truth with a certain type of falsehood that appears superficially as Truth. The former he calls *penimius* (internal Truth) and the latter *chitzonius*, referring to the focus on external appearances.

The contrast between the two modes of life goes back to Kayin and Hevel, at the very beginning of human history. Both brought sacrifices, but Hevel brought from the choicest of his flocks showing

---

6. Professor Cyril Domb. Professor Domb learned in Eitz Chaim Yeshiva, and was decades later a member of its board of directors.

Rabbi Moshe Orbach, who learned in Eitz Chaim in 1941 after having arrived in England from a camp in Poland for Polish citizens expelled from Germany, remembers it as a yeshiva where a boy who was interested in learning could certainly do so. Most of the students, however, were biding time prior to entering careers in business. The yeshiva's location in London's East End, near the docks, provided numerous potential distractions as well.

7. Rabbi Hillman was a close *talmid* of Rabbi Chaim Ozer Grodzenski and the recipient of a constant stream of letters from Reb Chaim Ozer over the years. His son-in-law Rabbi Yitzchak Isaac Herzog became the first Ashkenazi Chief Rabbi of Israel.

8. *Michtav Me'Eliyahu*, Vol. V, p. 504.

his real intention, while Kayin contented himself with the poorest offerings of his fields.

Later we find a similar contrast in Noach's sons Shem and Yefes. The latter, whose name means beauty, focused on external form. Shem, from whom the Jewish people are descended, on the other hand, was thus named because he was designated as the essence (*shem*) of Creation.

Still later, we find the same distinction between Esav and Yaakov. Esav could honor his father to an extraordinary degree even while thinking in his heart, "The days of mourning for my father will come soon, and then I will kill Yaakov my brother" (*Bereishis* 27:41). Yaakov, on the other hand, epitomizes for all time the quality of *Emes* (Truth); he was an *ish tam* (pure man) incapable of dissembling with respect to his true feelings.

That level of *Emes*, writes Rabbi Dessler to his father, could only be achieved after the complete separation from the non-Jewish nations — i.e., after a distillation process like that in which Yishmael and Esav were filtered out of the Jewish people for good.[9]

In those first years in London, Rabbi Dessler received fiery letters from his father decrying the prevalent materialism of both America and England. On the eve of Rabbi Dessler's journey to America in 1930, Reb Reuven Dov warned him that America would prove to be just the opposite of *Eretz Yisrael*, whose air makes wise the foolish. America, by contrast, was a country that "makes fools of the wise and hunts in its snares even the pure of heart."

From the spiritual point of view, America was, in Reb Reuven Dov's opinion, a land that "eats its inhabitants." The illusion that material success is the result of one's own efforts destroys the foundations of *bitachon* (trust in God), and the endless chase after material goods weakens any chance of in-depth Torah study.[10]

In another letter, Reb Reuven Dov again inveighed against the materialism sure to confront his beloved son on all sides:

---

9. Ibid., Vol. III, pp. 326-27.
10. Katz, Vol. V, pp. 149-50.

They call it the New World — a world in which money answers for everything.... Guard yourself not to become a flatterer.... Men of wealth [are treated] as gods of silver and gold, as if they have an influence above nature, to such an extent that people lower themselves in front of them.... [They] seek the favor of the Golden Calf in the hopes that the Golden Calf will save them a little part of its golden tail. But it does not occur to the calf to save part of itself for others. As the *Gemara* says, "The rich are stingy."... Learn not to flatter the rich and to recognize their weaknesses, ... for they are filled with disgusting desires and despicable *middos*. It would be a good idea to set aside fixed times to think about this using many examples and *meshalim*.[11]

Rabbi Dessler fully shared his father's disgust with the surrounding materialism. He repeatedly expressed his repugnance for a society in which everything was inevitably turned into a "business" — either a business of money or a business of *kavod* (honor). He expressed doubts as to whether the use of external motivations to eventually reach a true service of Hashem — מתוך שלא לשמה בא לשמה — was even possible in England. The use of external motivations, such as honor or money, could only be justified if one's ultimate intention is to reach the level where one acts solely out of the desire to do Hashem's will. But in a society in which the pursuit of money and honor was not even seen as a cause for embarrassment, Rabbi Dessler doubted that there was any hope that such incentives could ever lead to a higher spiritual level.[12]

The Rabbinate

RABBI DESSLER INITIALLY SECURED A POSITION AS THE RABBI OF the Ein Yaakov shul in London's teeming East End, the area of the city to which most new Jewish immigrants made their way. His salary was the princely sum of 10 shillings (half a pound) a week.[13]

---

11. Ibid., pp. 151-52.
12. *Michtav Me'Eliyahu*, Vol. III, 332-334.
13. Rabbi Aryeh Carmell.

In part, Rabbi Dessler's salary reflects the financial situation of his largely poor congregation. The congregants were by and large unlearned. Even though they treated Rabbi Dessler with respect, they had little appreciation of his stature. One congregant even offered Rabbi Dessler half a crown (⅛ of a pound) to wake him up in the morning for *selichos* (penitential prayers).[14]

On that paltry salary, Rabbi Dessler not only had to provide for his own very minimal needs but also send money back to his wife and children in Kelm and support his invalid father. In addition, he had to save money so that his family could eventually join him.

His meager salary offered him little hope of repaying the business debts, which had been the initial impetus for his coming to England. How heavily those debts weighed on him can be seen from a letter from Reb Chaim Ozer in 1931 in which he expresses his hope that "Hashem give [you] the ability to pay off all [your] creditors."[15] Not until 1937 would Rabbi Dessler be able to repay his last creditor. His *talmid* Mordechai Miller accompanied him to the solicitor's office on that occasion and still remembers Rabbi Dessler's joy at having finally repaid all his debts.[16]

Rabbi Dessler's letters to his father in his first years in his rabbinate are filled with worries that his life has become a "business" and that his activities lack even the smallest element of *lishmah* (for the sake of Heaven). In one letter, he discusses *Chazal's* injunction, "Let all those who labor for the public do so for the sake of Heaven." "Every other form of *yiras Shamayin* can at least be found in the nooks and crannies," he comments, "but this one is difficult to find even there. There is always the business of money and *kavod*."[17]

He acknowledges that a person's own spiritual level can be raised by the deeds of the community if the community's spiritual level depends upon him. But even that is not true if working for the public is "only a business." Once one's public activities are tainted by considerations of money and *kavod*, one loses whatever merit one

---

14. Rabbi Aryeh Carmell.
15. Sorasky, *Achiezer: Collected Letters*, Vol. II, Letter 343.
16. Rabbi Mordechai Miller, long-time head of Gateshead Seminary.
17. *Michtav Me'Eliyahu*, Vol. III, p. 312.

might have gained by being joined to the community.[18] Another letter to his father suggests that he had little satisfaction from his *drashos*, and felt compromised in some way by them. One who attempts to arouse others and remains untouched himself, he writes to his father, cannot be described as one "upon whom the merit of the public depends."[19]

No clearer evidence of Rabbi Dessler's unhappiness in his first years in the rabbinate is needed than his trip to America in the summer of 1930 in search of a more satisfying position. The trip had apparently been long contemplated, for in a series of letters the preceding year Reb Reuven Dov inveighed against the materialism of America. Already by *Elul* of 1929, Rabbi Chaim Ozer advised him that he should consider looking for a position in America.[20]

About Rabbi Dessler's time in America, we know next to nothing. He remained in America no more than two months, having departed England by ocean liner on June 25 and arrived back on September 4. While in America, Rabbi Dessler stayed with Reb Yaakov Yosef Herman, whom he described in the most effusive terms in a letter to his father:

> He is a businessman brought up in America. But he is an outstanding *y'rei Shamayim*, who observes the *mitzvos* of the Torah meticulously. He influences many people and guides them to become observant Jews. Reb Yaakov Yosef is known for strict adherence to the mitzvah of *hachnasos orchim*. On Shabbos, there are approximately twenty guests at his table.... We enjoyed each other's company immensely over Shabbos. He is not a rich man in money, but he is wealthy in good deeds.[21]

---

18. Ibid., p. 312.
19. Ibid., p. 331.
20. *Achiezer: Collected Letters*, Vol. I, Letter 180.
21. Ruchama Shain, *All for the Boss*, pp. 173-174.
   The year following Rabbi Dessler's trip to America, he was able to repay Reb Yaakov Yosef's hospitality. The latter appeared unexpectedly at his door late one night and asked whether Rabbi Dessler could possibly gather a *minyan* with whom he could

Rabbi Dessler did not find the sought-after position in America. Upon his return to England, Reb Chaim Ozer commiserated with him on his trials in America and promised to continue doing everything he could to secure him a position worthy of his talents.[22]

In 1934, Rabbi Dessler became the rabbi of the Montague Road Beis Hamedrash in Dalston in Northeast London. The Montague Road shul was a considerable step up from the small Ein Yaakov shul. It boasted three *minyanim* every morning at a time when many shuls could not gather a morning *minyan* at all. The shul maintained an excellent library. Among the congregants were a number of learned men, and the shul was open all day with people learning.[23] A Chevra HaShas met daily, and Rabbi Dessler frequently gave *shiurim* to the members.

On minor fast days, the Montague Road shul could count on at least a *minyan* of people fasting — a rarity in those days. Shavuos night, Rabbi Dessler gave an hour and a half *shiur* before the sunrise *davening*. Those *shiurim* were

The Montague Road Beis Hamedrash

---

daven. Despite the lateness of the hour, Rabbi Dessler succeeded in doing so.

Reb Yaakov Yosef had taken an airplane to London from his preceding destination because he realized that if he were to proceed by train and boat across the English Channel he could not possibly arrive in time to find a *minyan*. But as it turned out the substantial added price of an air ticket cost him nothing. He arrived in England without a proper visa, and the customs official only allowed him in because he had come by plane, which was a novelty in those days. Had he arrived by sea, he would have had to pay a large fine, exactly equal to the added price of a plane ticket. Ibid., p. 172.

22. Sorasky, *Marbitzei Torah U'Mussar*, p. 60; *Achiezer: Collected Letters*, Vol. II, Letter 340.

23. Reb Chaim Ozer wrote to Rabbi Dessler congratulating him on the fact that his congregation included some learned *baalebatim*. *Achiezer: Collected Letters*, Vol. I, Letter 123.

well attended, which would not have been true for many shuls in London at the time.²⁴

Despite the improvement in his situation with the move to Dalston, it does not appear that Rabbi Dessler ever had much satisfaction from his rabbinical duties. He taught in the shul's Talmud Torah. But he harbored little hope that much would come from the education provided in an after-school setting and was frustrated by his ability to reach only a small fraction of the youth. "Of all the hundreds of children attending our Talmud Torah," he told a group of his congregants, "the only real achievement is with the one we manage to send away to a full-time yeshiva. The rest will, unfortunately, probably not remember enough Hebrew even to say Kaddish."²⁵

In later years, Rabbi Dessler told the members of the Gateshead Kollel many bitter, funny stories, in which he expressed his scorn for the English rabbinate as it was then constituted. His congregants, he said, had approached his *drashos* as if he were an entertainer.²⁶

Being forced to earn his living as a rabbi galled Rabbi Dessler. The rabbinate, in his view, turned Torah into a commodity to be sold. Approaching life in terms of a "career" was anathema to him. To educate and influence others was the only goal he ever held out to his *talmidim*, but the moment that goal became wrapped up in considerations of career it became nothing but a business.

But if his duties gave him little pleasure, Rabbi Dessler was nevertheless scrupulous in their performance. The first piece of advice he gave *talmidim* who were going into the rabbinate was to treat their congregants' *sheilos* with the utmost seriousness. If the rabbi treated his congregants' questions as silly, he warned, they would stop consulting the rabbi altogether.

To illustrate the point, he would share a story from his days as a rabbi in England. A woman had come to him concerned that the fish she had just opened up to clean lacked a gall and might therefore be forbidden as a *treifah*. Even though there are no laws of *treifah* for

---

24. Professor Cyril Domb.
25. Rabbi Aryeh Carmell, "Eliyahu Eliezer Dessler," in *Guardians of Our Heritage*, Rabbi Leo Jung, ed.
26. Rabbi Zusia Waltner, one of the founding members of the Gateshead Kollel.

fish, Rabbi Dessler took down an imposing-looking volume from his bookshelf and read intently for a few moments before pronouncing the fish kosher.[27]

Another time, he was able to help a congregant solve the mystery of his "haunted house." Every night, it seems, the congregant's clock would fall off the mantle piece without any human agency, and the congregant was convinced that ghosts were responsible. Rabbi Dessler immediately recognized the cause of the clock's mysterious behavior, but nevertheless pondered the matter for several moments before offering a possible solution: The clock could not stand up for some reason and was therefore usually placed on its back. When the winding mechanism turned, it jarred the clock from its place.[28]

The demands on his time were great. "I didn't even have the spare time this week it would take to swallow," he writes to his father.[29] The multiple demands on his time weighed heavily on his spirit. If those who come on social visits and "steal my time for myself... knew how painful [their visits] were to me, they would surely desist," he confides to his father.[30]

The lack of time caused him to feel further and further removed from Kelm, with its emphasis on order and fixed schedules. "My lack of *seder* causes me great pain," he writes to his father, "and my letters are always written in the time snatched between other demands."[31] "I'm always in a hurry," begins another letter.[32]

Separation from Family

COMPOUNDING RABBI DESSLER'S DIFFICULT SITUATION UPON his arrival in England was the separation from his family. He found himself not only transplanted from the spiritual soil in which he had been nurtured, but far removed from those closest to him: his wife Bluma, his son Nachum Velvel, and his daughter Hennie.

---

27. Rabbi Yaakov Edelstein, one of Rabbi Dessler's closest *talmidim* in Ponevezh Yeshiva. Rabbi Edelstein succeeded his father as *rav* of Ramat Hasharon.
28. Rabbi Alter Halperin.
29. *Michtav Me'Eliyahu*, Vol. III, p. 317.
30. Ibid., p. 311.
31. Ibid., pp. 313-14.
32. Ibid., p. 314.

That separation pained him greatly, particularly the necessity of directing his children's development from afar. He wrote to his father for advice on how he could continue to guide his son Nachum Velvel. In his poignant response, Reb Reuven Dov replies that the greatest care and wisdom will be required in order for Rabbi Dessler to bind his 9-year-old son to him despite their separation.

He advises Rabbi Dessler to write to his son and inform him that he wishes to open a new page in their relationship and instruct him in the ways of wisdom. But before proceeding, Rabbi Dessler should first request from his son some indication that this is agreeable to him.

It is crucial, Reb Reuven Dov writes, that each letter should attempt to develop the boy's taste for wisdom in a pleasant fashion. Every letter from father to son should contain some new intellectual stimulation — a new idea, a psychological insight, a question in the Talmud, an observation on current events or the wonders of nature. In short, something that will arouse in Nachum Velvel a desire for deeper understanding.

These weekly letters from father to son, Reb Reuven Dov instructs Rabbi Dessler, should take priority over all other correspondence, even that to his wife. The crucial goal is to show Nachum Velvel that all his father's thoughts are constantly directed toward him.

At the same time, Nachum Velvel should be instructed to write his father every week. That letter must be neatly written, without erasures and corrections, and without jumping from one matter to another. Accompanying that letter, Nachum Velvel should submit a weekly report: how he learned, his degree of enthusiasm in his studies, his compliance with the times of the *yeshiva ketanah* and his attendance at *minyanim*, and his *derech eretz*. That report was to be signed by his mother and grandfather.

But above all, Reb Reuven Dov instructed his son, this letter writing must not be felt as a heavy burden imposed on Nachum Velvel, and he should be content with slow and steady progress.[33]

---

33. Rabbi Eliyahu Eliezer Dessler, ed., *Kisvei HaSaba Mi'Kelm*, Vol. II, Letter 47.

Rabbi Dessler's published writings furnish some inkling of how painful the separation from his children was for him and how he feared for the long-range consequences. Though his own children never sensed any effect on their relationship with their father as a consequence of the years spent apart, Rabbi Dessler's choice of examples that paralleled his own life is highly suggestive.

In perhaps his most famous essay, "Discourse on Lovingkindness: Giving and Taking," Rabbi Dessler considers the question of whether human beings give to others because they love them or they love them because they give. Contrary to what most people think, Rabbi Dessler asserts, the latter is true: Love is a consequence of giving. And he brings a proof from an incident that he had observed in World War I. That incident eerily foreshadowed his first years alone in London and his later separation from his wife and children for many years during World War II:

> I knew a young married couple whose little son was the delight of their lives. War overtook the town where they lived, and they were forced to flee. It so happened that the young mother was away from home on that day; the father fled with his little boy in one direction while the mother was forced to take the opposite route, and so the family was separated by warring armies. And so they remained, separated in sorrow and yearning, all the years of the war. At last the battlefronts grew quiet, peace returned, and they were reunited — and what a happy family reunion that was!
>
> But a remarkable thing came to light. They could no longer make good that which the years had taken away. The love between the father and his son was deeper and closer than that of the mother for the son.... [T]he potential "giving" of all those years was lost beyond recall. It was the father who had trained and reared the child and had lavished on him the thousand-and-one acts of tender care which normally fall to the lot of the mother. The love which springs from all that giving had passed completely to the father.[34]

---

34. *Michtav Me'Eliyahu*, Vol. I, pp. 36-7; *Strive for Truth*, Vol. I, p. 128.

RABBI DESSLER DID NOT LET THE DIFFICULTIES HE ENCOUNTERED in his early years in London — his lack of satisfaction in the rabbinate, loneliness, the separation from his family — deter him from continuing spiritual growth. His *menuchas hanefesh* was such that he eventually found ways in which to turn his situation in a spiritual wasteland into an opportunity for even higher levels of spiritual attainment.

Continuing Spiritual Aliyah

True, he lacked the time for intensive *Gemara* study that he had known in Kelm. And that lack of time for in-depth study obviously pained him greatly. Reb Chaim Ozer frequently expressed in his letters a desire to hear that Rabbi Dessler had established fixed times for study of *Shas* and *poskim,* and we can assume that his encouragement was in response to concerns expressed by Rabbi Dessler on this score.[35]

Yet it would be a mistake to imagine that his learning lacked either quality or quantity by anything other than his own exacting standards. Over a period of five years, from 1928 to 1933, he completed *Shas* once again with his student Solomon Sassoon. Many of the *chiddushim* recently published under the title *Chiddushei HaRav HaGaon Eliyahu Eliezer Dessler al HaShas* date from those years.[36]

In a letter to his father written in early 1931, Rabbi Dessler writes that he is "deriving a great deal of satisfaction from his learning

---

35. *Achiezer: Collected Letters*, Vol. II, Letter 353, 441.

36. Some of the recorded *chiddushim* were based on the notes of his student Rabbi Solomon Sassoon. Others were based on *shiurim* that he gave to the Chevra Shas in the Montague Road Beis Hamedrash. His method of preparation for the latter *shiurim* was to look through the various *achronim* (later commentators) on the topic he wished to address in search of a particularly difficult question. When he had found one, he would light a cigarette and begin talking the problem over with his student Aryeh Carmell until he had arrived at a solution. Many of the *shiurim* were based on difficulties raised by his great-grandfather, the father of Rabbi Yisrael Salanter, in his *Hagohos Zev ben Aryeh*. Rabbi Aryeh Carmell.

b'iyun (in depth)."[37] And in another letter from the same period, he mentions that he managed to complete four *kuntrasim* of *divrei Torah* that week, two of which are especially dear to him.[38] The extensive correspondence between Rabbi Dessler and Reb Chaim Ozer Grodzenski indicates that he frequently sent his uncle Torah *chiddushim*.[39]

Rabbi Dessler found ways to use the less than ideal environment in which he found himself to his spiritual advantage. He observes in *Michtav Me'Eliyahu* that if one determines to resist the influences of a bad environment in which he finds himself compelled to live, "he will emerge strengthened by having met and overcome the challenge." A person whose determination to remain unaffected by a morally bad environment is sufficient to overcome the environment "will find that the sight of evil arouses in him feelings of revulsion, and the more he sees of it, the greater his revulsion."[40] Those words surely applied to him.[41]

Even the isolation in which he found himself, cut off from the Beis HaTalmud of Kelm and the elevated souls who inhabited it, could be turned to advantage. Solitude, in his view, had its own spiritual advantages. "When one is in touch with his inner self, he must be alone with his thoughts," he writes. "All attachment to matters outside of

---

37. *Michtav Me'Eliyahu*, Vol. III, p. 314.
38. Ibid., p. 331.
39. See e.g., *Achiezer: Collected Letters,* Vol. II, Letter 375.
40. *Michtav Me'Eliyahu*, Vol. I, pp. 157-58; Carmell, *Strive for Truth*, Vol. II, p. 181.
41. At the same time, Rabbi Dessler pointed out in a letter to his student Solomon Sassoon, one must take care not to become inured to the morally offensive behavior one observes. Immediately upon his arrival in the summer of 1935 at the seaside resort of Margate, Rabbi Dessler concluded that he would have to find a place to hide from viewing the *pritzus* (licentious behavior) all around him. After fleeing from the place, he began to wonder whether there was really any danger that he "would learn from those whose disgusting actions reveal [them]. . . to have the understanding and feelings of animals."

As he contemplated that question, Rabbi Dessler recalled a letter from his father in which Reb Reuven Dov writes, "Every despicable thing that a person sees others doing causes a flicker of desire in him to imitate that behavior." Were that not true, the Torah would not have had to multiply its warnings to the generation that received the Torah not to imitate the idol worship of the nations they would encounter on their entry into the land. *Michtav Me'Eliyahu, Vol. IV, pp. 317-18.*

oneself diminishes ones inwardness." The Alter of Kelm learned from the advice of our Sages, "If a person has a worry in his heart, he should share it with others," that any idea that one tells another loses some of its power.[42] For that reason, the Alter would not share with his *talmidim* any *mussar* insight that still had the power to affect his own heart.[43]

The enforced solitude of London gave Rabbi Dessler the opportunity for refining his thoughts in the cauldron of his own soul. With few equals with whom to share his insights, there was less danger of them being prematurely expressed.

In his letters to his father, he refers frequently to the various "discoveries" that he has made and how dear they are to him. "A son runs to his father with everything he finds," he writes his father in one letter, quoting the words of *Chazal*.[44]

Many of the thoughts he conveyed to his father are not so much new insights as attempts to strengthen himself by sharing with his father his realization of the importance of *mussar*. "May Hashem grant me to immerse myself even a little in these words. If so, how happy I will be for eternity," he concludes one letter.[45] No doubt he understood that his father would be pleased by evidence that he still adhered fully to the path of *mussar*.

In a number of letters, Rabbi Dessler insists that without the deep reflection of daily *mussar* true *teshuvah* from the depths of the heart is impossible.[46] Without such reflection, we simply have no weapons to counter the *yetzer hara*, for we lack the ability to even recognize him at all. Rabbi Yisrael Salanter's great insight, writes Rabbi Dessler in one letter, was the identification of the hidden *yetzer hara*. At the beginning, a person recognizes the *yetzer* and his temptations. The *yetzer* presents itself in an easily recognized form: "the eye sees and the heart desires."

---

42. Rabbi Dessler frequently mentioned this principle to his students in Ponevezh Yeshiva. *Rabbi Naftoli Nebenzhal*, one of his early *talmidim* in Ponevezh Yeshiva.
43. *Michtav Me'Eliyahu*, Vol. I, p. 221; *Strive for Truth*, Vol. III, p. 36.
44. *Michtav Me'Eliyahu*, Vol. III, p. 328.
45. Ibid., p. 311.
46. Ibid.

But after having succumbed once or twice, our souls become like "dead flesh that does not even feel the knife." At that point, the *yetzer* is no longer something outside of ourselves, but becomes part of us. It is free to grow within us, only to reveal itself again later in a vastly strengthened form. Only *mussar*, as outlined by Reb Yisrael, gives us the power to bring the hidden *yetzer* to light and to uproot it.[47]

The intense reflection cultivated by *mussar* must pierce the heart; it must arouse feelings that have died within us. Then, and only then, is the greatest miracle possible: the miracle of *teshuvah*. Without heartrending *mussar*, not only is *teshuvah* impossible, even what we perceive as our greatest actions will reveal themselves as ugly deeds, for the *yetzer* knows how to use the ways of the Torah better than we do.[48]

Teshuvah, writes Rabbi Dessler, is the pinnacle of Creation. Even *techiyas hameisim* (revivification of the dead) cannot compare to *teshuvah*: The former brings a dead body to life, but the latter brings a dead soul to life.

The distance from Kelm also afforded Rabbi Dessler the opportunity to explore avenues of Jewish thought with which he would have been unlikely to come into contact in Kelm. Many *meshulachim* from Eastern Europe made the Dessler home their port of call in London. Among them was Rabbi Yitzchak Horowitz, who stayed with the Desslers for a week or more in the mid-30's. Rabbi Horowitz was universally known as Reb Itchie Masmid for his prodigious *hasmadah* (diligence in learning). He was rumored never to sleep in a bed from one Shabbos to the next. While he stayed with the Desslers, when Rebbetzin Dessler came to make his bed, she noticed that it had not been slept in.[49]

Rabbi Dessler spent as much time as he could with his guest that week soaking up his insights into *Tanya*, a work with which he was already familiar.[50]

---

47. Ibid., p. 323.
48. Ibid., p. 330.
49. Rabbi Yehoshua Geldzahler, Rabbi Dessler's son-in-law.
50. Ibid.

How great the impact of Reb Itchie Masmid's visit was can be discerned from a letter Rabbi Dessler wrote to his erstwhile guest in 1938. Rabbi Dessler writes that he has spent much time trying to determine whether there is a fundamental disagreement between the Vilna Gaon and the *Ba'al HaTanya* in their understanding of the Kabbalistic concept of *tzimtzum* (G-d's self-restriction to make room for the Creation). He concludes that their disagreement centered only on whether the concept of G-d's immanence could be used as a part of one's *avodah* (Divine service), or whether a focus on anything other than G-d's absolute transcendance carried too great peril.[51]

Reunited with Family

BY 1931, RABBI DESSLER WAS FINALLY ABLE TO BRING HIS FAMILY to England. Joining his wife Bluma and two children was his father Reb Reuven Dov. Reb Reuven Dov had very much hoped to live his final years in *Eretz Yisrael*, but Reb Chaim Ozer was unable to secure any position there for his brother-in-law. Declining health and the lack of any source of income left Reb Reuven Dov no choice but to join his son in England.

Rabbi Dessler's concern that he would not be able to reestablish his previous relationship with his children proved unfounded. His son Nachum Velvel and daughter Hennie never sensed any diminution in parental love as a consequence of their separation. Quite the opposite. "Growing up, we somehow had the feeling that our father loved us more than other fathers loved their children," remembers Rabbi Nachum Velvel Dessler. "The warmth of his letters was typical of the way he spoke as well."[52] Rabbi Dessler's daughter Hennie Geldzahler calls him simply "the best father there ever was."

---

51. *Michtav Me'Eliyahu*, p. 324.

   Rabbi Dessler's view that there is no fundamental difference between the *Vilna Gaon* and the *Ba'al HaTanya* with regard to *tzimtzum* was rejected by both sides of the debate: Rabbi Yoel Kluft, the late Chief Rabbi of Haifa, on behalf of the followers of the Vilna Gaon, and the late Lubavitcher Rebbe Yosef Yitzchak Schneerson, on behalf of followers of the *Ba'al HaTanya*. But see the lengthy defense of Rabbi Dessler's position by his son-in-law Rabbi Yehoshua Geldzahler in three long letters to Rabbi Aryeh Carmell. *Kodshei Yehoshua, Vol. V, siman 421-423, pp. 711-736*.

52. Rabbi Nachum Velvel Dessler.

"I never saw my father angry," Rabbi Nachum Velvel Dessler recalls. "I don't mean just that he never raised his voice. I never heard an expression of anger from him." Similarly, Rabbi Nachum Velvel attests that he never heard his father make a derogatory remark — not just about his children, but about any human being.

Rabbi Dessler did not oppose spanking children in theory. In fact, he was extremely critical of modern educational theories that stress developing the child's independence. He considered the desire of teachers and even parents to be friends with their students or children — "and all in order to teach them independence" — a fundamental mistake. "No wonder if the father strikes [a child raised with this philosophy], the child strikes the father or his younger brother back."

"What a child needs to learn is not independence but submissiveness," he writes. The child's natural tendency is to view the world in terms of "I and no one else," an attitude that leads to pride and murder. Rabbi Dessler quotes the Vilna Gaon and the *Ramchal* to the effect that spankings create an open and receptive heart, without which, in the Gaon's words, the parent is planting on stone.[53] But whatever his theoretical position on spanking, Rabbi Dessler never raised his hand to either of his children.

Even if Rabbi Dessler's relationship with his children was not adversely affected by his long separation from them, he did not find it easy to raise them as he wished in London. In a radical step for the time, he refused to send Nachum Velvel to public school, and had him tutored privately at home instead. The truant officer came around in time, but after testing Nachum Velvel, he did not bother the family again. The cost of those private tutors was a major drain on Rabbi Dessler's meager income, but he saw no choice.

Nor were there many children in London with whom Rabbi Dessler felt comfortable letting his children play. Among their only playmates were the children of Rabbi Elya Lopian, who had also spent their early years in Kelm. Rabbi Nachum Velvel Dessler tells a fascinating story about a Shabbos visit to the Lopians' home. On

---

53. *Michtav Me'Eliyahu,* Vol. III, p. 361.

Rabbi Elya Lopian's English passport photo

the way, he was almost hit by a car as he stepped off a curb. When he arrived at the Lopians, Reb Elya asked him if anything had happened to him on the way. When Nachum Velvel told Reb Elya about his near miss, the latter replied that he had seen an accident involving Nachum Velvel in a dream and had been *davening* for him. Returning home after Shabbos, Nachum Velvel noticed that his father was extremely relieved to see him. Later he revealed to his son that he too had had a dream in which Nachum Velvel was in an accident and he too had been fasting for him.[54]

Less than three years after being reunited with his family, Rabbi Dessler decided that England could not provide Nachum Velvel with

R' Yisrael David Gordon

the type of training in Torah and *middos* he would need if he were to grow to be a *gadol* in Torah. Thus Nachum Velvel was sent back to Lithuania prior to his bar mitzvah. He would return to London only intermittently thereafter.

Nachum Velvel departed for Wilkomir, where his father's first cousin Rabbi Yisrael David Gordon[55] was a *maggid shiur*, in 1933. With his departure, Rabbi Dessler was once again confronted with the task of guiding his son from a great distance. He made clear to

---

54. Rabbi Nachum Velvel Dessler.

55. Rabbi Gordon was the son of Reb Reuven Dov's sister Esther and Rabbi Moshe Gordon. The Gordon family lived in Minsk. Even after the Bolsheviks confiscated the Gordons' large house and forced them to live in the attic, the Gordons continued to defy the Bolshevik edicts against teaching Torah. They took abandoned children into their home and taught them Torah. Eventually Rabbi Moshe Gordon was arrested for his efforts. Only an international outcry succeeded in securing his release, along with 13 other rabbis, in exchange for a group of Soviet spies held by Great Britain. *Olshtein, Zichronos Chayai*, p. 19.

him how difficult the separation was for him: "You know that I am hundreds of miles away from you. And I cannot share in the joy of your bar mitzvah. Surely you understand that this is very difficult for me."[56]

As he would later do with his *talmidim*, Rabbi Dessler used his correspondence with his son to forge a bond of closeness. In one letter, he refers to himself as "your father, who loves you, and all of whose hopes depend upon you." About the nature of those hopes he left no doubt: "My entire soul yearns to see you a *gadol* in Torah and *yiras Shamayim*."[57] He built up Nachum Velvel, complimenting him on the quality of his *divrei Torah* and promising to respond soon to his questions.[58]

Rabbi Moshe and Esther Gordon, parents of R' Yisrael David.

But the biggest praise of all was judging his 14-year-old son worthy of receiving "a very great present, a priceless present to one who understands its value" — Reb Reuven Dov's notes of

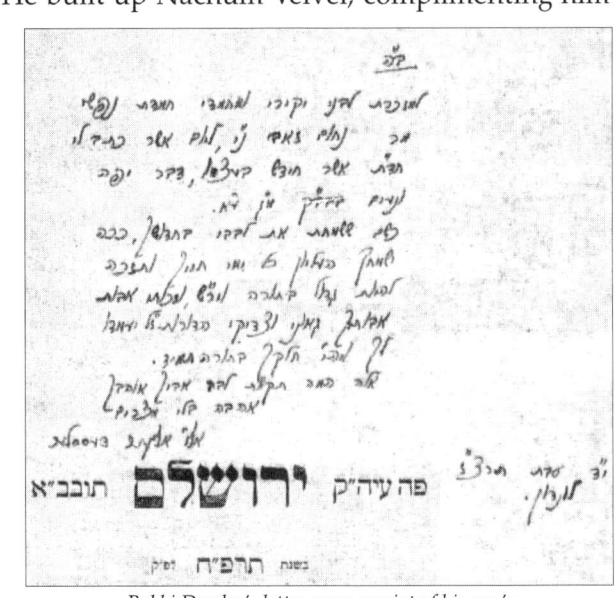

Rabbi Dessler's letter upon receipt of his son's chiddushim

---

56. *Michtav Me'Eliyahu*, Vol. IV, p. 310.
57. Ibid., p. 308.
58. Ibid., p. 316.

Chapter Nine: Stranger in a Strange Land / 133

the Alter's *sichos* in Grubin, written more than sixty years earlier. Rabbi Dessler himself painstakingly typed the entire manuscript and sent it to his son *Rosh Chodesh Elul*. He made it clear that he was entrusting him with a very great treasure — one that could not be read just one or two times, but required in-depth study. On the envelope containing the Alter's *shmuessen* the following words were written: "Do not read except with preparation and with a clear mind and a heart at peace."[59]

Even as he sought to develop Nachum Velvel's sense of himself as an adult, he was quick to point out failures in *middos* as they appeared. For Rabbi Dessler, correspondence was a form of *chesed*, and he reacted strongly to Nachum Velvel's failure one *Elul* to write with the promised frequency. It is possible, he conceded, that the strenuous efforts of *Elul* might have taken all Nachum Velvel's time. "But," he continued, "I have found that a weak resolve is more likely to cause laziness in correspondence than is a lack of time because one was so involved with strengthening oneself."[60]

Rabbi Dessler's letters to Nachum Velvel were filled with *mussar* similar to that which he had imbibed at the same age in Kelm. He stressed to his son that it is far easier to change oneself in youth before one has settled into fixed patterns,[61] and urged him to make for himself a *seder* (order) in all his activities "worthy of one who wants to fulfill the word of Hashem."[62]

In one letter, Rabbi Dessler shared with his son one of the Alter's insights on *teshuvah*. It is customary, he writes, to imagine that when we revert to former ways after Yom Kippur that we did complete *teshuvah* on Yom Kippur but subsequently the *yetzer hara* again succeeded in seducing us. But the truth is that we never really did

---

59. Ibid., p. 315.

    Rabbi Dessler considered those notes of the Alter's *shmuessen* his most precious possessions. He once told a young student in Ponevezh Yeshiva that in the event of a fire in his home he would instinctively rush first to the cabinet containing the Alter's *shmuessen* in order to save them.

60. Ibid., p. 313.

61. Ibid., p. 316.

62. Ibid., p. 310.

teshuvah, and that it why we quickly begin anew all those actions for which we beat our chests on Yom Kippur.[63]

Upon learning that Nachum Velvel had begun to put on *tefillin* in preparation for his bar mitzvah, Rabbi Dessler pointed out that there was an even more important type of preparation required: the development of *yiras Shamayim* (fear of Heaven). With *yiras Shamayim*, he writes, one can guard the entirety of the Torah; without it, one is defenseless the minute the *yetzer hara* has aroused his desire. All one's resolve to keep the Torah will dissolve, either out of laziness or due to a desire to act in ways contrary to the Torah. No matter how much Torah or *mitzvos* one acquires, without *yiras Shamayim*, he is like one who has built a beautiful mansion, filled it with precious items and then left the front door wide open and everything inside unprotected. *Yiras Shamayim* alone protects the wealth of Torah and *mitzvos*.[64]

In another letter, just prior to Reb Nachum Velvel's bar mitzvah, Rabbi Dessler emphasized that the only true riches in life are spiritual ones — a theme that was to become his central message to the young students he gathered around him in London.[65]

By *Elul* of 1936, Rabbi Dessler was not just concerned about his son's spiritual health, but also his physical safety:

> Last year only one nation openly expressed its hatred; the rest were embarrassed by their anti-Semitism. But today there is not a nation in which Jew hatred is not openly expressed. And in that one nation, the killing of Jews is an everyday event. Many congregations have lost all means of support.... And in Poland, *shechitah* has been outlawed for millions of Jews.... Less than a year ago, we thought of *Eretz Yisrael* as the one particularly secure place.... And now, all of a sudden, the Arabs are attacking from all sides.

Naturally, Rabbi Dessler sought the explanation of these calamities in the spiritual health of the Jewish people. He related to

---

63. Ibid., pp. 314-5.
64. Ibid., p. 308.
65. Ibid., p. 310.

Nachum Velvel a question that the grandfather after whom he was named, Rabbi Nachum Velvel Ziv — "a gaon in the depths of Fear of Heaven and *mussar*" — had in his youth asked the Alter: How can we say that Hashem is merciful and at the same time that He does not overlook any sin? The Alter answered that even the Divine judgment is a form of Divine mercy. Rosh Hashanah and Yom Kippur are designed to cause the evildoers to return to Hashem before they destroy the world.

R' Reuven Dov Dessler

Rabbi Dessler added that when the Torah recounts all the punishments that will befall the Jewish people when they stray from Torah, it states "these are the words of the convenant," not "these are the words of the curse." Thus we see that the calamities are forms of reproof, and even the punishments are forms of Divine mercy.

If all this has befallen our people since the preceding Rosh Hashanah, Rabbi Dessler writes his son, we must realize that this could never have occurred if even a small group had done complete *teshuvah* the preceding year. What, then does Hashem seek from us? "Just one truthful thought" — a thought that pierces to the depths of one's being and effects a lasting change.[66]

AROUND THE SAME TIME THAT RABBI DESSLER WAS CUT OFF once again from his beloved son, he was also about to lose the person whose advice he had always relied on most. In 1933, Reb Reuven Dov suffered a stroke that left him almost completely paralyzed. The Desslers could not afford much help and the burden of caring for Reb Reuven Dov over the next eighteen months fell almost exclusively on Rabbi and Rebbetzin Dessler, who was not a well woman herself.

Reb Reuven Dov Dessler's Petirah

---

66. Ibid., pp. 335-37.

Dr. Dov Heiman, who was the Desslers' personal physician at the time, was awed by the way that Rabbi and Rebbetzin Dessler attended to all Rabbi Reuven Dessler's personal needs. Their round-the-clock care for Reb Reuven Dov exemplified, in his opinion, *kibud av v'eim* (honoring one's parents).[67]

Reb Reuven Dov passed away on 14 *Teves* 5695 (December 1934). As soon as the *shivah* period passed, Rabbi Dessler wrote to Reb Chaim Ozer. In his letter, he did not mention his father at all other than to say that "we need a consolation." Reb Chaim Ozer immediately understood the implication of Rabbi Dessler's letter and wrote back asking for all the details. "My one consolation," he wrote to Rabbi Dessler, "is that Reuven did not die, for he left a son like him, that he raised to follow on his path in Torah and *yirah*. His memory will not be lost among his seed and his name will be a blessing from generation to generation."[68]

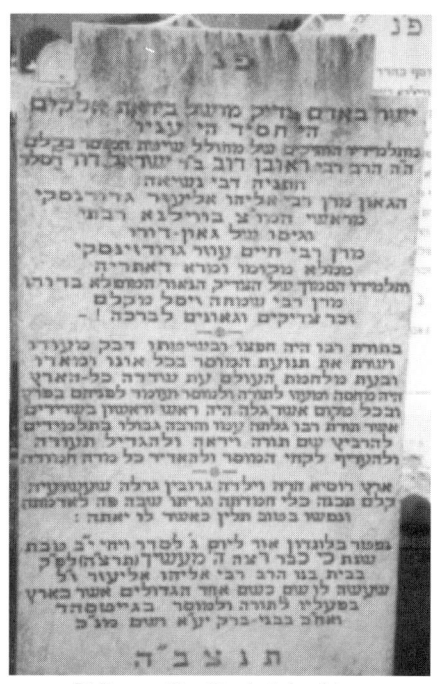

R' Reuven Dov Dessler's headstone

From Kelm, the heads of the Talmud Torah expressed their shock at the news of Reb Reuven Dov's passing. Both Rabbi Doniel Movshovitz and Rabbi Gershon Miadnik referred to the long chain of "trials and afflictions" that Reb Reuven Dov had suffered. "We saw that Hashem tests a *tzaddik* until he has no place to stand," wrote Reb Gershon.

Rabbi Yerucham Levovitz from Mir described what the loss of Reb Reuven Dov meant for the *mesorah* of Kelm. "There was between us the love of brothers, and I feel his loss very dearly," wrote Reb Yerucham.

---

67. Dr. Dov Heiman.
68. *Achiezer: Collected Letters*, Vol. II, Letters 364-65.

Chapter Nine: Stranger in a Strange Land / 137

"All the time that he was alive I felt that the root of our spiritual tree, the Saba Mi'Kelm, was still alive, and with his departure the honor and crown departed as well."[69]

Reb Reuven Dov was buried not far from the Alter's close friend Rabbi Eliezer Gordon.[70] In keeping with the custom of Kelm, Rabbi Dessler did not put up a headstone to mark his father's grave. Only thirty years later was one placed there by his relative Reb Eliyahu Eliezer Skolsky of London.

---

69. Katz, Vol. V, pp. 153-54.
70. Rabbi Gordon passed away in London on a fundraising trip for Telshe Yeshiva.

Chapter 10

Teacher of Youth

FORTUNATELY FOR RABBI DESSLER, HE WAS NOT CONFINED for long to the rabbinical tasks from which he had so little satisfaction. Not long after his arrival in London in September 1928, Dayan Shmuel Yitzchak Hillman, the *av beis din* of London, recommended him to David Sassoon as a suitable tutor for his two children, Flora (Pircha), 15, and Solomon David (Sliman[1]), 14. Thus began Rabbi Dessler's career tutoring a small group of young men that would constitute his principal occupation until the founding of Gateshead Kollel in 1941.

Initially, the Sassoon children were Rabbi Dessler's only pupils, and he used to travel three times a week to the family mansion in London's fashionable Mayfair district (where the Sassoons were virtually the only Jewish residents.) One by one, the circle of Rabbi Dessler's private students expanded. In a 1938 letter to Rabbi Avraham Yaakov Neumark in Tel Aviv, Rabbi Dessler described

---
1. Friends such as Aryeh Carmell knew Rabbi Sassoon as Silman, but he was called to the Torah as Sliman. Sliman is the name Rabbi Dessler always employed in his letters.

L. to r.: David Sassoon, Dayan Shmuel Yitzchak Hillman, David Hillman

The Sassoon residence at 32 Bruton Street

his delight in his private pupils:

Hashem has favored me … with precious students, who are dear to me, and of substantial merits. Among them are those who are *lamdanim* and people of great deeds. Of all my labor this is the only that gives me satisfaction.

Some are learned in science, and are exerting themselves in their Torah study. Others of great means are devoting their days and nights to learning, both in halachah and the depths of *Aggadata* to get to the root of the matter according to the words of their great predecessors in *chassidus* and *mussar*. The classes with them, which are mostly individual, last from early in the morning to near midnight.

Kelm's emphasis on the importance of education ensured that Rabbi Dessler found nothing demeaning about teaching young teenagers, most of whom had no substantial background in Torah learning. In an early letter to England, Reb Reuven Dov took pains to remind his son that "our teacher [the Alter], the light of the world, involved himself in teaching wild, young schoolboys at a time when he was involved in the deepest matters of *mussar*. He put aside his involvement in elevated *mussar* thoughts and ignored all those who opposed him, even though the matter was very strange in their eyes."[2] In a later letter on the same subject, Reb Reuven Dov recalls how the Alter used to say that the Talmud Torah in Kelm and later in Grubin were so dear to him that he made a point of collecting for them during the *Yamim Noraim*. "I was *mafkir* my soul for them," the Alter said.[3]

The Kelm attitude toward the importance of educating young Jews at any level of understanding is underscored by an exchange between Rabbi Chaim Dov Silver and his Rosh Yeshiva Rabbi Doniel Movshovitz, shortly before the former's departure from Kelm in 1940. Rabbi Silver was a British citizen and had already been informed that the British intended to evacuate all their nationals then in Lithuania to Australia. He asked Reb Doniel whether he should become a *rav* or *shochet* (ritual slaughterer) in Australia.

Reb Doniel replied that he should become neither, despite being eminently qualified for both positions, but rather a *melamed* (teacher of young children). When Rabbi Silver told him that as far as he knew there were no such positions in Australia at the time, Reb Doniel did not retract his advice. "If you gather a group of children together and tell them they are the children of Avraham, Yitchak and Yaakov and teach them *Aleph-Beis*, you'll be doing a lot," said Reb Doniel.

RABBI DESSLER WAS EXTREMELY FORTUNATE THAT HIS FIRST student, Solomon David Sassoon, was so suited to him by virtue of his brilliant and far-ranging intellect. Ten years after his original introduction to Solomon's father David, Rabbi Dessler wrote to Dayan Hillman, who had made the

Rabbi Solomon Sassoon — the First Talmid

---

2. *Kisvei HaSaba Mi'Kelm*, Vol. II, p. 564.
3. Ibid., p. 568.

introduction, to express his eternal gratitude. Rabbi Dessler details the tractates that he and Solomon have recently learned, and adds that Solomon is currently working on a rare old manuscript in the family's library. Solomon's powers to clarify the halachic subjects to their very depths and his expertise in comparing a number of extant versions of the same text constituted nothing less than a "wonder" in Rabbi Dessler's eyes.[4]

R' Dessler's lesson plan for studies with Solomon Sassoon, written in the "chatzi Kolmus" script then commonly used in the Sephardic community

Solomon, writes Rabbi Dessler, has a tremendous influence on the younger *talmidim*, and has developed into an excellent *darshan* (speaker), "bringing forth pearls filled with the deepest expressions of Torah and the Fear of Heaven." Rabbi Dessler also marveled at Solomon's depth in a wide variety of scientific subjects. "My soul has virtually fled from me upon hearing the thoughts that he lays before me," he writes. "He analyzes and investigates until the root the most complicated questions in these areas, without the purity of his spirit being touched in the slightest, *chas veshalom*."

Solomon Sassoon (left) with his parents. Typically, the young man is sitting with a sefer.

---

4. Avraham Ben-Yaakov, *Perakim B'Toldos Yehudei Bavel*, Vol. I, p. 194.

Solomon's character impressed Rabbi Dessler no less than the depth of his thought. Despite the closeness of our relationship, writes Rabbi Dessler, he uses all his considerable intelligence to hide from me the many great deeds he does in secret.[5]

The Sassoons were descended from one of the most distinguished families of Baghdad Jewry. Solomon's great-great-grandfather, known as Sheik Sassoon, was *nasi*[6] of the Jewish community from 1781 until 1817. In that position, he was the virtual ruler of the internal affairs of the Jewish community and a leading advisor to the pasha. Sheik Sassoon's son, the first David Sassoon, however, was forced to flee Baghdad in the 1820's in connection with one of neverending intrigues that plagued the pasha's court during that period. He arrived in Bombay, India in 1832.

David Sassoon became head of the local Jewish community in Bombay and a prosperous merchant. His descendants rose to prominence in Bombay society under the British raj, and to this day there are still buildings and streets in Bombay named after David Sassoon, the founder of the dynasty in Bombay.

Most of David Sassoon's eleven children and descendants eventually assimilated into British colonial society. The branch of the family headed by his son Solomon David, however, remained faithful to their ancestral traditions. Despite their great wealth and social standing,[7] this particular branch of the Sassoon family retained the strictest religious standards. Two rabbis lived with the family to tutor the children. Flora Sassoon, Solomon David's wife, was a very learned woman, widely conversant in Talmud. She used to prepare

---

5. Ibid., p. 203.

6. In that position, he was the virtual ruler of the internal affairs of the Jewish community and a leading advisor to the pasha.

7. The childhood playmates of David Sassoon, the father of Rabbi Dessler's pupil, included the grandchildren of Queen Victoria of England.

After moving to England in 1910, David Sassoon once saw Edward, Prince of Wales (and later Edward VII), on the other side of the street. His initial reaction was to cross the street to greet his childhood friend, but then he recalled the *Mishnah* in *Pirkei Avos* (2:3) that advises caution with respect to the ruling authorities, and he remained on his side of the street. *Rabbi Aryeh Carmell.*

Chapter Ten: Teacher of Youth / 143

lists of Talmudic questions for Dayan Hillman after moving to England in 1910.

The decision of David Sassoon (Flora's son) to engage Rabbi Dessler to tutor his children was in keeping with the family tradition of engaging the finest available tutors to provide religious instruction.[8] By the time Solomon started learning with Rabbi Dessler at age 14, he had already memorized much of *Tanach* and had been tutored in Talmud from the age of 7. He could speak Yiddish with Rabbi Dessler just as he could speak Judaeo-Arabic with a *Chacham* from Baghdad.

Solomon received *semichah* from both Rabbi Dessler and Dayan Hillman's son-in-law Rabbi Yitzchak Isaac Herzog when he was only 21. He and Rabbi Dessler had already completed Talmud Bavli twice by that time. Rabbi Dessler held his *talmid* in such high esteem that he hoped to travel with him to Vilna to receive *semichah* from Rabbi Chaim Ozer Grodzenski, but Reb Chaim Ozer replied that he never granted *semichah*.[9]

In time, Solomon Sassoon fulfilled all his early promise. His close friend Professor Cyril Domb described him, in a tribute written after his passing in 1985, as a fusion of so many worlds that one could point at him and say, "Here is the power of Torah to unite universes."[10] In one of his last letters, Rabbi Dessler describes Rabbi Sassoon's comments on the concept of "the lips speaking even in the grave" as written in the style of his ancestor the *Maharal* of Prague.[11]

---

8. The family followed the same policy with respect to general studies. Rabbi Sassoon, for instance, was extremely well versed in mathematics and the natural sciences, despite having had little formal education. As a child he studied with the finest tutors, and in later years when questions arose in the course of his voracious reading, he would invite professors from nearby Cambridge University to the family home in Letchworth to talk to him.

9. *Achiezer: Collected Letters,* Vol. II, Letter 382.

10. Professor Cyril Domb, "Rabbi Solomon David Sassoon: An Appreciation," *L'Eylah,* Rosh Hashanah 5747.

11. *Achiezer: Collected Letters,* Vol. IV, Letters 368-69.

Rabbi Sassoon's mother Selena (nee Prinz) was a granddaughter of the famous German Jewish rabbi and author Rabbi Marcus Lehmann, and a descendant of the *Maharal.*

```
                                    15, Sollershott East,
                                         LETCHWORTH,
                                            Herts.

                                    30th October, 1953.

Rabbi E. L. Dessler,
         P. O. B. 26,
              BENEI BERAK,
                   Israel.

Dear Rabbi Dessler,

      A thousand thanks for your beautiful letter, for which I was
most grateful.  I am also most glad that you found the books
useful.   I shall shortly be sending you a few more.

      I think I should tell you that recently I have been approached
from various quarters to put my name down as a candidate for the
Chief Rabbinate of Jerusalem, but I have refused.  My reasons
are many.

      First of all, there is the education of the children to think
of, and I fear they would be neglected by me if I took on my
shoulders this onerous duty.

      Secondly, there is the question of trans-planting the whole
family.

      Thirdly, it is not likely that I would be able to remit income
on which to live in Jerusalem, and the salary they paid the late
Chief Rabbi was hardly enough to keep him and his wife, and they had
no other dependents.

      Fourthly, since I had pneumonia I have not entirely recovered
my previous vigour, and would not physically be able to bear the
burden at the present moment (of course if this were the only
argument against accepting, I could always say that I would take it
up in a year's time).

      Fifthly, I do not know whether I could make a success of the
post.

      Sixthly, I think one of my main tasks would be travelling round
the world collecting money for all the more impoverished Institutions
and Yeshivoth; a task which I do not greatly relish.

      Seventhly, there must be a lot of problems which must appear to
be almost insolvable.

      Eighthly, there may be so many things which I cannot put
right that I should regret having taken the position.

      Ninthly, I am still rather young, and feel that when I am older
such a position may be easier for me to fill.

      Tenthly, I think that they will ultimately find a suitable to
fill this position.
```

```
Of course, points five, seven and
eight are very much the same arguments

     Also I feel that I shall be able
to be very much more helpful outside
that position than inside, as the
position might restrict me even more
than now, instead of giving me
greater freedom to help.

     I should be very grateful if you
would give me your feelings and opinion
on this whole question.

     With best wishes and kindest
regards,
                     Yours sincerely,
```

R' Sassoon's letter to R' Dessler regarding the offer of the position of chief rabbinate

Rabbi Sassoon was recognized as a Torah scholar of both great breadth and striking originality. At the age of 38, he was approached by then Ashkenazi chief rabbi Yitzchak Isaac Herzog about the possibility of becoming the Sephardi chief rabbi. Rabbi Herzog, who had granted Rabbi Sassoon *semichah* only 17 years earlier, wrote to him of his hope that he would "merit to see you sitting on the seat of the chief rabbinate of Israel together with me, your friend, who loves you heart and soul…."

Rabbi Sassoon wrote to Rabbi Dessler at that time expressing his many misgivings about the position and his reasons for rejecting the offer. Rabbi Dessler wrote back in full support of his beloved protégé's decision. The chief rabbinate, he suggested, required involvement in too many political matters far outside a rabbi's proper concern. In the effort to draw closer to the Torah many who have no interest in coming closer, Rabbi Dessler warned his student, he would inevitably be led to many very doubtful compromises.

Much of what Rabbi Dessler wrote applied to rabbinical positions in general and not just the chief rabbinate. He confided that many of the greatest rabbis later find themselves filled with regret for accepting rabbinical positions "from which the benefit is slight and the pain great." He confirmed Rabbi Sassoon's intuition that he could do more to advance the causes close to his heart as a private citizen than as a chief rabbi. Rabbis in our generation, wrote Rabbi Dessler, spend much of their time giving speeches at various occasions that are nothing but a "waste of time" and *"bittul Torah."*[12]

Tens years later, the offer to Rabbi Sassoon to become chief rabbi was renewed, but he once again turned it down. Though he rejected the position of chief rabbi, Rabbi Sassoon employed his vast Torah knowledge in service of the community in many ways. With his encyclopedic knowledge of *Tanach*, he was able to refute many of the theories of the so-called Bible "critics." His insights in *Tanach* were published posthumously under the title *Natan Chachmah L'Shlomo*. When the Steinhaus Yeshiva moved to Letchworth in 1952, Rabbi Sassoon and his brother-in-law Rabbi Asher Feuchtwanger took over the running of the yeshiva.

Rabbi Sassoon also put his scientific expertise to good use on behalf of Orthodox Jewry. He authored several scientific pamphlets

Students of the Letchworth Yeshiva in 1952

---

12. Unpublished letter from Rabbi Dessler addressed to Mrs. Solomon David Sassoon and dated 5 *Kislev* 5714 (November 19, 1953), little more than a month before Rabbi Dessler's passing. Typically, Rabbi Dessler wrote part of the aerogramme to Rabbi Sassoon's mother in English and the part for Rabbi Sassoon in Hebrew.

refuting charges that kosher slaughter of animals is inhumane. Copies of these pamphlets were duly mailed to every local councillor in England and played a major role in silencing proponents of a ban on shechitah. He was enthralled by the progress of modern science and kept himself abreast of developments in a wide range of fields. He saw a move towards a more spiritual view of the universe running through many recent scientific theories, and appropriately titled an address to the British Association of Orthodox Jewish Scientists, "The Challenge of Torah to Science," rather than the reverse. Many of his own thoughts on science were included in a volume published shortly before his death entitled *Reality Revisited*.

R. to L.: R' Solomon Sassoon, R' Ezra Attia (Rosh Yeshiva of Porat Yosef), and Isaac Sholom at Yeshiva Porat Yosef

The Sassoons also continued in their historical role as Jewish aristocrats. The mansion in Letchworth, which the family inhabited from 1940 until their move to Israel in December 1970, was the meeting place of leading figures from every part of the Torah world. There they might find themselves sharing a table with a beggar in tatters, for the Sassoon family had a long-standing tradition that whoever appeared seeking alms at mealtime was invited to stay for the meal.[13]

Though unostentatious in his own standard of living, on more than one occasion, Rabbi Sassoon confounded those seeking his support for their institutions by telling them that the sum they had requested was too small for such a crucial project. At the death of the great American philanthropist Isaac Shalom in 1968, Rabbi Sassoon assumed the leadership of Otzar HaTorah and its large network of Torah schools in North Africa and the Middle East. To support the work of Otzar HaTorah, he even parted with the most

---

13. Rabbi Nachum Velvel Dessler.

R. to L.: R' Yosef Drari, R' Solomon Sassoon, R' Yehudah Tzeddakeh (Rosh Yeshiva of Porat Yosef)

prized item in the family's magnificent library — a copy of the Maimonides' *Commentary on the Mishnah* written in his own hand — which Rabbi Sassoon had devoted much effort to authenticating over the objections of numerous scholars. The manuscript was sold to the national library for a million dollars, all of which went to Otzar HaTorah.

The Circle Widens

INITIALLY, SOLOMON SASSOON WAS RABBI DESSLER'S ONLY Talmud student. He would always remain the senior member of Rabbi Dessler's circle of private *talmidim*, and the student with whom Rabbi Dessler spent the most time.

Less than a year after Rabbi Dessler began teaching Solomon Sassoon, there were discussions between Rabbi Dessler and a group of *baalebatim* in Gateshead concerning a plan to open a yeshiva. (Unfortunately, our knowledge of these discussions is confined entirely to four letters written in the spring and summer of 1929 from Reb Reuven Dov to Rabbi Dessler.) Reb Reuven Dov was extremely excited by the prospect of creating a yeshiva in Gateshead, and seems to have had some familiarity with the town. In his first letter on the subject, he describes the project as one that would fully justify all his son's peregrinations to date. In the isolation of Gateshead, he writes, it might be possible to create an institution stronger and more elevated than anything then existing in London or Manchester.[14]

Reb Reuven Dov's next letter extolled the importance of teaching young boys and noted that the Alter had devoted the best years of his

---

14. *Kisvei HaSaba Mi'Kelm*, Vol. II, pp. 562-3.
15. Ibid., p. 564.

life to precisely that task.¹⁵ The chances of establishing a yeshiva to be headed by Rabbi Dessler seemed sufficiently good at that point for Reb Reuven Dov to begin offering suggestions on how it should be done. He advised his son to follow the model of Grubin where the youngest group was 12 or 13 years old. Great attention should be given, as in Grubin, to *seder* (order) and care in the performance of *mitzvos*. Not only should these matters be emphasized for the *talmidim* but for the staff as well. Educating others, Reb Reuven Dov warned his son, is first a matter of educating oneself.

A letter to the Sassoons from Rabbi Dessler in New York

By the following week, however, Reb Reuven Dov already showed some misgivings as to whether the whole project would come to anything. He seemed unsure between two possible paths: starting immediately, with a very small group (as the Alter had initially done), even before all the necessary financial arrangements had been worked out, or waiting until a solid basis for building a yeshiva was in place, lest the initial enthusiasm be quickly dissipated and the whole enterprise come to naught.¹⁶

We will never know which course Rabbi Dessler himself chose since there is no mention of the idea of establishing a yeshiva in Gateshead in any of his letters from that period. All that is known with certitude is that Reb Dovid Dryan, the *shochet* in Gateshead, did start a yeshiva after Sukkos of 1929 with less than a handful of boys, and that Rabbi Dessler, for whatever reason, had no part in that new enterprise.

After the disappointment of Gateshead, the Sassoons remained Rabbi Dessler's only students until his trip to America in the late

---

16. Ibid., pp. 565-7.

R. to l.: Nachum Velvel Dessler, Sliman Sassoon, and Aryeh Carmell at the Montague Road Beis Medrash

summer of 1930. Upon his return from America, however, Rabbi Dessler began to add to his group of students. Reb Reuven Dov wrote in the summer of 1931, in response to a letter from his son in which the latter expressed his pleasure from his students: "The One Who directs the steps of all men did not uproot you and bring you to London for nothing. And if you will remember, I tried to tell you this from the beginning."

In that same letter, Reb Reuven Dov reiterates one of the cardinal principles of Kelm: the quality, not quantity, of the students is crucial. "Don't let the number of your *talmidim* be a small thing in your eyes," Reb Reuven Dov adjures him, "for if they continue in their present path, they will, in time, do great things." He then quotes the *Gemara* (*Yevamos* 62b) that describes how Rabbi Akiva lost 24,000 *talmidim*, and the world was empty of Torah until he came and taught Rabbi Meir, Rabbi Yehuda, Rabbi Yosi, Rabbi Shimon, and Rabbi Elazar ben Shamua. The Alter used to learn from this *Gemara* that four or five people of great merit can by themselves build an entire world.[17]

One by one the circle of Rabbi Dessler's private *talmidim* grew. Among the very earliest *talmidim* were Sam and Fred Kahn, sons of Oscar Kahn, a successful printer and Torah benefactor, Moshe Weingarten and Wolf Bodenheimer. In 1932, the 15-year-old Aryeh Carmell joined the group. He would one day be the individual most responsible for the dissemination of Rabbi Dessler's thought as co-

---

17. Ibid., pp. 569-70.

editor and editor of the five volumes (to date) of *Michtav Me'Eliyahu*.[18]

Three years later, Mordecai Miller, then 14, was added to the roster of *talmidim*. Over more than fifty years as a teacher and principal in Gateshead Seminary and in Gateshead Yeshiva, he has taught Rabbi Dessler's thought to thousands of young men and women, many of whom spread Rabbi Dessler's ideas further in their own teaching careers.[19]

In time, the circle of students grew sufficiently large for Rabbi Dessler to maintain an informal *beis medrash* of his *talmidim* in the front room of his home or in the Montague Road Beis Hamedrash.

In the course of their two- to three-hour learning sessions, Rabbi Dessler would encourage his students to ask whatever questions might be bothering them. Yaakov Katz, for instance, who would later study philosophy at the Hebrew University, recalls as a young teenager discussing with Rabbi Dessler questions of theodicy and the proofs of Judaism vis-à-vis other religions in the course of their *Gemara* learning.

Mordecai Miller attended a school where he was one of the few religious students. His classmates frequently taunted him with questions, and he would bring these questions to Rabbi Dessler. Rabbi Dessler always answered them in a way that was so convincing that he could hardly wait to get back to school the next day to give them the answers.

Tired of hearing Mordecai Miller talking about Rabbi Dessler, three of his classmates decided to have some fun at the expense of someone they considered an old-fashioned European *rav*. One day

---

18. In addition to having been one of the primary editors of all five volumes of *Michtav Me'Eliyahu*, Rabbi Carmell has translated the first volume of *Michtav Me'Eliyahu* into three English volumes under the title *Strive for Truth*, and part of Volume II of *Michtav Me'Eliyahu* as *Sanctuaries in Time*. Volumes V and VI of the *Strive for Truth* series are comprised of essays of Rabbi Dessler on each of the weekly Torah readings and on every book of *Tanach*.

19. Rabbi Miller also authored two volumes of *Shabbos Shiurim* and one volume of *Yom Tov Shiurim*. Though highly original works, these volumes draw heavily on the thought of Rabbi Dessler and other thinkers whom Rabbi Dessler first brought to Rabbi Miller's attention.

they entered the *beis medrash* while Mordecai Miller was learning with Rabbi Dessler. The ringleader approached Rabbi Dessler, while his two partners stood at a distance smirking, and asked whether he could pose a question.

Rabbi Dessler nodded affirmatively. "What color is G-d?" the boy asked. All three boys then waited for the predictable explosion. None came. Rabbi Dessler put his head down for several minutes and appeared to be lost in the deepest thought. After a few minutes, he raised his head and told the fidgeting young man, "Color is a quality that attaches to physical objects. Since G-d has no physical aspect, the question is not legitimate with respect to G-d." The boys were as devastated by Rabbi Dessler's total self-control as the man who bet that he could cause Hillel to lose his temper.[20] Meanwhile Miller delighted in watching their discomfiture in the face of Rabbi Dessler's total self-control.

While Rabbi Dessler was always open to any type of question that his students asked, it must be emphasized that his principal activity with all his students was the study of Talmud. He was engaged to tutor them in Talmud, and that is what he did. Without a thorough grounding in classical texts, he realized, there would be no ground for *mussar* to take hold and to protect his charges against the intellectual forces around them. And he was a highly skilled *Gemara* rebbi whose highly analytical approach was well suited to most of his *talmidim*, as evidenced by those who later became accomplished scholars, despite a lack of early yeshiva training.

Rabbi Dessler's students had in most cases never met anyone remotely like him before, and the first meeting could be a little unnerving, even frightening. The first time Mordecai Miller met Rabbi Dessler was in the company of his father. Mordecai Miller's father asked a number of seemingly straightforward questions — e.g., How many times a week can you learn with my son? How much do you charge? After each question, Rabbi Dessler put his head in his hands and thought for what seemed like an eternity to the 14-year-old boy before answering.

---
20. See *Shabbos* 30b-31a.

Shortly after the incident in question, Rabbi Dessler explained to Mordecai Miller that when they first met, one of his *kabbalos* for the week was not to answer any question immediately without some reflection, and that is why he had hesitated before each of Mr. Miller's questions.

On another occasion, Miller was learning with Rabbi Dessler in the latter's home and a repairman came to repair a sash on one of the windows. Rabbi Dessler asked him whether the material he was using was of high quality, and the workman replied, "We use only the best." Rabbi Dessler startled the workman by telling him that he did not require the best but only that the material be serviceable.

Later he explained to his student that the repairman knew that he was renting the apartment and that the general practice was for renters to order the most expensive repairs and then deduct them from their rental payment. He wanted the workman to understand that a religious Jew does not take advantage of his landlord in such a fashion.

Both by example and instruction, Rabbi Dessler taught his students to be continually on the look out for opportunities for *Kiddush Hashem*. Chananiah, Mishael, and Azariah provided him with the model of "how great is the merit of bringing benefit to the masses" through *Kiddush Hashem*. According to the *Midrash*, the prophet Yechezkel himself ruled that they were under no obligation to throw themselves into the fire, especially since the only onlookers were non-Jews, in front of whom there is no *mitzvah* of sanctifying G-d's name.[21] They should have hidden, yet they did so because they understood that dying for the sake of *kiddush Hashem* would outweigh anything that they might achieve for the rest of their lives.[22]

Rabbi Dessler described the *mitzvah* of *kiddush Hashem* as an opportunity to do many *mitzvos* at the same time. He made the point with a *mashal*. No one can become a millionaire selling newspapers on the street corner. The profit on each paper is simply too small. But the owner of the paper, with hundreds of vendors in his employee,

---

21. *Shir Hashirim Rabbah* 7:1[8].
22. Letter to his father written in 1931 when he first started to gather a group of students around him. *Michtav Me'Eliyahu, Vol. III, pp. 318-19*.

can become a millionaire, even though he too only earns a few pennies on each paper. The key is volume. *Kiddush Hashem* is a chance to do *mitzvos* in volume. Indeed the *Midrash*[23] continues that when Chananiah, Mishael, and Azariah emerged unscathed from the fire, all the idol worshippers present went home and broke their idols.

Rabbi Dessler showed his *talmidim* in very concrete ways how they could cause G-d's Name to become beloved in the world. Mordecai Miller, for instance, used to travel to his lessons with Rabbi Dessler by double-decker bus. In those days, each bus had a conductor who went around collecting the fares. If one went up to the upper deck and the journey was short, there was a good chance that one would reach his destination prior to the conductor collecting his fare.

Rabbi Dessler told Miller to deliberately go up to the upper deck. When he reached his destination, he was to approach someone sitting nearby and in a voice that would be heard all around ask that person to please pay his fare to the conductor. In a similar vein, Rabbi Dessler instructed Aryeh Carmell that he should give a penny to each of the numerous beggars he passed on Southhampton Row on his way to his lectures in estate management.

---

23. *Shir Hashirim Rabbah* 1:15 [2].

Chapter 11

Drawing Close With Cords of Love

RABBI DESSLER SUCCEEDED IN BINDING HIS *TALMIDIM* to him as if they were his own children. He gave himself over completely to his students and was unsparing with his expressions of love in both writing and speech.[1] The opening of a letter to Solomon and Flora Sassoon was typical of the warmth he showed his *talmidim*. "Your departure, my dear and beloved students, was hard on me, especially in that the month of *Elul*, the period of preparation for *teshuvah*, has arrived. I miss each of you with spiritual yearnings."[2]

Over the years, letter writing became one of his primary means of developing an intense emotional connection with his students. Especially in later years, when he was geographically separated from his closest students, a profusion of letters poured forth from

---
1. Rabbi Dessler's son Rabbi Nachum Velvel Dessler says that his effusive warmth in writing was a perfect reflection of his speech.
2. *Michtav Me'Eliyahu*, Vol. IV, pp. 310-11.

his pen. Many a Thursday night was given over entirely to letter writing until dawn, and some mornings he would rise early and write ten letters before *Shacharis*.³

The effort he put into correspondence was enough by itself to make his students feel how much they meant to him. He concludes a typical letter to the Sassoons by noting that it is already 2 a.m. but that he felt compelled to stay awake because there was no other opportunity for writing during the day.⁴ Another letter to the Sassoons concludes with apologies for the number of writing errors caused by pushing off sleep "long past midnight" to write.⁵

When he could not write, his subsequent letters were filled with profuse apologies for not having done so. To Mordecai Miller, who was in Dublin during the war years, Rabbi Dessler writes in 1940, "Forgive me for not writing. No doubt I caused you to worry about me. Surely you know that if there had been any possibility of doing so, I would have, since writing to you is my greatest pleasure."⁶

In writing, Rabbi Dessler gave full vent to emotions that he might have hesitated to express in person for fear of embarrassing the recipient. The warmth of expression to young men a fraction of his age is astonishing. When illness prevented him from attending the *vort* (engagement party) of Rabbi Dov Steinhaus, he wrote a letter that the Steinhauses read and reread over the years:

> All day I have been in anguish — anguish that comes from joy. This is a strange thing: The heart rejoices and that very joy causes sorrow to rule the heart. And the more the heart rejoices the greater the pain. Yesterday I pictured all day how I would be with you tonight and rejoice so greatly in the rejoicing of your heart.... I said to myself how eagerly I looked forward to meeting the choice of your heart and her distinguished parents, for how could it be that you are so

---

3. Rabbi Dov Sternbuch.
4. Ibid., p. 312.
5. Ibid., p. 323.
6. Ibid., p. 333.

close to me and I have not previously met them...⁷

Each letter was carefully crafted, the Hebrew expressions reaching the level of poetry. In a 1941 letter to Rabbi Moshe Schwab, Rabbi Dessler apologizes profusely for the fact that his quick departure from Letchworth, where Rabbi Schwab's parents lived, prevented him from saying goodbye or thanking Rabbi Schwab for all his assistance. He beseeches Rabbi Schwab to forgive him "though I shall not forgive myself for the denial of the good done for me." He then informs the still unmarried young man of his next visit to Letchworth and expresses the hope that they will be able to spend a long time together in discussion: "My powerful desire to delight in your company makes preferable spending the night seated on a chair in your house to resting on a bed filled with fine pillows and expensive bedding somewhere else."⁸

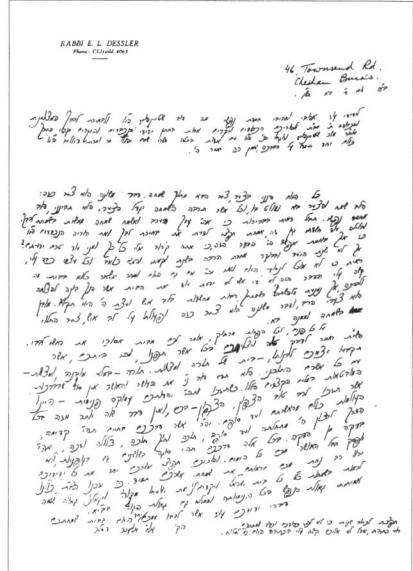

R' Dessler's letter to the Steinhaus family

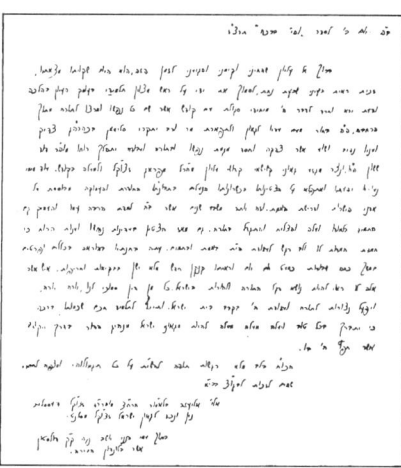

R' Dessler's letter to R' Schwab

Many of the letters were nothing more than expressions of longing

---

7. *HaRav Dov Zev Steinhaus* (Hebrew), p. 20. This work is a privately published pamphlet on the life of the late *Mashgiach* of Yeshivas Kol Torah in Jerusalem.
8. Unpublished correspondence dated *Erev Sukkos* 5701 (1940).

Chapter Eleven: Drawing Close With Cords of Love / 157

to see the recipient, even when he had just taken his leave of them. Thus after arriving in Margate for a brief vacation, he immediately sat down to write the *talmid* who had accompanied him to the train station:

> I am pained by the fact that while we were in the middle of the discussion with the conductor about my bag, the train arrived and we did not have a chance to say good-bye. *This sorrow accompanied me all my journey.* I arrived just five minutes ago. I came into Rabbi Cohen's house and immediately sat down to write you, my dear one....[9]

Letter writing was only one of Rabbi Dessler's means of expressing his love for his *talmidim*, for it was conveyed in everything he did. He was extremely considerate of others. The warmth he conveyed, remembers Rabbi Yosef Epstein, went "much deeper than good manners" or even consideration. He made everyone feel that he was vitally concerned with them and that he understood them.

Though lacking money himself, he showered his students with presents, almost invariably *sefarim* (books) from which he felt they could grow.[10] When the father of one of his *talmidim* lost all his money in a series of financial reversals, Rabbi Dessler very much wanted to continue teaching the young man and tried every stratagem to continue the lessons without payment.[11] During the war, when his *talmidim* were dispersed all over the British Isles, Rabbi Dessler made every effort to keep in touch with all of them and thought nothing of traveling five hours round-trip by train to visit a young *talmid*.[12] Above all, Rabbi Dessler devoted himself to answering all of his students' questions, whether of a personal or philosophical nature. "Whenever you needed help or an *eitzah* (piece of advice), or thought

---

9. *Michtav Me'Eliyahu*, Vol. V, pp. 504-5.
10. Rabbi Mordecai Miller.
11. Rabbi Yosef Epstein.
12. See Rabbi Aryeh Carmell, *Strive for Truth*, Vol. I, p. 208.

you did," remembers Rabbi Aryeh Carmell, "he lent the full weight of his powerful mind to whatever was bothering you."

Rabbi Dessler knew the secret of positive reinforcement, and was constantly on the lookout for praiseworthy developments in his students. An early letter to Solomon Sassoon praises him highly for setting aside fixed times to learn Torah even while on vacation and contrasts him favorably to others his age "who find their enjoyment in resting, going to the beach, and pretty scenery."[13] Another letter informs Solomon, "You have conquered my heart by virtue of your desire to learn." Rabbi Dessler made clear to him the high hopes that he held out for him:

> Why are you so dear in my eyes? I will tell you explicitly.... Because in the secret recesses of my heart I place the hope ... that you will be a *gadol b'Torah* in whom all of *Klal Yisrael* will be glorified.[14]

By pointing out Solomon's great potential, Rabbi Dessler sought to inbue him with a sense of obligation to realize that potential:

> It is incumbent upon you to know that Hashem demands of you, and it is your portion in this world, that when you reach adulthood, you will attain greatness in Torah and be among the *bnei aliyah*. Seeing you, many will follow your example. For surely it was not for nothing that Hashem has brought you to this point.[15]

Yet the praise was carefully measured — designed to spur further growth rather than stunt it by leading to pride and complacency. Rabbi Dessler was careful to tell Solomon that he had reached only the "beginning" of the love of Torah, the first level: finding pleasure in learning. A later letter to Solomon characterizes the British custom

---

13. *Michtav Me'Eliyahu*, Vol. IV, p. 304.
14. Ibid., p. 307.
15. Ibid.

of going on vacation during *Elul* as the work of the *yetzer hara* and draws a sharp contrast to the custom of the European yeshivos of traveling to vacation spots during *Tammuz* and *Av* so as to gather strength for *Elul* and the *Yamim Noraim*.[16] It would not hurt Solomon to know, Rabbi Dessler felt, that he still had a long way to go before reaching the level of a Eastern European *yeshiva bachur*.

When his *talmidim* produced worthy insights, Rabbi Dessler was effusive in his praise. He complimented Mordecai Miller, stranded by World War II in Dublin where he completed two law degrees, for having written "amazing things" in response to a *shiur* Rabbi Dessler had sent him on the "Root of *Mussar*." "Your thoughts and insights show you are growing in the straight path, according to the fundamental principles of faith," Rabbi Dessler writes, before concluding, "It has been a long time since I had such pleasure as in reading your letter."[17]

A Reluctant Critic

BY NATURE, RABBI DESSLER WAS RELUCTANT TO REBUKE ANYONE, including his students. Yet when he felt it was necessary, he could do so in very subtle ways. In response to Solomon Sassoon's complaint that he had failed to achieve his goal of learning six *blatt* (folios) while on vacation, Rabbi Dessler remarks dryly, "I received your postcard today. Thank G-d that you arranged your studies a *little* (emphasis added). From the beginning, I knew, my dear Sliman, that you would not fulfill your intention ... , but I gave you the chance to arrange things according to your desire. But now at least figure out what you can learn and make a fixed *seder* for that.[18]

That, however, was only a prelude to an even more subtle criticism. Rabbi Dessler reminded Solomon that in his previous letter he had informed him that he would soon be writing to him very deep words of Torah "in order that you could savor this present and prepare yourself for it." But there had been another purpose to this advance notice. Rabbi Dessler wanted to measure Solomon's

---

16. Ibid, p. 311.
17. Ibid., p. 336.
18. Ibid., pp. 316-17.

eagerness to receive the *divrei Torah*. When Solomon's return letter came back filled with discussions of boating with his sister and bicyle riding, but no mention of the forthcoming *divrei Torah*, Rabbi Dessler decided that he had not shown proper appreciation and therefore did not include his promised insights in his next letter.

He was careful to conclude, however, "Understand, my dear Sliman, that I speak out of love not anger, … but better open reproof when it flows from hidden love."

A lack of good *middos* was one of the few things guaranteed to elicit Rabbi Dessler's criticism. On one occasion, one of Rabbi Dessler's closest *talmidim* sent Rabbi Dessler a long letter with fourteen questions on different matters. Rabbi Dessler's reply dealt with only thirteen of the questions, and the *talmid* noted the omission in his return letter without a word of thanks for Rabbi Dessler's long letter.

Rabbi Dessler's response began with the same words he concluded his rebuke of Solomon Sassoon: "better open reproof when it flows from hidden love." After half a page dealing with a halachic problem the student had raised, Rabbi Dessler returned to the subject of reproof, without mincing words:

> I had great pain from your letter. I wrote you a very long letter, which you know is not easy for me. Yet I did not find a single word of thanks in your return letter. [I mention this] not because I need your thanks, but because of my love for you and concern that you not become a person who denies the good done for him. Recall what I wrote at the end of the "Discourse on Giving and Taking" concerning the words of our Sages: "Whoever denies the good done him by his friend will in the end deny the good *HaKadosh Baruch Hu* does him as well."
>
> Not only [was there no word of thanks], but at the beginning of your letter you reminded me that there was one question of yours to which I forgot to furnish an answer…. Was that the proper beginning to a letter of ten pages?

Rabbi Dessler went on to attribute his *talmid's* oversight to haste and a lack of concentration. That haste reflected a *bilbul hadaas* (confusion of thought) that was the very opposite of the *menuchas hanefesh* so prized by Kelm, and which Rabbi Dessler noted he had always found in his student in the past. Such confusion, Rabbi Dessler pointed out, is precisely the quality that gives the *yetzer hara* its power over people, which is why our Sages command us to separate ourselves from those who have no *daas*.[19]

When the student replied to Rabbi Dessler's reproof with a letter filled with contrition, Rabbi Dessler was quick to seize upon the exchange as a way of building up his *talmid* and bringing him yet closer. In his next letter, Rabbi Dessler informed his student, "You are dear and honored in my eyes because you accept rebuke.... I enjoyed your letter very much, my precious one."[20] And that letter was followed by another, expressing delight in the fact that "you are striving to go deeply and to understand."[21]

The rebuke directed to that particular *talmid* reflects the stress that Rabbi Dessler always placed on the importance of *mitzvos bein adam l'chaveiro*. At one point, for instance, Mordecai Miller wrote to him from Dublin with a problem: His mother, who was separated by the war from her husband, had asked her sons to accompany her to some light entertainment. Her sons considered attending such entertainment inappropriate due to the horrible suffering of Jews in Europe. Rabbi Dessler did not denigrate their sensitivity — indeed he praised it. But he pointed out, "Sometimes a person wants to do a *mitzvah*, and it is truly a *mitzvah*, but because of other things that are mixed in, it becomes an *aveirah*. Just as a positive *mitzvah* pushes off a negative prohibition, so does the Torah *mitzvah* of honoring your parents take precedence over your feelings.... For everything there is a time, and you must be very careful not to cause pain to your parents."[22]

Just as Rabbi Dessler exemplified *kibbud av* in his relations with

---

19. Ibid., Vol. III, pp. 340-42.
20. Ibid., Vol. IV, p. 333.
21. Ibid.
22. Ibid., pp. 333-4.

his father, so did he insist upon it from his *talmidim*. After the war, he brought one of the members of the Gateshead Kollel with him to Ireland. At one point in their visit, he asked the young man whether he had written to his mother and pointed out that doing so was the fulfillment of a *mitzvah d'oraisa*. He also remonstrated with the young man for having walked out in the middle of a *drashah* by the local *rav*.

In general, Rabbi Dessler preferred to guide his *talmidim* by personal example and with general words of *mussar* rather than by criticizing them directly. Only with the very closest of his *talmidim* would he ever permit himself to comment directly on their *middos* development. One Thursday night, Rabbi Dessler and a married *talmid* with whom he was staying spoke late into the night. Eventually Rabbi Dessler's host headed upstairs to bed, while Rabbi Dessler remained downstairs to write letters. As his host mounted the stairs, Rabbi Dessler called after him.

"When I was a young man," Rabbi Dessler told him, "I had a friend who told me, 'Even though you always stand in the background and never put yourself forward, in your heart of hearts, you still think you are the one.' I'm that friend." To this day, the *talmid* still has no idea whether the story Rabbi Dessler told about himself was true, or if he was just trying to soften the *mussar* by comparing his student to his younger self.

It was extremely rare for him to speak critically of anyone, even without mentioning the person's name. There is only one such example in all his printed correspondence, and even in that case, Rabbi Dessler breaks off in the middle of his narration to remind his correspondent, "It is not my way to give frequent reproof. I am well aware that there are few who can accept *tochachah*."

In that particular instance, Rabbi Dessler found himself together at a certain place with the brother of someone whom Rabbi Dessler knew from Eastern Europe. The brother in England had repeatedly ignored letters from his brother in the Mirrer Yeshiva, and the latter had written to Rabbi Dessler expressing his concern for his brother and asking him to look into the matter. When Rabbi Dessler approached the brother, the latter took the offensive, telling him that he knew very well what Rabbi Dessler wanted: "The Rav wants me to be a Zevulun to my brother's Yissachar. But I have no need for that. I too could learn if I wanted, but I have other *mitzvos*."

To Rabbi Dessler, the brother in England was a classic example of how a basically good person could deceive himself so deeply out of a love of money. And he rebuked him strongly to his face: "Listen to your own words, *'I can learn but I don't want to.'* All those other *mitzvos* of which you speak would be of a far higher quality if you learned. Certainly you would no longer ignore your brother, who takes precedence over all those others you benefit, and you would cease causing him such worries."[23]

A Relationship for Life

ONCE ESTABLISHED, VIRTUALLY EVERY ONE OF RABBI DESSLER'S close relationships lasted for his entire lifetime. And it was more often than not Rabbi Dessler who took the initiative in preserving the relationship when the passage of time or geographical distance had weakened the ties. One of his first students in Gateshead Seminary, who had since moved to America, was shocked one day to receive a letter of blessing from Rabbi Dessler congratulating her and her husband on the birth of their first son three and a half years earlier. The letter contained not one word of remonstration for not having informed him of the boy's birth.[24]

With every new undertaking, Rabbi Dessler went to extraordinary lengths to ensure that it would not be at the expense of his existing students. When he left London and its environs to establish the Gateshead Kollel, he did not abandon the students in London he had nurtured from youth. Rather, he devised an almost superhuman schedule in order that he could retain his connection with them. Similarly, when he left Gateshead for Ponevezh Yeshiva in *Eretz Yisrael*, Rabbi Dessler made an explicit condition that he be allowed to return to England several times a year.

Rabbi Dessler treated third and fourth cousins as if they were

---

23. Ibid., p. 320.
24. Rebbetzin Miriam Elias.

brothers and sisters,[25] and his *talmidim* like members of his immediate family. To fully appreciate what that means, however, one first has to know how he treated family. Shortly after the marriage of his much younger cousin Rabbi Simcha Zissel Dessler, Rabbi Dessler showed up at the home of the new couple in Jaffa carrying two beautiful, large silver candlesticks. He told the young couple that he had combed the length of Allenby Road in Tel Aviv in search of proper "*Litvishe licht.*"[26]

R' Dessler (l) at the wedding of R' Steinhaus (r)

Every week he made a special trip from Bnei Brak to Jaffa to visit his cousin and his family. He never came without presents for each of the children. Yet when one of the young Dessler children made the mistake of asking one week, "What did you bring us?" Rabbi Dessler replied, with his usual sweet smile, "I brought, but we do not ask that question, and today you won't receive."

On his visits, Rabbi Dessler would discuss with his cousin the talk he intended to give on Wednesday night. Mrs. Dessler was a teacher, and whenever she had a question on a *Midrash*, Rabbi Dessler would learn it with her. He also bought her a set of books on the *Midrash* inscribed "as a reminder of our love." Both Rabbi Simcha Zissel Dessler and his wife viewed Rabbi Dessler "like a father."

Rabbi Dessler also acted towards his students as if he were their father. The Steinhauses were surprised to receive from him shortly after their marriage a brief note informing them of his intention to

---

25. Rabbi Nachum Velvel Dessler.
   When he arrived in *Eretz Yisrael*, for instance, he took the time to look up and visit relatives of his daughter-in-law.

26. Those two candlesticks were the most prized possession of Rabbi Simcha Zissel's family. Many decades after Rabbi Dessler's passing, Mrs. Sarah Dessler returned

R' Dessler holding Dovid Sassoon, son of Solomon Sassoon

visit them "to see how they have established their new home for success and blessing."[27] Rabbi Dessler addressed the wives of his students by their first names or called them "*mein kind*," just as he did his daughter-in-law. In his letters to his close students, he invariably mentioned every child by name and inquired after their well-being.[28] Nor was there anything formulaic about the mention of the children. The children themselves treated him like a grandfather. He would hold them on his knee and carry them up and down the stairs. Rabbi Mordecai Miller recalls his two young daughters, ages 3 and 2, respectively, each grabbing hold of one of Rabbi Dessler's legs and yelling, "It's my Rabbi Dessler." Finally, the older one told the younger, "It's your Mommy, but my Rabbi Dessler."

Casting His Net

RABBI DESSLER'S GREATEST INFLUENCE WAS ON HIS PRIVATE students, but it was by no means limited to them. He was always searching for new ways to reach young Jews. Though he taught in the after-school Talmud Torah in the Montague Road Beis Hamedrash, he soon realized that any results from the Talmud Torah would be superficial at best. He therefore invested much effort in convincing parents to send their children either to Eastern European yeshivos or to Heide Yeshiva near Antwerp where Rabbi Feivel Shapiro, a great-nephew of the Alter of Kelm, was Rosh Yeshiva.

---

home one day from a short shopping trip to find that her apartment had been broken into and everything of value taken. Every cabinet and the writing table upon which the candlesticks stood (which was inherited from Rabbi Dessler) had been emptied of its contents, but for some reason the thieves had left the candlesticks, which stood there in plain view undisturbed.

27. *HaRav Dov Zev Steinhaus*, p. 24.
28. Rabbi Aryeh Carmell.

While Rabbi Dessler's successes in convincing parents to send their children to Eastern Europe were not many, he did not slacken and even raised money to support young men who wished to study in Eastern Europe. Yaakov Goldman, the son of the *shammas* in the Montague Road Beis Hamedrash, was one of those who did heed the call. He went to learn in Kelm. When the British evacuated all their citizens from Lithuania in 1940, he refused to leave — perhaps because the evacuation was scheduled to take place on Shabbos and perhaps because he wished to share whatever fate Providence had in store for his fellow *talmidim*.

Koppel Rosen was another young man who fell under Rabbi Dessler's influence and eventually went to study in Mirrer Yeshiva. Later he returned to England and founded Carmel College, a school for Jewish boys modeled on the exclusive British public schools, but which provided a modicum of Jewish education to boys who otherwise would have had none.[29]

In a well-known letter, Rabbi Dessler practically begs the father of a boy in whom he has spotted genuine potential to send him to Mir to learn. Rabbi Dessler begins by excusing himself for offering an unsolicited opinion, but states that his "heart filled with love" does not allow him to restrain himself.

"Has not your entire goal until now been that of a select few — i.e., that your children grow not just to be simple G-d-fearing Jews, but real *gedolei Torah?*" Rabbi Dessler asks. "I know your heart," he continues, "and you are not a compromiser. All that will come from compromises is the illusion of Torah."[30]

Rabbi Dessler also gathered a group of neighborhood boys for a once-a-week *Gemara shiur*. This *shiur* consisted of about twelve boys past the age of bar mitzvah. Most of them had little, if any, background in Talmud, but the group included a number of young men of exceptional intellectual promise.[31] Rather than learning straight

---

29. Rabbi Aryeh Carmell.
30. *Michtav Me'Eliyahu*, Vol. III, pp. 337-340.
31. One member the group was Solly Gross, who went on to be a senior member of the British diplomatic corps.

Chapter Eleven: Drawing Close With Cords of Love / 167

through a particular tractate on a once-a-week basis, Rabbi Dessler made his principal goal whetting his students' appetite for the study of *Gemara*.

He would take a specific problem raised somewhere in *Shas* — a *Tosafos* in *Temurah*, for instance — and explain it to his students. Then he would invite them to offer their own solutions using nothing but their logical faculties. When they were done, he would reveal how the *Gemara* resolved the issue — often in a way completely at variance with any of the solutions they had been able to offer — and explained the underlying logic of the *Gemara*.

In addition to the specific content of the *shiur* itself, the class enabled Rabbi Dessler to establish a much closer contact with a number of boys.

Cyril Domb, who went on to Cambridge University and to become a distinguished professor of physics at London University and Fellow of the Royal Society, was one of those in Rabbi Dessler's class. He remembers Rabbi Dessler as being eager to deal with any philosophical questions that were raised by his education. When Domb would see Rabbi Dessler on vacations from Cambridge, the latter would always ask him, "Do you have any problems?" The answers he gave inspired Domb with confidence that they were well based and authentic, not apologetic.

Nor would Rabbi Dessler confine his discussion to philosophical topics. He inquired about the Dombs' environment from a religious standpoint, and asked Domb whether there were other religious students with whom he associated. And he would encourage him to remain firm in his *mitzvah* observance. Two *halachos* (laws) which Domb recalls him stressing were not to carry a handkerchief on Shabbos and not to shave with a razor, both of which prohibitions were either unknown or widely ignored at the time.[32]

---

32. Today it might seem insulting to Professor Domb that Rabbi Dessler felt it necessary to remind him not to engage in actions which are prohibited by the Torah. Professor Domb, however, notes that in the context of the times, Rabbi Dessler's admonitions were a compliment and an indication that he viewed Professor Domb as a seriously committed young Jew, who would take his reminders to heart. Care with regard to such laws in those days represented the outer limit of religious observance.

Nor was Rabbi Dessler's teaching confined to young men. From the late '30s, he taught a weekly *shiur* in *Tehillim* to women in the house of Mrs. Devorah Sternbuch. When her husband Asher Sternbuch passed away in 1935, Mrs. Sternbuch was left with the daunting task of raising nine children alone. She turned to Rabbi Dessler for advice on all her affairs. He used to arrive an hour before each *shiur* to discuss with Mrs. Sternbuch whatever questions had arisen during the week.[33] Throughout the war years, the *shiur* drew thirty to forty women a week.

Many of those who attended were drawn from the ranks of German refugees for whom Rabbi Moshe Schneider had set up a special hostel. (In addition to his concern for these girls, who in most cases arrived in England without their families, Rabbi Schneider was also hopeful that some of the girls would prove to be suitable spouses for the older *bachurim* in his yeshiva.)

Kelm had always placed a strong emphasis on women's education. The Alter's daughter Nechama Liba was acknowledged to be one of the few who really understood her father's *shmuessen*, and the daughters of Rabbi Nachum Velvel Ziv, the Alter's son, were each highly educated in both Jewish and general subjects.

Rabbi Dessler fully subscribed to the Kelm belief in the importance of women being well versed in Torah thought and said so in his *shiurim* to women.[34] He spoke very seriously to the women, not at all as someone providing entertainment, with a bit of spiritual uplift. Mrs. Sarah Margulies, one of the Sternbuch daughters, remembers the *shiurim* as being on a very high level and that Rabbi Dessler revealed a psychological dimension to the words of King David. Some of the *shiurim* were subsequently included in *Michtav Me'Eliyahu*.[35]

---

33. Mrs. Sternbuch was a truly remarkable woman. All of her three sons — Rabbi Moshe Sternbuch, *dayan* of the *BaDaTz* of Jerusalem, Rabbi Eliyahu Sternbuch, *dayan* in Antwerp, and Rabbi Dov Sternbuch, one of the premier teachers in Gateshead Seminary for more than half a century — grew to be highly respected *talmidei chachamim*, and a number of her daughters married world-famous *talmidei chachamim*.

34. Mrs. Sarah Margulies, one of Mrs. Sternbuch's daughters.

35. See e.g., *Michtav Me'Eliyahu*, Vol. I, p. 81.

Around the same time that he began his *shiurim* for women, Rabbi Dessler also started a weekly *mussar shmuess* for a small number of advanced yeshiva students then learning in London. This new circle began on the initiative of Moshe Schwab, a German-born immigrant who had learned in Baranovitch and Kaminetz and one *Elul zman* in Mir. Upon his arrival in London in 1938, he immediately began searching for a regular *mussar shmuess*, like those he had heard from Rabbi Yerucham Levovitz in Mir Yeshiva. Everyone he asked mentioned the same name: Rabbi Dessler.

Schwab set about organizing a group of those interested in hearing Rabbi Dessler on a regular basis. The initial circle was no more than five or six *bachurim* drawn almost exclusively from the top *bachurim* in Rabbi Moshe Schneider's yeshiva.[36]

Rabbi Schneider's own style of *mussar* could not have been further removed from Rabbi Dessler's philosophical approach. He was extremely straightforward — this is what we must do; this is what we must be — and fond of illustrating his points with stories. He eschewed anything that was too "*philosphishe*," as he put it.[37]

Yet Rabbi Schneider recognized that there were young men who had a thirst for a deeper understanding.[38] Indeed his own son Rabbi Gedaliah and his future son-in-law Rabbi Alter Halperin were among those closest to Rabbi Dessler. Throughout the war years, Rabbi Dessler continued to meet with this group once a week at

---

36. Rabbi Alter Halperin.

37. Rabbi Naftoli Friedler.

Rabbi Dessler himself recognized that at some level many of the issues with which he dealt were dictated by a decline in the *emunah peshutah* (simple faith) that had characterized previous generations and which was exemplified in his day by the *Chofetz Chaim*, in whose path Rabbi Schneider followed. He once commented after proposing some particularly profound thesis, "Would that we never had this sort of problem! For those who in their innermost heart are really imbued with the spirit of the Torah, these are not problems at all ... ." Rabbi Aryeh Carmell, "Rabbi Eliyahu Eliezer Dessler," in *Guardians of Our Heritage*, Rabbi Leo Jung, ed. See also, *Michtav Me'Eliyahu*, Vol. V, p. 376, fn. 2.

38. On at least one occasion, Rabbi Dessler was invited to give a *shmuess* by Rabbi Schneider. He spoke on the happiness in this world of one who has the privilege of learning Torah with intensity. That study frees him from all those activities upon which most people are dependent to distract themselves from the emptiness of their lives. Rabbi Wolf Kaufman.

Rabbi Gedaliah Schneider's house, where Rabbi Dessler would spend the night.

During the winter of 1941-42 when the Gateshead Kollel was just beginning, Rabbi Dessler was so busy that he did not have time to meet with the circle from Schneider's. Alter Halperin, who was still a *bachur*, felt so keenly the loss of contact that he wrote Rabbi Dessler a letter demanding to know why Rabbi Dessler had not found time for them while he continued to meet with other *talmidim*. Rabbi Dessler correctly understood the young man's brazen remarks as an expression of how important the learning with Rabbi Dessler was to him, and rather than taking offense, he invited Halperin to spend that Pesach with him in Chesham.

In many ways, the weekly *shmuess* begun at the behest of Rabbi Moshe Schwab served as the bridge to the *shmuessen* Rabbi Dessler would say in the Gateshead Kollel just a few years later. Many of the early members of the Gateshead Kollel were drawn from this small group of exceptionally talented young men. The founder of the group, Rabbi Moshe Schwab, was one of the founding members of the Gateshead Kollel and subsequently the *Mashgiach* of Gateshead Yeshiva. Rabbis Alter Halperin,[39] Naftoli Friedler,[40] Shammai Zahn,[41] Dov Sternbuch,[42] Wolf Kaufman[43] and Elchonon Karnovsky were others who eventually joined the group and went on to learn for many years in the Gateshead Kollel.

For the first time, Rabbi Dessler was addressing a group of *talmidim* who were already well versed in Talmud, and some of whom had already learned in the great European yeshivos like Mir and Kaminetz.[44] The *shmuessen* were thus much closer in depth and

---

39. Rabbi Halperin succeeded his father-in-law as Rosh Yeshiva of Schneider's Yeshiva. He was also the prinicipal editor of the first volume of *Michtav Me'Eliyahu*.

40. Rabbi Friedler was Rosh Yeshiva for decades in Breuer's Yeshiva and in Yeshiva Ner Israel in Toronto.

41. Rabbi Zahn has been the Rosh Yeshiva of Sunderland Yeshiva for nearly half a century.

42. For nearly 50 years, Rabbi Sternbuch has been one of the principal teachers in the Gateshead Seminary.

43. Rabbi Kaufman is Rosh Kollel in Manchester.

44. Besides Rabbi Schwab, Rabbi Yosef Epstein, who arrived in England in 1939 via Italy, had learned in Kaminetz Yeshiva under the great Rabbi Boruch Ber Leibowitz.

style to those that he would one day give in Gateshead and Ponevezh than those which he had previously given to his circle of private students in London.

Rabbi Yosef Epstein, who had learned in both Mir and Kaminetz, remembers Rabbi Dessler's *shiurim* very vividly almost sixty years later. Many were based on the *Zohar*. Rabbi Dessler would cite a passage from the *Zohar* and then explain it. He was comparable to a Rabbi Chaim Brisker of *hashkafah*, recalls Rabbi Epstein, with a phenomenal ability to break things down into their basic principles. (The comparison to Rabbi Chaim Brisker in his analytical abilities is one cited over and over again by Rabbi Dessler's students.) The *shmuessen* were, in Rabbi Epstein's opinion, comparable in quality and depth to those that he had heard from Rabbi Yerucham Levovitz in the Mirrer Yeshiva, though each, of course, had his unique, individual style.[45]

The expansion of Rabbi Dessler's circle of students to include a group of budding *talmidei chachamim* can, in retrospect, be seen as part of the transition to the public stage as head of the Gateshead Kollel.

---

arrived with a set of Reb Boruch Ber's *shiurim*, and immediately began giving *shiurim* in Schneider's Yeshiva on the basis of those notes. He was subsequently interned as an enemy alien.

Rabbi Elchonon Blumenthal, who had learned in Telshe Yeshiva with Rabbi Dessler's son Reb Nachum Velvel and thereafter for a year in Kelm, lived with the Dessler family for a year after his arrival in England in 1938. Despite his friendship with the younger Dessler, Rabbi Blumenthal was amazed by the warmth with which he was received by the Dessler family, who, in his words, made him feel "just as if I were a member of the family." Blumenthal, *Trials and Challenges*, p. 54.

45. Rabbi Epstein's contact with Rabbi Dessler was not limited to the weekly *shiur*. Rabbi Dessler opened his home to the young refugee and offered him free access to perhaps his most precious possession: Reb Reuven Dov's copies of the *shmuessen* of the Alter of Kelm. He describes the nine months that he was in close contact with Rabbi Dessler as the most crucial in his *chinuch* (education).

Chapter 12
Separated Once Again

RABBI DESSLER WAS FORCED TO CALL HIS SON NACHUM Velvel back to London from Telshe Yeshiva in the summer of 1938. All his life, he had suffered from poor eyesight. By 1938 cataracts had so reduced his vision that he had no choice but to undergo surgery. Though both eyes were affected, Rabbi Dessler rejected the suggestion that they both be operated on. An operation on both eyes would have meant being unable to look in a *sefer* for two weeks, and that was unimaginable for him. "For my purposes," he told his cousin Simcha Zissel, "vision in one eye will be enough."[1]

Farewell to Reb Nachum Velvel

The surgery forced Rabbi Dessler to remain virtually immobile for six weeks. Nachum Velvel attended him during the entire recuperation process. During that time, letters poured in from Reb Chaim Ozer — nine in all.[2] Reb Chaim Ozer instructed Nachum

---
1. Rabbi Aharon Sorasky, *Marbitzei Torah U'Mussar*, Vol. III, p. 64.
2. Ibid., pp. 63-4; Sorasky, *Achiezer: Collected Letters*, Letters 393-401.

Nachum Velvel at the Telshe Yeshivah

Velvel to write him every three days detailing his father's progress,[3] and to Rabbi Dessler he wrote urging him to heed the orders of his doctors and not to write until they gave their permission.[4]

A story from Rabbi Dessler's period recuperating in the hospital gives us an idea of the kind of impression he made on people. His eye doctor was Dr. Levy, who had virtually no connection to anything Jewish. Yet he immediately recognized Rabbi Dessler as an extraordinary person. As a consequence, he offered to arrange a private room for him in the hospital at the same price Rabbi Dessler was then paying for a room he shared with other recuperating patients. Rabbi Dessler, however, absolutely refused to accept any such gift.[5]

Though immobilized for well over a month, Rabbi Dessler did not waste his time. While recuperating, he revised much of *Kuntras*

Nachum Velvel's British passport

---

3. *Achiezer: Collected Letters*, Vol. II, Letter 397.
4. Ibid., Letter 399.
5. Dr. Dov Heiman, Rabbi Dessler's personal physician at the time.

174 / RAV DESSLER

HaChesed (Discourse on Lovingkindness), which he had first begun formulating as far back as his marriage in Kelm. He used the eye surgery in another way as well: as a metaphor for the degree to which our opinions are the products of our own subjectivity. After the cataract was removed, he told his students, the entire world looked completely different to him. And so it is that our views of the world are heavily influenced by our individual perspectives.[6]

Once Rabbi Dessler's recuperation was complete, it was time for Nachum Velvel to return to Telshe. Neither father nor son could have dreamed at the time that it would be nearly nine years until they would see each other again.

Separation from Wife and Daughter

RABBI DESSLER'S WIFE BLUMA AND DAUGHTER HENNIE HAD planned a trip to Eastern Europe in the summer of 1938 for the purpose of visiting Rebbetzin Dessler's mother, Rebbetzin Pesha Ziv, and other relatives in Kelm. The trip, however, was postponed until the following summer because of Rabbi Dessler's eye surgery.

The media was already full of discussions of prospects for war at the time of Rebbetzin Dessler and Hennie's departure for Lithuania in August of 1939. There were discussions in the Dessler family about the dangers involved in traveling to Eastern Europe. But it was assumed that the threat of war would somehow blow over.

Within a month of their arrival in Kelm, the Nazis had invaded Poland. Despite the uncertain political situation, Rebbetzin Dessler and Hennie still traveled to Vilna during Chanukah of 1939 to visit Rabbi Chaim Ozer Grodzenzki. Reb Chaim Ozer offered Hennie some Chanukah *gelt* (money). The young girl told the *gadol hador* that she did not need any money. He explained to her, however, "Chanukah *gelt* is not given because you need it but because the giver loves you." He also gave her a bracelet that had belonged to his first wife, the sister of Rabbi Dessler's mother.[7]

---

6. Rabbi Yaakov Katz, a private student of Rabbi Dessler's in London and later in Gateshead Yeshiva.
7. Rabbi Yehoshua Geldzahler.

By 1940, the first rumors of the Nazi atrocities in Poland had reached England, and it was clear that the Jewish communities of Eastern Europe were in grave peril. Rabbi Dessler tried to calm his fears with the thought that as long as his wife and daughter were in close proximity to such a great *tzaddik* as his brother-in-law Rabbi Doniel Movshovitz they could come to no harm.[8]

Writing to his daughter in 1940, Rabbi Dessler did not share his worst fears with her, but he gave full vent to his own anguish over being separated from her. The five-page letter to his daughter, each page adorned at the top with another term of endearment, begins:

> Your letter in Hebrew finally arrived, and I have read it over and over. Every day I read it over as if I had just received it.... There are days when I feel I have almost seen you — you, your mother, and Nachum Velvel, all three together. Yet it is only in a dream I have seen you.... The joy is overwhelming, and then suddenly I awaken, and behold it was a dream. May Hashem grant that we shall again be together as in former times.
>
> Still we must give thanks to Hashem with all our heart that we are in good health, lacking nothing, [while] many of our Jewish brothers are suffering horribly in different places.

Even after the Nazi invasion of Poland made it impossible for his wife and daughter to return to England, Rabbi Dessler still tried to console himself that his daughter Hennie was being exposed to the same atmosphere of *kedushah* in which her parents had been raised, an air of holiness unique in all the world:

> You are now found in the environs of a holy yeshiva, and not just any yeshiva, but the holiest and most elevated place in the world — the Talmud Torah of Kelm.... And you even live within the yeshiva itself....[9] The holiness that you can

---

8. *Marbitzei Torah U'Mussar*, Vol. I, p. 72.

9. Rebbetzin Dessler and Hennie lived in the yeshiva, in the apartment formerly occupied by the Alter's daughter, Rebbetzin Nechama Liba, who later lived with Rabbi Doniel Movshovitz and his wife. The apartment was referred to as *die andere halbe* — the other half.

absorb there will provide you spiritual sustenance for your whole life. You hear there the voice of *tefillah* that has no parallel anywhere in the world. You now know the way they learn *mussar* to straighten their hearts for the service of Hashem....

The separation weighs heavily upon me. But when I consider the spiritual riches that your soul can now acquire, I am glad even for this difficult situation....

My daughter, my life, my eyes pour forth tears, warm tears, many tears, in reading your mother's letter that you are learning with great enthusiasm and desire. There are many girls who excel in the studies of the world. But there are few educated in purity and holiness to know and understand Torah and the emotions of a Jew.

The letter to Hennie conveys not only Rabbi Dessler's pain at the separation from his family, but how intense remained his sense of longing for Kelm twelve years after he had seen the *beis medrash* for the last time. He takes his daughter on a tour of the *beis medrash*, stopping along the way to point out how connected their family was to every inch of the house:

Ask and they will tell you where was my place in the *beis medrash* — there next to the window and the bookcase on the left side.... In earlier years there was no bookcase because that was the place of your great-grandfather, the Alter of Kelm, Reb Simcha Zissel, and when he died they put the bookcase there so that no one should stand in his place.

Do you know where was the place of your grandfather, your mother's father, or of your other grandfather, my father.... And who sat to his right near the window? Our teacher Reb Tzvi Hirsch Braude, the husband of your honored aunt Nechama Liba.

Have you seen the clock in Beis HaTalmud? The clock was brought into the *beis medrash* in the year 1895. It had been the clock in my family's house in Libau. And when my mother, who gave birth to me, died in that year, my father and teacher gave the clock as a remembrance for her soul. And for 45 years that clock has established the *sedarim* in the yeshiva....

Did you see the large *sefer Torah* in Beis HaTalmud? It belonged to my father's mother, and she gave it to the yeshiva. I read from that *sefer Torah* every Shabbos for years.

These memories ... I place before your eyes. This house is a part of our souls without doubt. Your great-grandfather the Alter obtained the plot in 1874 and established Beis HaTalmud, which has been standing in all its glory for sixty-six years. Our whole spiritual legacy is from there. Your mother's father learned there for twenty years. And my father learned there almost without break until his wedding. My father brought me there when I was about 13 years old, and I was privileged to be perfumed by its holy air until I came here at the end of 1928, except for the four years of the World War.

I came in 1906, two days before *Rosh Chodesh Shevat*, and I had the great privilege of sitting in the house of Hashem for 18 years. Anything we have within us is from there. Every hair, every fibre is connected to that place.[10]

Escape

UNDER THE 1939 RIBBENTROP-MOLOTOV TREATY BETWEEN Germany and Russia, the two countries divided up Eastern Europe between them, with the Russians receiving the Baltic states of Lithuania, Latvia, and Estonia. On *Motzaei Shabbos*, June 21, 1940, Russian tanks rolled into Kelm at 2 a.m., as part of the Russian takeover of the Baltics. The Russians wasted no time plundering all the shops, confiscating every business and placing their sympathizers in charge. Rationing was instituted for all essential goods.[11]

---

10. *Michtav Me'Eliyahu*, Vol. IV, pp. 328-30.

11. The following account of the Desslers' escape from Kelm is based almost entirely on an article by Shmuel Gorr in *Yiddishkeit Magazine, Tammuz* 5746, entitled "From Kelm to Melbourne."

Concerned that its nationals in Lithuania were in imminent danger, the British Consulate in Kovno invited all British subjects to come to Kovno a few weeks after the Russian takeover. The rapidity of the Russian conquest caught the British unprepared, and they were now hastily making plans to evacuate all British subjects from the war zone.

Rebbetzin Dessler and Hennie were told that the British government would soon close all its consulates in Lithuania, and that anyone seeking travel documents thereafter would have to travel all the way to Moscow. Even in Kovno, securing the necessary travel documents was far from a matter of course. The Soviets interviewed every foreign national about his reasons for seeking a travel permit. These interviews could be grueling. Rabbi Nosson Wachtfogel, a Canadian then studying in Kelm, was kept overnight in prison after his first interrogation.

Initially the British government recommended evacuation to Sweden for the duration of the War. Subsequently the group was informed that the evacuation might be to Canada. After *Tishah B'Av*, they were told that plans had changed once again and now the intention was to send British nationals to Australia.

After all these changes in plans, the Desslers and the other members of their group began to question whether they should leave at all. All of them found the thought of separation from their friends and colleagues in the Talmud Torah very difficult.

When Rabbi Elchonon Wasserman came to Kelm in *Elul*, he was approached and asked for his opinion concerning leaving Kelm. Reb Elchonon's first replied that the safety of Australia depended to a large extent on whether Japan entered the war. But in the middle of the conversation, he suddenly stopped and said, "Don't ask me any more. I can't see anything. Whatever you do, let it be with *hatzlachah* (success). But remember one thing — wherever you may be, even in Australia, you will never be exempt from the birthpangs of the Mashiach. They will follow you everywhere."

Reb Doniel, however, gave his blessing to the plan to depart for Australia. During the Ten Days of Repentance, the British Consul in Kovno informed the British citizens in Kelm that they would be leaving Kovno on Shabbos *Parashas Bereishis*. The group leaving Kelm included Rebbetzin Dessler and Hennie, Rabbi Chaim Dov Silver, a British citizen, his Kelm-born wife Channah Gisa, and their four children, and two Canadians learning in Kelm, Rabbi Nosson Wachtfogel[12] and Rabbi Shmuel Schecter. They left Kelm *Chol HaMoed Sukkos* for Kovno, where they stayed in the home of Rabbi Gedaliah Dessler. *Simchas Torah* was spent in the *mussar shtibel* in Kovno founded by Reb Gedaliah.[13]

Rabbi Silver was still uneasy about traveling on Shabbos, and he went to see the venerable *rav* of Kovno, Rabbi Avrohom Dovber Kahane, the most distinguished *posek* in Lithuania and author of *Dvar Avraham*. As soon as he heard the question, Rabbi Kahane jumped up and told Rabbi Silver emphatically, "How can you ask such a *shaylah* (question). Get on the train tomorrow. Don't you understand what is going on? It's *pikuach nefesh*."

The group from Kelm was joined by one from Telshe Yeshiva, which included Pinchos Berliner, Shmuel Bloch, Yehoshua Chinn, Rabbi Shlomo Davis, later a *maggid shiur* in Telshe Yeshiva, and Rabbi Chaim Gutnik, subsequently a *rav* in Melbourne and the father of the well-known philanthropist Reb Joseph Gutnik, and Monty Moore. They placed their belongings on the train Friday afternoon and departed the next morning for Moscow via Riga. Arriving in Moscow Sunday morning, they were met at the train station by a British consular official, who escorted them to the Transiberian Express, on which they would traverse Russia.

The journey across Russia to Vladivostok[14] on the Pacific Ocean took nine days. For food, the religious Jews had to content themselves with some fruit and tea. The Silvers had been told that there would be milk for their infant, but there was not. The group

---

12. Rabbi Wachtfogel also succeeded in securing with great difficulty a visa for his future wife Chava, to whom he was already engaged.

13. *Zichronos Chayai*, p. 27.

14. Rabbi Nachum Velvel Dessler also escaped from Lithuania via Vladivostok about a month earlier than his mother and sister. Traveling on a student visa provided by Yeshiva Torah Vodaath, he left Telshe in August. He spent Rosh Hashanah together with the Telshe Roshei Yeshiva and the Modzhitzer Rebbe in Yokohama, Japan. From Japan, he took a boat to San Francisco, landing on Simchas Torah.

was closely watched the entire journey by Intourist agents and under strict orders to talk to no one. At Vladivostok, the train cars with foreign nationals were detached from the rest and three armed guards were placed to watch it. Before the group departed by steamer from Vladivostok, the Russians confiscated all their valuables.

From Vladivostok to Australia took almost four and a half weeks by sea. The Desslers' group found themselves sharing the ship with 150 British subjects of Lithuanian descent, who soon enough proved that British citizenship had done little to dilute their traditional Lithuanian anti-Semitism. Rabbi Silver also discovered on board a Jewish missionary, whom he threatened to throw overboard if he attempted to missionize.

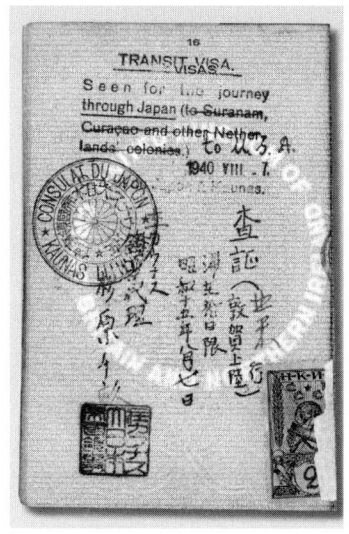

Nachum Velvel's Japanese transit visa

For food, the group had to content themselves with little more than tomatoes, eggs, and sardines. The lack of food made a stop in Hong Kong that much more welcome. The ship's captain had telegraphed ahead to Hong Kong that he had a contingent of religious Jews on board, and as a consequence, the leaders of the Hong Kong Jewish community came to greet the refugees bearing kosher food. They escorted their guests to the local synagogue and then on a tour of Hong Kong.

Eventually the group arrived in Brisbane, Australia, landing just before the onset of Shabbos. They were met and taken straight to the local synagogue. The next morning the rabbi announced that the arrival of real *bnei Torah* in the city was a historic moment for the community.

That opinion, however, was not universally shared. When the Board of Governors of the Australian Jewish community discovered that several Torah scholars had arrived in their midst, they were less than thrilled. Rabbi Wachtfogel and Rabbi Shmuel Schecter were offered first-class tickets if they would agree to proceed on from Australia to their native Canada.[15] (In light of the impact that Rabbi Wachtfogel would subsequently have on the flowering of Torah in America,[16] the Board of Governors' fear that he and Rabbi Schecter might introduce an undesired level of religious enthusiasm into the community was well founded.)

Australia

UNLIKE RABBI WACHTFOGEL AND RABBI SCHECHTER, THE Silvers and Desslers had no place else to go. For nearly six years, the two families would live together as one.[17] After nine months living in Brisbane, Rabbi Silver was fired from his job in the wartime censorship bureau for refusing to work on Rosh Hashanah. As a consequence, the Silvers moved to Melbourne where there was a far greater demand for Rabbi Silver's services. He was offered a number of positions as both a *rav* and as a *melamed*, but remembering Reb Doniel's advice, he refused all the rabbinic positions. In each of his teaching jobs, Rabbi Silver found himself accused of being an extremist for attempting to teach the students Talmud.

In Melbourne, the Desslers were reunited with one old friend under highly improbable circumstances. Prior to leaving Kelm, Rebbetzin Dessler had taken with her a quilt that her son Nachum Velvel's friend from Telshe Yeshiva, Elchonon Blumenthal, had left behind in Kelm.

At the time Rebbetzin Dessler left England, Rabbi Blumenthal was living in the Dessler home. Subsequently he was arrested as an enemy alien and eventually sent by ship to a detention camp

---

15. Rabbi Shmuel Schecter.

16. Upon arriving back in North America, Rabbi Wachtfogel, together with Rabbi Schecter — and with assistance of Rabbi Hillel Bishko, international president of Tiferes Bachurim — established what was likely the first kollel in North America in White Plains, New York. After the arrival of Rabbi Aharon Kotler in June 1941, this kollel became the nucleus of Lakewood Yeshiva, where Rabbi Wachtfogel served as *Mashgiach* for 47 years until his passing 2 *Kislev* 5759 (1999).

17. The account of the Desslers' life in Australia is almost entirely drawn from a short biography of Rabbi Chaim Dov Silver, which was privately published after his passing: *Orchos Chesed*, pp. 53-60.

for enemy aliens in Australia.[18] When Rebbetzin Dessler heard of a detention camp for enemy aliens after her arrival in Melbourne, she immediately inquired whether Rabbi Blumenthal was among the detainees and found out that he was.

As it happened, the prisoners were provided inadequate bedding in the camp for the cold nights and the quilt that Rebbetzin Dessler had transported all the way from Kelm could not have arrived at a more propitious time for Rabbi Blumenthal.[19]

Rebbetzin Dessler was "*Tante* (Aunt)" Bluma to the Silver children, whom she referred to as her "*Kelmer kinder.*" *Tante*, however, does not begin to capture her closeness to the Silver children, in whose upbringing she was actively involved. She instilled in them the traditional Kelm discipline and stressed, above all, the importance of avoiding anything in which there was the slightest possibility of *chilul Hashem*. That included making sure that their shoes were always polished and that any little tear in their garments was sewn. The youngest Silver child, Avigdor, can still remember his teacher placing him on a desk so all his classmates could see how neatly polished his shoes were.

When the time came for Avigdor to go to school, the Silvers were informed that the law prohibited him from wearing any form of head-covering in school. (There was at that time no full-day Jewish education.) Rebbetzin Dessler could not bear the idea of Avigdor being forced to go without a *yarmulke,* and went to the school to speak to the headmistress herself. She explained to the principal the significance to Jews of a head-covering.

Her words seemingly left the headmistress unmoved. The latter just repeated that the law was the law and there was nothing she could do about it. At that point, Rebbetzin Dessler could not contain herself, and she began crying. When the principal saw how much importance Rebbetzin Dessler attached to the subject, she agreed to

---

18. One of his fellow prisoners was Rabbi Asher Feuchtwanger, who later married Rabbi Solomon Sassoon's sister Flora, and who was also close to Rabbi Dessler in England.
19. Blumenthal, *Trials and Challenges,* pp. 65-6.

let Avigdor wear a hat outside at recess (where his classmates soon made a game of flicking it off his head).

Rebbetzin Dessler instilled the sensitivities of Kelm *mussar* in Hennie and the Silver children. Once she and Hennie were walking on the street when Hennie stopped to look in the window of a pawnshop. Rebbetzin Dessler immediately insisted that she move on. Each item of jewelry, she explained, represented a personal tragedy — some poor person had been forced by circumstances to part with some cherished possession out of financial desperation. It was forbidden, she told Hennie, to derive any pleasure — even the pleasure of viewing a beautiful piece of jewelry — from the suffering of others.[20]

The environment in Melbourne in the war years could hardly have been further removed from Kelm, and the Silver children were only allowed to play outside the house with the children of one other family, the Slonims. The presence of Rebbetzin Dessler in the house was thus crucial in preserving the atmosphere of Kelm.

Communication between Rabbi Dessler and his family throughout the war was very limited. From the time that Rebbetzin Dessler and Hennie left England in August 1939, until they were reunited with Rabbi Dessler more than six years later, they never spoke by telephone. And during the war, even letters between Australia and England were very sporadic. All mail was subject to wartime censorship, and over half the letters never even reached their destination.[21] Despite this, Rebbetzin Dessler never complained about the situation, or even spoke about it. She took the attitude that Hashem had decreed that the family should be separated and therefore complaining was useless.

For his part, Rabbi Dessler too rarely spoke about the pain of the separation. And if he did, it was only to emphasize his good fortune that his entire family had reached safety at a time when so many Jewish lives had been lost.

One morning, a letter from his wife and daughter in Australia arrived. From the shape of the envelope, it was clear that there were

---

20. Rabbi Yehoshua Geldzahler.
21. Rabbi Nachum Velvel Dessler.

photographs inside. Now, at last, he would have a chance to see how his daughter Hennie, who had left England as a girl, had grown into a young woman, already capable of teaching in the afternoon Talmud Torah headed by Rabbi Silver.

R' Danzig and R' Dessler

The mere sight of the letter set off a powerful emotional reaction in Rabbi Dessler. But he did not open the letter immediately. Rather he placed it on the mantle and waited for ten minutes before allowing himself the pleasure of reading it and looking at the photographs.[22] That response was pure Kelm: Any strong desire must be quelled and not given into, for once one is controlled by his desires, the *yetzer hara* has gained a foothold. Indeed in Kelm, they made a practice of not opening letters on the day they were received.

Chesham

MUCH OF LONDON'S JEWISH POPULATION, INCLUDING MOST OF Rabbi Dessler's private students, evacuated the city for the countryside, after the onset of the brutal German air strikes on the city. With his family gone and his students dispersed, there was little holding Rabbi Dessler in London. In 1940, he left the Montague Road Beis Hamedrash and moved to Chesham, where he had been preceded by Aryeh Carmell and some of his other close students. Most of the inhabitants of Chesham had never before seen Jews, whom they tended to identify with the Israelites of the Bible.[23]

In Chesham, Rabbi Dessler first lodged with Mr. and Mrs. Weinkoff, Aryeh Carmell's parents. Later, he rented the second floor

---

22. Rabbi Aryeh Carmell.
    Rabbi Mordechai Miller relates a similar story that took place after the war. Rebbetzin Dessler was abroad, and Rabbi Dessler was concerned that he had not heard from her for many days. One morning, Rabbi Miller asked him whether he had heard from his wife, and Rabbi Dessler replied that he had. But when Rabbi Miller inquired whether everything was well with her, Rabbi Dessler said he did not know yet because had decided not to open the letter until 10 a.m.
23. Rabbi Aryeh Carmell.

of the home of a non-Jewish woman. Sharing his small apartment with him was Rabbi Shimon Danzig, a fundraiser for the Kelm Talmud Torah, who, like Rabbi Dessler, had been cut off from his family by the outbreak of the war. Virtually the only possessions that Rabbi Dessler brought with him to Chesham were his *sefarim*. So large was his library that visitors joked that the floor of Rabbi Dessler's apartment looked like it was caving in under the weight of his books.[24]

The library was a true reflection of its owner. "The whole Torah library is for me," Rabbi Dessler once told his son-in-law Rabbi Yehoshua Geldzahler. In formulating his responses to the questions posed by his students, he looked everywhere for answers that were both well based and compelling. But even without the need to respond to issues raised by his students, Rabbi Dessler's own curiosity and breadth of outlook would have led him into every branch of Jewish thought.[25]

Rabbi Dessler made a deep impression on the Chesham community. He was particularly close to Rabbi Yisrael Ehrentreu, a *rav* in the community.[26] Rabbi Ehrentreu once said, "There were two great revolutions in my life: the first when I left home for the Nitra Yeshiva in Hungary, and the second when I met Rabbi Dessler in Chesham."[27]

---

24. Rabbi Naftoli Friedler.

25. Rabbi Dessler viewed every *sefer* in his library as a potential conduit of Divine inspiration. Rabbi Yitzchak Greenberg, the long-time Mashgiach of Lomza Yeshiva in Petach Tikvah, once asked to borrow a certain *sefer* from Rabbi Dessler. Rabbi Dessler explained that he could not lend his *sefarim* when he was busy preparing his *shmuessen*, because he never knew which one was destined to be a source of inspiration for the coming week. He described to his younger friend how every week he carefully wrote down each *sefer* that he looked at during the week and marked the exact spot to which he had opened. Treating each of these sources as a form of revelation from Heaven, he then proceeded to fashion his talks on the basis of all the places he had looked during the week. To lend a book, then, was to limit his potential sources of illumination. (Rabbi Dessler was quick to add that when he traveled during the intersession, Rabbi Greenberg was free to borrow any work he wished.)

26. Rabbi Ehrentreu was the son of Rabbi Chanoch Ehrentreu, who had been the chief rabbi of Munich.

27. Rabbi Aryeh Carmell.

Rebbetzin Ehrentreu used to prepare Shabbos meals for Rabbi Dessler. One Friday, Rabbi Ehrentreu delivered the Shabbos package to Rabbi Dessler's lodgings. When Rabbi Dessler saw who the messenger was, he refused to accept the package. Rabbi Ehrentreu was equally insistent that he would not take the package back. A "struggle" developed between the two, with Rabbi Dessler's student Aryeh Carmell watching in amazement. After Rabbi Ehrentreu left, Rabbi Dessler said to his student, "Doesn't he know that I'm doing this for his honor, not for mine?"[28]

R' Ehrentreu with R' Dessler

R' Dessler with R' Aryeh Carmell

In Chesham, Rabbi Dessler busied himself giving *shiurim* and continued with some of his private lessons. He spread his net to gather in new students as well. Among the new devotees were two young men who first met Rabbi Dessler while in Chesham to collect money for Schneider's yeshiva. Naftoli Friedler and Shammai Zahn knew that Rabbi Dessler was one of the finest products of Kelm, but they had heard that he did not dispense his Torah readily. Yet when they went to visit him, he told them that *bachurim* who were collecting for their yeshiva deserved to hear a good *shmuess*, and he spoke to them for over an hour on the importance of directing one's thoughts to a specific goal. Along with the

---
28. Ibid.

R' Dessler with his portable writing table, correcting stencils

shmuess, the two budding *talmidei chachamim* were very impressed by Rabbi Dessler's friendliness and the delicious hot chocolate Reb Shimon Danzig prepared for them.[29] Both men joined Rabbi Dessler within a few years in the Gateshead Kollel.

Because his close students were spread far and wide by the war, Rabbi Dessler began for the first time in Chesham to print his *shiurim* in the form of stencil sheets. These stencils were then sent out to *talmidim*. It was difficult for Rabbi Dessler to carry on his Talmudic learning with his students by mail, and he increasingly turned his attention to *hashkafah* (philosophic) topics. The necessity of putting his thoughts in writing also lent them a more formal structure than the ideas that he had previously conveyed to his pupils. Thus the stencil *shiurim*, which Rabbi Carmell helped him to prepare,[30] represent another transition step from his tutoring in *Gemara* to his emergence as the premier Jewish thinker of the second half of the twentieth century.[31]

Though the separation from his wife and children was very hard for Rabbi Dessler at the time, but for that separation Rabbi Dessler's name would not be a household word today. Had his wife and daughter remained with him, he could never have undertaken the schedule that he did in founding the Gateshead Kollel.

---

29. Rabbi Shammai Zahn.

30. One of Rabbi Dessler's lifelong traits was his eagerness to listen to the ideas of others. When *talmidim*, such as Rabbi Carmell, offered insights of their own in connection with a theme which Rabbi Dessler had treated, he was happy to incorporate them into the stencils that were distributed. *Rabbi Aryeh Carmell.*

31. In both Gateshead and Ponevezh, Rabbi Dessler continued this practice of sending stencil copies of his *shiurim* to distant students. These sheets were kept and bound by his students, and eventually formed the basis for much of the posthumously published *Michtav Me'Eliyahu.*

Rabbi Dessler himself pointed out the degree of *Hashgachah Pratis* (Divine Providence) involved. Less than two years after the Kollel first opened, he wrote to his former physician, Dr. Dov Heiman, "If it were not for the fact that I have been left without my family, I could not have done this."[32]

R' Dessler in Switzerland in 1938, at the wedding of his cousin Devorah Olshtein.

The destruction of European Jewry filled Rabbi Dessler with a passion to dedicate himself totally to the *Klal* (community) and to the rebuilding of Torah life. And ironically, it was his own private tragedy in being cut off from his family for over six years that enabled him to do so.

---

32. *Michtav Me'Eliyahu*, Vol. V, p. 509.

Chapter 13
The Founding of Gateshead Kollel

R' Dovid Dryan as a young man

An Implausible Dream

WE HAVE ALREADY DESCRIBED IN DETAIL THE arrival of a letter in Chesham in the summer of 1941 inviting Rabbi Dessler to participate in the establishment of the Gateshead Kollel (see Introduction). That invitation from Rabbi Dovid Dryan, the *shochet* of Gateshead, and Rabbi Dessler's response thrust Rabbi Dessler onto the public stage.

The immediate impetus for the idea of a kollel was the arrival in England of a handful of outstanding young Talmudic scholars in the late 1930's as a consequence of the deteriorating situation in Eastern Europe. Several of these young men had married into Gateshead families and were then living in Gateshead.

Mr. Ephraim Bloch, for instance, claimed two outstanding products of the Lithuanian yeshiva world for sons-in-law: Rabbi Chaim Shmuel Lopian, a product of Telshe Yeshiva and already famous in the yeshiva world as author of *Ravcha D'Shmaitza*, and Rabbi Aryeh Leib Grossnass, a student of Rabbi Boruch Ber Leibowitz in Kaminetz. Rabbi Yehuda Zev Segal,[1] who had learned in Mirrer Yeshiva for many years, was also living in Gateshead, as was Rabbi Kalman Pinsky, who was married to Rabbi Elya Lopian's daughter Chaya Ita. These young men gathered every day to learn in the house of Rabbi Naftoli Shakovitsky, the *rav* of Gateshead.

Eventually the small study group conceived the highly improbable idea of forming a kollel in Gateshead of outstanding young Talmudic scholars like themselves. The natural first step was to approach Rabbi Dovid Dryan, who had been the driving force behind the founding of the Gateshead Yeshiva twelve years earlier. They knew that once Reb Dovid committed himself to the project he would throw himself into it body and soul and not be deterred by any obstacle.

Reb Dovid adopted the idea enthusiastically. He quickly realized that for a kollel to succeed it would require someone of stature to head it, and accordingly drafted a letter describing the proposed kollel. That letter was sent to a list of prominent *rabbanim* then living in England, of which Rabbi Dessler was but one.

Reb Dovid communicated with twenty-two rabbis in all, many of whom he knew only by name or reputation. Their responses tell us much about the obstacles facing the proposed kollel. Eighteen of the recipients did not bother responding at all; three more responded that the establishment of a kollel was a wonderful idea, but totally impracticable in the midst of a war in which communities were in complete disarray and many Jews had left London.[2]

---

1. In 1941, Rabbi Segal became a *maggid shiur* in the Manchester Yeshiva headed by his father, and therefore never joined the Gateshead Kollel. Rabbi Segal did, however, become a close disciple of Rabbi Dessler, who visited Manchester weekly during World War II and afterwards as well.

2. Rabbi Aryeh Carmell.

Only Rabbi Dessler responded affirmatively, repeatedly expressing his gratitude to Reb Dovid for having offered him the opportunity to participate in such a "momentous matter upon which the entire world depends." "My heart sees a great light in the matter which Your Honor suggested — your merit is very great," he wrote.[3]

Though Rabbi Dessler would not receive final confirmation for another four years that his beloved Kelm was no more, there were already strong intimations of the destruction of Lithuanian Jewry. In his reply to Rabbi Dryan, Rabbi Dessler begins by describing the total destruction of all that had been built by the great leaders of the preceding generations. Even at that early date, the Kollel would become in his mind part of the effort to salvage some small remnant from the fire. He referred to it as a "little Yavneh," after the academy of scholars Vespasian granted R' Yochanan, just prior to the destruction of Jerusalem.[4]

Reb Dovid Dryan

IN RABBI DOVID DRYAN, RABBI DESSLER RECOGNIZED A KINDRED soul of untainted idealism. In that first letter, Rabbi Dessler addresses him as "*yedid nafshi*, a man of greatness and great deeds, ... upon whom the merit of the community rests, Moreinu HaRav Rabbeinu Rabbi Dovid Dryan."

Rabbi Dessler knew Reb Dovid as the driving force behind the founding of Gateshead Yeshiva, in which project Rabbi Dessler had come close to joining him. Not long after his arrival in Gateshead in the early 1920's from a small Welsh community in which he had previously served as a *shochet*, Reb Dovid conceived the remarkable idea that one of England's smallest Jewish communities would one day be home to a great yeshiva. Not everyone in the community was elated by Reb Dovid's dream. One of the communal leaders was frequently heard to remark, "We employ him as a *shochet* and *chazzan* and not for any of his other activities."

---

3. *Fifty Years of the Kollel Rabbanim of Gateshead* (Hebrew), pp. 31-2.
4. Ibid., p. 31.

Though a man of few words, Reb Dovid possessed an iron will when it came to his public projects. By 1929, he had assured himself of enough community support to travel to Leeds with the aim of persuading boys to come to learn in a "yeshiva" in Gateshead. His efforts netted him a grand total of two students. Those two boys and another from Gateshead were promptly installed in a small side room of the the Blechener (or Tin Hut) Shul that then serviced the small Gateshead community, and Gateshead Yeshiva was born.

R' Dovid Dryan

Within a few months, Reb Dovid had eight boys in tow, each of whom ate his meals with members of the local community. Reb Dovid collected the money, penny by penny, to support the fledgling yeshiva, which lacked both a building and students. He made frequent appeals for that purpose from the *bimah* of the Blechener shul. Despite the yeshiva's inaspicious beginning and less than abundant resources, Reb Dovid succeeded in persuading Rabbi Nachman Dovid Landynski, son of Rabbi Moshe Landynski, the Rosh Yeshiva in the *Chofetz Chaim's* yeshiva in Radin, to assume the position of Rosh Yeshiva.

Rabbi Landyski proved the perfect rosh yeshiva for a yeshiva of mostly younger boys. He was in the *beis medrash* for eight hours every day, and always knew precisely when each boy entered and left the *beis medrash*, and when they arrived for *davening*. One could learn from him what it means to sit engrossed over a *Gemara* for hours at a time, without moving.[5]

By 1931, Reb Dovid had even secured a building for the yeshiva, which then numbered twenty students. He and his wife Zlata devoted themselves entirely to the yeshiva. In the early years, when funds were lacking to pay someone to clean the floors, Reb Dovid thought nothing of undertaking the task himself. He and his wife were not blessed with children, and the young *bachurim* became for them surrogate children.

---

5. Professor Zev Low, a student in the pre-World War II yeshiva.

Chapter Thirteen: The Founding of Gateshead Kollel / 193

IN MANY RESPECTS, REB DOVID DRYAN PERSONIFIED THE SPIRIT of fierce independence and determination that characterized the Gateshead community from its founding. On its face, the small town of Gateshead would seem an unlikely center for the major Torah institutions of Western Europe. Yet there was nothing accidental about the lead role of the small Gateshead community in the development of English Jewry.

Gateshead

To describe Gateshead as nondescript would be overgenerous. In Rabbi Dessler's day, Gateshead was a poor, working-class suburb of Newcastle, to which it is joined by a bridge over the River Tyne. Gateshead's air was laden with a thick dust from the nearby coal mines. The grey drabness of the town was further accentuated by the cold and rainy climate.[6]

Nor could it be said that any notable intellectual ferment ever penetrated to Gateshead prior to the establishment of a Jewish community there. Such cultural life as may be found in that area of northeastern England belongs primarily to Newcastle. And even in Newcastle, the local soccer team and ale inspire far more fervent allegiance from the population than any pursuits of the mind.

Even as a center of Torah learning, Gateshead had to take a backseat to nearby Sunderland for most of its first half century. In the early 1930's, the daily *blatt shiur* in Sunderland's roomy shul building attracted fifty to sixty *baalebatim* a day. Sunderland's first Jewish settlers were drawn primarily from Lithuania, many of them from the *mussar* stronghold of Kretinga, and the community boasted a large number of members who had learned in the leading Lithuanian yeshivos.

And yet it was the smaller and less learned Gateshead community that became home to Gateshead Yeshiva, Gateshead Kollel, and Gateshead Seminary. This was not, as Reb Reuven Dov Dessler pointed out in a 1929 letter to his son, a "function of luck but of merit. And that merit comes from conducting one's actions with *daas, yiras Shamayim* and for the sake of Heaven." Knowing Gateshead only by reputation, Reb Reuven Dov nevertheless predicted, even at that

---

6. The following discussion of the history of the Gateshead community is based on Miriam Dansky's *Gateshead* (Targum Press, 1992).

early date, that there existed in Gateshead the potential to construct something stronger and more elevated than anywhere else in England.[7]

Above all, the members of the Gateshead community were distinguished by their fierce insistence on preserving the religious standards that they brought with them from Eastern Europe and Germany and their refusal to submit to the process of "anglicization" that had overtaken most Jewish immigrants and their offspring. The tone of the community was set for good by its founder, one Zelig Bernstone. Unwilling to accept what he viewed as the laxity of the Newcastle community, he crossed the bridge over the River Tyne one day in 1881 and took up residence in Gateshead.

Bernstone immediately set about encouraging like-minded Jews to join him. Upon his arrival in Gateshead, he found a number of large houses lying empty as the result of an overly ambitious building boom. With cheap rentals as an incentive, Bernstone was able to attract a handful of new immigrants arriving at Newcastle port from Eastern Europe and a few family members. By 1883, twelve males over the age of 13 dwelled in Gateshead, including Mr. Eliezer Adler, who would become the dominant figure in the nascent community.

From the very beginning, the community resisted all efforts to force it to submit to the authority of the chief rabbi of the British Empire. Dr. Hermann Adler, the chief rabbi at the time of the community's founding, recommended that the members continue to *daven* with the Newcastle community on days on which the Torah was read. But fearing that they would again be subsumed under the aegis of their less strict co-religionists in Newcastle, the Gateshead *minyan* refused. Their rejection of the chief rabbi's suggestion was abetted by a wealthy Jew from Nottingham, who donated a *sefer Torah*. That *sefer Torah*, however, remained hidden in a drawer, when not in use, so as not to bring the community into open rebellion against the chief rabbi.

The community's rejection of the authority of the chief rabbi, however, could not be hidden forever, and indeed it was not. The

---

7. *Kisvei HaSaba Mi'Kelm*, Vol. II, pp. 562-3.

hiring of a *shochet* for the community in 1908, without soliciting a candidate from the chief rabbi or submitting to his supervision, was one such act of defiance.

By 1912, the community was prepared to build a *shul*. A small parcel of land was purchased ten yards distant from a railway station, and there the Blechener *shul* was erected. The *shul*, which continued to serve the community until 1939, is best remembered for its tin roof, from which it derived its name. The roof sagged noticeably under winter snow and reverberated ominously during the heavy rains that frequently pelt northeast England. The shaking of the building every time a train rumbled past was a further threat to the concentration of those praying.

On a 1923 visit to Gateshead, the then chief rabbi, Dr. J. Hertz, was so astounded by the makeshift premises in which Gateshead's Jews prayed and learned that he offered the community the large sum of 2,000 pounds for the building a new *shul*. Fearful, however, that acceptance of the gift would entail acceptance of the chief rabbi's authority, the congregation politely, but firmly, turned the offer down.

Further conflict with the chief rabbi was not long in coming. The issue this time was the right of the Gateshead community to appoint a marriage secretary so that its marriages were recognized by Great Britain under an 1840 Act of Parliament. Appointment of a marriage secretary required certification by the president of the Board of Deputies of British Jewry that the synagogue in question was "a body of persons professing the Jewish Religion." And that certification was conditional on the synagogue adopting a set of by-laws recognizing the final authority of the chief rabbi over the appointment of the rabbi, *chazzan*, *shochet*, and any other religious functionaries.

In the course of the dispute, the chief rabbi asserted that his supervisory role was necessary for the protection of Judaism. The reply from Gateshead, signed by the community secretary Akiva Bell, was characteristically short on tact:

> My community cannot understand what you mean by the Sacred duty of the chief rabbi to protect Judaism, when they

see that the majority of your Ministers shave with a razor, have mixed choirs in their synagogues, and do not believe in *mikveh*....

Not until 1935 did Gateshead succeed in obtaining the right to register marriages, and even then only because the chief rabbi was forced to grant the right to a non-Orthodox congregation.

Gateshead's rejection of the supervision of the chief rabbinate, it

R' Naftoli Shakovitsky

must be emphasized, did not derive from any anti-authoritarian bias on the part of community members. Indeed there are few, if any, communities in the world in which the *rav's* authority is absolute, as in Gateshead. From the arrival of Rabbi Naftoli Shakovitsky from the famed Kovno Kollel in 1938, the *rav* has been consulted on every community initiative, and his word is law. When Rabbi Bezalel Rakov succeeded his father-in-law Rabbi Shakovitsky, he was greeted by a delegation representing the entire community upon his arrival by train in Newcastle. And at a subsequent reception in his honor, the heads of every communal organization rose one by one to publicly accept the authority of the new *rav*.

The universally accepted authority of the *rav* reflects the absolute unity of purpose that has characterized the Gateshead community from its inception. Those who are not prepared to conduct their lives according to the strictest halachic standards simply do not remain in Gateshead, which to this day, over a hundred years after its founding, is still home only to *shomrei Shabbos*.

It was to this remarkable community that Rabbi Dessler moved in late 1941. Gateshead would provide the setting for some of his greatest triumphs, and he, in turn, would have an impact felt to this day on every one of Gateshead's major institutions.

RABBI DESSLER HAD SHOWN GREAT ENTHUSIASM FOR THE IDEA of a kollel, but a good deal still remained to be worked out before he could commit himself to leaving Chesham. Uppermost on his mind was the question of what would become of his circle of *talmidim*. Whatever form his involvement with the proposed kollel took, it would obviously require him to move to Gateshead, which was at least five hours from London by train. In addition, his duties with the kollel would seemingly leave him no time for the students he had nurtured for nearly a decade in most cases.

Working Out the Details

He knew how dependent his *talmidim* were on him, and they were like sons to him. Simply abandoning them was out of the question. Eventually, he found the answer to his dilemma in a *Midrash*. *Bereishis Rabbah* (41:8) records an apparent argument between two Sages over *Avraham Avinu's* relations with his nephew Lot:

> Rabbi Yehudah said: The Holy One, Blessed is He, was angry with Avraham on account of Lot's departure, for the Holy One, Blessed is He, said, "Others you are able to draw close and not your own nephew Lot?"
>
> Rav Nehemiah said: The Holy One, Blessed is He, was angry with Avraham for [allowing] Lot to remain with him [for as long as he did], for the Holy One, Blessed is He, said, "I said to you, *'To your descendants will I give this land'* (Bereishis 15:8), and you keep Lot with you with the apparent intention of including Lot in your inheritance."

On their face, the two opinions in the *Midrash* seem irreconcilable. On the one hand, Avraham is criticized for sending Lot away; on the other hand, he is criticized for having let him remain in his house for as long as he did.

One of Rabbi Dessler's fundamental principles in intepreting *Midrash*, however, was that apparently conflicting opinions are but two sides of the same coin. Following his standard method of interpretation, Rabbi Dessler succeeded in reconciling the two opinions. As long as Lot remained on a comparatively low spiritual level, he explained, Avraham was adversely affected by his presence and should have separated from him (as noted by Rav Nehemiah). The solution, however, was not to send Lot away, but for Avraham to elevate himself to the point that he would be incapable of being adversely affected by Lot, which would allow him to lift up Lot to be a worthy member of his household.[8]

The lesson for Rabbi Dessler was that one must undertake any burden to ensure that those for whom one is spiritually responsible do not come to harm. That meant in Rabbi Dessler's case taking on an almost superhuman schedule of traveling through the night by train two or three nights a week.[9]

In his initial reply to Rabbi Dryan, Rabbi Dessler proposed that the two meet to discuss further the practical details of implementing Reb Dovid's dream. Rabbi Dessler suggested that they meet midway between Gateshead and London, but expressed his willingness to come to Gateshead if that was too difficult for Reb Dovid.

At that first meeting, Rabbi Dessler and Reb Dovid agreed that each would bear responsibility for raising half the Kollel's budget. Reb Dovid wrote three letters seeking initial backers for the idea, and each one responded with a check for £50, quite a large contribution in those days. Those favorable initial responses suggested that the Kollel was not a hopeless fantasy and convinced Rabbi Dessler of the financial viability of the project.[10]

Unfortunately, Reb Dovid never succeeded in securing another contribution, and the entire fundraising burden of the Kollel fell on

---

8. *Michtav Me'Eliyahu*, Vol. II, pp. 166-69.

9. Rabbi Aryeh Carmell.
   This lesson was one that Rabbi Dessler passed down to his *talmidim* as well. Rabbi Chaim Friedlander, his closest disciple in Ponevezh Yeshiva, served for many years as the *Mashgiach* in Yeshivat HaNegev in Netivot. Subsequently, he was offered the prestigious position of *Mashgiach* in Ponevezh Yeshiva, the same position once held by his revered teacher Rabbi Dessler.
   Though both positions were full-time positions, Rabbi Friedlander recalled the example of Rabbi Dessler. He agreed to accept the position in Ponevezh only on the condition that he could simultaneously remain in his position in Yeshivat Hanegev. He did this by traveling to Netivot every Sunday evening and devoting the entire day on Monday to the needs of the Netivot students.

10. Rabbi Aryeh Carmell.

Rabbi Dessler.[11] But if Rabbi Dessler had been deceived by the success of Reb Dovid's initial solicitations, the deception had obviously been from Heaven in order that Rabbi Dessler cast his lot fully with the Kollel.

In truth, Rabbi Dessler was unconcerned with the statistical probability of the Kollel succeeding and needed little encouragement before committing himself. The Kollel, he knew, was a spiritual undertaking, and as such its success or failure would be largely determined by the quality of the intentions of all those involved. In the early years of the Kollel, he frequently quoted his great-grandfather Rabbi Yisrael Salanter, *"Men darf nit oif tun, men darf tun; men darf nit optun, men darf tun; men darf nit noch tun, men darf tun* — Our task is not to accomplish, but to do; our task is not to be among the naysayers, but to do; our task is not to delay, but to do.

Rabbi Dessler answered Reb Dovid's call but not because he was sure of success. He knew as well as the pessimists did the many factors then arrayed against the establishment of a Kollel. No broad public yet existed in England with a deep appreciation of the importance of Torah learning. The few yeshivos that existed were small in size. (Gateshead Yeshiva itself did not begin to really grow substantially until the influx of many refugees into England.)

As a consequence, raising funds for the Kollel required a full-scale educational campaign as well. Even in Eastern Europe, the concept of a group of scholars supported after marriage by monies raised from the public was almost unknown, and no precedents whatsoever existed in England. Rabbi Dessler frequently told the first group of young men to join him in Gateshead that they most probably appeared in the eyes of the ordinary British *baalebos* like "men from Mars."

In addition, the potential supporters of the Kollel were few, and the economic uncertainty caused by war and the dispersion of potential donors over a wider area made collecting funds more difficult than it would otherwise have been. All in all, a prominent *rav* who told the early members of the Gateshead Kollel, "Hair will

---

11. Rabbi Aryeh Carmell.

grow from my palm before there will be a Kollel in England," seemed to have cold reality on his side.¹²

Yet despite the naysayers, the Kollel did succeed beyond anybody's initial expectations. In the years to come, Rabbi Dessler frequently asked himself how someone as lacking in merit as he believed himself to be had achieved so much. He answered, "[I]n times such as ours, when capable men are scarce, anyone who shows willingness to tackle a vital problem has Divine assistance heaped upon him. It turns the incapable into successively men, not because they deserve it but because the world needs them."¹³

A plaque in the Gateshead Kollel in memory of R' Dessler

"Sometimes we see with clarity that someone of no great ability succeeds in achieving something of the greatest importance to the entire world," he writes in one letter. "With what does he succeed to such a degree? Only because no one else understood the importance of the matter. And since he was the only one to come forward, all the joy [of success] falls to his lot."¹⁴

He was that one.

---

12. Rabbi Dov Sternbuch.
13. *Michtav Me'Eliyahu*, Vol. I, p. 19.
14. Ibid., Vol. V, p. 287.

Chapter 14

The Opening of the Kollel

ROSH CHODESH SHEVAT 5702, THE GATESHEAD KOLLEL officially opened its doors with little more than a handful of members. The initial group was diverse both in personality and background, though with the exception of the Hungarian-born Zusia Waltner all had learned in the major Lithuanian yeshivos.

In the beginning, the Kollel met in the home of Rabbi Chaim Shmuel Lopian, a son of Rabbi Eliyahu Lopian. Rabbi Lopian, a product of Telshe Yeshiva, was related by blood or marriage to over half the founding members of the Kollel. He and Rabbi Aryeh Leib Grossnass, a close *talmid* of Rabbi Boruch Ber Leibowitz in Kaminetz, were married to sisters. Rabbi Kalman Pinsky, a product of the Beis Yosef system founded by the Alter of Novordhok, was married to Rabbi Lopian's younger sister.

Shortly after the Kollel began, Rabbi Dessler persuaded Rabbi Leib Lopian, who was then the rabbi of a small congregation in a London suburb, to join the Kollel. Like his older brother, Rabbi Leib

Lopian had learned in his father's *yeshiva ketanah* in Kelm and then Telshe Yeshiva.

The other founding members of the Kollel were Pinchos Gard, a native of Brisk, who delighted in telling stories of his home town and its illustrious *rabbanim,* and Moshe Schwab. A native of Frankfurt, Moshe Schwab left his native city to learn in Baranovitch under Rabbi Elchonon Wasserman and subsequently in Kaminetz and Mir. Moshe Schwab and Zusia Waltner were the only two *bachurim* in the Kollel.

Rabbi Naftoli Shakovitsky, the *rav* of Gateshead, learned together with the Kollel all morning. Only when members of the community were present did he allow the members of the Kollel to address him by his title. But within the Kollel itself, he was simply Reb Naftoli just like every other member.

Rabbi Shimon Danzig, with whom Rabbi Dessler had shared his quarters in Chesham, accompanied Rabbi Dessler to Gateshead, where he served as the *shammash* of the Kollel.[1] Reb Shimon's whole family was trapped in Plungian, their fate unknown, and when he led the *davening* all the pain with which he lived could be heard in his prayers. But far from being further embittered by his role as *shammash,* Reb Shimon viewed it as a privilege to assist such distinguished *talmidei chachamim.*

A graduate of the famed Slabodka Yeshiva, Reb Shimon too was a full participant in the Kollel learning. He, perhaps more than any other member of the Kollel, still lived and breathed the air of Lithuania. When he went across the bridge into Newcastle on some errand or another, he often forgot himself and asked the Kollel members whether there was anything he could get for them in Kovno.[2]

The level of learning in the Kollel was extremely high. Every member was assumed to have already mastered the tractates of

---

1. Reb Shimon's duties included making sure that the *sefarim* in the Kollel were neatly arranged and that the *Gemaras* were ready on every *shtender* when the members arrived in the morning. In addition, he supervised the *bachurim* in the Kollel building, made sure their rooms were cleaned and their linens changed, and that their Shabbos meals were properly prepared.

2. Slabodka was a suburb of Kovno, to which it was joined by a bridge over a river, just as Gateshead was joined to Newcastle by a bridge over the River Tyne.

Nezikin and *Nashim* that are generally studied in yeshivos. As Rabbi Shakovitsky said at the outset, "We know how to learn. Now let's learn." From the beginning, the Kollel focused on the less frequently learned tractates of *Kodshim*, starting with *Menachos*, *Zevachim* and *Bechoros*. There were no *shiurim*, but each week one member of the Kollel would present a *chabura* (original composition), which his colleagues viewed as their solemn duty to refute.

The early development of the Kollel far exceeded even Rabbi Dessler's expectations. Writing to Dr. Dov Heiman, who had been his personal physician, months after the Kollel opened, he could not contain his delight "with the task Hashem has granted me." "The Kollel is producing those who learn with enthusiasm and deep insight," he writes. "The spirit, the desire to look into the depths of the Torah that rests upon the Kollel are quite remarkable."

After a long description of his role in the Kollel and its guiding philosophy, he adds in a postscript: "Who can conceive anything like our Kollel in our days? One who has not seen it could not imagine it — amazing *hasmadah*, with depth of penetration, which seems to me above the level of our generation."[3]

The works they produced and their subsequent careers attest to the remarkable talents of the Kollel's founding members. Rabbi Chaim Shmuel Lopian had already gained fame as a very young man for his commentary *Ravcha D'Shmaitesa*, on the classical work of *lamdus*, *Shev Shmaitesa*. His younger brother Rabbi Leib Lopian[4] left the Kollel to become the Rosh Yeshiva in Gateshead Yeshiva, in which position he remained until his passing over thirty years later. Rabbi Aryeh Leib Grossnass[5] assumed a position on the London Beis Din immediately upon leaving the Kollel, and he eventually succeeded Dayan Yechezkel Abramsky as *Av Beis Din*. The Kollel not only provided Gateshead Yeshiva with its long-time Rosh Yeshiva, but also with its Mashgiach, in the person of Rabbi Moshe Schwab.

---

3. *Michtav Me'Eliyahu*, Vol. V, pp. 509-10.

4. A great-granddaughter of Rav Dessler, Bluma Brudny, married Moshe Klein, a grand-nephew of Reb Leib Lopian.

5. His grandson Akiva Grossnass later married Rabbi Dessler's great-granddaughter Bluma Schiff.

Within a year, the Kollel also began attracting a series of younger *lomdim* from Rabbi Moshe Schneider's yeshiva in London. In contrast to the initial group, the second group were mostly refugees from Germany. They were younger than the founders of the Kollel, and came to Gateshead unmarried. This wave of younger *bachurim* was led by Rabbi Alter Halperin, who was already engaged to Rabbi Schneider's daughter when he came to Gateshead. He eventually succeeded his father-in-law as the Rosh Yeshiva in Schneider's Yeshiva.

Rabbi Halperin was soon followed by Rabbi Naftoli Friedler. Rabbi Schneider feared that the loss of Rabbi Friedler and Rabbi Halperin together would destroy his yeshiva, and he tried to convince Rabbi Friedler not to leave. Dayan Abramsky, however, realized that the young genius could grow much more in the Gateshead Kollel, and he intervened with Rabbi Schneider to secure permission for him to go to Gateshead. At the age of 25, Rabbi Friedler was already offered the position of Rosh Yeshiva in Gateshead, which he had to turn down for familial reasons. Over the next fifty years, however, he was a highly respected rosh yeshiva in Washington Heights, Toronto, and Monsey.

Rabbi Shammai Zahn led a second wave of *bachurim* from Schneider's Yeshiva who were eager to test themselves in the charged atmosphere of Gateshead Kollel. He was already a *maggid shiur* in Schneider's Yeshiva when he came to Gateshead, and from Gateshead he became the Rosh Yeshiva in Sunderland Yeshiva, in which position he has remained for over fifty years.

Other products of Schneider's Yeshiva who pursued their advanced learning in the Gateshead Kollel in Rabbi Dessler's day include: Rabbi Dov Sternbuch, one of the primary teachers in Gateshead Seminary for half a century; Rabbi Wolf Kaufman, the Rosh Kollel in Manchester; and Rabbi Bezalel Rakov, the *rav* of Gateshead since the early 1950's.

In a letter to Rabbi Mordechai Miller less than three years after the establishment of the Kollel, Rabbi Dessler describes the Kollel "as a unique place of Torah learning in all of Europe and perhaps the entire *galus*."[6]

---

6. Ibid., Vol. IV, p. 341.

Rabbi Dessler's Role in the Kollel

DURING THE EARLY YEARS OF THE KOLLEL, RABBI DESSLER WAS rarely present in Gateshead for more than two days a week. Yet the Kollel was stamped in his image. He created the air in which the remarkable group of young scholars flourished.

The unifying force of the Kollel, remembers Rabbi Zusia Waltner, was the *mussar* atmosphere and approach to character development that Rabbi Dessler instilled. Every night there was a half-hour *mussar seder* prior to *Ma'ariv* that might have reminded any visitor of the Talmud Torah of Kelm. The one native English *bachur* in the early days of the Kollel could never get used to the loud cries and sobs that went together with the recitation of the classic *mussar* texts.

Mussar ran deeply in the veins of the original Kollel members, quite apart from their contact with Rabbi Dessler. Three of the members were either sons or sons-in-law of Rabbi Elya Lopian, one of the great *mussar* figures of our time. Moshe Schwab, still a *bachur* and subsequently the *Mashgiach* of Gateshead Yeshiva, was widely viewed as the *tzaddik* in the group. Even in his sleep, he recited passages from Talmud, *Chumash* or *mussar* texts.

But if the members of the Kollel were hardly strangers to *mussar*, it was Rabbi Dessler who set the tone and served as a living exemplar of the *mussar* ideals. Every week he spoke for the members of the Kollel on Friday and for the entire community either at *Kabbalas Shabbos* or *Shalosh Seudos*. Those talks, many of which were subsequently published in *Michtav Me'Eliyahu*, had a profound impact on the Kollel members, particularly the younger *bachurim* from Schneider's Yeshiva.

It was not Rabbi Dessler's way to reprimand people or to address himself directly to their faults. Yet he inspired a desire to seek spiritual heights. An early letter to the Kollel members captures the striving for purity of motivation that he sought to instill.

From the letter, it would appear that some members of the Kollel were concerned that more top-quality *talmidei chachamim* had not yet joined them. Rabbi Dessler admonished them that all such concerns with external issues like the Kollel's finances or the number of members would only be at the expense of a proper focus on the real purpose of the Kollel.

He warned the Kollel members not to view their task as if it were to pave the way for those who would come after them. Nor should they think that they would be spiritually uplifted by others for whom they had prepared the way and made it possible to learn without distraction.

Rabbi Dessler accused himself of being the guiltiest of all in this respect and of "seeking to be built up spiritually by grasping on to the tip of the inner life of the Kollel." "I have acted," he writes, "as if my primary task — breaking the fortified walls of my *yetzer hara* — would be done for me by others!"

It is a dangerous illusion, he adds, to imagine that new members will be freer of external distractions than the present ones. Such thoughts are nothing more than an excuse provided by the *yetzer hara* for the present members to slacken in their own battles against distractions. Rather each member must keep in mind that "to be a member of a Kollel is a great level requiring much *mesiras nefesh* to separate oneself from every distraction, to go at the appointed times to the house of Torah and *avodah*." Those distractions can only be overcome by daily learning of *mussar*.

Had the members of the Kollel — himself chief among them — focused on the spiritual task incumbent upon them, he writes, the Kollel "would already be a place of glory." Instead of acting as if they would be elevated spiritually by the association with the scholars for whom they were laying the groundwork, Rabbi Dessler urges each member of the Kollel to feel "that the entire Kollel depends upon him, not only with respect to any slackening of determination but with respect to any positive growth as well." Only then will the Kollel succeed spiritually and financially.[7]

Rabbi Dessler personally raised every penny to cover the Kollel's expenses and was twenty years older than any other member. Yet he absolutely refused to accept the title of *Nasi* of the Kollel and always insisted that he was just another member of the Kollel, with no more say in its running than any other member.[8] At the Friday meetings

---

7. Ibid., Vol. III, p. 342-4.
8. As the Kollel grew in size, the decisions came to be made by a Vaad of those who

of the Kollel, the other members of the Kollel were more likely to tell him what he should do rather than vice versa.⁹

His tone was always that of one who was honored to be allowed to participate in the deliberations of such illustrious scholars. In a letter to the members of the Kollel, he addresses them as "my guides and intimates, my masters and teachers, and at their head the greatest of his brothers, the *rav* and *Av Beis Din* [Rabbi Shakovitsky]." The letter begins: "Forgive me, if I, the lowly one, whom you have honored by allowing you to join in this great *dvar mitzvah* that has been so blessed from Heaven, if in my lowliness I express an opinion."¹⁰

He was a consummate diplomat, who preferred working behind the scenes to direct matters as he wished. When he wanted someone to apply to the Kollel, he would never ask them directly, but would rather have a third party suggest the idea.¹¹

Before any major decision of the Kollel, Rabbi Dessler would go from one member to another to discuss the matter individually. Thus when the issue was raised in the Kollel, the outcome was usually a foregone conclusion, without Rabbi Dessler having even expressed his opinion publicly. Then Rabbbi Dessler would announce the "*daas hakol* (unanimous opinion)," as if he had had no special influence on the outcome.

Rabbi Dessler's insistence that he was but one member of the Vaad and that he had no more say in the direction of the Kollel than any other *avreich* was not a mere pretense. He viewed his self-effacement as crucial to the success of the Kollel. Any institution led by someone seeking honor or prestige, he believed, was doomed to failure. In *Michtav Me'Eliyahu* he describes people "who were great in Torah, extremely capable, meticulously observant of *mitzvos*, brilliant thinkers, who nevertheless never fully succeeded in imbuing their students with the spirit of a *ben Torah*. The reason is that they treated their yeshivos as a 'position' — a

---

had been in the Kollel at least two years, from which a smaller executive was selected.
9. Rabbi Zusia Waltner.
10. Ibid., p. 342.
11. Rabbi Wolf Kaufman.

source of livelihood and prestige. This approach will never succeed in changing others' basic attitudes."[12]

In addition, Rabbi Dessler believed deeply that it was forbidden to rule over *talmidei chachamim* such as the members of the Kollel: "My low level I know well, and how much worse to rule over *talmidei chachamim, gedolei Torah* and *yirei Shamayim*," he wrote to Dr. Heiman in New York. The proper foundation of a kollel, he insisted, is that the great rabbis learning in it should be *chaveirim* (colleagues) not *talmidim* (students). In the same letter, he praised the members of the Kollel for needing "neither a *rav* nor a leader nor an administrator. Each of them is an important *rav* in his own right and among them are those who are *gedolei Yisrael*."

He even speculated that a failed attempt to establish a kollel in America that Dr. Heiman mentioned in a letter to him was a consequence of conceiving of the kollel as a group to hear a *shiur* from a *gadol*.[13]

Only twice did Rabbi Dessler insist on his position in the face of opposition from some members of the Kollel. The first came about when he wanted to expand the Kollel and many of the members were reluctant to do so for fear that the resources would not be found. Rabbi Dessler's response was quite uncharacteristic. "You have a right to contract if you wish," he said. "But I cannot work for an organization that has contracted itself."[14] The second incident arose a few years later. Rabbi Dessler had succeeded in obtaining what was then a very large contribution of £400. Subsequently a representative of Gateshead Yeshiva solicited a contribution from the same benefactor, who responded that he had already given to the Yeshiva. Since there was always some fear on the part of the Yeshiva that the Kollel would draw away money from the Yeshiva, the matter created some tension.

The Vaad of the Kollel voted not to return the gift on the grounds that it had been given personally to Rabbi Dessler. But Rabbi Dessler

---

12. Ibid., Vol. I, p. 139; *Strive for Truth*, Vol. II, p. 126.
13. *Michtav Me'Eliyahu*, Vol. V, pp. 509-10.
14. Rabbi Naftoli Friedler.

felt that the principle of avoiding any trace of *machlokes* (dispute) with the Yeshiva was more important than the money, and he insisted that the gift be handed over to the Yeshiva. Since the full responsibility for raising the funds was on his shoulders, the other members of the Vaad eventually acquiesced.

Rabbi Dessler's Schedule

FROM THE BEGINNING, GATESHEAD KOLLEL DEPENDED ON the almost superhuman endurance of Rabbi Dessler. Always in frail health, he undertook a schedule throughout the war years that would have destroyed a far younger man in more robust health.

Every week, Rabbi Dessler had to achieve three objectives. From the beginning, he conditioned his acceptance of responsibility for the Kollel on the understanding that he would continue teaching his private students in the London area. He refused to take any money from the Kollel, and the private students remained his only source of income.

In addition to his private teaching, he continued to give public *shiurim* and to meet with small groups of close *talmidim* in London, Chesham, and Manchester. He also found the time to prepare a weekly *shmuess* for the Kollel and a public *shmuess* in Gateshead. At least in the early years of the Kollel, he also took his turn delivering a *chabura* on the tractate the Kollel was learning.

And finally, he had to raise the entire week's budget for the Kollel — which soon exceeded £100 a week. One of his principles from the beginning of the Kollel was that the Kollel should incur no debts and that the stipends should be paid on time. Somehow he was able to fulfill both conditions, even though at the beginning of each week, he usually found himself starting again with the coffers nearly empty.

To do all this, Rabbi Dessler embarked on a schedule that left him in Gateshead only from Friday morning to Saturday night.[15] Two nights every week, and frequently more, he slept on train cars filled

---

15. After Gateshead Seminary opened in 1944, he added Thursday in Gateshead, much of which was spent teaching in the Seminary.

with members of the British armed forces. In one letter, he describes himself as "one whose dwelling is the train."[16] He spent so much time on trains during the Gateshead years that he even developed a device to alert the engineer to upcoming signals before he could see them visually.[17]

Solomon Sassoon learning in the garden at Letchworth

Motzaei Shabbos, he would take a midnight train from Gateshead to London. In his valise, he carried three or four large cakes baked specially for him by Stenhouse's bakery in Gateshead, with saccharin in place of sugar. These cakes constituted his principal food for the week.[18] Sunday morning, he arrived at the Sassoon family mansion in Letchworth where he spent half a day each week learning with Solomon Sassoon.[19] Sometime in the middle of the week, he would travel by train from London to Manchester and return to London by night train. Late Thursday night it was back to Gateshead by overnight train from London.[20]

---

16. *HaRav Dov Zev Steinhaus*, (Hebrew), p. 16. This work is a privately published pamphlet on the life of the late *Mashgiach* of Yeshivas Kol Torah in Jerusalem.

17. He told Rabbi Elchonon Karnovsky that he patented the device but did not have the money to maintain the patent, and it was eventually taken over by British Railways.

18. Rabbi Aryeh Carmell.

19. So familiar a figure was Rabbi Dessler at the Sassoon estate that even the servants knew him well and came to him with their complaints. During World War II, the Sassoons took in four young women from Germany. (One of them, Alice Benjamin, eventually married Rabbi Solomon Sassoon.) Miss Thompson, a non-Jewish nanny, who had been with the Sassoon family since before Solomon's birth, resented the fact that the Jewish refugees were invited to eat with the family on Shabbos and she was not. It was obvious to her that the only person who could intercede on her behalf was Rabbi Dessler, and she took her complaint to him.

A few years later, shortly after the birth of David Sassoon, the same Miss Thompson became very ill and the doctors lost hope for her recovery. Rabbi Dessler, however, assured her that she would live to see David married. And so it was. She recovered and did not die until three weeks after David's wedding. *David Sassoon*.

20. While they were still learning in Schneider's Yeshiva, Rabbi Alter Halperin and Rabbi Dov Sternbuch used to spend a couple of hours with Rabbi Dessler at Kings Cross station on Thursday night, prior to his overnight train back to Gateshead.

Rabbi Dessler spent several nights a week in Chesham, where he shared an apartment with Rabbi Dov Stenhouse, until the latter's marriage in 1943. Even those nights he did not travel, Rabbi Dessler often stayed up most of the night teaching and writing letters.[21] One night a week, he gave a *shiur* at the home of Rabbi Gedaliah Schneider to a group of students in Schneider's yeshiva.[22] Another night, he learned with Dr. Avraham Adler, while the latter served as an air-raid fire marshal.[23] Yet a third evening was spent with a small group of *talmidei chachamim* in Manchester, including Rabbi Yehudah Zev Segal, Rabbi Yisrael Ehrentreu, and Reb Herschel Goldstein.[24] In Chesham, he also gave classes to a small group of men and women one evening. Another morning, he taught *Tehillim*. He would then write out the lessons he had taught and send them to his daughter Hennie in Australia.[25]

Though in large part Rabbi Dessler's schedule was dictated by the overwhelming demands on his time, he appears to have also sought some level of identification with the suffering of his Jewish brethren on the Continent. "My brothers sleep on the ground," he once commented to someone who asked him why he drove himself as he did.[26]

Rabbi Moshe Schneider told his students that throughout the war years Rabbi Dessler did not undress or take off his shoes when he went to sleep.[27] Nor did he purchase any new clothing. "Perhaps,

---

21. Of course, Rabbi Dessler's schedule did change from time to time. When Gateshead Seminary opened, for instance, in 1944, he added another day a week in Gateshead. Thus it is not clear that each of the classes mentioned took place for the entirety of the war years. Indeed it is clear that they could not have all taken place simultaneously, particularly after the opening of the Seminary.

22. Rabbi Leizer Zahn.

23. Dr. Sam Adler.
   Prior to learning with the senior Dr. Adler, Rabbi Dessler would spend an hour and a half learning *Chiddushei Rabbeinu Chaim HaLevi* with Dr. Adler's son, Sam, who was then in medical school.

24. Rabbi Mordechai Miller.
   He also gave public *shiurim* in Manchester, and the private *shiur* likely followed that.

25. Mrs. Thea Pozen, one of the participants in that class.

26. Rabbi Alter Halperin.

27. Rabbi Wolf Kaufman.

when my family is here, I'll think about that," he would say. "Until then, I'm thinking about others."[28]

"If it were not for the fact that I am without my family," he wrote to Dr. Heiman, "I could not have undertaken this." But he refused to think about his personal situation, and even saw in the fact that he had been freed for the task of supporting the Kollel an indication of the importance of the matter in the eyes of Heaven. "The great miracle that Hashem has done for us is that He has given everything from His storehouses in proportion to the importance of the matter," he continued.[29]

It would be hard to imagine anyone less suited by temperament to bear the entire fundraising burden of Gateshead Kollel than Rabbi Dessler. Besides his poor health, he was by nature shy and reserved. Though capable of great warmth, there was nothing of the hale-fellow-well-met quality about him. His words were always measured and chosen with care — the antithesis of the glib, fast-talking salesman.

Yet as difficult as fundraising was for him, he did not spare himself when the cause was one in which he believed. Even as a rabbi in Dalston, he had gone out every Thursday night to collect for poor families in the congregation, and his address was one of those that Rabbi Chaim Ozer Grodzenski gave to anyone collecting for the Eastern European yeshivos.

The fundraising for the Kollel was filled with constant humiliations, for there was as yet no appreciation of the value of a Kollel in England. Almost the entire funding of the Kollel was based upon gifts of £5 or less solicited door-to-door.[30] At least here, Rabbi Dessler's natural modesty made the humiliations of fundraising more bearable. As he once told Rabbi Zusia Waltner, "It is impossible to throw me down because I don't climb high."

---

28. Rabbi Alter Halperin.
29. *Michtav Me'Eliyahu*, Vol. V, p. 509.
30. One member of the Kollel had a rich uncle who once made a gift of £1000 on the condition that only the interest be used for Kollel expenses, but such gifts were extremely rare.

Chapter Fourteen: The Opening of the Kollel / 213

The uncertainties and dislocations caused by the war should ostensibly have made collecting more difficult, but Rabbi Dessler found a way to turn the situation to his advantage. One of his constant themes was the transient nature of all material possessions. The idea that the first task in life is to establish a firm financial base was one learned from the gentiles, he wrote to a father whom he was trying to convince to send his son to yeshiva. Those who followed that approach first lost any connection to advanced Talmudic scholarship, then even a straightforward learning of Talmud, and had ended up contenting themselves with a simple observance of halachah.

And what were the fruits of the pursuit of economic security? Precisely in that land in which there had not been a poor Jew to be found, a land in which every Jew was educated for a life of economic success, arose the great oppressor of the Jews. What did the great professors, who were lucky enough to escape, know of window washing and the other jobs they now had to gladly accept?[31]

The nightly bombings to which London was subject brought home the same message with great clarity to British Jewry: not only one's possessions but one's very life hang by a hairsbreadth. As Rabbi Dessler writes, "There were people who thought that the material basis of their lives was firm and secure for all time. Then they saw it shattered in front of their eyes."[32] Rabbi Dessler used the lesson of the bombings to convince people to invest their money in things that would pay eternal returns.[33]

As unsuited as he may have been for large-scale fundraising, Rabbi Dessler succeeded. On more than one occasion, he confronted a large deficit looming only days away. Yet somehow the precise amount of money needed was always found. Not once did the Kollel miss its payroll. Rabbi Dessler viewed his success in this regard as a Heavenly sign of approval for his activities on behalf of the Kollel.[34]

---

31. *Michtav Me'Eliyahu*, Vol. III, p. 339.
32. *Strive for Truth*, Vol. II, p. 15.
33. Rabbi Dov Sternbuch.
34. Rabbi Aryeh Carmell.

Far too modest to attribute his success to his own merits, Rabbi Dessler attributed the Kollel's flourishing to its importance to *Klal Yisrael*. The merit of the *Klal* was a recurrent theme in his talks:

> A community may be in dire need of a person to come to its rescue or help it in some other way, material or spiritual, but there is no one at hand who is really suited to the task. We then find that Hashem will shower heavenly aid in extraordinary measure upon anyone who volunteers for the task, even though judged on his own merits he is far from being worthy of this. Though he is not suitable, he will be made suitable. What has brought about this amazing change? The merit of the community which needs him.[35]

The physical and emotional drain on Rabbi Dessler from his non-stop schedule of teaching and fundraising exacted a heavy toll on him. "I have given up my health and my soul to undertake this task without help from others," he wrote to Rabbi Mordechai Miller in *Elul* of 1944. The pressures were so great, he confided, that he could not even afford the luxury of staying in Gateshead between Shabbos and the *Yamim Tovim* in the middle of the week.[36]

Yet as great as the pressures on him were, they were not the heaviest price extracted by his activities on behalf of the Kollel. *Chazal* say that one who travels loses his name. "Name," Rabbi Dessler explained in a letter to Rabbi Zusia Waltner, refers to a person's spiritual level. He felt acutely the loss of his own spiritual *madreigah* (level) as a consequence of his travels.

But he had no regrets. There could be no greater sacrifice than one's own spiritual level, and thus no greater privilege than to have been found worthy to be the one to "*mafkir* his personal spiritual worth *leshem Shamayim* (for the sake of Heaven)." [37]

---

35. *Michtav Me'Eliyahu*, Vol. I, p. 151; *Strive for Truth*, Vol. II, p. 159.
36. *Michtav Me'Eliyahu*, Vol. IV, p. 341.
37. Ibid., Vol. V, p. 506.
   Elsewhere, however, Rabbi Dessler points out that one who pours himself out in *chesed* to others does not, in fact, give away his very self. "[I]n truth, he loses nothing. On the contrary, those to whom he has given so much are now in a sense "his"; they are "called by his name" because his being has extended into them all. *Michtav Me'Eliyahu*, Vol. I, pp. 151-2; *Strive for Truth*, Vol. II, p. 160.

Chapter 15

In His Image

RABBI DESSLER WAS A FIGURE OF AWE IN THE EYES OF THE Kollel members, and his personality was indelibly stamped on them. While few, if any, of the Kollel members followed Rabbi Dessler's lead in concentrating on *Aggadata*, his ideals became the defining ideals of the Kollel and those by which the members guided their lives.

They hung on his every word. His speech was *gefiddled*, like listening to a perfectly structured piece of classical music, says Rabbi Dov Sternbuch. Many of those who grew to maturity listening to Rabbi Dessler's *shmuessen* found that they were never again able to listen to anyone else.[1]

To the members of the Gateshead Kollel, Rabbi Dessler was simply the *gadol hador* in *hashkafah* (Jewish thought). In their descriptions of him, the members of the Kollel repeatedly revert to the same comparison: He was the Rabbi Chaim Brisker of *Aggadata*. Upon being shown some of Reb Chaim's early *chiddushim* by his

---
1. Rabbi Yaakov Katz.

father, Rabbi Yisrael Salanter is said to have remarked, "He will be the Rosh Yeshiva for the coming generation." Reb Chaim showed an analytical depth in *Gemara* that could compete with any intellectual ferment the secular world had to offer. And Rabbi Dessler, in the eyes of the Kollel members, did the same in the area of *Aggadata*.[2]

Rabbi Bezalel Rakov relates how some of the younger members of the Kollel once asked Rabbi Dessler whether Reb Yerucham Levovitz could possibly have been a deeper thinker than he. Rabbi Dessler was horrified by the question,[3] and explained to them that what they perceived as greatness was really a reflection of the decline of the generations: The teachers of each generation have to reveal more and more because what was self-evident to previous generations is no longer known. The question nevertheless captures Rabbi Dessler's stature in the eyes of the Kollel members.

Rabbi Yitzchak Hutner once said that there are those who lift a *ma'amar Chazal* from its context and use it to make their own point. And there are those who read their own thought into the *ma'amar Chazal*. But there is also the *ma'amar* itself. Rabbi Dessler's greatness lay in his ability to break each *ma'amar* down to its component parts, ask the fundamental questions, and then reconstruct the worldview of our Sages.[4]

"I never met another person with his phenomenal ability to plumb a subject to the depths," remembers Rabbi Dov Sternbuch. "His *koach ha'iyun* (capacity for sustained deep thought) was incomparable. His face would go red with exertion when he was working on a problem." Rabbi Dessler once told Rabbi Zusia Waltner that he had spent three years learning just the first ten pages of R' Yitzchak Isaac Chaver's kabbalistic work *Pischei She'arim*.[5]

---

2. Rabbi Alter Halperin.

3. Rabbi Dessler held Rabbi Yerucham Levovitz in the highest esteem, and described him as "one of the most profound thinkers I have known, wise and saintly...." *Strive for Truth*, Vol. II, p. 67.

4. Rabbi Mordechai Miller.

5. Rabbi Yitzchak Isaac Chaver, *av beis din* of Suvalk, was a *talmid* of Reb Mendel of Shklov, who had learned kabbalah together with the Vilna Gaon.

Chapter Fifteen: In His Image / 217

The Ideals of the Kollel

BOTH INDIVIDUALS AND INSTITUTIONS, RABBI DESSLER FELT, have to be built on the same fundamental principle: only quality counts; numbers are meaningless. In a lowly generation, the concern is always with numbers: More and bigger are always better. But for him it was always the opposite. "Large" and "many" were inherently suspect. That was the legacy of Kelm.

On the individual level, the focus always had to be on the point of truth, of *lishmah*, no matter how small. Let it be as fine as the point of a needle, as long as it passes from one side to the other without obstruction, without taint. As long as that point of truth exists, there is a basis for unlimited spiritual growth; without it, there is no hope. And above all, do not despair upon discovering that the rest of the world seems headed in the opposite direction. Truth is always hidden, always the minority, always the exception.[6]

And on the societal level, Rabbi Dessler stressed that the only unit of measure is the individual. Jewish history begins with a solitary individual on one side against the entire world. One lonely man of faith triumphed over the multitudes. That was the lesson Avraham implanted in the Jewish people for all time. As the prophet puts it, "One alone I summoned him [Avraham] and will bless him and make him many" (*Yeshaya* 51:2).[7]

In his very first letter to Rabbi Dovid Dryan, Rabbi Dessler returned again and again to the same point: the foundation of the Kollel must be quality. "The world errs," he begins, "in thinking that from a large quantity comes quality. The truth is the exact opposite."

Two conditions, he writes to Reb Dovid, are necessary for the success of the Kollel. First, clear thinking — so that the Satan has no entry to steal the inwardness and weaken the *quality*. And second, very great eagerness (*zrizus*) — so that the matter not be allowed to grow cold. If both those conditions are met, the Kollel could be the instrument of hastening the redemption, for "anyone who increases the *quality* (emphasis added) of Torah and *yiras Shamayim* in the world helps [bring the *geulah*], and how much more so a community."

---

6. Rabbi Moshe Shapiro on the occasion of Rabbi Dessler's fortieth *yahrtzeit*.
7. Ibid.

Rabbi Dessler instilled in the members of the Kollel a disdain for anything besides finding the point of truth, internalizing it and living one's life accordingly. He himself was completely removed from the material world. Someone once explained to him that for the same amount of money that he was paying in rent on an apartment in a two-flat building, he could buy the building. All he had to do was take out a mortgage and purchase the building. For what he was now paying in rent, plus rent from the building's other tenant, he could then pay off the mortgage, and in ten years, the building would be his without any encumbrances.

Rabbi Dessler listened politely as the man explained this opportunity, before replying that he had no interest in becoming an owner rather than a renter. "*Chas ve'shalom*, that I should be so connected to anything in the material world," he said. He noted incidentally that in *lashon HaKodesh* (the Holy Tongue) there is no word for owning.[8]

The same attitude filtered down to all the members of the Kollel. "He was a living example of what is important and what is not," remembers Rabbi Wolf Kaufman. "He made us embarrassed to talk about money at all." He could be very sharp when poking fun at the pretensions of the world. Once people had dirt floors, he told the members of the Kollel. Then they started covering the dirt with wood to hide the dirt. Now they have carpets to hide the wood, and plastic covers on top of the carpet to protect them from dirt.[9] He scoffed at those who searched for carpets with warranties longer than the purchaser's life expectancy.

One time Rabbi Dessler and Rabbi Mordechai Miller were traveling together by train. Rabbi Miller was not feeling well, and took a first-class compartment where he felt he would have a better chance of being able to sleep. In the morning, Rabbi Dessler asked him how he had enjoyed his compartment, Rabbi Miller replied enthusiastically. Upon hearing that his student was not instinctively repulsed by luxury, Rabbi Dessler cried out, "*Oy, shlecht*! (Oh! Terrible!)"

He created such an atmosphere of spiritual striving in Torah that the young Kollel couples were able not only to endure but to ignore

---

8. Rabbi Mordecai Miller.
9. Rabbi Shammai Zahn.

Chapter Fifteen: In His Image

very strained circumstances. Many of the *yungeleit* did not have chicken for Shabbos and every cigarette in the Kollel was divided into three, but the excitement of spiritual growth made the poverty seem trivial.

The members of the Kollel had absolutely no doubt that learning in the Kollel was the most important thing they could possibly be doing.

When Rabbi Naftoli Friedler was offered a position as a rosh yeshiva in Gateshead Yeshiva, for instance, he did not view the offered position as a step up from being a member of the Kollel. If one could learn *lishmah* in the Kollel, there was no higher level to which one could aspire. Even when Rabbi Grossnass left the Kollel to accept a position on the London *Beis Din*, his fellow Kollel members had a hard time understanding why he would do such thing. And when Rabbi Binyamin Zev Weiss accepted a rabbinic position in Zurich, he was too embarrassed to even share the news with his colleagues.[10]

On occasion offers of positions to Kollel members, even when they were directed to specific individuals, were discussed by the Vaad of the Kollel to determine who, if anyone, would be well suited to it. The point was that every position had to be evaluated from the point of view of *Klal Yisrael*, not any particular individual. The only justification for taking a particular position was what one could do for *Klal Yisrael*, not what one could gain personally from the position.[11]

Any ambition other than growth in Torah learning was disdained. Rabbi Dessler was highly skilled at puncturing all the pretensions of the world, and rarely was his wit so withering as when he described the folly of those whose lives centered around the pursuit of a *shtella* (position). To the members of the Gateshead Kollel he told the story of a woman who always referred to her husband as a civil engineer when he was in fact a washroom attendant. "But at least he had a *shtella* with a uniform," Rabbi Dessler concluded.[12]

---

10. Prior to coming to the Kollel, Rabbi Weiss had already been the *rav* of a congregation in Blackburn.
11. Rabbi Mordechai Miller.
12. Rabbi Shammai Zahn, Rosh Yeshiva of Sunderland Yeshiva.

He attributed the premature departure from the Kollel — and subsequent loss to Orthodoxy — of one brilliant, young *bachur* to the fact that he was a "careerist," eager to progress to the top of the English rabbinic establishment. One of the students closest to Rabbi Dessler once came to him to discuss an offer he had received to become the principal of a day school in London. He patiently explained all the reasons why he felt the job presented a real opportunity and what he hoped to achieve. But when he had completed the presentation, Rabbi Dessler deflated him with just one sentence, "All I hear is your *kavod* (desire for honor) speaking."

And to those who needed an additional incentive to fight against the temptations of a prestigious position, Rabbi Dessler was more than happy to share from his supply of stories of the humiliations he suffered as a congregational rabbi.

RABBI DESSLER LIVED IN EXTREMELY CLOSE CONTACT WITH THE Kollel members. When he was in Gateshead, he ate his weekday meals together with the *bachurim*,[13] and he was a frequent visitor to the homes of the *avreichim*.

An Exemplar in Middos

He became for the members of the Kollel a living example of every positive *middah*. He personified, in their eyes, a *ba'al mussar*, someone in complete control of himself. His ability to set the ideals for the Kollel flowed directly from the Kollel member's admiration for his person.

The Kollel members saw in him someone far removed from any sense of self and immune to the blandishments of society in which most people place so much store. He studiously avoided anything which smacked of a trace of *chitzonius* and calling attention to oneself. In *davening*, he stood perfectly still like a stick.[14] At the same time, the veins on his head literally bulged out from the intense concentration that he brought to every *tefillah*.

Like the Alter of Kelm, he eschewed any titles of honor. He not only refused the title of Rosh Kollel, he would not allow himself to be called for an *aliyah* as *Rabbeinu*.

---

13. Rabbi Bezalel Rakov.
14. Rabbi Dov Sternbuch.

Rabbi Dessler instinctively hid from any public notice. On a trip to America in the early '50s, Rabbi Joseph Elias, whose wife had been the first student in Gateshead Seminary, invited Rabbi Dessler to speak for a group of Zeirei Agudath Israel. Knowing how Rabbi Dessler abhorred titles of any kind, he inserted a one-line notice in *Der Morgan Journal*: "Rabbi E.E. Dessler will speak at .... " But even that was too much for Rabbi Dessler, who told him that it would have been better not to speak at all than to have one's name in the newspaper. All attention, he told Rabbi Elias, is bad for a person. In that vein, he once asked a rabbi who insisted on holding a door for him, "Are you trying to poison me?"[15]

Rabbi Dessler used to describe Rabbi Shimon Danzig as the *shammas* of the Kollel and himself as the *unter-shammas* (the assistant *shammas*). That description provoked Rabbi Naftoli Shakovitsky to protest that Rabbi Dessler was going too far, and would lessen the honor of Torah by appearing to denigrate himself in this fashion. Yet Rabbi Dessler, in fact, did not hesitate to act as a *shammas* for the members of the Kollel. He would bring meat and other packages from parents in London to their sons in Gateshead.[16] And in the days before long-distance telephone calls were commonplace, he often found himself playing the role of messenger between engaged couples. He would bring regards from the *chassan* learning in the Kollel to his *kallah* in London, and her regards back to Gateshead. He thought nothing of taking the time from his packed schedule to make the necessary phone calls.

Rabbi Dessler seemed to give no thought to himself or his personal situation. One Pesach, he joined Rabbi Naftoli Friedler and his wife for the *Seder*. At the end of the *Seder*, Rabbi Friedler was so excited at the experience of having Rabbi Dessler that he expressed the hope that they would merit to be together with Rabbi Dessler next year too. Rabbi Dessler gently reprimanded him. "You should have wished me," he said, "that next year my family and I would be reunited at our own *Seder*." But such references to his separation from his wife and children were exceedingly rare, and on that occasion

---

15. Rabbi Mordecai Miller.
16. Rabbi Bezalel Rakov.

his remark was almost surely aroused by the poignant memory of the Dessler family gathered for the *Seder* in years past.

Another Kelm *middah* that Rabbi Dessler personified for the Kollel members was his *menuchas hanefesh*. Nothing caused him to lose his composure. Once a Chassidic *rav* called him up in the middle of a *shiur* in Gateshead Seminary and criticized him sharply for spending his time teaching girls. Rabbi Dessler listened politely, without responding, and when the man was done he thanked him for his comments. The next time that particular *rav* came to Gateshead, Rabbi Dessler made a point of going to hear him speak in the main shul, something he almost never did.[17]

Rabbi Elchanan Blumenthal once witnessed a similar incident in London. Not only did Rabbi Dessler refuse to respond to someone who had spoken rudely to him, he continued to smile the entire time his attacker was speaking. Rabbi Blumenthal wondered how such self-control was possible. Rabbi Dessler told him, "Do you think I was born that way? By nature, I am both an angry man and a stubborn one, but, *Baruch Hashem*, I have overcome these traits and trained myself to treat every person … pleasantly."[18]

One time, while in New York, Rabbi Dessler went to visit Rabbi Avrohom Yaffen, the Novordhok Rosh Yeshiva, together with Rabbi Naftoli Friedler. As they went through the subway turnstile, Rabbi Friedler heard the subway pulling into the station below and started to run. Rabbi Dessler, however, held him fast. "If it's not this train, it will be the next one," he said. "Never do anything in this world with *behillus* (hurriedly)."

Rabbi Dessler was a master at conveying a lesson to those close to him in the subtlest fashion. No member of the Kollel was closer to Rabbi Dessler than Rabbi Zusia Waltner. Rabbi Dessler was the Waltners' *shadchan*, as he was for many other members of the Kollel, and he lived in an attic apartment above the Waltners for more than four years.

---
17. Rabbi Mordechai Miller and Rabbi Dov Sternbuch.
18. Blumenthal, *Trials and Challenges*, p. 55.

Reflecting on the most important lessons he learned from Rabbi Dessler, Rabbi Waltner mentions self-discipline. Not only did Rabbi Dessler provide a real-life example of a person with absolute self-control, he taught others how to attain that self-discipline.[19]

During the war, the British government ran various auctions at which items donated by rich people were sold to raise money for the war effort. One such sale was scheduled to take place near Gateshead on a Friday afternoon, and Rabbi Waltner decided to go to see if there was anything on sale that would be suitable for beautifying Shabbos. He allocated no more than £1 for that purpose.

Rabbi Waltner told Rabbi Dessler where he was going, and to his absolute amazement Rabbi Dessler expressed an interest in joining him. Soon after they arrived at the sale, Rabbi Waltner's eyes lit on a beautiful handcrafted silver plate that was selling for the ridiculously low sum of 10 shillings. Rabbi Waltner immediately picked it up and went to pay. But before he could do so, Rabbi Dessler mentioned that he would very much like that silver plate for himself. Rabbi Waltner could not refuse him, and Rabbi Dessler purchased the silver plate.

A short time later, Rabbi Waltner spotted candlesticks for only £1. He picked them up, only to hear Rabbi Dessler once again say, "Oh, I like that very much. May I purchase it?" Rabbi Waltner found himself for the first time in his life getting angry with his teacher and guide, but was incapable of refusing a request from Rabbi Dessler.

A few minutes later, the whole sequence of events was repeated yet a third time with a large silver cup on sale for only ten shillings. By the time that Rabbi Dessler had also commandeered the silver cup, Shabbos was already fast approaching, and Rabbi Waltner had no choice but to return home dejectedly, with nothing to show for his efforts. He still could not figure out what possible use Rabbi Dessler could have had for the items in question, with his family

---

19. Part of the *mussar* approach was to devise stratagems to combat the wiles of the *yetzer hara*. When Rabbi Dessler gave up smoking, for instance, he told every *talmid* that he met that day that he had done so. He thereby used the fear of embarrassment in front of his students to fortify his resolve. *Rabbi Azriel Schwab.*

abroad, especially inasmuch as he had never before shown the need for anything more than his small writing table, a bed and his large library.

As he prepared for Shabbos, Rabbi Waltner found himself more and more perplexed by Rabbi Dessler's actions. Just then, Rabbi Dessler appeared in the Waltner apartment bearing the silver plate, the candlesticks, and the silver cup. He handed them to Rabbi Waltner with the words, "These are presents for you. Use them in happiness."

Noticing the confused look on Rabbi Waltner's face, he explained why he had acted so out of character. "I noticed that as soon as you saw these things," he said, "you were filled with a tremendous desire to buy them. That is not good. I wanted to teach you self-restraint and the ability to wait and evaluate, without being swept away by your first look at something."

A True Giver

IN HIS "DISCOURSE ON LOVINGKINDNESS,"[20] RABBI DESSLER divides people into two major categories — givers and takers. The latter are those who have never worked to improve their character or to gain mastery over their desires. They are spiritually empty inside. That inner emptiness reflects itself in an urge to acquire more and more material objects in the mistaken belief that objects external to oneself can somehow fill up what is lacking inside. The lack of inner substance of the "takers" paradoxically causes them to focus exclusively on themselves, and they are characterized by their selfishness.

The "givers," on the other hand, eschew the pursuit of material goods, which by definition can never become truly part of oneself. They focus instead on their spiritual growth. As they grow spiritually, they overflow the narrow confines of their own selves and enter into deep connection with other people.

Rabbi Dessler exemplified the portrayal of the "giver" in his essay. At the simplest level, he enjoyed giving presents despite the fact that he always himself lived on the bare minimum. At a time when few *sefarim* were printed in England and they were very hard to

---

20. *Michtav Me'Eliyahu*, Vol. I, pp. 32-51; *Strive for Truth*, Vol. I, pp. 118-158.

> ב"ה
> רחמים, תרצ"ה
>
> לחביבי   ישראל
> כהן-הלוי   ישמרך הא-ל
> הש"ס הזה לך למנה
> בהיותך שלש עשרה שנה
>
> * * *
>
> הלא   אם-כן
> אם גם ימה של מרגית תמיד   מה גדול ורחב הוא יום-התלמוד
> ערי קץ ציר צפון תגיע   אשר חכמה בלי קץ יבע
> ועתה
> אזור גבורתך   להרחיב ידיעתך
> ותרבה עבודתך   ולהעמיק הבנתך
> ואז
> כל מגמתך   ימי היותך
> יהי בתורתך   על אדמתך
> והתורה,   ובשכרה,
> על גפי מרומים תעלה אותך תגיע אלי תפארת גדולתך
> וגם כשתגדל,   לא תחדל
> אך   אף
> תלמוד   שתדרעהו
> בתלמוד   ותבינהו
> כי הכל בו   כי אין חקר לו
> ולא יקראוך עוד ישראל   כל ימיך
> אלא רבנו גדול בישראל   יהיה שמך
>   כברכת אוהבך
>   אד"א

The text of an inscription for a bar mitzvah gift

find, he gave a set of *Chiddushei Rabbi Akiva Eiger* at every *bris* in the Kollel, together with an elaborate inscription to the newborn recipient. One Friday night, shortly after their marriage, Rabbi Naftoli Friedler and his wife invited Rabbi Dessler for a meal. He noticed that they had only six very cheap knives that would rust easily. The next Friday night, Rabbi Dessler came again for dinner, and this time he brought with him six new stainless steel knives.

But the many presents were the least of his giving. He gave of himself. In the early days of the Kollel, most of the *bachurim* were penniless refugees from Germany, who had arrived in England without their families. Even those whose families had also escaped to England were in little better shape financially. Moreover the Kollel only paid stipends to those who had already learned there for at least two years. As a consequence, many of the young Kollel couples began married life with virtually nothing.

Rabbi Dessler took on the extra burden of raising money for the newlyweds. Though he lived without any frills whatsoever, he tried to make sure that new couples began married life in a respectable style. He provided the Waltners, for instance, with their furniture after the wedding.

Rabbi Dessler was very involved in all aspects of the *shidduchim* of the members of the Kollel. Convincing Zusia Waltner's wife, a girl from a proper German-Jewish family and a graduate of the Wurzburg Teachers' Seminary, that she would find happiness with a brilliant Hungarian-born *chassid* was his first triumph in this regard.

The first time Rabbi Naftoli Friedler met his wife was at Rabbi Schneider's home in London.[21] Present in the room were Rabbi Schneider, Rabbi Dessler, and Mrs. Friedler's father, who had just arrived from Germany. Apparently no one had remembered to inform the latter that this was a *shidduch*, and he remained in the room even after Rabbi Schneider and Rabbi Dessler had discreetly removed themselves. After it became clear that her father had no intention of leaving, Mrs. Friedler gently nudged him with her foot under the table. The older gentleman, however, misinterpreted the signal and thought that he was being called upon for a *dvar Torah*, which he then proceeded to deliver.

And so it was that on their first meeting the Friedlers managed to spend no time alone. The second meeting was little more successful, as Rabbi Friedler was accompanied by a cousin serving in the American army and then on leave in London. Eventually, however, the young couple did manage to find some time alone to get to know one another. After a few meetings, Rabbi Dessler invited them to accompany him to the London train station prior to his Thursday night return to Gateshead. There he took each aside separately and asked how things were progressing. Each gave approximately the same answer: Thus far, everything seems fine. Hearing that, Rabbi Dessler called them together and wished them a *Mazel Tov* on their engagement.

Rabbi Dessler also took an active role in the financial arrangements for the young couples. Rabbi Shammai Zahn was another Kollel member who married the daughter of recent German immigrants, who had come to England with nothing. Rabbi Dessler traveled to Manchester to meet the *kallah's* father, who was eager to help his son-in-law, but lacked the wherewithal to do so. Nevertheless, when Rabbi Dessler returned from Manchester, he told Rabbi Zahn, "Your father-in-law *macht* (is making) a bankruptcy," meaning he had agreed to extend himself to the utmost.

---

21. Rabbi Schneider had opened up a dormitory for young refugee women. The young women worked during the day, and several nights a week they had *shiurim*. One of Rabbi Schneider's goals was to find proper wives for the advanced *bachurim* in his yeshiva. Mrs. Friedler was one of these young women.

Rabbi Dessler was prepared to give up his long-established *hanhagos* (ways of conducting himself) for the benefit of others. To further a *shidduch*, for instance, he once sacrificed a practice that was very dear to him. Every year, he stayed in Gateshead the week of his father's *yahrtzeit* so that he could spend the week immersed in learning and lead the *davening* in the Kollel. One year, however, on the very evening of his father's *yahrtzeit*, he asked Rabbi Waltner to accompany him to the train station. There were no cabs available, and they had to walk all the way to the Newcastle train station. Rabbi Dessler absolutely refused to permit his younger friend to carry his bag despite the very long walk.

On the steps of the train, Rabbi Dessler explained why he was departing precisely at the moment when he should be *davening* at the *amud*. He told Rabbi Waltner that he had received a call from a rosh yeshiva in London that a *shidduch* between a girl in Gateshead Seminary and a *yeshiva bachur* in London had run into difficulties, and that Rabbi Dessler might be able to save it. "I thought to myself," said Rabbi Dessler, "what better *Kaddish* can I send my father than to help establish a house of Torah?"[22]

Rabbi Dessler had an almost preternatural sensitivity to the needs of others. One day at breakfast, he noticed that Rabbi Friedler seemed downcast and asked him what was the matter. Rabbi Friedler was surprised that his internal mood was so evident, but confided to Rabbi Dessler that he was being pressured concerning a *shidduch* in which he was not interested. Rabbi Dessler assured him that he was under no obligation to proceed. Fifty-five years later, Rabbi Friedler still recalled the feeling that a 200-pound weight had been lifted from his heart.

Rabbi Dessler and Rabbi Bezalel Rakov were walking down the street one day when Rabbi Dessler suddenly stopped to stare into a shopwindow and write down the price of some children's clothing in his notebook. His curiousity piqued, Rabbi Rakov asked him what he was doing. Rabbi Dessler explained that he was often invited to the homes of Kollel families for Shabbos and felt that he

---

22. Rabbi Dessler succeeded in his mission of reuniting the couple. *Rabbi Zusia Waltner.*

should have something of particular interest — like a sale on children's clothes — to discuss with the woman of the house in return for her hospitality.

In general, he was particularly sensitive to the needs of the young Kollel wives. At the outset of a *Seder* at the Waltners, he noticed that Mrs. Waltner was exhausted from all the preparations leading up to the *Seder*. Rabbi Dessler insisted that they conduct the *Seder* rapidly so that Mrs. Waltner could stay awake for the entirety, and then sent her to sleep while he and Rabbi Waltner did the dishes.

Praise, Rabbi Dessler knew, was often the most precious gift, and he was not sparing with it. Even the pickled herring served by Rabbi Gedaliah Schneider's mother-in-law during one of the late night study sessions at Rabbi Schneider's home did not escape the effusion of his praise.

Two weeks after Rabbi Shammai Zahn's wedding, Rabbi Dessler was the Zahns' Shabbos guest. The young couple were very poor, and six silver-plated place settings were virtually the only wedding presents they received. Before the meal began, Rabbi Dessler took the silverware in hand, turned it over carefully, as if considering it from every angle, and then told his hosts how beautiful it was.

The "giver" as portrayed by Rabbi Dessler, makes strenuous efforts to never benefit from another without somehow returning the benefit. In his personal life, Rabbi Dessler went to great lengths to never ask anyone to do anything for him.

And if the "giver" does receive benefit from someone else, he never regards it as his due, but is filled with *hakaras hatov* (gratitude) for the good done to him. Rabbi Dessler's *hakaras hatov* for even the smallest favor knew no bounds. No sooner had his train pulled out of Gateshead station than he was found writing letters to the Waltners or other members of the Kollel. One typical letter, written on the way from Gateshead to Manchester, begins, "You have captured my heart, Reb Zusia, with the goodness of your heart by preparing a glass of tea that was waiting for me on my return from shul."

The letter continues with thanks to Mrs. Waltner for rising early to implore Rabbi Dessler to eat a wide variety of foods she had prepared.

Dr. Chalk

Though his stomach had not permitted him to eat them then, he informs Mrs. Waltner that he has now eaten and enjoyed the cakes she baked.[23] In another letter to the Waltners, Rabbi Dessler notes that the letter will likely arrive in Gateshead after he does. Nonetheless he feels compelled to write out of his *hakaras hatov* for all the Waltners have done for him.[24]

One particular incident, related by Rabbi Waltner, conveys just how far Rabbi Dessler's sense of *hakaras hatov* went. One winter he was bedridden with a severe flu. Late at night, he called to Rabbi Waltner and asked him to fetch a doctor. That alone was quite frightening to Rabbi Waltner because Rabbi Dessler normally refused to permit anyone to do anything for him. At that time, there were few private phones in Gateshead, and Rabbi Waltner had to go several blocks to the home of Mr. Ephraim Bloch in order to call Dr. Chalk, the Gateshead doctor.

After making his call, Rabbi Waltner noticed that Mr. Bloch looked as if he were deeply troubled by something. Rabbi Waltner asked him what the problem was, and Mr. Bloch replied that he had a £900 tax bill due the next day and no money with which to pay it. (The weekly Kollel stipend was then £4.)

When he returned back home, Rabbi Waltner told Rabbi Dessler of the situation with Mr. Bloch. As soon as Dr. Chalk had completed his examination, Rabbi Dessler sat down to write two notes, even though he could barely hold the pen in hand. The first was addressed to Mr. Steinhaus, owner of the local bakery, and the other to Mr. Fritz Nussbaum, one of the leaders of the Gateshead community. The note requested loans of £500 and £400, respectively, with Rabbi Dessler as the guarantor.

Though it was 3 a.m., Rabbi Dessler instructed Rabbi Waltner to bring the notes to Mr. Steinhaus and Mr. Nussbaum immediately

---

23. *Michtav Me'Eliyahu*, Vol. V, p. 507.
24. Ibid., pp. 506-7.

and to take the money directly to Mr. Bloch. When Rabbi Waltner returned home an hour later, his mission accomplished, Rabbi Dessler felt it necessary to explain his departure from his normal custom of never asking someone else for help.

He told Rabbi Waltner that Mr. Bloch had been over the years one of the most devoted supporters of the Kollel, and he was also the father-in-law of Rabbi Chaim Shmuel Lopian and Rabbi Aryeh Leib Grossnass. "It is forbidden for a Jew who has done so much for Torah to find himself in anguish even one night more than necessary," said Rabbi Dessler. "And I wanted you to have a part in this great *mitzvah* of bringing him relief."

Chapter 16
Builder of Torah

RABBI DESSLER IS BEST KNOWN AS THE AUTHOR OF *Michtav Me'Eliyahu*. Far less well known is his role as one of the premier builders of Torah institutions in the postwar years.

Yet when Rabbi Yechezkel Abramsky sought to describe the achievement of Rabbi Aharon Kotler, the architect of the entire American yeshiva world, he could think of no higher accolade than to compare Reb Aharon's impact on America to that of Rabbi Dessler on England. "What Rabbi Dessler did in England, Rav Aharon did in America," said Rabbi Abramsky.[1]

From the founding of Gateshead Kollel, Rabbi Dessler devoted himself completely to the needs of *Klal Yisrael*, without any regard for his own personal life. His uncle Rabbi Chaim Ozer Grodzensky was his model. In his *hesped* for Reb Chaim Ozer, Rabbi Dessler focused on Reb Chaim Ozer's complete devotion to *Klal Yisrael*, noting how the *Chofetz Chaim* used to say "Reb Chaim Ozer is *Klal Yisrael*."

---
1. Rabbi Moshe Mordechai HaLevi Shulsinger, *Penini Rabbeinu Yechezkel* (Hebrew), p. 27.

"For fifty-seven years, from the day of his wedding to the day of his death, his life was one unified, unbroken record of efforts on behalf of *Klal Yisrael*," said Rabbi Dessler. "No praise can be added to that, for *Moshe Rabbeinu* himself is similarly praised [for his complete devotion to *Klal Yisrael*]."

The need for every Jew to attach himself to the community and to identify completely with the needs of that community had long been a favorite theme of Rabbi Dessler. But the destruction of Eastern European Jewry gave it a new centrality and urgency. Thereafter, he demanded from himself total identification with the fate of *Klal Yisrael*. His almost superhuman schedule on behalf of the Kollel throughout the war years reflects a man driven to overcome all concern with self.

"We are in the midst of a conflagration," he wrote to Dr. Dov Heiman in the middle of the war. "I feel childish if an everyday thought even enters my mind in the midst of this terrible fire in which the majority of our people and its foundation stones have been consumed."

"Where is the Torah? And by whom has it found protection?" he asked. In the present situation, he stressed: "Any coldness of heart is treason. A betrayal of *Klal Yisrael*, its Torah, and its G-d."[2]

Rabbi Dessler demanded the same devotion from all those under his influence. In the midst of the war, his son Rabbi Nachum Velvel Dessler wrote that he had been asked by Rabbi Elya Meir Bloch, the founder of Telshe Yeshiva in America, to open a yeshiva day school in Cleveland. Reb Nachum Velvel was then the *rebbi* of the *mechinah* in Telshe Yeshiva, which he enjoyed very much. He was still unmarried and had no desire to give up his own full-time learning to become the principal of a new school. Nevertheless

R' Nachum Velvel when he was teaching in Telshe

---

2. *Michtav Me'Eliyahu*, Vol. V, pp. 509-10.

Chapter Sixteen: Builder of Torah / 233

The faculty and talmidim of the Telshe Yeshivah in Cleveland, 1945

Rabbi Bloch, who was very eager to build a yeshiva day school and high school in Cleveland, was putting great pressure on him.

Reb Nachum Velvel wrote to his father for advice. Rabbi Dessler asked whether there was anyone else who could undertake the task. When his son replied that there was no one, Rabbi Dessler told him that he had no choice: "After what was destroyed, our obligation is to build."[3]

Rabbi Dessler took great interest in his son's pioneering efforts, and gave him frequent encouragement. After receiving some favorable reports, he wrote Reb Nachum Velvel, "My own work has taught me that nothing is impossible with *siyata d'shamaya*. And when one acts with *mesiras nefesh* to advance the learning of Torah, Hashem helps in a miraculous fashion."

In the current world situation, he continues, spreading Torah is not just the most important task, it is the only one.

---

3. Rabbi Nachum Velvel Dessler.

Every person who has a heart should turn from every other activity and from every other thought concerning his material future, and make himself *hefker mamash* for the cause of spreading Torah in *Klal Yisrael*. So much has been destroyed that the obligation is upon us to build.

We lost not just bodies but holy souls. The places of Torah were uprooted and destroyed. If we don't strive to rebuild with more than our natural strength, we will be considered great sinners. Huge pieces of *Olam Haba* are today to be found like stones in the street, and yet no one understands enough to claim them.

As he had with Dr. Heiman, Rabbi Dessler described any personal concerns as nothing less than treason. "One would have to be a complete fool," he writes, "not to realize that anyone who thinks of his own material position at at time like this is nothing less than a traitor to Hashem":

How can any individual be so brazen as to think about his private needs at a time like this. Only a rebellious one could think like that, and [such a person] will end up being called a despicable traitor. We will be compared to animals. Woe, from that humiliation.

The Torah calls out to her children: Save me! . . . Today the nation will not listen except when it sees great actions performed with *mesiras nefesh*. Let us throw aside all thought of arranging our material sustenance. Rather let us be from among those who follow in the path of our ancestors of whom *HaKadosh Baruch Hu* Himself said, "I remember the *chesed* of your youth, the love of your betrothal, when you followed after Me into an unplanted desert"(*Yirmiyahu* 2:2). [They went out] without any provision for the way. On that merit, our ancestors merited redemption and the giving of Torah.[4]

---

4. Ibid., Vol. III, pp. 344-46.

MOST OF RABBI DESSLER'S ENERGIES WERE DEVOTED TO LAYING the foundations for the Gateshead Kollel. But he left his mark on

The Gateshead Teachers' Seminary

every Gateshead institution, and played a leading role in the founding of the world-renowned Gateshead Seminary.

The transformation of Gateshead Yeshiva from a yeshiva for younger boys to a *yeshiva gedolah* owed a great deal to the influence of Gateshead Kollel and to Rabbi Dessler's gentle urging in that direction. Even though the Kollel could only take a handful of outstanding *bachurim* in its early years, its existence stirred the ambitions of many young men eager to be among those select few. In one letter, Rabbi Dessler estimates that within a few years of the opening of the Kollel, the number of *bachurim* learning in Gateshead Yeshiva grew fivefold.[5]

Nor was Rabbi Dessler's influence only indirect. He played a major role in bringing Rabbi Leib Lopian into the yeshiva. When he decided that it was time for Rabbi Lopian to start saying a regular *shiur* in the yeshiva, recalls Rabbi Dov Sternbuch, he talked about the idea constantly to Rabbi Nachman Dovid Landynski, and the latter agreed. He brought Rabbi Moshe Schwab into the Yeshiva, as the Mashgiach, in much the same fashion.

Rabbi Aryeh Leib Gurwicz, a product of Baranovitch and Mirrer Yeshivos, was already a *maggid shiur* in London's Eitz Chaim Yeshiva and *rav* of a congregation in London's East End when Rabbi Dessler decided that he too should be a *maggid shiur* in Gateshead. Together Rabbi Dessler and Rabbi Gurwicz's brother-in-law Rabbi Leib Lopian urged him to move to Gateshead. Over a period of months, Rabbi Dessler visited Rabbi Gurwicz a number of times before succeeding.[6] When Rabbi Landynski was forced to seek medical attention for a sick child in America, Rabbi Leib Lopian and Rabbi Leib Gurwicz — "my two lions," Rabbi Yechezkel Abramsky used to call them[7] — became the *roshei yeshiva* of Gateshead Yeshiva. Over

---

5. Ibid., p. 356.
6. Rabbi Zusia Waltner.
7. A play on the name Leib, which means lion in Yiddish. On other occasions, Rabbi Abramsky referred to England standing on "three lions" — the third being Rabbi Leib

the next thirty years, they guided the yeshiva to the front rank of world yeshivos.

Rabbi Dessler's greatest influence was unquestionably on the world-famous Gateshead Seminary. The only picture to adorn the walls of the seminary, during the lifetime of Mr. Avrohom Dov Kohn, its first head, was one of Rabbi Dessler, in silent testimony to his crucial role in the creation of the seminary.

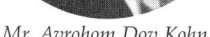
Mr. Avrohom Dov Kohn

Rabbi Dessler and Mr. Kohn together conceived the idea of a Teachers Seminary in Gateshead. German born and raised, Mr. Kohn also studied for a number of years in leading Hungarian yeshivos, before earning his teaching degree from the famous Wurzberg Teachers Seminary. He began his teaching career in the Jewish school of Nuremberg just before the Nazis expelled all Jewish students from the public schools.

After fleeing Germany for Czechoslovakia, the Kohns were fortunate to escape from Czechoslovakia to England on March 8, 1939, just six days before the Nazi takeover of Czechoslovakia. After taking up residence with his family in Wales, Mr. Kohn was placed in an internment camp for "enemy aliens," and only released December 31, 1941.

Upon his release, Mr. Kohn was invited to head the local afternoon *cheder* in Gateshead on the strength of the recommendation of a former student from Nuremburg, who was then learning in Gateshead Yeshiva. At that time, the local *cheder* consisted of afternoon classes taught to boys by Rabbi Shakovitsky and Rabbi Dovid Dryan. They were eager to find a younger educator who could better relate to the students in the *cheder*.

Though he had been invited to Gateshead to teach boys, Mr. Kohn soon realized that the situation of girls' education was even

---

Grossnass, another product of the Gateshead Kollel and Rabbi Abramsky's successor as head of the London *Beis Din*.

more disastrous. The education for girls was then a purely private affair, and many did not even know Hebrew. Mr. Kohn and his wife raised eyebrows by opening up official classes for girls.

Meanwhile Rabbi Dessler was concerned about the lack of suitable spouses for the unmarried young men learning in the Kollel and all those who aspired to enter the Kollel. There were then virtually no English girls willing to marry young men determined to devote their lives to learning and teaching Torah. Rabbi Dessler's concerns on this score dovetailed nicely with Mr. Kohn's worries about the low state of Jewish education throughout England. A teachers' seminary offered a partial solution to both problems, and the two men discussed the idea over a long period of time.

Rabbi Dessler knew that the success or failure of any proposed seminary would largely depend upon the quality of the person heading it, and he spared no effort to ensure that Mr. Kohn was that person. He set up a regular learning schedule with Mr. Kohn on Shabbos morning before *davening* that continued for over a year prior to the opening of the seminary.[8] In addition, he was a frequent visitor in the Kohn home, explaining to Mr. Kohn on one occasion that the visits were crucial so that he could judge "how someone who will be responsible for the education of Jewish girls runs his own home. How does he influence his children? Do his own children evidence good *middos*? And does the house have the air of *mussar*?"[9]

Mr. Kohn passed the test with flying colors, and Rabbi Dessler's wisdom in selecting him as the appropriate head for the new seminary was fully demonstrated over the forty years that Mr. Kohn headed the Seminary. The refinement of his *middos* was reminiscent of Kelm. One former student remembered him as a man of "utter integrity," whose every action was "correct and perfect. He was a perfectionist, and he demanded perfection from us." But, she added, he also "cared for each of us like a father." Another former student recalled her awe of his dignity and perfection: "In front of him, one could not act improperly."

---

8. Rabbi Aryeh Carmell.
9. Rabbi Zusia Waltner.

In his self-effacement too, Mr. Kohn could also have been mistaken for a product of Kelm. After his death, the following note was found among his papers: "I never felt myself to be the head of an institution. I never sat at the head — nor even in the middle — of the dais. I never insisted on having my way against the opinion of my colleagues on the staff, and I never made others feel that I was the principal."

Without Rabbi Dessler's full and complete support, it is doubtful that the seminary would have ever come into being. Many in Gateshead, including some important communal leaders, looked askance at the entire idea. Only Rabbi Dessler's prestige in the Gateshead community allowed Mr. Kohn to overcome that opposition.[10] In his diary, Mr. Kohn noted, "I undertook with the great help and advice and moral support of Rabbi Dessler to set up the seminary."

As it was, the seminary opened its doors in 1944 with only one full-time student, Miriam (Eisemann) Elias, who boarded in the Kohns' home. Another six or seven local girls also attended night classes. Miriam Eisemann was joined after three months by her cousin Hennie (Eisemann) Rosenthal, and by the end of the first year there were six full-time students. That number had grown to 13 by the end of the second year, almost all from German refugee families.[11]

Rabbi Dessler did not just lend his support to the seminary; he promised Mr. Kohn from the beginning that he would teach the young women. That teaching was fully consistent with the emphasis of the Alter and his son Rabbi Nachum Velvel Ziv on a firm foundation in *hashkafah* for their daughters.

Rabbi Dessler taught a *Chumash-Rashi shiur* on Thursday or Friday morning. Part of the *shiur* was devoted to an oral examination of the girls on Rashi's commentary on the *parashah*.[12] On Thursday night, he spoke on a particular topic in Jewish thought. That class was open to all the women in Gateshead, and the room was usually packed. At the latter *shiur*, Rabbi Dessler would address

---

10. Mrs. Miriam Elias.
11. Ibid.
12. Mrs. Esther Adler.

any topic that his students requested. For instance, he once devoted a series of lectures to evolution.

The seminary students were required to write their own synopsis of the night *shiur* every week, and Rabbi Dessler would himself personally go over their essays and write little comments in the margins, such as, "If that's your attitude, you'll go far."[13]

At the beginning of each talk, Rabbi Dessler would lower his head briefly before beginning, as if considering what he wished to speak about. Usually, he would begin with an intriguing question such as: If you meet someone in the desert, how can you tell whether he is Jewish? When he was done, each woman in the room felt as if he had been speaking directly to her.[14] The talks inspired his listeners with the desire to immediately put his lessons into action. After a speech on the power of giving, one student recalled, "You wanted to immediately do something for someone else."[15]

The young women in the *shiur* did not, of course, always appreciate the depth of Rabbi Dessler's thought. He spoke so clearly and simply that they often had no idea that he had said anything original. Mr. Kohn, who attended almost every talk, however, took pains to enlighten them as to the depth of what they had just heard. He would clap his hands together at the end of the *shiur* and exclaim, "Ah, girls! You have no idea — such a deep *inyan*. I never heard such a masterpiece."[16] Mr. Kohn fostered such an aura of respect around Rabbi Dessler that the girls dressed specially for his *shiur*.

Whether the girls fully appreciated Rabbi Dessler's depth or not, they found over time that their whole outlook on life was based on what they had received from him. They would discuss with him outside of class any problem — philosophic or personal — that was bothering them.[17]

He also provided them with a model of the *middos* with which he sought to imbue them. One day in class, he painted a detailed word

---

13. Mrs. Naomi Pels.
14. Mrs. Thea (Eisemann) Posen.
15. Mrs. Naomi Pels.
16. Ibid.
17. Ibid.

picture of what it was like for the Generation of the Desert to journey and encamp upon the explicit command of Hashem. He described a mother who had just put her children down to sleep and was about to confront a pile of ironing when suddenly the Clouds of Glory lifted and the trumpets blew announcing that it was time to decamp.

At that point, one of the young women raised her hand and pointed out that Rashi writes that they did no ironing in the desert because that work was done by the Clouds of Glory. Rather than being embarrassed, Rabbi Dessler complimented her on the observation. Shortly thereafter, when he gave a similar *shiur*, to a mixed group of men and women in Manchester, he went so far as to cite the student's correction and even mentioned her by name.

Rabbi Dessler's influence in the seminary was not confined to his own teaching. With his encouragement, a number of the Kollel members taught in the seminary. In fact, members of the Kollel comprised almost the entire early staff of the seminary. Among the first teachers in the seminary were: Rabbi Aryeh Leib Grossnass, Rabbi Naftoli Friedler, Rabbi Binyomin Zev (Theodore) Weiss, and Rabbi Shammai Zahn.

The influence of Rabbi Dessler on the seminary continues to the present day through two of his closest *talmidim*, Rabbi Mordechai Miller and Rabbi Dov Sternbuch. The two have been the mainstays of the seminary for the past half-century, with Rabbi Miller succeeding Mr. Kohn as principal. The seminary is justly famed for its emphasis on *hashkafah* (Jewish thought), and Rabbi Dessler's thought is one of the principal foundations of that *hashkafah*. Seminary graduates, saturated with Rabbi Dessler's ideas, as they heard them from Rabbi Dessler himself or from Rabbi Miller, have, in turn, made those ideas the basis of the seminaries which they founded or in which they taught.

The Gateshead Jewish Boarding School (Mechina LaYeshiva) opened during World War II, for the purpose of preparing boys for entry into the yeshiva. The boarding school was under the informal auspicies of the Kollel. Most of original students in the boarding school were refugees. The initial student body of twelve quickly expanded, and the school began to draw boys living in areas where only minimal Jewish education was available from all over England and from other places in Europe.

Rabbi Dessler brought Rabbi Moshe Aryeh Bamberger to Gateshead from his position as a provincial *rav* to head the boarding school.[18] He also convinced Mr. Yona Mantel and his wife, whom he had known in Chesham, to oversee the home in which the boys lived. The latter role was of great importance since so many of the students were either orphans or had been long separated from their parents.[19]

Rabbi Bamberger's salary was paid directly by the Kollel, and he was officially listed as one of its members. At one point, the Kollel's financial situation was extremely precarious, and the suggestion was made that those working for other institutions should have their salaries paid by those institutions. When it became clear, however, that the boarding school was in no position to raise Rabbi Bamberger's salary, Rabbi Dessler insisted that he remain on the Kollel list, despite the extra fundraising burden that decision imposed on him.[20]

Besides bringing Rabbi Bamberger to Gateshead and paying his salary, Rabbi Dessler also raised funds for the boarding school. Not all his efforts in that regard met with success. The neighboring Newcastle community numbered many well-to-do Jews among its members, but they never supported any Gateshead institution. On one occasion, Rabbi Dessler did succeed in arousing the sympathy of a few Newcastle *baalebatim* for the plight of the refugee children in the boarding school, and they agreed to come to Gateshead for a meal in their honor.

---

18. Rabbi Bamberger was a great-grandson of the Wurzberger Rav, Rabbi Yitzchak Dov Bamberger, a contemporary of Rabbi Samson Raphael Hirsch and one of the foremost German *poskim* (halachic decisors) of his time. After graduating from the Wurzberg Seminary, Rabbi Moshe Aryeh Bamberger learned in Slabodka Yeshiva, where he received his *semichah* from the Rosh Yeshiva, Rabbi Moshe Mordechai Epstein. Prior to fleeing to England from Germany, he was the *rav* of Mainz.

19. Rabbi Raphael Posen, one of the first teachers in the school.

20. Rabbi Bezalel Rakov.

In His Footsteps

THE CONTEMPT FOR THE PURSUIT OF A "POSITION" THAT RABBI Dessler instilled in the Kollel members did not mean that the Kollel members were expected to learn in the Kollel indefinitely. Indeed the Kollel was loosely patterned on the famed Slabodka Kollel, whose members were required to become communal *rabbanim* after five years in the Kollel. Contempt for "positions" simply meant that the needs of *Klal Yisrael*, and not the quest for personal security, should be the paramount consideration in choosing one's life work.

Rabbi Dessler not only set the goal of a lifetime of service to the *Klal*, he trained the Kollel members for a future in which many would head their own institutions. In the first years of the Kollel, Rabbi Dessler bore the entire fundraising burden himself. Thus it was quite a shock to the Kollel members when he announced at one of the Kollel Vaad meetings that the Kollel's financial situation was such that it would be necessary for the *avreichim* to also devote time to soliciting for funds.

Rabbi Moshe Schwab and Rabbi Zusia Waltner, for instance, were dispatched to Wales. The sight of two bearded Jews was so unusual in those days that the local hotel refused to give them a room, and they spent their first nights in Wales sleeping in the train station. The head of the local community added insult to injury when they approached him on behalf of the Kollel. He threw them out of his house, but not before expressing his low opinion of yeshiva students.

Shaken by their initial foray into the world of fundraising, the two young rabbis returned to Gateshead. Rabbi Dessler strengthened their resolve, and shared with them the basis of all successful fundraising: Never forget that you are benefitting those whom you solicit for money for holy causes, and that you are the givers.

Their resolve steeled, they set off again in search of funds. By the second week, they had already secured letters of introduction and addresses, and had soon perfected their fundraising pitch.

Some time later, Rabbi Dessler revealed the real reason he had been eager for the Kollel members to undertake some of the fundraising responsibility. He had been concerned that something

Chapter Sixteen: Builder of Torah / 243

L-R: R' Wolf Kaufman (now Rosh Kollel in Manchester), R' Chaim Shmuel Lopian, R' Yechezkel Abramsky, R' Laizer Zohn (Rosh Yeshiva of the Sunderland Yeshiva), R' Babad (Rav of Sunderland), and R' Leib Lopian

that one receives for free loses value in the recipient's eyes. "I wanted the *avreichim* to feel that the Kollel is theirs," he told Rabbi Waltner. His second consideration was to provide the training in collecting that the Kollel members would one day need when they headed institutions of their own.[21]

The prediction that the Kollel members would one day found their own institutions was soon proven correct. The first such institution was a yeshiva in neighboring Sunderland. Rabbi Zusia Waltner and Rabbi Aryeh Leib Grossnass opened Sunderland Yeshiva just after the war for young survivors from Europe. Rabbi Grossnass traveled to Prague to bring back the first group of survivors. The horrors that these boys had been through had left their mark. For six months after their arrival in England, Rabbi Waltner had to sleep with them every night in order to calm them when they awoke with terrible nightmares.

Not long after that first trip to Prague, Rabbi Grossnass decided that he wished to remain in the Kollel for the time being, and Rabbi Dessler and Rabbi Shakovitsky chose Rabbi Shammai Zahn to assist Rabbi Waltner in running the yeshiva. He has been there ever since.[22] Rabbi Chaim Shmuel Lopian, one of the original members of the Kollel, also served as a rosh yeshiva in the Sunderland Yeshiva for many years.[23]

---

21. Rabbi Zusia Waltner.
22. Sunderland Yeshiva, however, has since relocated to Gateshead.
23. Ibid.

One of the rules that Rabbi Dessler gave Rabbi Waltner at the inception of Sunderland Yeshiva was not to follow the accepted British practice of placing the administration of the yeshiva in the hands of a committee of *baalebatim*. That practice, he felt, had been responsible for the failure of Eitz Chaim Yeshiva in London to ever reach its full potential, despite the great *talmidei chachamim* who taught there.

Not surprisingly, the local *baalebatim* in Sunderland were not happy at this denial of what they considered to be their prerogatives as members of the host community. They called a meeting and invited Rabbi Dessler to attend. Since many of the Sunderland families were originally from Kretinga, a *mussar* stronghold, he began with a story about his great-grandfather Rabbi Yisrael Salanter.

After Reb Yisrael passed away, he said, his wife was asked whether she had found it difficult living in the presence of such a great *tzaddik*. She replied that there had never been a problem because at the beginning of their marriage, Reb Yisrael had laid down a clear rule: All *mili d'alma* (everyday matters) were to be her province and all *mili d'Shamaya* (spiritual concerns) his. In the course of time, however, she discovered that for Reb Yisrael everything was *mili d'Shamaya*.

Rabbi Dessler's point — that the administration of a yeshiva in all its aspects is a holy undertaking and *baalebatim* cannot have the decisive say — was not lost on his listeners. At that point, one of the local *baalebatim* announced that he too would give him a *drashah*. Rabbi Waltner stood up and shouted at him for his *chutzpah* (impudence) and pandemonium broke loose.

Sunderland Yeshiva proved to be merely the first of the institutions Rabbi Waltner would create. In the late '40s and early '50s, Sunderland Yeshiva began to serve as a place of refuge for Jews eager to leave North Africa. Rabbi Waltner traveled to Tangiers, Morocco and brought back with him 25 young boys eager to learn in a yeshiva. The next year he brought back another 25. On his third trip, Rabbi Shmuel Toledano, one of the leaders of the local community, asked him to stay in Tangiers and establish a school system there.

By then, Rabbi Dessler had already left Gateshead for Ponevezh, but Rabbi Waltner would not do anything without consulting him first. Rabbi Dessler told him that he could only consider the move if he could secure for his son teachers who were capable of bringing him to the level of understanding the questions of Rabbi Akiva Eiger by himself.[24]

Rabbi Dessler gave Rabbi Waltner another crucial piece of advice. Every institution, he said, needs its own "but" — a quality that distinguishes it from other similar institutions. In other words, the head of the institution should clearly identify what makes his institution unique, so that he can immediately tell those who wished to know, "Yes, we have that too, *but* we also have . . . ."

During his more than two decades in Tangiers, Rabbi Waltner created a network of schools from kindergarten through a Beis Yaakov Teachers Seminary, yeshivah gedolah, and kollel. Thousands of youngsters passed through this system, including many of the leading Sephardi *rabbanim* today in *Eretz Yisrael*.

Neither Sunderland Yeshiva or the network of schools created by Rabbi Waltner in Tangiers fit traditional models of schooling for children from normal religious homes. Both were created to save individuals and communities whose *Yiddishkeit* was under threat. The survivors of the Holocaust, for whom Sunderland Yeshiva was created, had to confront after the war the decision whether to resume the religious life they had known before the war. The presence of those actively concerned with a young survivor's future could often be the determinative factor in that decision.

The religious life of North African Jewry was no less under threat in the late '40s and early '50s. Without a well-developed religious educational system, the youth were easy prey for the Alliance schools and for Youth Aliya, which used every possible inducement to bring young North African Jews to Israel without their parents, where they could be placed in non-religious *kibbutzim*.

---

24. Rabbi Waltner fully succeeded in this regard. His son Rabbi Meir Waltner learned for many years in Lakewood Yeshiva, and is today a *rosh kollel* in Jerusalem.

Rabbi Dessler's *talmidim* were also involved with a third group of those who did not fit into existing models of religious schooling for those from religious homes: *baalei teshuvah*. Almost from the beginning Gateshead Seminary attracted a number of young women with little religious training. One of the first students was the daughter of Viscount Herbert Samuels, the only Jew ever to serve as the British High Commissioner of Palestine. She was already in her late 20's when she arrived in Gateshead, and had explored various spiritual regimens prior to her arrival. She did not speak Yiddish, and the other girls had to translate Rabbi Dessler's talks for her, an exercise they found beneficial for themselves as well.[25]

The first students in Gateshead Seminary were, by and large, from proper German-Jewish homes. They were followed by a large influx of young women from France and North Africa. Many of these were from traditional, but not strictly observant, homes, who were attracted to Gateshead Seminary by its reputation for being at an intellectually high level.

One of the best students in the early '50s was a French journalist, who first arrived in Gateshead on Shabbos, with a pen and notebook in hand, in order to write a story about Gateshead. She ended up staying to learn about Torah for the next three years. The products of those years themselves went forth to establish new schools of their own in Tangiers, Paris, Aix-les-Baines, Lucerne, Zurich, and throughout England.

Rabbi Dessler had personal contact with a number of *baalei teshuvah*, and the contact had a profound effect on them. There was a girl from Morocco in the seminary, who was engaged to a Moroccan boy, who was pursuing a post-doctorate degree in chemistry from the Sorbonne. Both were from observant, but unlearned, families. The girl, however, had become inflamed with enthusiasm for Torah while in Gateshead.

Her fiancé came to visit her in Gateshead. While in Gateshead, he was dismayed to find that he could not even keep up with young

---

25. Mrs. Naomi Pels.
   Another student from that period, Mrs. Esther Adler, remembers Rabbi Dessler translating word for word for Miss Samuels.

boys in learning. Rabbi Mordechai Miller advised him to speak to Rabbi Dessler. The young man told Rabbi Dessler that he wanted to learn Torah, but that it seemed impracticable at the moment. Rabbi Dessler asked him, "Do you really mean that *leshem Shamayim?*" When the young man replied that he did, Rabbi Dessler told him that he should spend the year after marriage in Gateshead and not worry about the future. "Hashem fulfills the will of those who fear Him" *(Tehillim* 145:20), Rabbi Dessler assured him.

The couple returned to Morocco and married. Ignoring their families' objections, they then headed back to Gateshead. In Paris, they had to switch train stations, and as the cab took them from one station to another, they passed the Sorbonne. The young man remembered that he had not taken leave of the professor who headed his program, and he asked the cab to stop so that he could do so.

The professor was quite taken aback by the announcement that the young man, who had shown great promise, was taking an indefinite leave from his program. But he wished him well. As the young man was getting back into his cab, the professor came running after him waving a piece of paper. The paper turned out to be an invitation he had just received from Durham University, located right next to Gateshead, for an exchange student from the Sorbonne. The offer included a stipend, and the professor wanted to know whether his student would be interested in taking the position.

The young man could think of nothing else as his professor spoke than Rabbi Dessler's words, "Hashem fulfills the will of those who fear Him." He was still concerned, however, how Durham University would react when it was discovered that he did not speak a word of English. As soon as they arrived in Gateshead, he went to see the professor who was looking for a research assistant. He explained that he spoke only French, and the professor replied in French.

That concern removed, the young man asked how many other research assistants there would be, and ascertained that he would be the only one. He and his new bride did a quick calculation that if they lived very frugally, they could make do on far less than the fellowship being offered. The young man asked whether he might take a smaller stipend in return for working fewer hours, and the professor was agreeable. Living on one third of the original fellowship, the young man was able to learn almost full-time in Gateshead that year. Just as Rabbi Dessler had predicted, Hashem had found the way for him to learn without financial worries.

Rabbi Dessler was one of the first to foresee a widespread phenomena of *baalei teshuvah*, and even predicted that there would one day be *baalei teshuvah* who would reach the front ranks of Torah learning and teaching. One day he was sitting together with Rabbi Yitzchak Greenberg, the *Mashgiach* in Lomza Yeshiva in Petach Tikvah, when a young woman came to speak with him. She spoke to Rabbi Dessler for twenty minutes, and he listened intently. When she left, Rabbi Dessler told Rabbi Greenberg that she was a *baalas teshuvah*, who had arrived in Gateshead knowing almost nothing. Now she was ready and eager to draw others back to their Judaism.

Rabbi Dessler continued speaking enthusiastically about the future of the *teshuvah* movement, which he saw as another aspect of the period of *ikvesa d'Mashiach*. He revealed to Rabbi Greenberg plans for a variety of spiritual revolutions. Among them, he intended to visit Italy at the invitation of a high-level judge who had become a *baal teshuvah*.

A number of Rabbi Dessler's closest *talmidim* were similarly infused with his enthusiasm for reaching out to Jews who had never been exposed to the depths of Torah learning. Rabbi Osher Westheim, a member of the small circle of *talmidim* who met with Rabbi Dessler weekly at Rabbi Gedaliah Schneider's home and subsequently a member of the Gateshead Kollel, later opened up a Jewish Center in Paris.

The Jewish Center was one of the first institutions of its type to be specifically designed for those with minimal religious background. Fittingly, the mainstay of the curriculum was the thought of Rabbi Dessler.[26]

---

26. Rabbi Westheim possessed voluminous notes of talks that he had heard from Rabbi Dessler. These proved very useful in the compiling of *Michtav Me'Eliyahu*. Rabbi Aryeh Carmell.

Chapter 17

Transitions

THE END OF WORLD WAR II BROUGHT WITH IT SIGNIFICANT changes in Rabbi Dessler's life. By far, the most

War's End important was the long-awaited reunification with his wife and daughter. Not until February 1946 were Rebbetzin Dessler and Hennie finally able to reach England. Over six years had passed since Rabbi Dessler had last seen them. When they departed for Lithuania, Hennie was little more than a girl, and now she returned to her father a mature young woman. No words can describe the rush of emotions that overwhelmed

Rabbi and Rebbetzin Dessler and their daughter

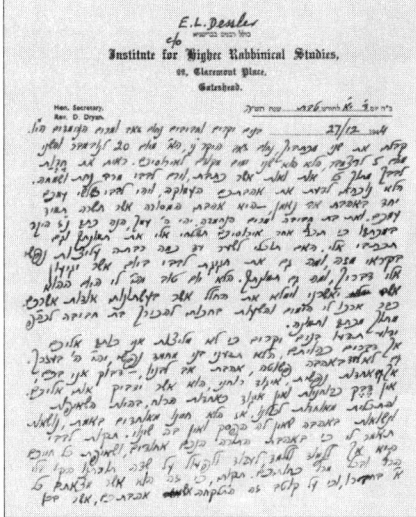

Letters from Rabbi and Rebbetzin Dessler to R' Nachum Velvel and his kallah

father, mother, and daughter now that they were finally reunited.

Yet the Dessler's joy at being reunited after so many years could not but be dampened by thoughts of those not present. Reb Nachum Velvel was still far away in Cleveland, and neither Rabbi nor Rebbetzin Dessler had even met their daughter-in-law Miriam. In December 1944, Nachum Velvel and Miriam became engaged. Letters from Rabbi and Rebbitzen Dessler poured in expressing their love, delight and gratitude, and welcoming their future daughter-in-law. Rabbi Dessler's moving and affectionate reference to her as "*my schnurale, perl* (my daughter-in-law, my pearl)" and "*Miraleh, mein gold* (Miraleh, my golden one)" are but a few indications of his great longing to his son and daughter-in-law.

Chapter Seventeen: Transitions / 251

A photo and a note sent to the young couple upon their marriage

Even more poignantly felt was the absence of all those whom they would never see again. Throughout the years, reports from Eastern Europe led Rabbi Dessler to fear the worst concerning the fate of all the loved ones he had left behind in Kelm. His worst fears were now confirmed. From Beis HaTalmud no one had survived: not Rabbi Dessler's beloved brothers-in-law, Rabbi Doniel Movshovitz and Rabbi Gershon Miadnik; not Rebbetzin Dessler's mother Rebbetzin Pesha Ziv, nor her sisters Chaya and Frieda, nor Reb Gershon and Frieda's children, nor her aunt, Rebbetzin Necha Liba Braude; not any of the families connected to Beis HaTalmud.

In one of the last communications from Kelm to the outside world, a friend of Rabbi Chaim Dov Silver wrote to him in Melbourne. The letter, dated June 6, 1941, describes the care with which Reb Doniel Movshovitz read Rabbi Silver most recent letter and the great pleasure he derived from the warmth of Rabbi Silver's words. "An overwhelming love was seen on his face as he read," writes Rabbi Silver's friend.[1]

There was no hiding the bitterness of the situation. The Nazis had not yet invaded Lithuania, but the invasion seemed imminent. Despite the fearful stories of mass exterminations reaching Lithuania from Poland, few Jews in Kelm availed themselves of the opportunity to flee deep into the Soviet Union. For the most part they

The photo R' Nachum Velvel sent his parents of his prospective kallah

---

1. *Orchos Chesed* (Hebrew), p. 33.

tried to convince themselves that they would be able to establish normal relations with the invading German army as they had in World War I.[2]

Reb Doniel, however, did not share their hopes. "This week," Rabbi Silver's friend confided, "Reb Doniel quoted the verse, 'Woe, who will survive when He imposes these [judgments]?' (*Bamidbar* 24:23)."

The actual Nazi invasion of Lithuania took place on June 22, 1941. Virtually all the Jewish homes in the center of Kelm were destroyed by the German bombardment. By the next day, the Red Army had completely fled the area, leaving the way clear for the unimpeded entry of the Germans into Kelm on June 24. On July 1, all the able-bodied men between 14 and 60 years of age, including the men of the Talmud Torah, were ordered to gather in the granary of Zundel Luntz, a successful Jewish farmer, whose farm was on the outskirts of the town. The Jewish men of Kelm were put to work, by Lithuanian nationalists, clearing away rubble. The Nazi conquerors felt justifiably confident leaving the Lithuanians in charge.

The night of the fifth of *Av*, Reb Doniel dreamt a horrible nightmare, and the next morning (July 29), he broke from his normal custom and recited *hatavos chalom*. As he was doing so, a group of Lithuanian fanatics broke into the granary and ordered all the men to gather.

Already the Lithuanians had savagely killed a number of Jews in Kelm. From the looks on the faces of the Lithuanians that morning, their victims could have had few doubts as to what lay in store for them. But as they marched at gunpoint, the men of the Talmud Torah sang and danced as if it were *Simchas Torah*. They were enraptured in the songs they had sung so often — "*Vetaher libeinu l'ovdecha b'emes*, Purify our hearts to serve You in truth," and "*Ashreinu ma tov chelkeinu*, How fortunate are we, how good is our lot." Held high on a chair was the Alter's daughter Rebbetzin Nechama Liba, whom they carried just as if she were a *sefer Torah*.[3]

---

2. *Kelm   Eitz Karus* (Hebrew), p. 52.

3. One of the great tragedies of destruction of the Talmud Torah of Kelm is that it came

When they reached their destination, the executioners ordered the men to start digging a large pit — a pit in which they would soon be buried. When the pit was completed and the extermination about to begin, Reb Doniel sought permission to address his flock for one last time. He quoted the *piyut* recited on Yom Kippur that recounts how the angels themselves cried out upon seeing Rabbi Akiva's flesh raked by metal combs, "This is Torah, and this is its reward." Hashem replied, "If I hear another word, I'll return the world to the primordial void."

At that moment, Reb Doniel explained, the world had lost any merit to justify its continued existence. Yet Hashem had promised not to bring another Flood, wiping out all of mankind, and so had chosen the Ten Martyrs mentioned in the *piyut* as an atonement for the rest of the world. If the angels forced Hashem to restrain His hand and spare the Ten Martyrs, they would, in effect, force G-d to destroy a world no longer worthy of existence.

Turning to his students, Reb Doniel told them that they stood at that moment in exactly the same position as the Ten Martyrs: The world had lost the merit to exist. Only through the atonement of their deaths would Hashem stay His hand and not return it to *Tohu Vavohu*. Therefore, he urged his students, "Let us be neither confused nor frightened, but rather let us accept upon ourselves this awesome responsibility with love."

With that he turned to the chief of the murderers and told them, "I have finished. Now you can begin."[4]

---

very close to being saved. On a 1939 trip to Palestine to visit his parents, Rabbi Chaim Dov Silver met Rabbi Hillel Vitkind, Rosh Yeshiva of Yeshivas Beis Yosef in Tel Aviv, on the street one day. The latter was ecstatic. He had just succeeded in obtaining visas and immigration certificates for all the rabbis and students of Beis HaTalmud.

When he returned to Kelm, Rabbi Silver immediately rushed to share the news with Rabbi Doniel Movshovitz. The latter was also very excited. He told Rabbi Silver that if the yeshiva merited to reach *Eretz Yisrael*, he would not reestablish it in Jerusalem or Tel Aviv. Rather he would build on Har HaCarmel, for from there Eliyahu had vanquished all the prophets of Baal with the "point of truth."

Ultimately, however, the Talmud Torah did not make its way to *Eretz Yisrael* due to fear that Rebbetzin Nechama Liba was in no condition to survive the arduous journey. *Orchos Chesed*, p. 32.

4. This account became known immediately after the war to the former *talmidim* of

The mass extermination of July 29 and a second on August 22 were carried out exclusively by Lithuanians. The only German participation was that of photographers taking pictures for Goebbel's Museum of the Final Solution. The Germans knew that they could count on the Lithuanian nationalists to act with unrestrained savagery, and they were not disappointed.[5]

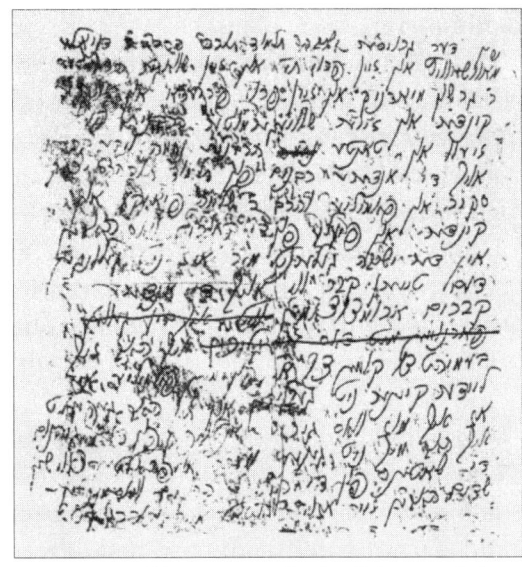

A portion of the testimony of Yaakov Zak, transcribed by R' Dessler

On the night of July 29, the executioners, who were by now all completely drunk, gathered their relatives for a festive meal on beautifully decorated tables in the local high school. Their wives and children came already attired in clothes taken from the Jewish victims that day. In front of their families and a handful of Jewish waiters, the Lithuanian murderers recounted their deeds in gory detail and boasted of how their hands had run red with Jewish blood.[6]

Upon receiving final confirmation of the loss of so many of those most dear to him and the destruction of the entire world in which

---

Kelm, including Rabbi Dessler and Rabbi Eliyahu Lopian. Rabbi Dessler and Rabbi Lopian both told the story on a number of occasions. The exact source, however, is unclear since none of the survivors of Kelm who left written accounts mention the end of the Talmud Torah specifically.

5. *Kelm — Eitz Karus*, p. 64.
6. Ibid., p. 85.
   Yaakov Zak, one of the few Jews from Kelm to survive the War, served at this macabre feast. After the war, he provided one of the most detailed eyewitness accounts of the destruction of Kelm Jewry. Eventually Zak came to *Eretz Yisrael* where Rabbi Dessler visited him and took down his testimony in his own hand.

Chapter Seventeen: Transitions / 255

he was formed, Rabbi Dessler described the tragedy in a letter to his son Reb Nachum Velvel.

He recounts how those who inhabited the Talmud Torah had always assumed that "this holy house would surely stand until the coming of *Mashiach*," for so had its builder, the Alter prayed. But it was not to be: "This small house [whose every corner was filled with truth] did not survive the decree of destruction."

"Why and for what?" had a place filled with so much holiness come to an end, Rabbi Dessler sought to understand. And he gave the only answer possible: "For the sins of the generation.... For such sins even the *Beis HaMikdash* could not stand, so how could this sanctuary in Exile survive?"

Memories flooded over him of *Simchas Torah* more than forty years past, "when our *rebbei'im* went through the gate of the [Talmud Torah] to dance toward the town with all their strength, with such spiritual arousal, singing in powerful voices, "*Ashreinu. Ma tov chelkeinu* — How happy we are! How good is our portion!"

Now those joyous memories were supplanted by other images of spiritual arousal:

> Who can even evaluate what they did then? They strengthened their hearts, and aroused themselves with a great rejoicing that they had been called upon to sanctify G-d's name. And in place of tears, they danced and sang, "*Ma tov chelkeinu...*" How happy are we to be Jews and to be killed because we are Jews. All the way to the killing field.
>
> Why did they have to pay with their lives? was the insistent question. They did not even have the merit of giving their lives to avoid a decree of *shmad* (a decree specifically designed to cause Jews to violate their religion), for the killers "did not seek any profession of false belief from them, but only to kill and destroy them, the believer and the heretic together, and to kill them because they were Jews."

A memorial to the slain Jews of Kelm

Yet, Rabbi Dessler concludes, they had passed the greatest test of all: "the test to discover who is true in his heart, who sanctifies Hashem in his heart as well, and will turn his heart completely toward Hashem, without withholding anything. Who will truly rejoice in the afflictions of death?"

"These men of truth," who passed this awesome test, Rabbi Dessler insists, did not die, "for they had no part in the decree of destruction":

> The outer garment has fallen but the inner still lives — a portion of Hashem from Above.... The general rule is: Everything that has absorbed within itself the truth does not die. Rather it casts off the outer garment and ascends in level towards Heaven. That is what *Chazal* mean: "The righteous are even greater in death than in life" (*Chullin* 7b).[7]

Meeting the Ponevezher Rav

EVEN AFTER THE ARRIVAL OF HIS WIFE AND DAUGHTER IN Gateshead, Rabbi Dessler continued to travel constantly.[8] The travel and the continued responsibility for the financial and spiritual direction of the Kollel proved to be an increasing strain on his health.[9]

Thus when Rabbi Yosef Shlomo Kahaneman, the Ponevezher Rav, first began to discuss with Rabbi Dessler the possibility of his coming to *Eretz Yisrael* to serve as the *Mashgiach* of Ponevezh Yeshiva, Rabbi Dessler did not dismiss the suggestion out of hand.

The two men met for the first time on one of the Ponevezher Rav's fundraising trips to England. Rabbi Dessler obviously made a very powerful impression on the Ponevezher Rav, for immediately after Rabbi Aba Grosbard, the *Mashgiach* in Ponevezh Yeshiva, passed away in *Av* of 1946, Rabbi Kahaneman offered the position to Rabbi Dessler.

Rabbi Dessler wrote to Solomon Sassoon just after Rosh Hashanah discussing the offer. On the one hand, he writes, he cannot consider leaving the Kollel without direction. On the other

---

7. *Michtav Me'Eliyahu*, Vol. III, 346-48.
8. Rabbi Bezalel Rakov, *rav* of Gateshead.
9. Rabbi Shmuel Schecter.

Rebbetzin Bluma Dessler

hand, he wonders whether there might not be someone capable of taking over his responsibilities.

He describes how he cast the *Goral HaGra* to determine what course to follow. The *Goral HaGra* came out on Yosef's instructions to his brothers after he has revealed himself, "Hurry — go up to my father ...." (*Bereishis* 45:9). Rashi explains that the word "go up" specifically refers to *Eretz Yisrael*, which is higher than all other lands.

Nevertheless, Rabbi Dessler did not interpret this verse as a directive to accept the Ponevezher Rav's offer. As he noted to Rabbi Sassoon, the *aliyah* (going up) that Yosef referred to was only a temporary one in preparation for Yaakov and his entire family descending to Egypt. He did, however, understand the *Goral HaGra* as a hint that he should at least visit *Eretz Yisrael,* and he began making plans with Rabbi Sassoon to travel together. At the same time, he expressed a determination not to travel at Rabbi Kahaneman's expense so as not to be obligated in any way prior to reaching some decision on the latter's offer.

As matters developed, the negotiations that preceded Rabbi Dessler's coming to Ponevezh Yeshiva were long and complicated. Not until after Pesach of 1949 would Rabbi Dessler finally settle in Bnei Brak. From the beginning, Rabbi Kahaneman was eager for Rabbi Dessler to sever his ties with Gateshead and to come to live in *Eretz Yisrael* on a permanent basis. Rabbi Dessler, however, knew that the Kollel was still dependent upon him and would not consider any step that might endanger an institution into which he had poured his life blood.

The Ponevezher Rav also wanted Rabbi Dessler to supervise the *bachurim* in the yeshiva on an individual basis, something Rabbi Dessler refused to do. He would agree only to give *sichos* in *aggadata* and *hashkafah*.

As a consequence of Rabbi Dessler's refusal to fill the classical role of *mashgiach*, the Ponevezher Rav also considered offering the position to Rabbi Yechezkel Levenstein, who was then the *Mashgiach* of Mirrer Yeshiva in Brooklyn, and who was much more of the traditional type of *mashgiach*. Rabbi Kahaneman confided to some of the *bachurim* who were close to him that in actuality the yeshiva needed both Rabbi Dessler and Rabbi Levenstein, but that it would be impossible for the two such luminaries to function at the same time in one yeshiva.[10]

Though the negotiations between Rabbi Dessler and the Ponevezher Rav would prove arduous, there was much drawing the two men together. Both had been saved by Divine Providence from the fire, and both were driven by a single-minded dedication to rebuilding the citadels of Torah. Neither would give in to the prevailing pessimism that all had been lost.

Starting with only six *bachurim* in 1944, the Ponevezher Rav nevertheless envisioned a yeshiva with 1,200 *talmidim*. He did not have any money to build such a yeshiva — nor were there even half that number of serious yeshiva students in all of *Eretz Yisrael* in those days. But at least he could build a stairway up to the entrance big enough to one day accommodate so many *yeshiva bachurim*. And that is what he did.

Those with whom the Ponevezher Rav shared his vision considered him a hopeless dreamer. Yet in the judgment of Rabbi Dov Wein, one of the early *talmidim* in Ponevezh and a prominent rosh yeshiva today, if it were not for the Ponevezher Rav's vision, the remarkable rebirth of Torah learning in *Eretz Yisrael* would never have come to pass, and the Torah world would have been confined to a few isolated pockets of the old *yishuv*.

Part of the Ponevezher Rav's vision was that he wanted only the top people in their respective fields for his yeshiva. He opened the Yeshiva with Rabbi Shmuel Rozovsky and Rabbi Dovid Povarsky as

---

10. Rabbi Yaakov Edelstein, one of the original six *bachurim* in Ponevezh Yeshiva.
   The Ponevezher Rav's remark proved prophetic, and indeed Rabbi Levenstein succeeded Rabbi Dessler as *Mashgiach* after the latter's *petirah* in the winter of 1953.

roshei yeshiva, and as soon as the opportunity presented itself added Rabbi Eliezer Menachem Shach as a third *rosh yeshiva*.

And he was equally determined that Rabbi Dessler come to Bnei Brak as the *Mashgiach*. When a group from the Gateshead Kollel protested his efforts to lure Rabbi Dessler away from Gateshead, he replied, "Do you know who Rabbi Dessler is? He is Reb Chaim in *Aggadata*. There are 400 *bachurim* in Ponevezh waiting to hear him."[11]

THE PONEVEZHER RAV WAS UNABLE TO PERSUADE RABBI Dessler to leave Gateshead permanently for Bnei Brak, but Rabbi Dessler did agree to come to *Eretz Yisrael* for *Elul* of 1947. Rebbetzin Dessler and his daughter Hennie were in Cleveland staying with Reb Nachum Velvel Dessler and his family, and it was therefore easier for Rabbi Dessler to travel to *Eretz Yisrael* than it otherwise would have been. In 1947, six weeks after Reuven Dov's birth, Rebbetzin Dessler had come to Cleveland with Hennie and spent close to a year in the home of Nachum Velvel and Miriam. Seeing Reuven Dov grow, and hearing him speak, was a source of great enjoyment and *nachas* to her.

First Visit to Eretz Yisrael

From the moment he set foot on shore, Rabbi Dessler was enraptured by *Eretz Yisrael*. Shortly after his arrival, his first cousin Rabbi Simcha Zissel Dessler asked him how he could have such a powerful reaction without having traveled in the country. Rabbi Dessler replied that his impression had nothing to do with physical vistas but with the

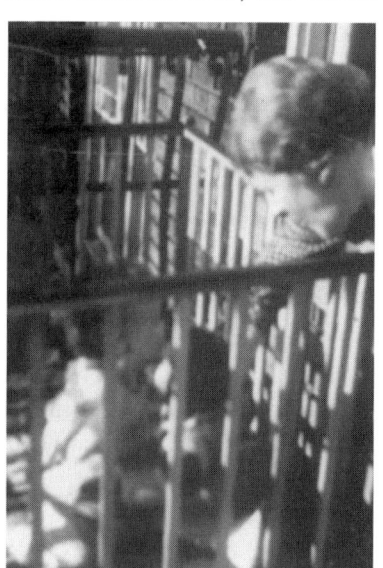

Rebbetzin Dessler with her grandson Reuven Dov

---

11. Rabbi Naftoli Friedler.
Ever the visionary, the Ponevezher Rav saw the *beis medrash* as if it were already filled with the 400 *bachurim* he knew would one day arrive. It is doubtful that the number of Ponevezh *talmidim* ever exceeded 200 in Rabbi Dessler's lifetime.

level of insight he found himself able to achieve. Difficulties in understanding that would have taken him weeks to achieve in *chutz l'aretz,* he said, required only a few hours in *Eretz Yisrael.*[12]

Rabbi Shammai Zahn, who came to Ponevezh very soon after Rabbi Dessler's arrival on a permanent basis in 1949, even noticed a change in his physical appearance in *Eretz Yisrael*. Rabbi Dessler was short, but in Ponevezh, he stood straighter, and seemed to Rabbi Zahn "twice as tall." Rabbi Zahn saw another change as well. In Gateshead Kollel, there had been little rhetorical flourish to his *sichos*. Before two hundred students in the Ponevezh *beis medrash*, however, Rabbi Dessler was transformed into an orator of rare power.

In later years, Rabbi Dessler told his students that the Torah he taught in *Eretz Yisrael* was deeper than that he had taught in *chutz l'aretz*. Even at our lowly spiritual level, he said, the spiritual influence of *Eretz Yisrael* is palpable. Not only were his insights deeper, he also found it easier to arouse his heart through *mussar* study.[13]

Shortly after settling in Bnei Brak, he wrote to his daughter and son-in-law, "I feel here the truth of the words of Rabbi Yehudah HaLevi, 'The air of your land is the air of holiness'…. True, there are places even here where the holiness is hidden and is not easily discovered. But in the places of Torah, the *kedushah* (holiness) can be sensed completely…. Here we are free of the nations, of their approach to life and *weltanshauung,* free of their stupidities…. The holiness causes rejoicing without end."[14]

To his beloved student Aryeh Carmell, he wrote that every Jew should at least come to see the land that Hashem chose for the Jewish people and for which we always longed. At the same time, he warned Rabbi Carmell that if he wanted to live in *Eretz Yisrael* he should not come first for a trial period. Those who do so, Rabbi Dessler said, do not succeed. "Only those who come determined to stay without any calculations and questions, with *mesiras nefesh* and ready to suffer, remain."

---

12. He later told his daughter-in-law Miriam Dessler how moved he was to find streets names after *gedolei Yisrael* throughout the generations.
13. Rabbi Chaim Friedlander.
14. *Michtav Me'Eliyahu,* Vol. V, pp. 519-20.

Prior to his arrival in Ponevezh, one of the *bachurim* went around telling everyone that he would be very strict and that "even the best would not be good enough for him." Yet the *bachurim* soon found out that he was the warmest and gentlest of men.[15] Indeed, there were those who complained to the *Chazon Ish* that he was not strict enough. The *Chazon Ish* replied, "*M'shichah* (drawing something towards one) is a stronger *kinyan* (means of acquisition) than *chazakah* (showing one's control over an object)."[16]

After his first meeting with Rabbi Dessler in *Eretz Yisrael*,[17] the *Chazon Ish* commented, "Kelm is not a rushing river. Rather it is a stream that stands in its place, a spring which is always renewing its waters."[18] That meeting was the beginning of what developed into a very close relationship between Rabbi Dessler and the *Chazon Ish*.

The *Chazon Ish* once described Rabbi Dessler as the last person to understand the *tochen* (inner content) of *mussar* and not just its *chitzonius* (superficial appearance).[19] Another time he told someone who said he was looking for a *mashgiach* like Rabbi Dessler, "Many places need a Rabbi Dessler, but not many Rabbi Desslers are born."[20]

For his part, Rabbi Dessler was in awe of the *Chazon Ish*.[21] On his return to England, after his initial

R' Dessler with the Chazon Ish

---

15. Rabbi Meyer Munk.
16. Rabbi Simcha Zissel Dessler.
17. It is possible that Rabbi Dessler had previously met the *Chazon Ish* on one of his visits to Vilna to see Rabbi Chaim Ozer Grodzenski.
18. Rabbi Shraga Grosbard, the longtime head of Chinuch Atzmai in *Eretz Yisrael*.
19. Rabbi Shalom Ulman.
20. Rabbi Naftoli Nebenzahl.
21. Rabbi Nachum Velvel Dessler.

At Yeshivas Hasharon in Hertzlia in 1953. From left: R' Shmuel Rozovsky, R' Yaakov Halperin (founder of Zichron Meir), the Chazon Ish, R' Dessler

three-month stay in *Eretz Yisrael*, he referred to the *Chazon Ish* as "the *Urim V'Tumim*."[22]

At one point, Rabbi Sassoon wrote to Rabbi Dessler seeking his opinion of the suitability of a certain rabbi for a particular position. Rabbi Dessler had reservations, but when he presented the matter to the *Chazon Ish*, the *Chazon Ish* noted that even if the rabbi in question was not an outstanding scholar, he was certainly the best candidate available for the position. Writing back to Rabbi Sassoon, Rabbi Dessler could not contain his admiration for the depth of the *Chazon Ish's* insight. "How wondrous is this matter and how incumbent is it upon us to ask the *gadol hador*," he wrote, "for how greatly would I have erred but for him."

One time the *Chazon Ish* told Rabbi Dessler that he should discuss the wonders of the Creation more in his lectures.[23]

Rabbi Dessler's impact on Ponevezh Yeshiva was immediate. In his very first public *shmuess* he shocked his listeners by discussing the sin of *Adam HaRishon*, as elucidated by Reb Tzadok HaKohen of

---

22. Rabbi Dov Sternbuch.

23. For an example of how Rabbi Dessler used his scientific knowledge in his *shmuessen* see *Michtav Me'Eliyahu*, Vol. III, p. 76, describing the production of rainfall.

Lublin.²⁴ The topic and his approach were completely new for his audience. At that time, the standard yeshiva *shmuess* consisted primarily of exhortations concerning one's obligations.²⁵

Dayan Nissim Karelitz describes Rabbi Dessler as having made nothing less than a "revolution" in the understanding of *Aggadata*.²⁶ He made basic concepts of *emunah* — e.g., *Mashiach, Olam Haba* — real in a way they never had been before, remembers Rabbi Meyer Munk, who was only 17 at the time. He revealed a depth of meaning of the words of *Chazal* that was available nowhere else in *Eretz Yisrael* at that time.²⁷

The most advanced students in the yeshiva became very attached to him, and drank thirstily of his Torah. The leader of this *chabura* (study group) was Rabbi Chaim Friedlander, who was already 23 years old when Rabbi Dessler arrived. Rabbi Friedlander had previously begun

A group of young men from Ponevezh, Purim 1947. Right to Left: Chaim Friedlander, Shlomo Berman, Baruch Dov Povarsky, unknown, Shlomo Noach Kroll, Meir Yakobovitz, Yaakov Edelstein

---

24. Rabbi Naftoli Nebenzahl.
25. Rabbi Dovid Tzvi Hillman, one of the first students in Ponevezh Yeshiva.
26. Ibid.
27. Rabbi Moshe Shapiro.

to delve on his own into many of the areas in which Rabbi Dessler would subsequently light the way. Among the others in the group were Rabbi Shimshon Harari,[28] Rabbi Simcha Kessler, and two brothers, Rabbi Gershon Edelstein and Rabbi Yaakov Edelstein.

At the end of Rabbi Dessler's three-month stay in Ponevezh, the *chabura*, with Rabbi Friedlander doing most of the speaking, approached Rabbi Dessler and told him that they were his *talmidim* and as such must insist on receiving regular *sichos* from him in England. Rabbi Dessler replied that his schedule in England allowed him nary a free minute, but he undertook to stay up one night a week to write over one of his lectures for them.

Return to England

UPON RETURNING TO GATESHEAD IN LATE 1947 FROM PONEVEZH, Rabbi Dessler was still not convinced that it was possible for him to move permanently to *Eretz Yisrael*. No replacement to take over any of his duties in the Kollel had yet presented himself.

Around that time he had a dream in which the *Ba'al HaTanya* appeared to him and repeated the verse: המושל תעלה עליך מקומך אל תנח אם רוח — "If the spirit of the ruler rises against you, do not abandon your place" (*Koheles* 10:4). The ruler in this case could easily have been understood as the Ponevezher Rav and Rabbi Dessler's place as Gateshead.

Rabbi Dessler reassured the members of the Kollel that even though the Ponevezher Rav was eager for him to move permanently to *Eretz Yisrael* and cut all his ties with England, he would never agree to do so.

Rabbi Dessler did not, however, return to England for long. Rebbetzin Dessler and Hennie were still with Reb Nachum Velvel and family in

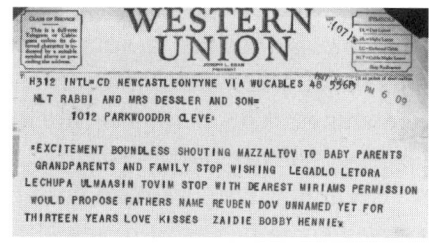

Congratulations upon the birth of Reuven Dov

---

28. After the *petirah* of Rabbi Aba Grosbard in *Av* of 1946, Rabbi Harari and Rabbi Friedlander took on unofficial responsibility for the supervision of the younger *bachurim*, even though both were still unmarried.

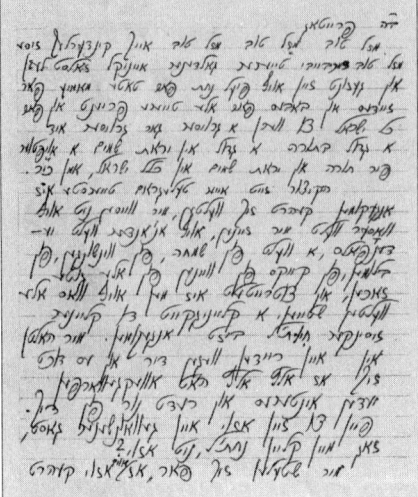 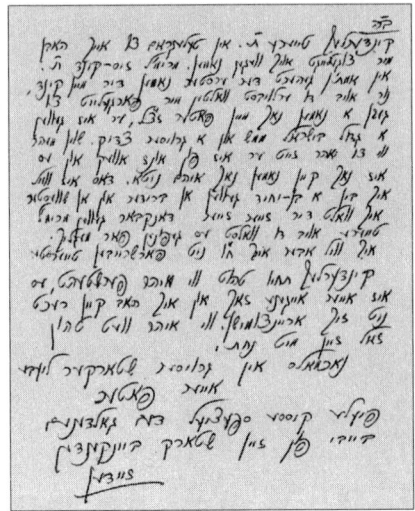

R' Dessler's letter upon the birth of Reuven Dov   Letter to R' Nachum Velvel and Miriam asking that they name their son Reuven Dov

Cleveland, and he was eager to join them and to see his son Reb Nachum Velvel again. Reb Nachum Velvel was a young *yeshiva bachur* of 18 when Rabbi Dessler last saw him, nearly nine years earlier. Now he was a married man heading a major Torah institution in Cleveland. Rabbi Dessler had never met his daughter-in-law nor his infant grandson, who had been named Reuven Dov at Rabbi Dessler's request.

Rabbi Dessler arrived in America during *Shevat* of 1948. At customs, he was asked whether he had anything to declare. He replied that he was bringing a set of rubber blocks for his grandson. The customs authorities assumed that anyone who declared rubber blocks must be carrying contraband. They spent the next two hours searching all his belongings before concluding that he was just an exceptionally honest person.[29]

Upon his joyful reunion with his son in New York, Rabbi Dessler presented Reb Nachum Velvel with a copy of *Givas Shaul*, which was bound together with *Teshuvos HaRif*, one of the few *sefarim* returned to the Dessler family by the Bolsheviks after they confiscated the entire family library. The work was especially dear to Rabbi

---

29. Rabbi Nachum Velvel Dessler.

Dessler because the Czarist censors had removed the last two chapters of the work, and his stepmother — "my mother and teacher" — had copied them into this volume from an old copy.[30]

One of Rabbi Dessler's first questions for his son was: Who had helped him during the many years that he had been all alone in America? Reb Nachum Velvel mentioned Reb Shraga Feivel Mendlowitz, the *menahel* of Mesivta Torah Vodaath, where he had learned upon arriving in America, and Rabbi Shlomo Heiman, the late Rosh Yeshiva. He also told his father that Rabbi Eliezer Silver, *rav* of Cincinnati and head of both Agudath Israel of America and Agudas HaRabbonim, had extended himself on his behalf. Rabbi Silver had been a close *talmid* of Rabbi Chaim Ozer Grodzenski, and when he heard that a great-nephew of Reb Chaim Ozer was in America, he did everything he could for the young man.

Rabbi Dessler immediately told his son, "We must thank him."

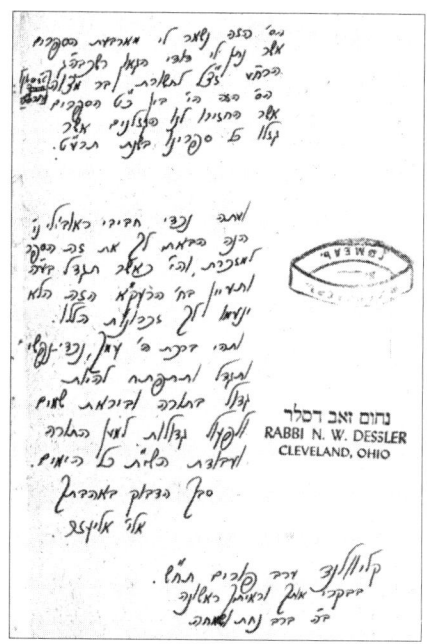

R' Dessler's inscription in a Chiddushei R' Akiva Eiger, presented to his infant grandson Reuven Dov when they first met

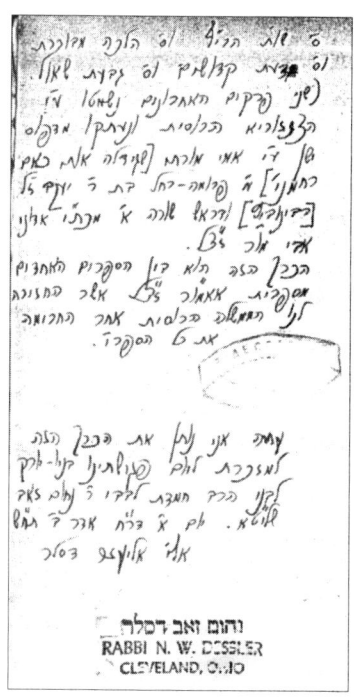

The inscription in Sefer Givas Shaul

---

30. *Michtav Me'Eliyahu*, Vol. V, p. 534.

Chapter Seventeen: Transitions / 267

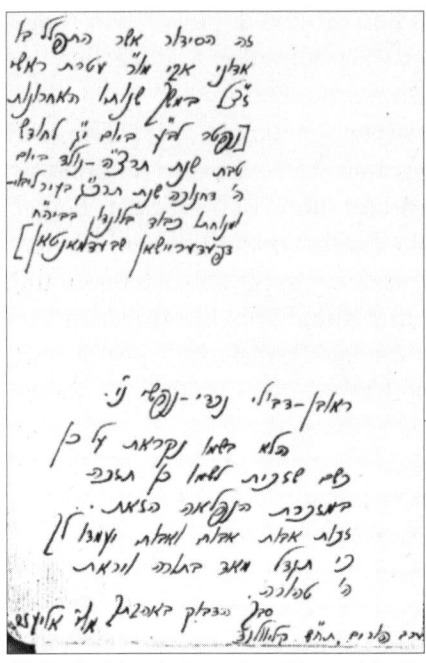

R' Dessler's inscription in the siddur used by his father, which he presented to his infant grandson Reuven Dov

Hearing that, Reb Nachum Velvel took his address book from his pocket and gave his father Rabbi Silver's address and telephone number. Rabbi Dessler, however, would consider nothing less than a personal expression of *hakaros hatov*, and insisted that Reb Nachum Velvel accompany him by train to Cincinnati, a trip of approximately nine hours.

The Desslers arrived in Cincinnati around 5 a.m. in the morning and went straight to Rabbi Silver's house. They sat patiently on the front porch until Rabbi Silver came out on his way to *davening*. Reb Nochum Velvel introduced his father, and the three proceeded to shul. After *davening*, Rabbi Silver invited his guests back to his house for breakfast.

"So, Rabbi Dessler, what brings you to Cincinnati?" Rabbi Silver asked his guest. Rabbi Dessler told him that he had come for no other reason than to express his great appreciation for all the kindness that Rabbi Silver had shown his son. Rabbi Silver mulled over this response for a few more minutes before asking again, "*Nu*, Rabbi Dessler what really brings you to Cincinnati?"

Again Rabbi Dessler insisted that he knew nothing of Cincinnati and had come for only one purpose: to express his *hakaros hatov* in person. For several minutes the conversation went off in other directions, until Rabbi Silver could no longer contain himself and asked again, "Rabbi Dessler, what can I do for you?" When Rabbi Dessler repeated for the third time that he had not come to seek anything from Rabbi Silver, but only to convey his gratitude in person, Reb

Leizer finally gave up and muttered, "This must be *mussar*."

The visit to America turned out to be an especially joyous one for Rabbi Dessler. Not only did he meet his daughter-in-law Miriam and grandson Reuven Dov for the first time, his daughter Hennie became engaged to Rabbi Yehoshua Geldzahler, one of the outstanding members of the Kollel of Beis Medrash Elyon, then the premier Kollel in America.[31]

Rabbi Dessler took particular delight in the fact that his new son-in-law was well versed in concepts of *chassidus* and *kabbalah*. Rabbi Dessler and Rabbi Geldzahler immediately commenced an extensive correspondence in these areas.[32]

Reuven Dov Dessler about the time R' Dessler first saw him

Rabbi Dessler returned to England just after Pesach, which the whole family spent together in Cleveland. It was truly a most joyous occasion for the family to once again be together for *Yom Tov*. Back in England, Rabbi Dessler continued to be torn with respect to the future. It was clear to him that he was still needed in some capacity in the Kollel. By *Elul* of 1948, however, he was writing to his *talmidim* in Ponevezh, "I hope that Hashem will grant me the merit of coming to live in *Eretz Yisrael* on a permanent basis." He still added pointedly that the matter was contingent upon his duties in the Kollel.[33]

The group of his close *talmidim* in Ponevezh were already quite dear to him. For the entire year and a half from his departure from

---

31. Rabbi Geldzahler was the rosh yeshiva of Yeshiva Ohr Yisroel in Queens, New York for over forty years and is the author of the five-volume work on *Seder Kodshim*, *Kodshei Yehoshua*.
32. Some of that correspondence has been published in Volume V of *Michtav Me'Eliyahu*.
33. *Michtav Me'Eliyahu*, Vol. V, p. 531.

Chapter Seventeen: Transitions / 269

Ponevezh until his return after Purim of 1949, he was in constant contact with them. He sent his *sichos* back to the *chabura* on a regular basis, as he had promised.

As soon as a letter with his *divrei Torah* arrived in Ponevezh, Rabbi Chaim Friedlander would convene the *chabura*, and they would sit down to study the *ma'amar* with study partners. After they finished studying Rabbi Dessler's words, the group would gather together and discuss any issues that they felt required further clarification. Rabbi Friedlander would write down all the questions that the group could not resolve by itself and send them to Rabbi Dessler for his response.[34]

Rabbi Yehoshua Sklar, a member of the *chabura*, recalls how they awaited Rabbi Dessler's letters with *kilyon einayim* (eyes filled with longing). When each pair of study partners had finished going over every word of Rabbi Dessler's letter, he says, they knew it like they knew a *sugya* in *Shnayim Ochzin*.[35]

At least one response of Rabbi Dessler to questions from the group has been printed. He had written to the *chabura* that "prayer reaches higher than we can perceive," and his students asked what was the benefit of something that reaches beyond our level of attainment. Rabbi Dessler replied that there are attainments of the heart and those of the mind, and the former can be higher than the latter. Thus we can have no intellectual knowledge of Hashem because our thoughts are inevitably in terms of forms. Nevertheless there is an attaining of the heart through *deveikus* (cleaving) to Hashem. Prayer at its highest level can be such an act of cleaving. Intellectually we can know only that Hashem exists and that He controls the world, but in prayer we can turn towards His essence.

He also explained how it is possible to pray for help in our service of Hashem and how that service can be of merit even if it depends on Divine assistance and not on the unfettered exercise of one's free will. One aspect of *siyata d'Shamaya*, he writes, is that when we reach a certain level of insight we should not find ourselves confronted by

---

34. Rabbi Yaakov Edelstein.

35. The first chapter in *Bava Metzia* and one of the most frequently learned chapters in yeshivos.

too many obstacles in our efforts to integrate that insight into our lives. "Prayer," Rabbi Dessler writes, "has the power to remove the obstacles even before we reach them."[36] The closeness of the bond that Rabbi Dessler had formed with his *talmidim* in Ponevezh is evident in the many letters that he wrote from England and America. The separation was particularly painful during Israel's War of Independence in 1948. "Since the troubles started there has not been a single night that I did not wake up in confusion from some nightmare," he writes.[37] In his nervous agitation over the fate of his students, he begged them to write as frequently as possible.[38]

Rabbi Dessler felt unworthy of writing words of *chizuk* while "far away and standing on the outside," and when he himself was beset by fears. Nonetheless his "feverish worry" over both the spiritual and physical state of his *talmidim* compelled him to write those things which he felt were absolutely clear. All the trials that the Jewish people had so recently witnessed and were again witnessing, he insisted, are those of *Ikvasa D'Mashicha* and must be recognized as such. "Do we think that the slaughter and destruction was for nothing? Is there no power in our millions of sacrifices to make an impression and bring about an improvement? Anyone who says it was mere happenstance is a *kofer* (a denier)...."[39]

But even as we recognize the Divine hand in the destruction, so must we recognize Hashem's power to change our situation from one extreme to another in an instant, he told his *talmidim*. Hadn't the Jews of *Eretz Yisrael* seen that during the war when they were trapped between two German armies? And then suddenly came the German defeats at El Alamein and in the Caucasus Mountains.

---

36. *Michtav Me'Eliyahu*, Vol. V, pp. 528-29.

37. Ibid, p. 527.

38. Ibid., Vol. IV, p. 349.

39. See Ibid., Vol. II, pp. 203-4 (*Strive for Truth*, Vol. II, p. 305), where Rabbi Dessler demonstrates how impossible it is to attribute the Nazis' rise to chance:

> It is unheard of — or was unheard of until our time — that a group of nameless and uneducated layabouts, meeting by chance in some obscure beer cellar, should suddenly turn out — without exception — to be capable of governing a nation and in fact, in a relatively short time, to actually rule vast nations.... We have seen how the Haman of our time (may his memory be accursed) and his gang ... overnight became outstandingly capable rulers with uncanny efficiency for evil.

In the birth of the State of Israel, he also saw Divine Providence. At a time in which hatred for the Jew was still rampant everywhere in the world, the nations of the world nevertheless said, "Let us place Israel in its Holy Land." "Is that the natural course?" he asked his students.[40]

Back to America

THE DESSLERS RETURNED ONCE AGAIN TO AMERICA AFTER THE *Yamim Noraim* of 1948 for Hennie's *chasunah* (wedding). In a letter to his future son-in-law, Rabbi Dessler describes how he had been torn between the desire to spend the *Yamim Noraim* together with his son in Cleveland, which would have allowed for moving up the date of the wedding, and the feeling of responsibility to the Kollel in Gateshead.

In the end, no decision was necessary because Rabbi Dessler was unable to obtain tickets prior to the holidays. He took this as a sign from Heaven that "even the small benefit to the community from my being here has pushed away any private considerations."[41]

Here Rabbi Dessler returned to one of his recurring themes: the necessity for each person to attach himself to the community. "If a person learns to place himself within the *Klal* completely," he wrote to Rabbi Geldzahler, "he will be forced to act for the benefit of the *Klal*." That compulsion, he felt, was the greatest possible protection against the wiles of the *yetzer hara*, which always attacks the individual through his selfish desires.[42]

After the Geldzahlers' marriage just before Chanukah, Rabbi Dessler neither returned immediately to England nor did he make a fi-

---

40. *Michtav Me'Eliyahu*, Vol. III, pp. 350-51.

See also ibid., Vol. IV, pp. 348-49. In that letter Rabbi Dessler writes to his students in Ponevezh: "Certainly everyone must see the miracles that Hashem is doing for us now, especially in *Eretz Yisrael*. Things are far from ordinary."

Virtually all the *gedolim* of Rabbi Dessler's day saw the creation of the State of Israel as, in the Brisker Rav's words, "a smile from Heaven," an opportunity to be seized if we were only worthy.

But see ibid., Vol. III, pp. 217-18, in which Rabbi Dessler described the situation in *Eretz Yisrael*, in a 1951 talk in Ponevezh Yeshiva, as "the last test of *Galus* (Exile), the hardest test ever …."

41. Ibid., Vol. V, p. 515.
42. Ibid., Vol. IV, p. 351.

nal decision to accept the position in Ponevezh. Rather, he remained in America until just before Purim of 1949. That delay suggests that the Ponevezher Rav had not yet fully agreed to his conditions for coming to Ponevezh, and thus Rabbi Dessler had made no final decision about his future. Perhaps he even considered remaining in America, where his children, from whom he had been separated for so long, were living.

R' Dessler with R' Yisrael Ehrentreu

While in America, Rabbi Dessler responded affirmatively to an appeal from Rabbi Avraham Kalmanowitz that he teach a group of boys recently arrived at Mirrer Yeshiva from Morocco. Rabbi Dessler's fluent Hebrew made him uniquely suited to communicating with this group of boys. During this period, he also gave *shmuessen* in Telshe Yeshiva in Cleveland, Beis Medrash Elyon in Monsey, and in Lakewood that are still remembered today by those who were present.

Yet for all his monumental achievements in England, Rabbi Dessler was far from a household name in America. Only with the rapid expansion of the yeshiva world in the '60s and '70s and the posthumous publication of *Michtav Me'Eliyahu* would Rabbi Dessler's fame spread throughout the Orthodox world.

Leaving Gateshead

SHORTLY AFTER HIS RETURN TO GATESHEAD BEFORE PURIM OF 1949, Rabbi Dessler informed the members of the Kollel that he had decided to accept the Ponevezher Rav's offer. Though the Ponevezher Rav had agreed to his stipulation that he be allowed to return to Gateshead twice a year, most of his time would henceforth be spent in *Eretz Yisrael*.⁴³ Rabbi Dessler's announcement of his imminent departure occasioned crying in the Kollel, especially among the younger members, for whom the eagerness to have Rabbi Dessler as a spiritual guide had been one of the primary attractions of the Kollel.⁴⁴

Rabbi Dessler kept his promise to maintain his ties with Gateshead and to return frequently. When he did, there was a stiff competition among those eager to host him. Rabbi Mordecai Miller, Rabbi Moshe Schwab, and Rabbi Moshe Aryeh Bamberger all vied for the right to host him. In support of his position, Rabbi Miller argued that the other two had each learned under great men — Rabbi Schwab in Kaminetz and Rabbi Bamberger in Slabodka — but for him Rabbi Dessler was everything. "I'm in the position of a child competing with his uncles to host his own father," Rabbi Miller told them.

Rabbi Schwab accepted this argument, but Rabbi Bamberger was not so easily convinced. "I could forgo the pleasure of Rabbi Dessler's company," Rabbi Bamberger conceded, "but I cannot simply renounce the spiritual growth that comes from being in his presence." In the end, however, Rabbi Dessler stayed with Rabbi Miller.

Even after his departure, Rabbi Dessler continued to be consulted on important issues concerning the Kollel and the other institutions in whose formation he had played such a crucial role. One such issue involved a plan formulated by Mr. Kohn to open a teachers' seminary for young men in Gateshead that would offer an external college degree from a nearby university.

Rabbi Nachman Landynski, the Rosh Yeshiva, had already started a small teachers' seminary for young men interested in pursuing careers in Jewish education. He hoped thereby to improve the low standard of Jewish education that then prevailed throughout England. Mr. Kohn's innovation, after Rabbi Landynski's departure to America, was to add the possibility of earning a college degree at

---

43. The Ponevezher Rav also accepted Rabbi Dessler's condition that he not be asked to supervise individual *bachurim*.
44. Rabbi Bezalel Rakov.

the same time. He hoped to thereby increase the stature of those involved in Jewish education.

When Mr. Kohn broached the subject with Rabbi Dessler, however, the latter strongly opposed his plan. Rabbi Dessler acknowledged that the plan could be "both a *Kiddush Hashem* and the salvation of *nefashos* [for those boys who would in any event have attended university]" but feared the medicine would ultimately do more harm that the disease it sought to cure. Rabbi Dessler's primary objection was that the presence of such a seminary in Gateshead would weaken the yeshiva by providing an incentive for many boys to terminate their studies prematurely.

He made clear that he entertained no doubts that the new institution would be run with the purest *yiras Shamayim* (Fear of Heaven). Indeed that was precisely the problem: "Won't it be a terrible temptation when the yeshiva students see the first graduating class of the new institution with their degrees, their *yiras Shamayim*, and even *semichah* (rabbinical ordination)?" The danger of destroying a large yeshiva and a large Kollel together was simply too great in Rabbi Dessler's opinion.

Rabbi Dessler styled the issue as a choice between the worldview of Frankfurt and that of the Lithuanian yeshiva world. He made his adherence to the latter view absolutely clear. He admitted that adherents of the *Torah Im Derech Eretz* philosophy of Frankfurt had remained staunch in their *mitzvah* observance, even after pursuing university studies. But making university studies a desideratum, he argued, had resulted in a rapid depletion of the number of *talmidei chachamim*.

The approach of the Lithuanian yeshivos, by contrast, was to emphasize the exclusive goal of producing *gedolei Torah* and *yirei Shamayim*. And that could only be done by students concentrating all their intellectual efforts on Torah study. Those who headed the Lithuanian yeshivos knew very well that there would be spiritual casualties from their approach, but they viewed that as a price that had to be paid. "They did what they could for those who could not remain *bnei Torah*, but not at the cost of having others follow after them," Rabbi Dessler wrote. He explained that they followed the rule of the Rambam that the first priority must be to produce great scholars, even though others might suffer in the process.[45]

Mr. Kohn was fully prepared to accept Rabbi Dessler's opinion, but he now had an additional problem. The program had already begun, and he felt that he had a commitment to those who had already enrolled. Rabbi Dessler consulted with both the Ponevezher Rav and the *Chazon Ish*. "It is not my practice to take [the *Chazon Ish's*] time with simple matters," Rabbi Dessler wrote, but he was unwilling to *pasken* questions with financial implications.

The *Chazon Ish*, however, fully concurred with Rabbi Dessler that there should be no mixture of university and Torah studies. He told Rabbi Dessler that Mr. Kohn should simply tell those already in the program that he was forced to terminate the program based upon the *psak* from *Eretz Yisrael*.

Mr. Kohn fully accepted the decision of the *Chazon Ish*, showing in the process the exceptional *erlichkeit* that had drawn Rabbi Dessler to him in the first place. "The *gadol hador* (the great man of our generation) ruled against our program, and therefore our decision was also clear," he said. But he confided to his diary:

> I was convinced that the program was necessary and would increase *k'vod Shamayim*. I thought it was "right" but the *gedolim* said it was "left." What can I do? It says in the Torah one must accept what the *chachamim* say even if they tell you that what is right in your eyes is left....
>
> By listening to the *chachamim* I feel that I'm losing out on a one-time opportunity. I'm forgoing a matter in which I had invested a great deal of my *avodas hakodesh* (holy work). Naturally, it is extremely difficult for me to annul my will before their wisdom.

But annul his will, Mr. Kohn did. And with love. In the end, he found consolation in the fact that the greatest Torah scholar of the generation had considered his question worthy of his consideration, and that he had the "merit" of accepting his determination.

---

45. Ibid., Vol. III, pp. 355-57.

With that realization, his acceptance became an "acceptance with love."

Just before Rabbi Dessler left Gateshead, his father came to him in a dream. In the dream, his father told him, "They are satisfied with you here [in *Gan Eden*]."

The Heavenly Court had good cause for that satisfaction. In little more than seven years, Rabbi Dessler had launched from Gateshead a revolution in Torah life in England and the rest of Western Europe. And similarly, his arrival in Ponevezh Yeshiva would mark the beginning of a new stage of the growth of Torah in *Eretz Yisrael*.

Chapter 18

The Power of His Word

FROM THE TIME HE ARRIVED IN PONEVEZH YESHIVA, Rabbi Dessler set the tone in the yeshiva, much as Rabbi Yerucham Levovitz, the Mirrer *Mashgiach*, was the dominant figure in the pre-war Mirrer Yeshiva.

RABBI DESSLER'S GREATEST IMPACT IN PONEVEZH YESHIVA WAS through his thrice-weekly *sichos*. He spoke every Wednesday night,

A Speaker Nonpareil
leil Shabbos, and again on *Motzaei Shabbos*. The Shabbos and *Motzaei Shabbos* talks were often a continuation of the theme of Wednesday night, though on Shabbos, when there were far fewer in attendance from outside Ponevezh, he was far more likely to include a specific *mussar* message concerning the yeshiva.[1] Initially, each talk lasted approximately 45 minutes, but that soon expanded to an hour or more.[2]

---

1. Rabbi Shalom Ulman, who lived in Rabbi Dessler's home after the passing of Rebbetzin Dessler.
2. Rabbi Meyer Munk.

The talks became major intellectual events for the still nascent yeshiva world in *Eretz Yisrael*. Every Wednesday night, the hill surrounding Ponevezh Yeshiva was filled with taxis from Tel Aviv and even Jerusalem.[3] The *Chazon Ish* himself sent somebody to the *sichos* to report back what Rabbi Dessler had said.[4] His nephew Rabbi Chaim Shaul Karelitz used to come on Wednesday night. "A *shmuess* from Rabbi Dessler is *Olam Haba* (the World to Come)," he would say.[5]

Each talk was the product of meticulous preparation. Rabbi Dessler told students that he prepared between eight and ten hours for every talk. Most of that time was spent deciding precisely how to present the main ideas. Ideas that might take Rabbi Dessler less than a minute to summarize could take forty-five minutes to develop in the course of the talk.[6]

Every detail of the delivery was carefully considered in advance. Speaking once in Beis Medrash Elyon in Monsey, Rabbi Dessler used a piston engine as a metaphor for the way that actions generate reactions in the opposite direction. The natural tendency of any speaker demonstrating the thrust of a piston engine is to thrust his hand outward. Rabbi Dessler, however, pulled his hand towards him so that the outward thrust was seen from the perspective of his audience.[7]

In addition to the time spent on the technical presentation of his ideas, Rabbi Dessler prepared and tested himself to ensure he was on a sufficient spiritual level to speak on elevated matters. He once told Rabbi Yaakov Edelstein that because he was not learning Torah all day, it took him at least twelve hours of preparation to feel worthy to address an audience of *bnei Torah*.

Rabbi Dessler was a masterful speaker, and each talk was a carefully constructed tour de force. "As a speaker, he was without

---

3. Rabbi Berel Povarsky.
4. Rabbi Moshe Shapiro.
5. Rabbi Naftoli Nebenzahl.
6. Rabbi Meyer Munk.
7. Rabbi Nisson Wolpin.

compare," remembers Rabbi Dovid Zvi Hillman, one of the early students in Ponevezh. "There was no one like him." All those who heard him in Ponevezh attest that even the enormously influential *Michtav Me'Eliyahu* (which is largely based on his talks) does not begin to capture the emotional power of his speech. Those who heard the original talks can easily recall them from *Michtav Me'Eliyahu*, but the effect is still not the same.[8] A talk of an hour and a half, when stripped of its wealth of anecdote and illustration, might consist of no more than ten or twelve written paragraphs.[9]

Despite his slight stature, Rabbi Dessler required no amplification to be heard throughout the packed Ponevezh *beis medrash*.[10] His daughter-in-law Miriam was astounded the first time she heard him speak that someone so soft-spoken spoke so forcefully.

All the rhetorician's means were at his command. He would raise and lower his voice to dramatic effect.[11] Rabbi Dessler employed humor sparingly but to great effect. It was not uncommon for the talks to be punctuated by loud laughter from the audience, as Rabbi Dessler ridiculed the ugliness of a bad *middah* or the foolishness of worldly pursuits.[12] He once proposed a simple test for all those who convinced themselves that all their business endeavors were the fulfillment of a *mitzvah* of "six days shall you labor": "Do spiritual thoughts occur to them in the middle of business or do thoughts of business intrude in the middle of their *Shemoneh Esrei*?"[13]

One time he spoke while the Maccabiah Games were taking place in Tel Aviv, and he had been informed that a number of *bachurim* were tempted to go.[14] Rabbi Dessler responded with a vivid description of

---

8. Rabbi Menachem Cohen.

9. Lion Carmell, "Rabbi Eliyahu Eliezer Dessler," in *Guardians of Our Heritage*, Leo Jung ed., p. 686.

10. Rabbi Moshe Turk.

11. Rabbi Yaakov Edelstein.

12. Ibid.

13. *Michtav Me'Eliyahu*, Vol. I, p. 188; *Strive for Truth*, Vol. II, p. 266.

14. That temptation itself is an indication of the vast gulf between the small Israeli yeshiva world of Rabbi Dessler's day and the present one. Today almost all students enter yeshiva from *yeshiva ketanos* and come from families in which the fathers and even the grandfathers learned for many years in yeshiva. In those days, most *bachurim* arrived in the yeshiva from religious high schools combining secular and religious studies.

a soccer game. He pictured eleven people running after a ball. The one who runs fastest gets to the ball first and kicks it. The crowd cheers, and they set off once again in pursuit of the ball. By the time he had finished describing the scene, recalls Rabbi Meyer Munk, all taste for attending the Maccabiah games had disappeared.

A popular New Year's card, portraying three mussar giants: R' Dessler, R' Yechezkel Levenstein, and R' Elya Lopian

Humor was only one of the ways in which Rabbi Dessler's ability to describe a scene in words revealed itself. To combat a certain laxity in the *Erev Shabbos seder* in the yeshiva, he once pictured in great detail how the *bachurim* had greeted Shabbos in the yeshivos of Europe. All pre-Shabbos preparations were completed by midday so that the *bachurim* could greet the Shabbos Queen amidst Torah learning. And on Shabbos itself, there were those who did not sleep all day in order not to miss any of the *kedushah* of the day.[15]

Frequently, Rabbi Dessler would portray figures from *Tanach* or *Tannaim* in a way that cast them in an entirely new light and made them come alive for the *bachurim*. Once he described in great detail how Yosef's brothers each came through a separate gate into the city where the royal granary was located and how each was singled out from among the throngs and brought to Yosef's palace. He built up, step by step, their confusion over everything that happened to them, until they heard the words, "I'm Yosef ...."[16]

But for all Rabbi Dessler's rhetorical power, the primary appeal of his *sichos* was intellectual. The oratory was nothing more than

---

15. Rabbi Meyer Munk.
16. Ibid.

seasoning. Rabbi Dessler's clarity of presentation was such that every listener gained something from the talk, even if he could not understand the depth of his meaning. It was said in the yeshiva that even those who were inattentive during the *shmuessen* did not remain unaffected.[17] He would break down the fundamentals of Jewish belief into their most basic components, and provide strong definitions of each concept.[18]

"I'm speaking before an audience of *lomdei Torah*," he used to say, "and I have to ask questions that excite, that create intellectual tension." He did. "His questions were questions, and his answers were answers," says Rabbi Berel Povarsky, today a rosh yeshiva in Ponevezh Yeshiva.

Rabbi Dessler's language was rich and philosophical, and enabled him to attract many from far outside the orbit of the yeshiva.[19] Two young men from Ramat Gan — one the head of the left-wing Mapai Party branch in the city and the other a local pharmacist — were walking one day in Bnei Brak when they saw the large Ponevezh Yeshiva. Their curiosity piqued, they decided to go inside. They entered in the middle of one of Rabbi Dessler's Wednesday night talks, and were so struck by what they heard that they asked when the next talk would be. Eventually they began coming every Wednesday night and *Motzaei Shabbos*, which required more than an hour walk. They sat right up front opposite Rabbi Dessler.[20]

The power of Rabbi Dessler's talks is best gauged by the testimony of those who heard them. Many of those who heard Rabbi

---

17. Rabbi Menachem Cohen.

18. Rabbi Yaakov Edelstein.

19. A group of *bachurim* once approached the *Chazon Ish* and asked him how they could positively influence other *bachurim* to remain in learning. The *Chazon Ish* told them to ask Rabbi Dessler because he was the expert in how to influence others. *Rabbi Gershon Edelstein*, rosh yeshiva in Ponevezh today.

20. Rabbi Dessler eventually developed a personal relationship with the pharmacist. When the latter started to put on *tefillin*, he was embarrassed to be seen with them by his children and came to Rabbi Dessler for advice. Once he missed one of the *sichos*, and Rabbi Dessler contacted him to make sure that everything was all right with him. *Rabbi Shalom Ulman*.

Dessler speak in Ponevezh Yeshiva can still recall the *shmuessen* almost word for word today, in some cases fifty years after they were given. For Rabbi Dov Landau, rosh yeshiva of Slabodka Yeshiva, the anticipation every Wednesday before Rabbi Dessler's *shmuess* was like that preceding a *Yom Tov*. It was a day of rejoicing and uplift. "He electrified the audience," says Rabbi Landau.

During one talk on *Motzaei Shabbos Shuvah*, Rabbi Menachem Cohen was so moved by Rabbi Dessler's words that he felt the urge to jump up on the *bimah* and kiss him. He had to consciously restrain himself from doing so.

The *sichos* were completely engrossing, and afterwards many of those present would stand around for a long while discussing what he had said.[21] Though *davening* was supposed to begin immediately after the Wednesday night *shmuess*, no one approached the *amud* for fifteen or twenty minutes: the intellectual tumult in the *beis medrash* made it impossible to start *davening*.[22] Meanwhile the Rosh Yeshiva, Rabbi Dovid Povarsky, would circulate among the *bachurim* encouraging them to return to their Talmudic studies to no avail.[23]

The *roshei yeshiva* feared that Rabbi Dessler made the learning of *aggadata* so interesting — almost like a Reb Chaim Brisker in *hashkafah* — that the *bachurim* would be distracted from their learning.[24] Indeed, Rabbi Berel Povarsky remembers that as a *bachur*, he tried to avoid Rabbi Dessler's *sichos* when he was learning well for fear that he would become so absorbed in Rabbi Dessler's words that he would be unable to return to his learning.

At the same time, Rabbi Povarsky attests that he was never able to listen to anyone else speak on matters connected to *hashkafah* after Rabbi Dessler. He credits Rabbi Dessler with having changed his entire life with one explanation. The *Gemara* in *Bava Basra* (10b) describes *Olam Haba* as a reversal of this world: "Those who are above will be below and those who are below will be above." The *Gemara* is traditionally interpreted to mean that the rich in this world will be

---

21. Rabbi Moshe Turk.
22. Rabbi Avraham Tzvi Leichtman.
23. Rabbi Naftoli Nebenzahl.
24. Rabbi Yitzchak Rabe.

below in the World to Come, and the poor in this world will be above.

Rabbi Dessler, however, explained the *Gemara* in a different fashion. He described two boys coming to yeshiva. One is an *ilui* (genius). He marries the rosh yeshiva's daughter, and eventually becomes the rosh yeshiva himself. Though recognized as a great scholar, he never has to push himself because of his great natural gifts. The second boy is blessed with no special intellectual gifts but he is a phenomenal *masmid* (diligent student).

The World of Truth is for souls, Rabbi Dessler explained. The reward there is knowledge of Torah according to the effort invested in its attainment in this world. All gifts that a person is born with — even intellectual gifts — are connected only to the body, and the body has no part in the reward of the next world. Thus what a person accomplishes in this world solely by virtue of his natural endowments confers no reward in the World to Come. There the *masmid* is on top and the *ilui* on the bottom.[25]

Rabbi Povarsky's statement that he was never able to listen to anyone else speak about *aggadata* after Rabbi Dessler echoes an oft-repeated sentiment of his *talmidim*. Once another well-known *mashgiach* spoke at an event in place of Rabbi Dessler. The Ponevezh students, who were used to hearing Rabbi Dessler, were so disappointed that they could not restrain themselves from complaining to Rabbi Dessler. In his next talk, he dwelt on the words of the other *mashgiach* to demonstrate how much depth of understanding was contained in his words.[26]

His Impact Within the Yeshiva

ABOVE ALL, RABBI DESSLER INFUSED LIFE INTO A DISPIRITED generation. From the perspective of today, the state of the Torah world of fifty years ago is almost inconceivable. Today the Torah world of *Eretz Yisrael* is numerous and well established, with hundreds of yeshivos and tens of thousands of *talmidim*. Then there were at most a few hundred *bachurim* learning in a handful of advanced

---

25. See *Michtav Me'Eliyahu*, Vol. III, p. 20.
26. Rabbi Dov Wein.

yeshivos. Today we are witnessing the third and fourth generation of families in which intense Torah learning is the norm. Then, except for a handful who came from families of local *rabbanim*, most of the yeshiva *bachurim* came from homes of simple Jews struggling to eke out a living and often finding little time for intense Torah learning. By and large, the *bachurim* came from high schools with both secular and religious studies, not *yeshivos ketanos* as today. Even those learning in yeshiva expected to learn for a couple of years at most before entering the business world.

Today children are immunized from an early age against all philosophies of "by my strength and the might of my hand" (*Devarim* 8:17). Then Jewish nationalism reigned supreme and pulled many believing Jews in its wake. The future seemed entirely with the nationalists, and both within and without the small Torah world, it was widely assumed that there would soon be nothing left of the old *yishuv*. Israel's political leaders, wrote Rabbi Dov Landau, rosh yeshiva of Slabodka Yeshiva, were viewed, even by most observant Jews, as the true leaders of the nation and the ones who would secure the continued existence of the Jewish people.

It would take decades and the efforts of many great leaders before the tides changed. But the influence of Rabbi Dessler in Ponevezh Yeshiva, one of *Eretz Yisrael's* two premier yeshivos in those days, was a major factor. More important than any specific insight that he conveyed, says Rabbi Dov Landau, was the attitude he instilled. "What I remember most was the way he made us feel: And his heart was lifted up in the ways of Hashem' (*Divrei HaYamim* II 17:6)."

He provided a sense of purpose, a goal, to the generation of young men who drank in his words. That goal was nothing less than to build up a generation of *lomdei Torah* (Torah scholars) to replace that which was lost. But that would not be easy, and would require a full measure of idealism from each and every one of those privileged to learn in yeshiva.[27]

"Ours is not like other generations," he told them. "Ours is a generation of destruction." Nevertheless, he insisted, "Perhaps, it is still possible to return sparks of holiness to the face of the earth!

At the engagement of R' Baruch Dov Povarsky. Top photo, at right, R' Dovid Povarsky and R' Dessler. Bottom photo, at right, R' Baruch Dov Povarsky, R' Shmuel Rozovsky, R' Elazar Menachem Schach

If we feel that way, then we are not yet dead. If there still exists within in us a desire for life, we are still living....

"Know one thing clearly: If we sacrifice ourselves to the fullest extent, we will again see among us the *kedushah* that we once saw.... It is in our hands! True *mesiras nefesh* is demanded! True [*mesiras nefesh*] — no fake, no simulacrum!... Come, let us go up, higher, and not retreat!"[28]

Rabbi Dessler created a *"shtrebung"* (a striving for excellence) in Torah that had not existed. He used to repeat: *"Es iz da Torah, un nor Torah, un kein shum zach chutz miTorah* — There is Torah, and only Torah, and nothing else besides Torah."[29] At one of the *yahrzeit* gatherings for Rabbi Dessler in Ponevezh, a prominent rosh yeshiva commented that if had not been for Rabbi Dessler he would never have remained in Torah learning. He had come into Ponevezh expecting to learn for one or two years at most. But when he heard Rabbi Dessler describe what Torah learning is, he told his parents that he had made up his mind: He would never leave the yeshiva.

---

27. Rabbi Shmuel Shulsinger, *rav* of Kiryat Ata.
28. Ibid., Vol. I, pp. 70-71.
29. Rabbi Shmuel Shulsinger.

Rabbi Dessler also convinced many parents that their children were worthy of remaining in Torah learning.[30]

To a downtrodden and beleaguered generation, Rabbi Dessler gave hope. Two days after the second elections in Israel, which had only strengthened the antireligious forces in the country, he put matters into perspective. Quoting the *Maharal,* he told his *talmidim* that *HaKadosh Baruch Hu's* guidance of the world is such that there is a limit to how far the forces of evil can go, and thus they had nothing to fear from its ultimate triumph.[31]

He taught *bnei yeshiva* how to strengthen one another by forming themselves into a community. One of the great failings of young *bachurim,* he wrote to his future son-in-law Rabbi Yehoshua Geldzahler, is that each one views the yeshiva as if it were a random association of individuals, who just happened to arrive there at the same time. That is false. A yeshiva is a collective unit, and each student is like a limb on the body.

Recognition of the essential unity of the yeshiva or any other community, he felt, protected against the *yetzer hara.* Just as the limbs of the body have no opinion apart from the body itself, so one who sees himself as part of a community submerges his individual opinion in that of the community. By suppressing his individual desires, he thwarts the *yetzer hara,* which always preys on the isolated individual by arousing his selfish, personal desires.[32]

Summarizing Rabbi Dessler's impact on Ponevezh, Rabbi Yaakov Edelstein describes him as an *"or gadol* — a great light. He opened up a new world. He could elevate with a word. He demonstrated that this world is nothing and that the only reality is the reality of the spirit."

Rabbi Dessler showed his *talmidim* how to discern the spiritual cause behind every thing that happens. That spiritual cause he

---

30. Rabbi Dov Wein and Rabbi Shalom Ulman.
31. Rabbi Shmuel Shulsinger.
    See *Michtav Me'Eliyahu,* Vol. III, pp. 202-207, for the *shmuess* given a week later on *galus Edom* and its end.
32. Ibid., Vol. IV, pp. 350-51.

referred to by such terms as the *"nekudas hap'nimis"* (the point of inwardness) or the *"nekudas haemes"* (the point of truth). Each person would be judged, he told his students, precisely by his degree of awareness of the "point of truth," after all the outer coverings have been removed.[33]

He sensitized his students to recognize how common ways of thinking and talking obscure the underlying spiritual reality of the world. A prominent political leader's boast after the Dunkirk evacuation, "We left nothing to chance," for instance, served as example of hubris that leaves no room for G-d.[34] When his wife was in the hospital with her final illness, one of the nurses told Rabbi Dessler that "she was in good hands," referring to the quality of her doctors. That chance remark too occasioned an entire *shmuess* on how foreign such reliance on the doctor's skill is to the believing Jew.

No matter what he spoke about, Rabbi Dessler inevitably left his audience with a heightened awareness that the world is governed according to a spiritual calculus. And that awareness was not confined merely to the realm of the intellect. The *tefillos* (prayers) immediately after his *sichos*, remembers Rabbi Shalom Ulman, were the most powerful of the week. Rabbi Naftoli Nebenzahl likens the *davening* after one *shmuess* to that of *Ne'ilah* on Yom Kippur.

A New Derech

RABBI DESSLER PIONEERED A NEW PATH OF JEWISH THOUGHT seen by admirers and critics alike as a radical departure from the standard *mussar shmuessen* of the time. Both the form of his *sichos* (talks) — his rigorous analytical approach to *aggadata* — and the wide diversity of sources from which he drew were innovations.

Even those who considered themselves opponents of the entire *mussar* approach were attracted to his talks.[35] Prior to Rabbi Dessler, many of the *bachurim* in Ponevezh viewed *mussar* as something dry and uninteresting.[36] "We thought of a *mussar shmuess* as requiring

---

33. Rabbi Yitzchak Greenberg.
34. Ibid., Vol. I, p.188.
35. Rabbi Shlomo Wolbe.
36. Rabbi Dov Wein and Rabbi Dovid Tzvi Hillman.

nerves of steel and the patience to hear the same idea repeated twenty times," recalls Rabbi Dovid Tzvi Hillman. But Rabbi Dessler was different — elevating, not boring.

Rabbi Dessler was convinced that the task he had set himself of explicating *aggadata* was of the greatest importance. The *aggadata* found throughout the Talmud were designed, in his view, to provide a path in *mussar* and service of Hashem. (He viewed kabbalah in the same light.)[37]

"*Aggadata* is to enlighten the heart," he wrote to Rabbi Aryeh Carmell, "and if it does not do so because of our lowly understanding, we are not obligated to involve ourselves in its study,[38] until we reach a sufficient level of understanding.... So long as we have not attained that level of understanding, there is no value to our continued involvement, since it will only lead us to false conclusions.... We cannot base our service of Hashem [on *aggadata*] if we don't understand them."[39]

For the first time since Kelm, Rabbi Dessler had the opportunity to immerse himself, without outside distractions, in plumbing the depths of Torah thought. As a consequence, he began to reveal increasingly deeper levels of Torah. In a letter to Dr. Dov Heiman, Rabbi Dessler conveys the excitement with which his efforts filled him, and his sense that he was one of few engaged in the crucial task of uncovering the true meaning of *aggadata*:

> *Baruch Hashem*, work in the Yeshiva has swallowed me up whole .... I could never have anticipated ... the *nachas ruach* of being surrounded by those who drink thirstily in these matters, young and old alike. On what merit have I been privileged to this?

---

37. Rabbi Yehoshua Geldzhaler.

38. In contradistinction to halachah, which one must keep studying no matter how deficient one's understanding.

39. Ibid., Vol. IV, pp. 353-4.

Rabbi Carmell had written to Rabbi Dessler seeking an explanation of R. Shmuel HaNaggid's distinction in *Mevo HaTalmud* between halachah and *aggadata*. The study of the former is incumbent on every Jew; the study of the latter only to one of sufficient understanding.

The Satan was successful and all the great scholars put their full energy into the study of halachah, and in that area there are many who are capable of teaching. But they have left aside the area of aggadata, *and separated from that which enlightens with sparks of truth every corner of the soul. There is much cause for concern in this. For if those who can explain [it] have so decreased with what will we influence the p'nimius of anshei Torah* (emphasis added).⁴⁰

Rabbi Dessler introduced a new analytical depth to *ma'amarei Chazal* (the words of the Sages). His approach could almost be termed scientific, and he taught his students to think in a rigorous, abstract fashion.⁴¹ The underlying message of Rabbi Dessler's teaching was that *aggadata* must be learned just as one learns any other *sugya* in the Talmud⁴² — with sharp questions, clear resolutions, and proofs for everything.⁴³ He did not make *drashos*, but rather sought to clarify the thought of *Chazal*. For that reason he would only use those *midrashim* that he found quoted in earlier sources.⁴⁴

Following the path of the *Maharal*, whose insights were a mainstay of his *shiurim*, he showed his students how to extract depths of meaning from every word of the Sages.⁴⁵ He would turn over and over a complicated matter, like the sin of King Davd, until suddenly all the various *ma'amarei Chazal* would arrange themselves in order and cry out, "This is what *Chazal* meant."⁴⁶

Rabbi Dessler's second great innovation was to draw from a far wider range of sources than anyone had done previously. The whole library of Jewish thought was open in front of him, and he did not hesitate to employ it fully. Upon meeting Rabbi Dessler for the first

---

40. Ibid., Vol. V, pp. 510-11.
41. Rabbi Dovid Tzvi Hillman.
42. Rabbi Avraham Tzvi Leichtman.
43. Rabbi Moshe Shapiro.
44. Rabbi Avraham Tzvi Leichtman.
45. Rabbi Shalom Ulman.
46. Rabbi Dovid Zaretsky.

time, Rabbi Reuven Grozovsky, Rosh Yeshiva of Bais Medrash Elyon, told Rabbi Yehoshua Geldzahler, "Your father-in-law is the one person I ever met without a recognizable *nusach*. Everyone has certain works that excite him and those that do not. But he finds *ta'am* (taste) in everything."

Dovid Zaretsky, the greatest Hebrew and Yiddish writer of the day, nicely captured Rabbi Dessler's originality in his ability to draw from such a wide range of sources:

> He revealed things that no ear had heard among the *talmidim* in yeshivos, ... combining *mussar* with the fire of *chassidus* to create something entirely new.... He wanted to empty all the treasure houses filled with hidden treasures of Jewish thought.
>
> Anyone who heard even one talk knew that he was listening to someone who was presenting a different approach in very deep waters.

One of Rabbi Dessler's fundamental principles in the interpretation of *aggadata* was that even when two *Tannaim* or *Amoraim* appear to disagree, they are merely expressing two ways of looking at the same coin. "*Tikkunei Zohar* makes clear," he wrote to his closest *talmidim* in Ponevezh, "that in matters of *aggadata* and *kabbalah* no argument is possible — only two vantage points of the truth."[47]

The same principle applied, Rabbi Dessler felt, to the great Jewish thinkers of later generations as well. He told Rabbi Yitzchak Greenberg that all "the *gedolim*, whatever their backgrounds, were at the depths speaking one language. Only the outer expression differs. But as one penetrates to the depths of their understanding one recognizes the differences in expression as nothing more than outer clothing."

---

47. Ibid., Vol. III, pp. 353-4.
  Rabbi Dessler cites the Vilna Gaon in support of this proposition. Thus the Gaon in *Even Shleimah* interprets the well-known dispute between Rav and Shmuel over what the days of *Mashiach* (Messiah) will be like, not as a dispute at all, but as two distinct stages in the process. Shmuel, who said the only difference would be the end of subjugation to foreign rule, writes the Gaon, is talking about *Mashiach ben Yosef* and Rav, who sees the days of *Mashiach* as the fulfillment of all Biblical prophesies, is describing *Mashiach ben David*.

Thus Rabbi Dessler felt comfortable drawing from a remarkably wide-range of Chassidic thinkers. He enjoyed, for instance, showing his *talmidim* that Rabbi Chaim of Volozhin and the *Tzemach Tzedek* offer the same explanation of the verse, "All Israel *saw* the thunderclaps ... and the sound of the shofar" (*Shemos* 20:15): At Sinai, the people perceived the spiritual universe with the clarity usually associated with sight, not hearing.[48]

Rabbi Dessler was well versed in the early writings of Chabad, those of Reb Nachman of Breslav, and of the *Sefas Emes*. The works of Reb Tzadok HaKohen of Lublin particularly influenced him. Almost every *shiur* included something from Reb Tzadok, even though this might not be clear to the uninitiated.[49] Once he gave ten straight talks on Samson based on Reb Tzadok.[50] Rabbi Mendel of Vitebsk was another Chassidic thinker who was especially dear to Rabbi Dessler. He treated Reb Mendel's *Pri Ha'Aretz* with the same precision that one reads a *Rishon* and frequently mentioned the work in his talks.[51]

Rabbi Dessler's heavy reliance on the *Zohar* was another departure from the traditional sources for *mussar shmuessen*. The *Zohar* was integral to Rabbi Dessler's thought, and not just a source of piquant quotations. He had a regular *chavrusa* in Bnei Brak with Rabbi Yitzchak Berman in kabbalistic works.[52]

Nor did he discourage certain special *talmidim* from acquiring knowledge of the Hidden Torah. Even as a young man, Rabbi Shalom Ulman, who shared a room with Rabbi Dessler after the *petirah* of his wife, had a great interest in kabbalah. Rabbi Dessler noticed this interest, but said nothing to him about it. Over time,

---

48. Rabbi Naftoli Nebenzahl.

49. Rabbi Shalom Ber Lipshitz, a close *talmid* in Ponevezh and a leading activist in P'eylim.

50. Rabbi Shalom Ulman.

51. Rabbi Shmuel Shulsinger.

52. Rabbi Dov Landau.

Rabbi Berman was the father of Rabbi Shlomo Berman, the son-in-law of the Steipler Gaon and widely considered the greatest *ilui* (genius) in Ponevezh Yeshiva in Rabbi Dessler's day. Rabbi Shlomo Berman later became a rosh yeshiva in Ponevezh Yeshiva.

however, he gave Rabbi Ulman several works of Rabbi Moshe Chaim Luzzato from his own library: *Adir Ba'Marom* and *138 Gates of Wisdom*. Rabbi Dessler filled in with his own hand missing words or passages that had become erased from these volumes over time. Eventually, he gave Rabbi Ulman a complete set of *Zohar* as well.

Not surprisingly, those used to the prevalent style of *mussar* did not react with equanimity to the innovations introduced by Rabbi Dessler. They objected both to the range of sources from which he drew and to his departure from the focus of traditional *mussar*. On a visit back to England, Rabbi Dessler told his *talmidim* in Gateshead that his talks were considered *"nit mussar* — not mussar" by the *mashgichim* of *Eretz Yisrael*.[53]

Rabbi Dessler, however, was unshaken in his conviction that the path he had chosen was necessary for the generation. Due to a decline in the generations, he felt, it was no longer possible to speak directly to the heart. Before one could speak to the hearts of the present generation, Rabbi Dessler realized, it was first necessary to win their attention. They had to be shown the depths of Torah, and only then would it be possible to address practical applications to their lives.

When asked why in Kelm they had not learned all the works upon which he drew, he replied with a *mashal*. A philosopher once approached the king with a request, and fell at the king's feet. The king told him that it was not befitting a philosopher to act in such a servile fashion, and that he should speak into his ear. The philosopher answered that he was speaking into his ear.[54]

With that *mashal*, Rabbi Dessler meant that one must find the proper language for one's own generation. The purpose of *mussar*, he said, והשבת אל לבבך, to internalize one's *emunah*. In Kelm, they were already at a very elevated level and so only needed a few *sefarim* to reach this level.[55]

---

53. Rabbi Bezalel Rakov.
54. Rabbi Shlomo Noach Kroll, son-in-law of Rabbi Yaakov Landau, Rav of Bnei Brak.
55. Rabbi Yehoshua Geldzhaler.
　Compare *Nedarim* 22b: If *Klal Yisrael* had not sinned, they would have only needed *Chumash* and *Yehoshua*.

When describing the decline of the generation, Rabbi Dessler did not exclude himself. Once Rabbi Aharon Cohen, rosh yeshiva in the Chevron Yeshiva, asked him why he never spoke simple words of faith in Hashem. Rabbi Dessler replied that such words only have an effect when spoken by an *erlicher Yid*, one who is at one with the words that he is saying. And he did not feel that he was at that level — the level of "words that go out from the heart enter the heart." The nature of his talks, however, was such that even if he was not worthy, the elevated content would itself leave an impression.[56]

Despite the criticism of Rabbi Dessler's pathbreaking approach, he held to his path with tenacity. A well-known *mashgiach* once reproached him sharply for his departure from the content of *mussar*. Rabbi Dessler stood there silently with his shoulders slightly bent, his hands clasped together, and leaning towards the one offering the reproof, in the manner of Kelm for receiving *tochachah*.[57] Yet despite his high personal regard for the one offering the criticism, Rabbi Dessler was not swayed. He replied that there was no one left capable of listening to old-fashioned *mussar*. "What should I do?" he once asked rhetorically. "If I give them *mussar* as they once did, they'll just run away."[58]

Rabbi Dessler's analytical approach to *aggadata* paralleled Rabbi Chaim Soloveitchik's new approach to Talmud study. In an age of increasing analytical sophistication in many areas of life, it was necessary to show the same depth of analysis in Talmudic learning in order to combat the attraction of secular disciplines.[59] Similarly, by showing the depth of *aggadata*, Rabbi Dessler hoped to sweeten its

---

56. Rabbi Dov Yaffe, *Mashgiach* of Yeshivas Knesses Chizkiyahu, Kfar Chassidim.

57. Rabbi Moshe Shapiro in a *hesped* given in Gateshead Kollel on Rabbi Dessler's fiftieth *yahrtzeit*.

58. Rabbi Naftoli Nebenzahl; Rabbi Levi Shainin.

59. See *Michtav Me'Eliyahu*, Vol. III, p. 55, where Rabbi Dessler explicitly compares the change in the style of Talmudic learning from that of *pilpul* to the analytical methodology of Reb Chaim Brisker with a new approach to *aggadata:* "In our generation, the generation of the birthpangs of the Messiah, the great ones of the generation have revealed the methodology of in-depth analysis both in halachah and *aggadata,* for it enlightens even those of a lowly level and little worth."

study to the point where it could affect the heart.[60] Only by first arousing the intellect — even by speaking far above the understanding of his audience[61] — would it be possible to inspire his listeners to the real goal of *mussar:* the purification of the heart.

Yet the goal remained, as always, the integration of one's intellectual knowledge into one's heart, the seat of a deeper knowledge informing one's every action. "In our weak generation," he wrote to his *talmidim* in London, "it is necessary to use one's mind to understand the truth and to understand the importance of Torah."

But at the same time, one must not forget that *avodah*, Divine service, is always referred to as "service of the heart," not "service of the intelligence." Richness of intellectual knowledge, at best, remains only preparation for *avodah*, not the *avodah* itself. By itself it will do more than enable a person to justify continuing to do what he has been educated to do.[62]

In the same vein, he wrote to Rabbi Aryeh Carmell, that if we could remove the blockage of sin from our hearts, then that which we apprehend with our intelligence would enter our hearts. Yet so long as our hearts are blocked, our intellectual knowledge remains external to ourselves.[63]

The acuity of Rabbi Dessler's analysis of the needs of his generation has been fully demonstrated by the huge popularity of his *Michtav Me'Eliyahu*. It has proven the most influential work of Torah *hashkafah* of the last fifty years — a work speaking to both the heart and mind of Jews around the world.

---

60. Rabbi Menachem Cohen.
61. Rabbi Dov Yaffe, *Mashgiach* of Yeshivas Knesses Chizkiyahu.
62. *Michtav Me'Eliyahu*, Vol. IV, p. 361.
63. Ibid., p. 356.

Chapter 19
The Power of His Example

Rabbi Dessler held the official title of *Mashgiach* in Ponevezh Yeshiva, but he always insisted that the title did not fit him. "I am not the *Mashgiach*," he would say. "That title is reserved for someone who is involved with every single individual. I give *shiurim* in *Hilchos Dei'os*."[1]

Not a Mashgiach

The Ponevezher Rav continually pressed him to become more involved with individual *bachurim*, but he insisted with incredible firmness that he was incapable of doing so. He refused to be a policeman. "He had been raised among those for whom it was enough to simply point out the light in the Torah and man," wrote Rabbi Yitzchak Greenberg soon after his *petirah*.

The entire focus in Kelm was on producing individuals of the most elevated character, and in this Rabbi Dessler remained true to his roots. In the spiritual world, Kelm taught, all counting is from the multitude down to the solitary individual. "Large" and "many"

---
1. Rabbi Yitzchak Greenberg.

are terms of the physical world, but they are meaningless in a spiritual context. The spiritual world is defined by its unity, represented by the number one, or the solitary individual.

Quantity has meaning, as far as Kelm was concerned, only when its starting point is a solitary point of perfection, no matter how small. Quality can produce quantity, quantity can never produce quality.

Any emphasis on numbers was repugnant to Rabbi Dessler.[2] He stressed rather repairing oneself and only then influencing others. A poem entitled "*L'Atzmi* — To Myself" expressed his attitude:

> To myself I record
> in order that I can review the truth that I saw
> I guard it and remember it ...
> Is this [guarding for myself] not the outgrowth of self-love?
> That is what the superficial view claims. [But the true view is]:
> If my heart does not learn, how will it teach?
> Only that which goes out from the heart — a heart overflowing its banks — can enter the heart of another.[3]

Following the principles of Kelm, Rabbi Dessler worked with a small group of *talmidim*, whom he saw as having the potential to influence others. In this regard, he had a particularly sharp eye. His closest disciple, Rabbi Chaim Friedlander, was one of his successors as *Mashgiach* of Ponevezh Yeshiva and was recognized, in time, as one of the leading Jewish thinkers and teachers of our generation.

Among those who learned privately with Rabbi Dessler were: Rabbi Berel Povarsky, Rabbi Moshe Shimon Diskind, and Rabbi Dov

---

2. Rabbi Moshe Shapiro.
3. *Michtav Me'Eliyahu*, Vol. III, p. 299.

Landau. All subsequently became prominent *roshei yeshiva*. Rabbi Povarsky and Rabbi Diskind each learned the *Ramban's* commentary on *Chumash* with Rabbi Dessler once a week. In one year, Rabbi Povarsky remembers they almost reached the fifth *aliyah* of *Bereishis*. With Rabbi Dov Landau, he learned the *Radvaz's Ta'amei Hamitzos*. They would share a single text, and as they read, the thoughts would just flow forth from Rabbi Dessler. Rabbi Landau doubts that they even finished the first mitzvah in this fashion.[4]

While Rabbi Dessler worked individually with a handful or so of close students, the actual supervision of *bachurim* in Ponevezh Yeshiva was left to Rabbi Chaim Friedlander and Rabbi Shmuel Harari, two members of the circle of Rabbi Dessler's close *talmidim*. Rabbi Friedlander officially assumed the task of assistant *Mashgiach* in 1952 at the behest of the Ponevezher Rav. He and Rabbi Dessler ate breakfast together every morning, and Rabbi Dessler would give his young protege certain guidelines for his task. Afterwards they learned the works of Rabbi Moshe Chaim Luzzato (the *Ramchal*).

His entire life, Rabbi Dessler was reluctant to give rebuke, and that did not change in Ponevezh Yeshiva. Instead of rebuke, he preferred to describe the elevated nature of good *middos* and how ugly and ridiculous are bad *middos*. His ridicule of defective *middos* could provoke hysterical laughter, but he always insisted that he was merely exaggerating some fault he found within himself.[5]

On at least one occason, however, Rabbi Dessler did publicly rebuke a group of *bachurim*.[6] There was a kiosk near the yeshiva where the *talmidim* used to buy milk and other small items on credit. The students learned that there would be a devaluation of the Israeli

---

4. In addition to his *sichos* and his learning with individual *bachurim*, Rabbi Dessler also led a number of *vaadim* (smaller groups). (How many such *vaadim* there were is a matter of some dispute among the *talmidim* from those years.) These *vaadim* were less formal presentations than the *sichos*, and Rabbi Dessler was freer in turning his scorn on the vanities of the world. The *vaadim* would focus on a particular topic, like *tefillah* (prayer). *Rabbi Menachem Cohen and Rabbi Meyer Munk.*

5. Rabbi Simcha Zissel Dessler.

6. The rebuke was not personal. It is unlikely that Rabbi Dessler even knew whom he was speaking about. His intention was to describe the type of behavior that is unacceptable for any yeshiva student using an example that had been brought to his attention.

currency. Rather than paying their debts immediately, they waited until after the devaluation so that they could repay in devalued currency. The owner of the kiosk complained to Rabbi Dessler about what had happened. In response, Rabbi Dessler publicly labeled the use of trickery to profit at another's expense as extremely ugly behavior, even if it was halachically permissible.[7]

Though Rabbi Dessler did not have personal contact with most of the *bachurim* in the yeshiva, his personality made a great impression on all those who were privileged to be within his close circle. "His *middos* and his whole personality," wrote Rabbi Chaim Friedlander, "made a deep and lasting impression on all who came in contact with him. Each one felt that they were the recipients of a special closeness." Those who drew close found him easy to speak with on any subject. He possessed the ability to make the person with whom he was speaking feel that a deep connection existed between them.[8]

He treated his *talmidim* with the utmost *kavod* (respect). When they came to visit him on *Chol HaMoed,* he would exclaim, "What an honor that you came to visit me." Then he would take out of an old cabinet some silver cups and some wine. "I made this wine myself," he would tell them, "and I only take it out for my most important guests."[9] Once, after Rebbetzin Dessler had passed away, Rabbi Yaakov Edelstein visited Rabbi Dessler. When no milk could be found to serve with the coffee, Rabbi Dessler proudly demonstrated his technique for whitening a cup of coffee using an egg instead.

Such treatment was not reserved for his students alone. Once Rabbi Shlomo Wolbe was in Rabbi Dessler's home. When it came time to leave, Rabbi Dessler was distraught that he could not find anything to serve his guest. Finally, he found a chocolate candy in the kitchen. When Rabbi Wolbe departed, Rabbi Dessler told him that he too had to go out, so that the younger *mashgiach* would not be embarrassed to have Rabbi Dessler accompanying him. Rabbi

---

7. Rabbi Dov Wein.
8. Rabbi Moshe Shapiro, the youngest of Rabbi Dessler's close disciples in Ponevezh Yeshiva.
9. Rabbi Dov Wein.

Dessler did not specify his destination and walked alongside Rabbi Wolbe to the bus stop, where he remained until his visitor's bus arrived.

As eager as Rabbi Dessler was to honor others, he did everything possible to avoid asking others to do anything on his behalf. Even though Shalom Ulman was his official house *bachur,* after the death of his wife, Rabbi Dessler would not let him so much as make a cup of coffee for him. Similarly, he refused to consider the young man's offers to polish his shoes or to help him with the preparation of raisin wine for Shabbos. More than Ulman served Rabbi Dessler, it was said in the yeshiva, the latter served him.

The highest honor that Rabbi Dessler paid to his students was the seriousness with which he took their ideas. Rabbi Dessler and Shalom Ulman used to eat every *Shalosh Seudos* together, and at the meal, Rabbi Dessler would relate what he planned to say on *Motzaei Shabbos.* He actively sought Rabbi Ulman's critique, and encouraged him to ask questions and offer his own ideas on the subject. Rabbi Dessler always offered to repeat Shalom Ulman's insights in his name, but the young man begged him not to do so. Nevertheless, if Rabbi Dessler mentioned the insight, he was always careful to state that it was not his but someone else's.

Often, Rabbi Dessler would tell a *talmid,* "You provided me with the *yesod* (the fundamental principle) for the entire *shiur.*" Yet when the *talmid* subsequently heard Rabbi Dessler repeat the *yesod* attributed to him, he often found it unrecognizable.[10] On several occasions, Dov Landau mentioned a certain idea of his or something interesting that he had read to Rabbi Dessler, only to have the latter immediately sit down, take out his notebook, and enter the idea in it.

Rabbi Dessler once received a letter from his old friend Rabbi Moshe Schneider in England. Rabbi Schneider pointed out that the Chofetz Chaim had, in his time, expressed the desire to go to war against the Bolsheviks, just as the Maccabees has warred against the Seulicid Greeks in their day. If so, Rabbi Schneider demanded to

---

10. Rabbi Dov Wein.

know, why were observant Jews in *Eretz Yisrael* not waging a battle against efforts to separate new immigrants from religion?

Rabbi Dessler shared the letter with Dov Landau, and asked him how he would answer Rabbi Schneider's question.[11] With little gestures like these, and by showing such respect for their opinions, Rabbi Dessler built up the self-confidence of his young followers.

The same honor that Rabbi Dessler extended to his students, he extended to their parents as well. Dov Wein and his mother were in disagreement over how to handle a *shidduch*, and Mrs. Wein expressed her intention to discuss the matter with Rabbi Dessler. Wein was mortified at the thought of her doing so and did everything in his power to convince her that it would be inappropriate.

His efforts were to no avail. One night he was learning together with Rabbi Dessler, when there was a knock on the door. Wein went to answer the door and to his horror found his mother standing there. He begged his mother to leave, but she refused. Wein's delay in returning brought Rabbi Dessler to the door. The young man had no choice but to introduce his mother, but he apologized to Rabbi Dessler, "I explained to her that she couldn't just come and talk to Rabbi Dessler."

Rabbi Dessler responded that, on the contrary, nothing could be a greater honor than a visit from "the mother of Reb Dov." He sat and talked to her at great length and repeated a number of times what a pleasure it was to talk to the mother of a budding *talmid chacham*. Rabbi Dessler's behavior made a tremendous impression on Rabbi Wein, and in his subsequent career as a rosh yeshiva, he has made it a practice whenever the mother of a *talmid* is present to solicit her opinion first.

Even for those in the yeshiva who had no direct personal contact with Rav Dessler, merely being faced with the constant image of so spiritually refined a person made an important impression.

Paradoxically, the first impression that many of the *bachurim* had of Rabbi Dessler was highly misleading, but in a way that made it

---

11. Rabbi Landau does not recall what, if anything, he answered at the time or whether Rabbi Dessler ventured an answer. But the fact that Rabbi Dessler asked his opinion left a lasting impression.

easier for them to integrate into the yeshiva. In those days, a large percentage of the incoming students, even in Ponevezh Yeshiva, were *tichonistim* (products of religious high schools). These students tended to think of *rabbanim* as out of touch with the times and yeshivos as a way station, at most, before entry into the "real" world.

When those students spoke with Rabbi Dessler and discovered that he possessed wide knowledge of the modern world, including a familiarity with recent scientific discoveries, their stereotypes of *talmidei chachamim* being completely detached from the world were broken down. They were relieved to discover that they need not choose between serious yeshiva studies and any knowledge of the world around them.[12] In time they discovered that Rabbi Dessler was, in Rabbi Dov Wein's words, "the *frumest* of the *frum*." And in that process of discovery, the *talmidim* learned that the highest spiritual demands were not incompatible with worldly knowledge.

The dominant impression left by Rabbi Dessler was of somone engaged in the most intense spiritual striving with a minimum of external show. The *talmidim* saw, for instance, how controlled and inward his *davening* was. Every *Shemoneh Esrei* looked to the outside observer exactly the same as every other. Each lasted precisely the same amount of time. All but the most obtuse students understood that such prayer could only be the product of intense concentration and never allowing one's mind to wander.[13]

On Rosh Hashanah, *Shabbos Shuvah,* and Yom Kippur, he did not speak at all.[14] After *Tashlich*[15] on the first day of Rosh Hashanah, the *bachurim* would return to a darkened *beis medrash* and hear Rabbi Dessler repeat over and over the same *ma'amar Chazal*: לא דיין לרשעים שאינן חרדין ועצבין מיום המיתה, אלא שלבם בריא להם כאולם — "It is not enough for the wicked that they are not fearful and forlorn about the

---

12. Rabbi Dov Wein and Rabbi Shmuel Shulsinger.

13. Rabbi Menachem Cohen, who sat next to Rabbi Dessler every day in *davening*.
   In his early years in Ponevezh, Rabbi Dessler did not sit in the front row, but in a seat off to the side in the very back row.

14. Rabbi Meyer Munk.

15. Rabbi Dessler himself did not perform *Tashlich,* in accordance with the custom of the Vilna Gaon and the *minhag* of Kelm.

day of death, but their hearts are as robust as a large hall" (*Shabbos* 31b). The sound of his voice not only pierced the silence in the darkened *beis medrash*, it pierced hearts as well.[16] One of the Torah world's leading *ba'alei hashkafah* credits that experience with awakening him to the power contained in every word of our Sages.

The stories that circulated about Rabbi Dessler revealed a person of acute spiritual sensitivity. Before Rebbetzin Dessler joined him in Bnei Brak, he ate his meals in the orphanage established by the Ponevezher Rav for survivors of the Holocaust. Mrs. Munk, who ran the dining hall, used to show her high regard by saving some small delicacy for him that she did not serve to others. That made Rabbi Dessler acutely uncomfortable, and he asked Mrs. Munk on a number of occasions to refrain from doing so.

One day as he was coming into the dining room, Rabbi Dessler saw a young boy running out. He stopped him and asked him why he was running away. It turned out that the boy had stolen a cherry left out for Rabbi Dessler. When he realized what had happened, Rabbi Dessler turned to Mrs. Munk and told her, "Either I eat exactly the same as everyone else or I can't continue."[17]

Rabbi Dessler once told Rabbi Yaakov Edelstein that he could look at a person's face and tell whether he had learned Torah that day. Rabbi Edelstein immediately challenged him to say whether he had learned so far that day. Rabbi Dessler replied that he had — a fact which Rabbi Edelstein denied. Rabbi Dessler, however, was unconvinced and demanded that Rabbi Edelstein repeat everything he had done that morning from the time he awakened. In the course of his recitation, Rabbi Edelstein remembered that he had gone to the Ponevezh *beis medrash* prior to his meeting with Rabbi Dessler, and there two *bachurim* had approached him and asked him to resolve a difficulty in the *Gemara* they were then learning. Rabbi Dessler was delighted to have been proven correct.

Even Rabbi Dessler's external appearance conveyed to the *bachurim* a taste of Kelm's emphasis on a neat and orderly appearance. His clothing was of the simplest possible quality, but always

---

16. Rabbi Shmuel Shlusinger.
17. Rabbi Meyer Munk and Rabbi Dov Wein.

immaculate. While Rebbetzin Dessler was still alive, she used to personally inspect him and brush off his hat and tie before he departed for the yeshiva.[18] After she passed away, Rabbi Dessler would always carefully examine his beard in the mirror to make sure it was neatly combed before leaving the house. The *bachur* who lived with him was initially surprised to see him show so much concern with his physical appearance. Later, however, he realized that Rabbi Dessler's concern was a reflection of Kelm's emphasis on avoiding anything that might cause a *chilul Hashem* in any way.[19]

The Beauty of His Ways

AS WE HAVE NOTED, RABBI DESSLER DIVIDED PEOPLE INTO TWO basic categories: "givers" and "takers." Most people are not purely one or the other, but possess an admixture of both tendencies. Sometimes they are givers and sometimes takers. Rabbi Dessler, however, was as close to the pure giver as is imaginable.

Rebbetzin Dessler in Australia

His own effort or time seems not to have been a factor to be considered as soon as he identified someone whom he was in a position to help. He once met a lonely woman in Bnei Brak, who had lost her immediate family in the war. In the course of their conversation, she mentioned that she might still have one distant relative in a small town in England. The next time Rabbi Dessler was in England he traveled many hours by train just to find the relative and to put the two in contact with one another.[20]

Five days before his death, he called Rabbi Shalom Ber Lifshitz to

---

18. Rabbi Avigdor Silver.
19. Rabbi Shalom Ulman.
20. Sorasky, *Marbitzei Torah U'Mussar*, Vol. III, p. 70.

ask him for information concerning a possible *shidduch* for a girl from Gateshead Seminary. At the time, he could not even sit up, but he was still fully involved in trying to help the girl.[21]

Rabbi Dessler's desire to give manifested itself as much in the small gestures as the large. Every time he visited Jerusalem, he brought with him eggshells he had collected to feed the chickens the Silvers raised and a box of special biscuits — then unavailable in Jerusalem — for the Silver children.[22]

He had an uncanny sensitivity to the feelings of others. For instance, he never put down the phone until he was absolutely sure that the other party had already hung up. One time in a *shmuess*, he asked a rhetorical question and answered it: "What will become of such a person? He'll become a *kneplach macher* (a buttonmaker)."

Unfortunately someone in the audience happened to be a manufacturer of buttons, and he was convinced that Rabbi Dessler had intended to rebuke him in some way. He told Rabbi Dessler, "I know you meant me," and despite all Rabbi Dessler's protestations to the contrary, the man remained unconvinced. Rabbi Dessler was greatly embarrassed by the incident, and mentioned it privately several times as an example of how careful one must always be to avoid speech that could possibly hurt anyone, however unintentionally.[23]

One time Rabbi Dessler heard that the head of World Agudath Israel, Moreinu Yaakov Rosenheim, whom he had known well in England, was visiting in *Eretz Yisrael*. Rosenheim had a granddaughter living in Bnei Brak, and Rabbi Dessler asked the granddaughter's husband to inform him when Moreinu Rosenheim was to visit them so that he could come over and pay his respects.

---

21. Rabbi Dessler was actively involved in many *shidduchim* though, as a rule, he only suggested a *shidduch* when he knew both parties personally. One such match was that of Rabbi Shalom Ulman, who shared his room after the passing of Rebbetzin Dessler, with Avigayil Silver, who had lived in the same house with Rebbetzin Dessler in Melbourne.

When Rabbi Naftoli Shakovitsky's daughter was considering marrying a young man in *Eretz Yisrael*, the only opinion that the Shakovitskys would rely on was that of Rabbi and Rebbetzin Dessler. The Desslers made a special trip to Zichron Yaakov, where the prospective groom, Rabbi Yitzchak Greenberg, was the *Mashgiach,* in order to put their stamp of approval on the match.

22. Rebbetzin Avigayil Ulman.
23. Rabbi Moshe Turk.

Chapter Nineteen: The Power of His Example

Later Rabbi Dessler realized that Moreinu Rosenheim had too many grandchildren in the country to visit each one individually, and that he might have placed the granddaughter in the awkward position of having to admit that her grandfather would not visit her. To avoid that, Rabbi Dessler traveled into Tel Aviv to personally call on Moreinu Rosenheim. Afterwards he made a big point of telling the granddaughter's husband that he need not tell him if Reb Yaakov visited since he had already met with him in Tel Aviv.[24]

In his "Discourse on Loving-Kindness," Rabbi Dessler distinguishes between "takers" and "receivers." Without someone to receive, he notes, there could be no "givers" in the world either. The difference between a "taker" and a "receiver" lies in their respective attitudes to the benefits they receive from others. The former views everything that others do for him as if it was coming to him by right. He has no compunction about being the recipient of other's largesse. The latter, by contrast, lives by the rule "one who hates presents shall live" (*Mishlei* 15:27) and is filled with *hakaros hatov* for the slightest benefit conferred upon him.

Rabbi Dessler personified the receiver. He tried as much as possible to avoid reliance on others. The first time he met his daughter-in-law Miriam in Cleveland, she marveled how he hesitated to trouble her even for something as simple as a cup of tea. It took him minutes to verbalize the request and when the tea arrived he thanked her profusely for any exertion he had caused her. Those who witnessed the way he thanked his wife with tremendous enthusiasm for bringing him a cold drink on a hot day never forgot it.[25]

The slightest act of *chesed* done for him by one of his students invariably elicited a profusion of thanks. When the students protested that he was being excessive and begged him to stop, he replied, "Also that little thank-you you want to take from me? You'll make me into a debtor, and eventually I'll have to give *din v'cheshbon* (a spiritual accounting) on that."[26]

Kelm inculcated a certain fineness in its products. They conducted

---

24. Rabbi Moshe Turk.
25. Rabbi Meyer Munk.
26. *Marbitzei Torah U'Mussar*, Vol. III, p. 70.

themselves like aristocrats of the spirit, and few more than Rabbi Dessler. Rabbi Moshe Turk once came to visit him around 9:30 in the morning. In the course of their conversation, Rabbi Dessler whispered something in the ear of a yeshiva student who was present. The student then told Rabbi Turk that Rabbi Dessler had not yet eaten and needed to do so. Rabbi Dessler simply could not bring himself to tell Rabbi Turk directly that he could not continue the conversation.

He never lost his temper or even showed any signs of irritation. Among the many *shiurim* that he gave around *Eretz Yisrael* was one which he delivered in Jerusalem for a group of people with academic backgrounds. The educated audience did not simply accept Rabbi Dessler's conclusions on the basis of his authority, especially when he touched upon subjects in which they considered themselves to be equally expert. Nor did they show him the deference to which he was accustomed in yeshiva circles. Yet no matter how challenging their tone or comments, remembers Professor Zev Low, who was a member of the group, Rabbi Dessler never allowed himself to become excited. At most, if someone spoke to him in a particularly provocative fashion, he would delay for a few seconds before responding to him.

Kelm emphasized an honest searching within one's self and a rigorous avoidance on any action that might be in any way questionable. Rabbi Dessler was once waiting at a bus stop in a driving rain when Katriel Munit, a former student of the yeshiva, drove by in a van. He stopped and offered Rabbi Dessler a ride. But before he would get in, Rabbi Dessler asked who owned the van and whether he had permission to pick up passengers. Munit assured Rabbi Dessler that his employer was a religious Jew and that permission was implicit in such circumstances.

Rabbi Dessler remained reluctant to accept the lift, and Munit continued to insist that giving lifts within the city was an everyday practice in the trade. For a moment Rabbi Dessler was persuaded and put his leg up on the dashboard, but he quickly changed his mind and went back to standing in the rain.[27]

---

27. Rabbi Yaakov Edelstein.
 Rabbi Dessler's actions on that occasion were reminiscent of those of Reb Leib

The ultimate enemy of the self-scrutiny demanded by Kelm was self-love and an elevated opinion of one's own attainments. Anything leading to self-love — for example, honor or flattery — had to be avoided, and *anavah* (humility) cultivated. Few succeeded to the same extent as Rabbi Dessler. He once came to visit the Chazon Ish in the latter's sukkah, and the Chazon Ish stood up for him when he entered the sukkah. Unable to conceive that the Chazon Ish was standing for him, Rabbi Dessler instinctively stepped to the side, and turned around to see what distinguished *talmid chacham* had entered behind him.

Rabbi Dov Yaffe once addressed Rabbi Dessler in the third person as "HaRav." Rabbi Dessler told him, "You can injure a person speaking like that." Another time, Rabbi Shalom Schwadron, the famous *maggid*, approached Rabbi Dessler on the street in Jerusalem and said, "When can I come to speak to the *Mashgiach?*" Again Rabbi Dessler looked behind him, as if checking to see who was being addressed, and then explicitly asked Rabbi Schwadron whom he was addressing. When Rabbi Schwadron indicated that he was speaking to Rabbi Dessler, the latter replied, "Whenever it is convenient for you."[28]

Anavah, however, did not mean for Rabbi Dessler merely an awareness of one's faults. If such an awareness did not serve as a spur to action, it was of itself of no value. As he wrote to the organizer of the Beis HaMussar in Jerusalem:

> There is *anavah* and there are those who merely know all their internal contradictions. The latter is not called *anavah*.

Chassid of Kelm in similar circumstances. It is even possible that Rabbi Dessler may have heard of Reb Leib Chassid's behavior during his younger years in Kelm.

In his later years, Reb Leib used to take a daily walk on the road between Kelm and Tavrig. One day a young man passed in his wagon and offered Reb Leib a ride. Reb Leib asked him whether he had permission from his father to pick up riders.

"Do I really need permission?" the young man asked.

"Yes," said Reb Leib, "without permission you are stealing from your father."

Many years later, the young man in the story told Rabbi Yaakov Kaminetsky that the exchange left a lifelong impression on him, and that he had learned from Reb Leib Chassid to flee from any "monkey business."

28. Rabbi Dov Wein.

> A humble person is a *ba'al madregos* (person of stature) who cannot bear the internal contradictions and corrects them. One who sees the contradictions and doesn't correct them, however, is nothing…. [It is merely] laziness masquerading as modesty.[29]

The rigorous self-examination to which Rabbi Dessler subjected himself was the prod with which he formed a personality whose beauty was apprehended by everyone he met. The Chazon Ish himself attested to the level of perfection attained by Rabbi Dessler when he applied to him the words of the Sages: "*HaKadosh Baruch Hu* saw that the truly righteous would be few. [What did He do?] He planted them in every generation."[30]

---

29. *Michtav Me'Eliyahu,* Vol. IV, p. 363.
30. *Marbitzei Torah U'Mussar,* Vol. III, p. 50.

Chapter 20

In the Public Eye

B**Spreading the Word** Y NATURE, RABBI DESSLER WAS A SHY, UNASSUMING man, whose greatest joy was to stay in one place immersed in his books. Yet from the moment he stepped onto the public stage, he drove himself from place to place and from one project to another.

In Ponevezh, he no longer had any fundraising responsibility. And he finally had the opportunity to spend eight hours or more preparing for each talk. Yet he remained a volcano of activity. He traveled back and forth to England twice a year to maintain contact with his *talmidim* and to oversee the institutions that he had helped create.

In addition to his three *shiurim* every week in Ponevezh, he spoke in various locations throughout *Eretz Yisrael* to a diverse array of groups. And he served as inspiration and guide to the young activists of Peylim in their efforts on behalf of new immigrants from Yemen and North Africa.

Rabbi Shraga Grosbard, long-time head of Chinuch Atzmai, described in a written eulogy the impulse that drove Rabbi Dessler to exert himself as he did. Rabbi Dessler's power to convey the vision of the Torah to others, he wrote, was not some technical ability but an expression of his soul, a reflection of his ability to devote himself entirely to others. It was his desire to give to others that led him to clarify the most difficult theological issues as he did.

Teaching Torah was for him the highest form of giving, an obligation from which he could not escape. The world measures greatness, wrote Rabbi Grosbard, in terms of how many people are at one's beck and call. But the Torah view is exactly the opposite: Greatness is measured by how many people one serves. Noach proves the point. Only because he was a *tzaddik tamim* (a perfectly righteous man) was he chosen to serve the lowliest animals in the ark. Rabbi Dessler lived with that sense of obligation to others.

The Chazon Ish once said that when Hashem takes pity on a lowly generation he brings down someone like Rabbi Dessler who is capable of influencing the entire generation.[1] Rabbi Dessler always professed to be amazed that there were those who wished to hear Torah from his lips. He insisted that any power he possessed to influence others was purely a function of the great men from whom he had been privileged to learn. In his mind, he was nothing more than a sponge that absorbs from others and returns the water when squeezed.[2]

Nevertheless as soon as he realized that he had the power to influence others, he also felt obligated to spread his influence as far as possible. As he wrote, "Someone who can affect his environment is responsible for that environment to the degree and extent his influence is felt."[3]

Rabbi Dessler opened his spiritual treasure house to all who could appreciate its riches. He spoke of the same deep matters with *baalei teshuvah* and great scholars, with *yeshivah bachurim* and the young women in Gateshead Seminary.[4] At one point, he even considered printing certain of his talks for distribution to Israeli high-

---

1. Rabbi Yitzchak Greenberg.
2. Ibid.
3. *Strive for Truth*, Vol. II, p. 158.
4. Ibid.

school students to show them how the words of Torah continue to provide guidance for our lives in the modern world.⁵

Over the years, he laboriously copied over in his own hand large numbers of his *shiurim* for students he felt would benefit from them. And he was a pioneer in the use of stencils and mimeographs to distribute his *shiurim* to his farflung *talmidim*.

Rabbi Dessler even sought to tape his *shiurim* in Ponevezh Yeshiva and send the tapes back to England. The idea of a tape recorder in the *beis medrash*, however, was still novel in those days, and he was advised not to do so.⁶

All his public life, Rabbi Dessler attracted those who had wide exposure to secular knowledge. His earliest *talmidim* in England, as we have noted, almost all went on to pursue university degrees, and in *Eretz Yisrael* too he also had wide-ranging contacts with Jews with advanced academic backgrounds.

After Rabbi Dessler's passing, Professor Ernest Simon, a professor of Jewish thought at the Hebrew University, sent a letter to both the Gateshead Kollel and the *hanhalah* of Ponevezh in which he described himself as sharing in their sorrow and that of many Jews "searching for the path of the light of Torah and *emunah*." Simon relates how he and Rabbi Dessler had gotten to know each other the previous summer in Gateshead, where everywhere he went he heard the praises of Rabbi Dessler. Thereafter they met once in Bnei Brak and another time in Jerusalem to discuss matters "standing at the height of the universe." A third meeting had already been scheduled in Jerusalem for 25 *Shevat*, Rabbi Yisrael Salanter's *yahrtzeit*, when Rabbi Dessler planned to speak at the Beis Hamussar in Jerusalem.

Rabbi Dessler gave a regular *shiur* to academics in Haifa that was organized by Max Rowe, a former German refugee to England,

---

5. Rabbi Dovid Zaretsky.
   The Israeli Ministry of Education did eventually print Rabbi Dessler's "Discourse on Lovingkindness" for use in Israeli schools. *Rabbi Aryeh Carmell*.

6. Among those who advised him that such use of a tape recorder would mark him in the Torah world of *Eretz Yisrael* as "*modernish*" was Rabbi Chaim Friedlander. In later years, Rabbi Friendlander frequently lamented his role in preventing Rabbi Dessler's *shiurim* from being recorded for posterity.

whom Rabbi Dessler had been close to in Chesham. Rowe headed the Rothschild Foundation in *Eretz Yisrael*.[7] And every week for an extended period of time, he spoke in Jerusalem in the house of Dr. Dov Shapira, a native of Dvinsk who had learned in Slabodka Yeshiva. The *shiur* was comprised mostly of doctors, and all the members had advanced academic training.[8]

In some sense, these *shiurim* were a continuation of Rabbi Dessler's work with his first *talmidim* in London. Then his concern had been to provide bright young men with answers to the questions raised by exposure to new developments in science and Western thought. With his more mature students in Haifa and Jerusalem, Rabbi Dessler sought to show the eternal relevance of Torah to modern life, and to demonstrate that the Torah had nothing to fear from the latest "findings" of the secular disciplines.

Rabbi Dessler deliberately addressed himself to topics related to the areas of expertise of the members of the Jerusalem group. He gave, for instance, two classes contrasting the Torah psychology of his great-grandfather Rabbi Yisrael Salanter and Freudian psychology. Before Freud, he noted, Reb Yisrael had pioneered awareness of the unconscious. Indeed much of the *mussar* regimen is devoted to planting certain ideas and habits deeply in the subconscious.

But, unlike Freud, Reb Yisrael knew that there is something in man much deeper than the level of the subconscious. That sub-subconscious might be described as the quest of the soul for connection to its Creator. (Many people so avidly pursue worldly pleasures, said Rabbi Dessler, out of a subconscious desire to still "the pangs of spiritual hunger — the longing of the soul for its state of perfection."[9])

Rabbi Dessler spent his life investigating the workings of the mind and how the *yetzer hara* and the *yetzer hatov* do battle at the level of the

---

7. Rabbi Shalom Ulman.
    Rowe was one of those who drew close to Rabbi Dessler while living in Chesham during the war.
8. Professor Zev Lev.
9. *Strive for Truth*, Vol. II, p. 13.

conscious and unconscious.[10] He did not hesitate to use psychological terminology to describe this struggle. Thus he could describe the voice that Elisha ben Avuyah heard, telling him, "Repentance is open to all, except for *Acher*," as the internalized voice of his *yetzer hara*.

Elsewhere he describes how the *yetzer hara* can use the promptings of conscience for its own purposes. "Radical denial" and "self-deception" are the *yetzer hara's* frequent response to the pangs of conscience.[11] Similarly, what we often lazily describe as "forgetfulness" is often a much more subtle unconscious process by which the *yetzer hara* seeks to conceal from us the gravity of our sins.[12]

Each *middah* with which a person is born, Rabbi Dessler showed, has both its positive and negative side. For instance, man's innate sense of his own independence, which causes him to rebel against divine commandments and to attribute everything he achieves to his own abilities, also has its positive side. Without that sense of independence, man would lack awareness of his own free will. He could not exercise his *bechirah* (free will) — the very purpose for which he was created. A person's feeling of independence protects him from despairing of ever being able to change himself.[13]

Only with a proper understanding of the tactics of the *yetzer hara*, Rabbi Dessler felt, was one armed for the struggle. But he insisted that with that knowledge every single human being has the capacity to apprehend the truth: "[E]veryone can get to the truth *if he wants to*…. [B]ias never completely obscures the truth…. This inability of the *yetzer* to obscure the truth completely is a direct outflow of the Creator's lovingkindness."[14]

---

10. Rabbi Moshe Shapiro.

11. *Strive for Truth*, Vol. II, p. 95.

12. Ibid., pp. 99-100.

  At the same time, the conscience is never completely stilled unless negative thoughts are reinforced by negative actions. When thought is converted into action it reinforces the inner defilement and creates the situation described by King Solomon, "A city broken open without walls; a man without restraint to his will" (*Mishlei* 25:28). *Strive for Truth*, Vol. II, p. 107.

13. *Michtav Me'Eliyahu*, Vol. IV, p. 27.

14. *Strive for Truth*, Vol. II, p. 276.

  At the same time, our ability to discern the truth means that we shall be held to account for every taint of impure motivation because we "could have discerned it." Ibid., p. 101.

Each of us, Rabbi Dessler taught, has an inborn ability to distinguish between proper and improper motivations. The trick is to sensitize ourselves to the measuring rods Hashem has given us. When confronted with a moral dilemma, for instance, a righteous man will not hesitate, while the one whose *yetzer hara* still holds sway over him will experience shame. Shame, then, becomes a useful sign that one's motivations are lacking in some respect.[15] And after one exercises his free will, if he feels victorious and satisfied, it is a sign from Heaven that he chose well. Embarrassment, on the other hand, is a sign of having chosen poorly.[16] Another test, Rabbi Dessler devised, was to always ask oneself how did a certain idea come to mind. If it arose hastily, its likely source is the *yetzer hara*.[17]

Rabbi Dessler's psychological acuity and his use of psychological terminology gained him a wide audience among those outside the world of the yeshiva. Those with academic training were also drawn by his willingness to confront and discuss issues and challenges posed to Torah by modern thought and science. He labored to find answers for his young *talmidim* in London and later for those already embarked on academic careers in Jerusalem. Occasionally that required him to read works of science or psychology.[18] His willingness to do so gave him a credibility he would otherwise have lacked.

Each generation had to be addressed at its own level, Rabbi Dessler believed. And he was therefore prepared to speak to all those whom he felt were genuinely seeking the truth in whatever idiom made Torah most accessible for them. One such technique, for instance, was to often explain deep matters of *kabbalah* at the level of *kochos hanefesh* (man's innate spiritual potential).[19]

The large number of those with academic backgrounds drawn to Rabbi Dessler, however, had nothing to do with his support for ad-

---
15. *Michtav Me'Eliyahu* Vol. II, p. 64.
16. Rabbi Mordechai Miller.
17. *Strive for Truth*, Vol. II, p. 269.
18. Rabbi Shmuel Shulsinger.
 See, e.g., *Michtav Me'Eliyahu*, Vol. IV, pp. 357-58 (discussing the problems with evolutionary theory based on the fossil record.)
19. Rabbi Yehoshua Geldzahler; Rabbi Dov Yaffe.

vanced secular training. On the contrary, from the time that he came to England, Rabbi Dessler discouraged his students from pursuing post-secondary studies, except as needed for purposes of earning a living. He had only indifferent success in this regard in light of the strong parental pressures in the opposite direction.[20]

Even if he could not prevent his students from pursuing university training, he still sought to undermine the prestige of secular thought in their eyes. He frequently expressed his skepticism about the latest findings of modern psychology. He had, for instance, only contempt for childraising theories that encouraged parents to treat their children as equals or friends. That approach would only produce "little *chutzpadik* Hitlers," he charged. Such theories led him to warn of "how careful we have to be to ignore all the new findings of the social scientists in connection to psychology and *chinuch* (education)."[21]

At the opposite end of the spectrum from Rabbi Dessler's private classes for the groups of academics were his frequent appearances at the *batei mussar* of Tel Aviv and Jerusalem. In certain respects, he found it more difficult to speak at the *batei mussar*. When a Beis HaMussar was organized in Meah Shearim, and he was asked to be one of the first speakers, he initially declined. Houses of Mussar, he wrote to the organizer, had never been primarily places for hearing *shmuessen*. Rather they had been gathering places for people to pour

---

20. Mrs. Nechama Kahn, wife of Sam Kahn, one of Rabbi Dessler's first pupils in England, once asked Rabbi Dessler how he explained the fact that so many of those closest to him had learned in universities given his outspoken opposition to such studies.

Sam Kahn himself was a good example of the phenomenon. Though he was a professor of English literature at the Hebrew University, he was never heard to speak about non-Torah topics outside the classroom. From the early '30s, he used to study the esoteric aspects of Torah together with Rabbi Dessler. After Rabbi Dessler moved to *Eretz Yisrael*, they used to continue those sessions once a week in Kahn's apartment in Jerusalem. In his later years, Kahn learned all day in his Bayit Vegan apartment with an almost nonstop flow of *chavrusas* from the neighborhood and nearby Kol Torah Yeshiva.

21. *Michtav Me'Eliyahu*, Vol. III, pp. 361-2.

At the same time, Rabbi Dessler was mindful of *Chazal's* words, "If you hear that there is wisdom among the nations, you may believe it...." (*Eichah Rabbasi* 2:13). He met, for instance, with the famous Swiss child-psychologist Jean Piaget on several occasions. *Rabbi Shalom Hoffman.*

out their souls individually and to make a *cheshbon hanefesh* (spiritual accounting).

More repugnant to him, however, was the idea of having different speakers on successive weeks, or even worse, a number of speakers on the same night. "Only in places of lightheadedness — theaters and the like — do they bring together groups of clowns and comedians. But in *divrei Torah, chas v'shalom*. Where is the *kavod haTorah* in that? ... There is no place [in *mussar*] for an audience to hear a new speaker every week...."[22]

Nevertheless Rabbi Dessler acquiesced to the practice of rotating speakers as he found it in the Beis HaMussar of Tel Aviv, and upon occasion he even agreed to speak on the same program with other prominent *mussar* personalities. In the latter case, however, he was almost always filled with remorse afterwards. On one occasion, he begged the organizer to make sure Rabbi Yechezkel Levenstein's talk preceded his on the grounds that he would be embarrassed to speak in front of him.[23]

On another occasion, he agreed to speak together with several other prominent personalities. Not long after, he wrote the organizer:

> *Oy*, for the humiliation and shame that I should take a place among *gedolim*, and how much more so in front of them.... Why have I let myself place my head between these great mountains. Have I chosen such *mitzvos* ... for myself before Rosh Hashanah? It was childishness on my part that I responded favorably to your first letter.
>
> But what can I do. The announcements have been printed....[24]

Besides his private *shiurim* in Haifa and Jerusalem and his talks in the *Batei Mussar* of Tel Aviv and Jerusalem, Rabbi Dessler was often

---

22. *Michtav Me'Eliyahu*, Vol. IV, pp. 359-60.
23. Once while speaking in the Tel Aviv *Beis HaMussar*, Rabbi Dessler stopped in the middle when a leading Mashgiach — probably Rabbi Eliyahu Lopian — walked in. *Rabbi Moshe Turk*.
24. Ibid., p. 364.

R' Dessler addressing a conference of Zeirei Agudath Israel

called upon to address large gatherings. At a conference of Zeirei Agudath Israel, he profoundly moved the audience with a far-ranging speech on the purpose of Creation, the purpose of a human being, and the specific mission of the Jewish people.[25] His last public appearance was a speech at an emergency gathering on behalf of Chinuch Atzmai.

Efforts to Uproot Religion Among the New Immigrants

IN ADDITION TO HIS TEACHING IN VARIOUS FORUMS AND TO A wide array of different groups, Rabbi Dessler played a major role in efforts to rescue the new immigrants from Yemen and North Africa from spiritual destruction in Israel. To understand the significance of those efforts, some background information about the absorption of immigrants from Yemen, North Africa, Iraq and Iran in the late '40s and '50s is necessary.

In the summer of 1949, Rabbi Dovid Zvi Pinkus, a religious member of the Knesset (the Israeli Parliament), charged that a spiritual inquisition was being conducted by the government and the Jewish Agency in the absorption camps. He characterized the assault on the religious practices of the new immigrants as nothing less than the murder of the culture and religion of one of the tribes of Israel.[26]

Pinkus's remarks created an uproar. Chief Rabbis Herzog and Uziel and the Chief Rabbi of Tel Aviv, Rabbi Isser Yehudah Unterman, personally visited a number of the camps in which the

---

25. Rabbi Dov Wein.
26. *Kol Chotzeiv* (the biography of Rabbi Shalom Mordechai HaKohen Schwadron, the Jerusalem Maggid, published by Machon Daas Torah), pp. 473-474.

new immigrants were housed, and they confirmed the substance of Pinkus's charges. A mass demonstration at Manhattan Center in New York City protesting against the new state's disregard for the religious beliefs of new immigrants greatly embarrassed the government of Prime Minister David Ben Gurion, which was heavily dependent on the financial and political support of world Jewry.[27]

In an attempt to quiet the situation, on January 17, 1950, Ben-Gurion appointed a special investigative committee headed by Gad Fromkin, a former justice of the Supreme Court. The other members of the committee were Yitzchak Ben-Zvi, later the second president of Israel, Knesset member Avraham Elmaliach, Rabbi Kalman Kahane, and Rabbi Avraham Chaim Shaag. Nearly five months later, on May 9, 1950, the committee issued its findings.

That committee report gave little solace to the prime minister in his efforts to deflect criticism. Among the committee's conclusions were: (1) The shearing of *peyos* (sidelocks) of immigrant boys was not a chance occurrence, but a methodical practice; (2) the disturbance of traditional religious study was also a methodical practice; and (3) insufficient care was taken in the observance of the Sabbath and prayer, and there were even incidents where prayer was disturbed.[28]

The committee heard testimony from over one hundred witnesses, and the evidence on all these points was so overwhelming that even the nonreligious members could not deny the facts. In one camp after another, religious teachers were harassed or barred entirely. Mr. Aldama, the head of the Ein Shemer refugee camp, announced that the teaching of Torah was forbidden, and that the only subjects to be taught were Hebrew, math, and Zionism.[29] Young people from a religious school in Pardes Chana were denied entry for a *Tu B'Shevat* celebration while the teenagers from nearby Kfar Vitkin had ready access to the camps to conduct mixed Israeli dancing.[30]

Vaad HaYeshivos sent two teachers to the Machane Yisrael camp after a hundred families in the camp requested religous education

---

27. Ibid., pp. 474-5.
28. Moshe Schonfeld, *Genocide in the Holy Land*, p. 400.
29. Ibid., p. 380.
30. Ibid., p. 372.

A Peylim activist teaching Yemenite youngsters.

for their children. They taught in the camp synagogue, until the director of the camp ordered the synagogue locked. Holy books and textbooks were strewn outside. One of the teachers was dragged to the entrance to the camp, his hands held behind his back, and bodily thrown out of the camp. When he attempted to return, he was threatened with a rifle.[31] In Be'er Yaakov the camp director removed all the benches from the synagogue to make it impossible to conduct religious instruction.[32]

A large number of parents in Amka requested religious schooling for their children, but when Rabbi Yitzchak Winkelstein and a group of teachers sent by Agudath Israel responded to their request, they were threatened if they persisted in seeking entry to the camp. The next day, as Rabbi Winkelstein was teaching thirty youngsters in the synagogue, an armed man burst in, announced that the Arabs had attacked the camp, and ordered everyone down on the floor and the lights shut off. Only hours later, when they were finally allowed to leave, did those in the synagogue discover that there had been no attack and everything had continued as usual in the camp. The camp watchman told Rabbi Winkelstein that the whole scenario was a ruse to prevent the Yemenite children from studying Torah.[33]

---

31. Ibid., p. 373.
32. Ibid., p. 375.
33. Ibid., pp. 377-788.

Religious teachers in Atlit were told that they were forbidden to teach without the authorization of the Department of Culture. On November 14, 1949, the camp director, accompanied by policemen, entered one of the synagogues (another had already been appropriated for Hebrew lessons) and ordered all the religious teachers detained in his office for two hours. The teachers were then turned over to the police from Zichron Yaakov for further questioning.[34]

Parents who insisted on religious instruction for their children were subjected to intense pressure to change their minds. Professor Yeshayah Leibowitz testified before the committee that in Liftah parents were told explicitly that if they asked for religious classes, they would not receive food and clothing for their families and would not find jobs.[35]

The Mizrachi daily newspaper *HaTzofeh* published a form letter sent by the Labor Council of Nes-Ziona to a parent who had registered his child for religious schooling:

> Dear Member:
>
> We learned that you registered your child with the Agudath Israel/Mizrachi school.
>
> We assume that you did that due to an error and you are asked, therefore, to demand immediately from the registration clerk of the city council to have your child transferred to the workmen's school.
>
> If you do not do so right away, your membership in the Histadrut will be considered void.[36]

Besides discouraging all forms of religious education, the directors of the aborption camps took many steps designed to destroy the religious faith and practice of immigrant children. Children slept in special quarters away from their parents, which dramatically

---

34. Ibid., p. 375.
35. Ibid., pp. 382, 384.
36. Ibid., p. 385.

An absorption camp

decreased the ability of their parents to protect their religious beliefs and practice.

For the Yemenite Jews, their long *peyos* had always been a sign of Jewish distinctiveness. In order to instill the Yemenite youngsters with the idea that all such religious practices were no longer necessary in Israel where everyone was Jewish, many camp directors waged systematic campaigns to remove the *peyos* of immigrant children. The committee found a recurrent pattern of systematic removal of *peyos* in "Ein Shemer, Rosh HaAyin, Beit Lid and probably other places."[37]

No camp head waged a more determined assault on *peyos* than Tzipporah Zahavi in Beit Lid. Children who refused to have their *peyos* cut were denied the right to go on organized trips, and even those who refused often had their *peyos* removed against their will. When the first group of children from Beit Lid were brought to Ponevezh Yeshiva, the Ponevezher Rav was astonished to hear them add a special *HaRachaman* prayer to their *bentsching* (the blessing after eating bread) calling for Hashem to take revenge against Tzipporah. Only when he inquired as to the origin of this

---

37. Ibid., p. 396.

HaRachaman, did he learn who Tzipporah was and what she had done.

The cutting of *peyos* was only the first step in the assault on all religious practice. Zahavi told the children in her charge that their blessings after eating in the lunchroom were disturbing and that "prayer is not necessary in *Eretz Yisrael*." [38]

On a Shabbos walk in Beit Lid, the counselor encouraged the children to walk beyond the Shabbos boundary and to pick from the fruits in the orchard. When the children refused to do so, the counselor told them not to be afraid. He then picked the fruit himself while explaining to the children, "There is no Shabbos in *Eretz Yisrael*."[39]

Peylim Is Born

IT WAS LEFT PRIMARILY TO A HANDFUL OF YOUTHFUL ACTIVISTS in Ponevezh and Hebron Yeshivos to attempt to thwart the designs of the government and Jewish Agency. Until Peylim, religious Jews in *Eretz Yisrael* tended to see themselves only as passive victims. Peylim instilled, for the first time, that it was possible to resist efforts to uproot religion.[40]

Though they had neither the numbers nor the resources to save the culture and religion of most of Oriental Jewry, whatever was saved from that period is due largely to them. The phenomenal growth of Shas (the Sephardi Torah Guardians Party) in the last decade reflects the deep bitterness left over from the cultural annihilation of the period. At the same time, the existence of a nucleus around which a Sephardi religious party could be formed more than thirty years later represents the fruits of the efforts of a dedicated band of yeshiva *bachurim* in those days.

Sometime in the winter of 1949-50, a tall Nitra Yeshiva student named Yosef Gobitz walked into Ponevezh Yeshiva during *Shalosh Seudos*. In the presence of the Ponevezher Rav, he banged on the table and demanded the attention of all those present. He then began to describe what was taking place in the immigrant absorption

---

38. Ibid., p. 386.
39. Ibid., p. 396.
40. Rabbi Moshe Tzviyon, one of the principal Peylim activists.

Chapter Twenty: In the Public Eye / 323

camps nearby, including the cutting off of the *peyos* of children in Beit Lid.

When he had finished, the Ponevezher Rav asked who was willing to investigate the story and to bring children back to the orphanage he had established if the charges proved true. Shalom Ber Lifshitz and Yitzchak Yacobovitz[41] answered the call. Motzaei Shabbos they traveled to Beit Lid, and under the cover of darkness, dug under the barbed-wire fence surrounding the camp.

Shlomo Noach Kroll with a young boy in Ein Shemer.

Once inside, they began speaking to the parents. The parents complained that the camp authorities forced their children to violate the Torah and that the female counselors were immodestly dressed. After the two *bachurim* described the purpose of their mission, one of the parents volunteered to go to the children's house and to bring out some young boys. At 1 a.m., Lifshitz and Yacobovitz arrived at the orphanage established by the Ponevezher Rav, accompanied by six boys. Most of the yeshiva, including the Ponevezher Rav himself, was still waiting up to greet them. The Ponevezher Rav personally kissed each of the boys.

By early the next morning, however, the disappearance of the boys had already been discovered and the police were at the yeshiva searching for the culprits. They threatened Lifshitz and Yacobovitz with jail for kidnapping, despite their protestations that they had only taken the children with the explicit permission of their parents.

---

41. In addition to being one of the founders of Peylim, Rabbi Lifshitz is also the head of the Yad L'Achim antimissionary organization and a *rav* in Petach Tikva. Rabbi Jacobovitz is the *rav* of Hertzliya.

The two *bachurim* were forced to return to Beit Lid with their charges. There they explained to the parents that they would have to declare their desire to send their children to Ponevezh to the camp administration. The administration tried every possible stratagem to dissuade the parents. They told the parents that their children would receive no medical care, food or clothing. The most vociferous was a young counselor wearing a knitted *kippah*, who told the parents that their children would be left unable to earn a living if they entered the *chareidi* educational system.[42]

Nevertheless the parents remained firm. One mother, who was asked why she wanted to consign her son to such an educational system, pointed towards Heaven and recited the verse, "Cast upon Hashem your burden, and He will sustain you" (*Tehillim* 55:23).[43]

Those six children rescued from Beit Lid were just the beginning. A small group of Ponevezh *bachurim* visited the handful of yeshivos then in existence in search of dormitory space for more children from the camps. Rabbi Isaac Sher, Rosh Yeshiva of Slabodka Yeshiva, had twenty spaces; Rabbi Hillel Vitkind, Rosh Yeshiva of the Novordhok Yeshiva in Tel Aviv, had room for fifty, but no beds. The *bachurim* went around collecting in Bnei Brak until they had gathered fifty beds and the necessary bedding.[44]

In those early days of activity, the young activists did not even have money for busses, and they had to hitchhike from one place to another. When they would return to Ponevezh after long days in the field, Mrs. Munk, the cook, made sure that they were fed.[45]

In almost every camp, the yeshiva students had to resort to subterfuge to enter. In early 1950, Shlomo Noach Kroll[46] and Noach Berman, two Ponevezh *talmidim*, were detained and locked up by the camp administration in Ein Shemer. A large crowd of Yemenite Jews, some of them brandishing the stakes used to secure the tents,

---

42. Rabbi Shalom Ber Lifshitz.
43. *Kol Chotzeiv* pp. 464-67; Rabbi Shalom Ber Lifshitz.
44. *Kol Chotzeiv*, p. 468; Rabbi Shlomo Noach Kroll.
45. *Kol Chotzeiv*, p. 469.
46. Later he became Rav of Chemed and son-in-law of Rabbi Yaakov Landau, Rav of Bnei Brak.

A newpaper account of the killing of Yaacov Gerbi

gathered to demand their release, and in the ensuing confrontation shots were fired by the camp guards.

Kroll begged the Yemenites to stop and warned them that they were dealing with murderers. His words proved prophetic. A month later, in the midst of a similar confrontation with the camp authorities over the detention of one of the Yememite women for questioning, a Yemenite Jew by the name of Yaacov Gerbi was shot dead by a camp guard.[47]

By early *Nissan* of 1950, the need for an organization to direct the rescue activities in the camps and in the villages and *ma'abarot* (slums of tin huts) to which the immigrants were sent from the camps was widely recognized. Rabbi Isser Zalman Meltzer, Rosh Yeshiva of Eitz Chaim Yeshiva in Jerusalem, issued a call for a meeting of leading *rabbanim* and community activists. Signing with him were Rabbi Dov Berish Wiedenfeld, the Tchebiner Rav; Rabbi Eliezer Yehudah Finkel, Rosh Yeshivas Mir; Rabbi Yechezkel Sarna, Rosh Yeshivas Chevron; Rabbi Akiva Sofer, *av beis din* of Pressburg, and Rabbi Yaakov Moshe Charlop.[48]

At a large gathering of yeshiva *bachurim*, *Chol HaMoed Pesach*, the three main speakers were Rabbi Isser Zalman Meltzer, Rabbi Yechezkel Abramsky, and Rabbi Eliezer Yehudah Finkel. Rabbi Isser Zalman demanded from each *yeshiva bachur* present a commitment of at least two weeks in the course of the year to the rescue work in

---

47. Ibid., pp. 476-9.
48. Ibid., p. 481.

the camps and the neighborhoods where the new immigrants congregated. Most dramatically, Rabbi Isser Zalman promised those assembled that their own learning would not be harmed as a consequence. It was impossible, he said, that those who devoted themselves to the Torah learning of others would lose their own as a consequence.[49]

A new organization known as Peylim was established at that gathering. Over 100 yeshiva students and thirty seminary students answered Rabbi Isser Zalman's initial call. But the hardcore activists at any given time numbered no more than ten. The others were involved primarily during *bein hazemanim* (intersession), or as needed.[50]

Peylim carried on the battle on many fronts.[51] The leading activists — Shalom Ber Lifshitz, Shlomo Noach Kroll, Noach Berman, Moshe Tzviyon, and a few others — continued to be active in the immigrant camps. But, in addition, Peylim was involved in organizing new schools. The organization's volunteers devoted much time to registering students for the fledgling Chinuch Atzmai system. Every *bein hazemanim* (intersession) fifty or so students from Ponevezh, Hebron, and Vishnitz went around the country signing up children for religious schools.

R' Sholom Schwadron visiting the Peylim Yeshivah in Beer Sheva

---

49. *Kol Chotzeiv*, p. 483; Rabbi Shlomo Noach Kroll.

50. *Kol Chotzeiv*, p. 484.

51. Peylim continued to be extremely active with new immigrants throughout the 1950's and beyond. The idealism of the young activists eventually became known in America, and an American branch of the organization was established. The most active member was Rabbi Shlomo Freifeld, and among the other members who came to *Eretz Yisrael* at one time or another were other well-known figures such as: Rabbi Berl Schwartzman, Rabbi Elya Svei, Rabbi Nisson Alpert, Rabbi Chaim Dov Keller, and Rabbi Yaakov Weisberg. *Rabbi Shlomo Noach Kroll.*

Peylim established *yeshivos ketanos* for high-school-age students in Afula, Acco, Beer Sheva, and Taoz, from which most of the graduates continued on in more advanced yeshivos. Many residential educational facilities were established in the early '50s for new immigrant children, as the only way to rescue them from the social environment of the *ma'abarot*.

Other volunteers were involved in assisting the older immigrants in making the adjustment to life in Israel and in organizing night *shiurim* for them. The *Chazon Ish*[52] was asked whether it was appropriate for *talmidei chachamim* to teach basically unlearned Jews *Chumash* and *Mishnah*. He replied that it was not only permissible but an obligation of "learning for the purpose of teaching." As a consequence, a number of distinguished kollel scholars would travel to different settlements to teach *shiurim* from 5 p.m. to 7 p.m. Young Beis Yaakov girls instructed immigrant women in the laws of *terumos* and *ma'aseros* (tithes).

Peylim volunteers taught the new immigrants to demand their rights. They were instructed how to press for religious schooling and other religious services, like *mikvaos*, and how to keep their daughters from being drafted into the army. The new immigrants greatly needed such advice since the Jewish Agency and government resorted to a slew of ploys to thwart the immigrants' desire for religious education for their children.

For instance, the Jewish Agency refused to construct religious schools in the *ma'abarot* on the grounds that they were only temporary. Yet many of the original residents were still in the *ma'abarot* more than a generation later. In cities where both religious and nonreligious schools were built, the former were almost universally in more remote areas of the town or city and consisted of nothing besides classrooms while the nonreligious schools were larger, better equipped, and contained many special purpose facilities. In Beit Shemesh, for instance, the secular school, with 240 children, occupied a modern two-story

---

52. The *Chazon Ish* took an active interest in the activities of Peylim, and the principal activists and younger *roshei yeshiva* involved in its activities consulted with him frequently. *Kol Chotzeiv*, p. 498. The Brisker Rav too was kept constantly abreast of the activities of Peylim. *Rabbi Shlomo Noach Kroll.*

53. *Genocide in the Holy Land*, p. 412.

building while the government's religious school, with 350 students, was housed in an inadequate little building.[53]

In some smaller villages, the Jewish Agency built only one school, which automatically went to the secular system. Even if the overwhelming majority of the parents voted to transfer the school to the government's religious system, their request would only be granted if there were at least 25 children for the school in first and second grade. That was rarely the case in smaller settlements where the total number of school-age children was between 80 and 100.[54]

Just how successful the Jewish Agency and government were in denying religious schooling can be seen from the fact that the percentage of children in religious schooling did not increase after 1953, even though a large majority of the immigrants in those years were from religious communities in North Africa.[55]

Rabbi Dessler's Involvement in Peylim

WE DO NOT KNOW PRECISELY WHEN RABBI DESSLER BEGAN his intense involvement with Peylim. He was not present at the first large gathering *Chol HaMoed Pesach* 1950, but was at the next gathering six months later.

But if we do not know with certainty when Rabbi Dessler's involvement began, we do at least know the triggering event. One day he was coming down the stairs from Ponevezh Yeshiva when he met Rabbi Ezra Brizel, who was at that time a young *maggid shiur* in Yeshivas Tiferes Tzvi and active in Peylim.

Filled with a sense of the urgency of the rescue work, Rabbi Brizel challenged Rabbi Dessler to become involved in the work in the absorption camps. "What are you achieving there?" he asked, pointing to Ponevezh Yeshiva. "At most, you improve the spiritual level of two hundred young men who are already studying Torah. But do you know that a few miles from here they are feeding *treifos* (improperly slaughtered meat) to Jewish children, cutting off their *peyos*, and forcing them to violate the Shabbos?"

---

54. Ibid., p. 408.
55. Ibid., p. 422.

Rabbi Dessler replied, "Ezra, you have given me something to think about. I will not sleep tonight."[56]

From that time on Rabbi Dessler's commitment to the work of Peylim intensified greatly. Once he saw a group of *bachurim* eagerly involved in the selection of their Four Species for Sukkos, and he commented, as if to himself, "They worry so much about their *esrogim*, but not about the descendants of the *Rambam* and the *Beis Yosef* (Rabbi Yosef Caro)."[57]

The winter of 1950-51 was a bitter one in *Eretz Yisrael*, with heavy snow and frost. By that time, *chadarim* had been established in Rosh HaAyin and a few other locales, but the Jewish Agency declared that it would only provide winter garments to the families of those whose children were studying in nonreligious schools. In response, a large group of Ponevezh Yeshiva students went around Bnei Brak collecting winter clothing in big bags slung over their shoulders.

When they reached Rabbi Dessler's house, he took out every piece of warm clothing he had brought from Gateshead — every sweater, every coat, every piece of thermal underwear. Rebbetzin Dessler was astonished to find the closets empty when she returned home.[58]

Two truckloads of clothing were brought to Rosh HaAyin. Fearing that the Jewish Agency would confiscate the clothing, the Peylim volunteers unloaded the trucks at a distance from the camp and spent hours stuffing it through a little opening in the fence. When they were done, they spent the rest of the night walking back to Bnei Brak. Arriving back in Bnei Brak, Rabbi Dessler personally prepared breakfast for them in his home, as he did on many occasions after similar missions.[59]

As *Mashgiach* in Ponevezh Yeshiva, Rabbi Dessler could not and did not encourage every *bachur* to become actively involved in the Peylim work, at least during the *zman*. His oft-proclaimed stance in the yeshiva was that the *bachurim* would have the greatest impact on

---

56. *Kol Chotzeiv*, p. 467; Rabbi Aryeh Carmell.
57. Rabbi Shlomo Noach Kroll.
58. *Kol Chotzeiv*, pp. 490-92; Rabbi Shalom Ber Lifshitz.
59. *Kol Chotzeiv*, pp. 492-93; Rabbi Shalom Ber Lifshitz.

Peylim activists distributing clothing from the clothing drive

the world through their own self-completion. He continually emphasized that nothing superseded the importance of Torah, and that the entire world depends on the learning of Torah.[60] Nevertheless, he did encourage the half a dozen or so *bachurim* who were already actively involved and whom he considered suited to the work. These were without exception young men who could be depended upon to return to the *beis hamedrash* even after the most exhausting days filled with physical danger and draining travel. In time, almost every member of this group was recognized as a leading *talmid chacham*, despite the fact that they had each given up several years of full-time learning to Peylim.

Rabbi Dessler became the spiritual guide for this core group of activists. Others, like Rabbi Yaakov Landau, the long-time *rav* of Bnei Brak, were more involved in the nitty-gritty of their daily plans, but it was Rabbi Dessler to whom they turned for overall guidance.

He began by establishing a few basic principles. First, the work must be done as quietly as possible, with an absolute minimum of publicity. Any fanfare, he was convinced, would signal the death

---

60. *Kol Chotzeiv*, p. 469; Rabbi Shlomo Noach Kroll.

knell of the organization. In driving home this point, he compared the work of Peylim to the *luchos* received by *Moshe Rabbeinu*. The first *luchos* were received amidst thunder and lightning, and they were broken; the second set of commandments were given in private, and they survived.[61]

Anything false, or smacking of self-interest, was anathema to Rabbi Dessler, and he instilled similar feelings in his close followers. "He taught us to think honestly and without falsehood," remembered Rabbi Shlomo Noach Kroll. "If he heard anything false, he would make certain almost involuntary movements as if to indicate how *pasul* (unacceptable) such falsehood is."

The activists in Ponevezh Yeshiva viewed Rabbi Dessler as exceptionally incisive in his analysis of what needed to be done. But he was very resistant to giving them instructions and telling them what to do. He would cross-examine them in detail about their plans to make sure that they had thought out the options and likely consequences. But once assured that they had, he preferred instead to let them work out the solutions for themselves.[62]

The only thing that he insisted on was that whatever decisions they reached should have unanimous approval. *Avodas haKodesh*, holy work for the benefit of the *Klal*, he taught them, must be done with unity. The *siyata d'Shamaya* (Divine assistance) enjoyed by those engaged in such work derives from the power of the *Klal*, Rabbi Dessler felt, and is therefore lost through strife and disagreement, which are the antithesis of the inherent unity of *Klal Yisrael*.[63]

Rabbi Dessler related to the small group of activists with a fatherly solicitude. He was involved in every aspect of their lives. Rabbi Shlomo Noach Kroll, for instance, slept in Rabbi Dessler's house almost every night in 1953 and ate breakfast with him every morning. One time Rabbi Dessler asked him whether he was worried that being out of the study hall might not hurt his marriage prospects. Rabbi Kroll replied that he only needed one wife and that

---

61. Rabbi Shlomo Noach Kroll. See, *Midrash Tanchuma Ki Sisa* 31; *Rashi* to *Shemos* 34:3.
62. Rabbi Shalom Ber Lifshitz; Rabbi Shlomo Noach Kroll.
63. Rabbi Shlomo Noach Kroll.

he was sure that she had already been picked out for him in Heaven. Rabbi Dessler liked the response.

Another time, Rabbi Dessler and Rabbi Kroll were approached by a poor man, feigning that he was crippled, as they came out of morning *davening*. Rabbi Dessler commented, "He's healthier than I am," but was immediately filled with remorse that he had spoken disparagingly about a fellow Jew. A short time later, while Rabbi Dessler was preparing breakfast, the same poor man knocked on the door. Rabbi Dessler was overjoyed by the opportunity to make amends for his earlier comment. He went outside to greet the man as if he were a long-lost brother and to entreat him to stay for breakfast.[64]

At some point, Peylim decided to establish a *yeshiva gedolah* for the graduates of its four *yeshivos ketanos*, and Shalom Ber Lifshitz was assigned the task. He was then still a *bachur* and doubted whether he was suitable for the task. He went to consult with Rabbi Dessler.

Rabbi Dessler told him a story involving Rabbi Chaim Volozhiner. A certain major contributor specified that he wanted his contribution to Volozhin Yeshiva to go to the support of the *talmidim* and not to buying a carriage or new suit for the yeshiva's fundraiser. Reb Chaim told him that the money contributed finds its proper place according to the intention of the one who gave it, and he need not worry. Similarly, Rabbi Dessler told Rabbi Lifshitz, if things have arranged themselves so that you have been selected for this task, it is because you are the one best suited for it.

In addition to his direct contact with the principal activists in Ponevezh, Rabbi Dessler headed for a period of time a group of younger *roshei yeshiva* and *talmidei chachamim* who served as the Vaad HaRabbonim of Peylim. These included: Rabbi Simcha Zissel Broide, Rabbi Avraham Farbstein, Rabbi Tzvi Markowitz, Rabbi Eliyahu Mishkovsky, Rabbi Shalom Schwadron, the Strikover Rebbe, and Rabbi Avraham Yaakov Zaleznik.

As the senior member of Peylim's formal administrative structure, one of Rabbi Dessler's primary tasks was to represent Peylim in talks

---
64. Ibid.

At a gathering for Peylim, Chol Hamoed Pesach 1951. Right to left: R' Sholom Schwadron, R' Dessler, R' Zalman Sorotzkin (speaking), R' Yaakov Landau.

with other religious groups. On one occasion, for instance, Peylim sought some financial assistance from Agudath Israel. But Rabbi Dessler was insistent that the work of Peylim not be seen as connected to anything political. In a meeting with Rabbi Zalman Sorotzkin, the Lutzker Rav, who was then the head of Agudath Israel in *Eretz Yisrael*, he demanded that certain forms containing both the name Peylim and Agudath Israel be redone and the name of Agudath Israel removed.[65]

After three years of activity, Peylim had acquired quite a reputation for itself, and a certain older, better-established organization sought to incorporate Peylim within its existing framework. The young activists of Peylim were not eager to lose their independence and did not believe that the older, more staid organization really understood the work in the field. Rabbi Dessler led a delegation of the young activists to Jerusalem to the offices of the other organization. Once there, he told his companions to leave the room, but behind the closed doors, they heard him say, "Do you know what these *bachurim* have accomplished? Stay out of their way and let them work."[66]

---

65. Ibid.
66. Rabbi Shalom Ber Lifshitz.

Rabbi Dessler's impact was immediately felt on the Vaad. His first meeting as head of the Vaad HaRabbanim was called for 7 p.m. at the Peylim office in Tel Aviv. The secretary of the Vaad, who had the keys to the building, arrived five minutes late to find Rabbi Dessler already standing outside by himself. The secretary told Rabbi Dessler that in the future he should come half an hour after the time called for the meeting, but Rabbi Dessler replied that he could not do that. Within three weeks, all members of the Vaad were arriving on time.

When he took on the position as head of the Vaad HaRabbanim, Rabbi Dessler made two conditions. The first was that he too must become an activist. It was impossible, he asserted, to be associated with an organization named Peylim (literally, those who do) and not be active oneself.

He suggested that perhaps the organization needed a "white beard." And that is what he became. When, for instance, the young activists of Peylim needed someone who could win the confidence of the *Chachamim* of the Yemenite community, they would bring Rabbi Dessler to meet them. Rabbi Kroll took Rabbi Dessler to *hachnasos sifrei Torah* all around the country. Since the only thing Peylim could promise parents was that their children would grow up to be *yirei Shamayim* (G-d-fearing), and not like the other children they saw on the street, it was important for the new immigrant parents to see someone of Rabbi Dessler's stature. At these gatherings, Rabbi Dessler would discuss *Zohar* with the Sephardi Chachamim.[67]

Rabbi Dessler's second condition for joining the Vaad was that he not be disturbed on Wednesdays and Fridays for the eight hours prior to his *sichos* on those nights. That condition turned out, however, not to be inviolable. One time the Vaad had a Thursday-night meeting, and it was decided that something very urgent needed to be done the next day in Jerusalem. But no one present was available to undertake the mission. One lived in the North and would not have time to reach Jerusalem and return home before Shabbos began; another was a neighborhood rabbi and had to be home to

---

67. Rabbi Shlomo Noach Kroll.

R' Sholom Schwadron dancing with Ezra Brizel

answer *shaylos* that arose during the pre-Shabbos preparations.

When it became clear that no one could go, Rabbi Dessler volunteered. Everyone protested that it was impossible. His need to prepare for his Friday-evening talk in the yeshiva was known to all, and it had not even occurred to any of the other members of the Vaad to ask him. But Rabbi Dessler pushed aside their objections.

"We all decided that this must be done," he explained, "and since no one else can do it, I must go." That, the secretary of the Vaad recalls, was the last time any of the members ever said that they could not do something on *Erev Shabbos*.

How important was Rabbi Dessler's contribution to Peylim? It is impossible to quantify. But one anecdote from *Kol Chotzeiv*, the recently published biography of the Jerusalem Maggid, Rabbi Shalom Schwadron, casts some light. One day, Rabbi Schwadron and his good friend Rabbi Ezra Brizel were standing on Rechov Raavad in Bnei Brak when they fell to reminiscing about the founding of Peylim.

Rabbi Schwadron reminded his friend how they had been together the day that Rabbi Brizel approached Rabbi Dessler and demanded that he become more involved in Peylim. "You brought in Rabbi Dessler, and from that time things began to move in the Holy Land," Rabbi Schwadron told his friend. "If so, it was you, Ezra, you ..." Hearing these words, Rabbi Brizel, no longer a youngster, kicked up his heels and began dancing in the middle of Rechov Raavad.[68]

---

68. *Kol Chotzeiv*, pp. 467-68.

Chapter 21

The Final Years

RABBI DESSLER'S LAST YEARS WERE NOT EASY ONES. Never in robust health, his health continued to decline. An even greater blow was the loss of his life partner Rebbetzin Bluma Dessler two years before his own *petirah.*
Yet neither the decline in his health nor the loss of his wife caused him to desist from his busy schedule. The day he died, he busied himself all morning with travel plans to England for one of his regular visits to the institutions he had brought into being. After his death, a half-completed letter informing his *talmidim* in England of his travel plans was found among his papers.

In those last two years, he was involved on a day-to-day basis with the young Peylim activists. He also spent much time working on a plan to completely reorganize the *kollelim* in *Eretz Yisrael* in order to greatly increase the subsidies for kollel scholars from charitable organizations like the Joint Distribution Committee.[1] And he continued to give his regular *shmuessen* in Ponevezh Yeshiva up until the very end.

---
1. Rabbi Yitzchak Greenberg.

In December 1950, Rabbi Dessler was told that he would need surgery. His long-time friend Rabbi Yitzchak Hillman and the latter's son-in-law Ashkenazi Chief Rabbi Yitzchak Isaac Herzog wired Solomon Sassoon in England for £500 to pay for Rabbi Dessler to travel to the United States for the surgery.

Yet despite the urging of many of those closest to him, in particular Rabbi Yechezkel Sarna, the Rosh Yeshiva of Hebron Yeshiva, that he travel to America for the surgery, Rabbi Dessler eventually decided against it. In early 1951, he wrote to Rabbi Sassoon:

> It is halachically permissible to leave *Eretz Yisrael* in a case of great necessity, in particular for an operation which entails a certain amount of danger. Nevertheless since the operation is also performed here, almost always successfully, and since, in any event, there is a certain amount of danger, and one needs Divine mercy, perhaps it makes more sense to worry about whether it is proper to leave *Eretz Yisrael*. I fear that it would reflect a lack of *bitachon* [to go abroad], especially in light of the special merit of *Eretz Yisrael*.

In addition to his concern about the propriety of leaving *Eretz Yisrael*, Rabbi Dessler was worried about the effect his going abroad would have on Rebbetzin Dessler. He doubted whether his wife was physically strong enough for a trip abroad. And were he to go by himself, he knew that she would be beset by worries the whole time that he was away.

After consulting with the *Chazon Ish*, who fully agreed with his reluctance to leave *Eretz Yisrael*, Rabbi Dessler decided to undergo the surgery at Shaarei Tzedek hospital in Jerusalem. Rabbi Berel Povarsky spent the entire Shabbos after the surgery with him in Shaarei Tzedek hospital. The doctors told Rabbi Povarsky that the pain from the surgery was very intense. Yet Rabbi Dessler never once mentioned the pain he was in.

We can gauge that pain from a letter written to Rabbi Sassoon three weeks after the operation. Rabbi Dessler had still not fully recovered. The surgery brought in its wake an excruciating attack of gallstones. Rabbi Dessler complained to Rabbi Sassoon that he could not concentrate his thoughts at all. Even reading a newspaper was beyond his powers of concentration, and to write a letter to Rabbi Sassoon, he had to write a few lines, rest, and then start again.

No sooner had Rabbi Dessler recovered from his operation than Rebbetzin Dessler learned that she too would need surgery. On November 15, 1951, Rabbi Dessler wrote to Rabbi Sassoon's mother declining an invitation to visit the Sassoons in England because Mrs. Dessler would soon be undergoing surgery.

Two weeks later, he again wrote the Sassoon family. "It is almost impossible to sit down and write, nevertheless, taking into consideration your devotion to us, it is even more impossible not to write," he began. Just as Mrs. Dessler had been about to be released from the hospital, she developed an embolism that entered her lung and blocked the flow of blood to the heart. Rabbi Dessler revealed that he had already asked the yeshivos in Israel and England to pray for her. In a postcript dated December 19, Rabbi Dessler wrote that the situation had worsened and that he had called in another specialist.

Even in her last days, under an oxygen tent, the habits of nobility did not desert Rebbetzin Dessler. She apologized to everyone who had to serve her in any way, whether family, friends, or the hospital staff.

Rebbetzin Dessler did not recover. *Leil Shabbos*, 23 *Kislev*, Rebbetzin Dessler passed away with Rabbi Dessler at her side. Just like her grandfather and father before her, her last moments were ones of total calm. She asked to recite *vidui* (the confessional prayer). Rabbi Dessler instructed her to say, "Let my death be a *kapparah* (atonement)." Those were her last words.

Rabbi Dessler was staying with his friends, the Silvers, with whom Rebbetzin Dessler had lived for over five years in Australia. He knew that they would be devastated by her passing, and could not bring himself to cause them that pain. He walked around the neighborhood for a long time Shabbos night to avoid returning to the Silvers' home. Even when he did finally enter, he

Chapter Twenty-one: The Final Years / 339

did not mention the disaster that had befallen him, but waited for the Silvers to discern it for themselves.[2]

On the outside, he gave no sign of his loss, in keeping with the injunction against public displays of mourning on Shabbos. When Rabbi Simchah Zissel Schapiro[3] greeted him the next day, Rabbi Dessler told him that he could not answer him because he was an *onein* (a mourner during the period before burial). Rabbi Schapiro had been unable to see that something was wrong from Rabbi Dessler's external demeanor. Only on *Motzaei Shabbos*, after *Havdalah*, did Rabbi Dessler finally give full vent to his tears over his beloved wife.

Sunday morning, the day of the *levayah* (funeral), Rabbi Silver was shocked to find Rabbi Dessler polishing his shoes. Rabbi Dessler explained, "She was always meticulous that my clothes should be spotless before I left the house, and now I'm fulfilling her will." Chief Rabbi Herzog, who had known Rebbetzin Dessler well in England and *Eretz Yisrael*, eulogized her as a "rare mixture of simplicity, humility, and modesty combined with a greatness of soul and the most elevated spirit." Rebbetzin Dessler was buried in Sanhedria, Jerusalem in an unmarked grave in keeping with the traditions of Kelm, which she had honored so greatly in her lifetime.[4]

Rebbetzin Dessler's kever

---

2. Rabbi Aharon Sorasky relates a story that Rabbi Dessler went to visit Chief Rabbi Yitzchak Isaac Herzog that night. Rabbi Herzog did not realize that anything had happened until he began to ask Rabbi Dessler about Rebbetzin Dessler's health, and the latter failed to answer his questions. Rabbi Herzog asked in amazement, "Why didn't you tell me?" To which Rabbi Dessler replied, "It's Shabbos. And it is forbidden to speak about painful matters on Shabbos." *Marbitzei Torah U'Mussar, Vol. III, p. 87*.

I have not been able to locate the source for this story or discern what could have brought Rabbi Dessler to Rabbi Herzog's house other than to inform him of the Rebbetzin's passing.

3. Rabbi Shapiro was a grandson of the Alter of Kelm's younger brother.

4. Rabbi Dessler too was buried in an unmarked grave. Years later, however, Rabbi Elya Lopian told Rabbi Nachum Velvel Dessler that he should put up headstones for his parents since no one today is capable of understanding the customs of Kelm.

After the Rebbetzin's *petirah*, Rabbi Dessler changed his normal conduct in two ways. Those changes reveal much about the great respect he had for his wife and his sensitivity to her desires. The Desslers had received a beautiful *kiddush* cup as a wedding present from Rabbi Chaim Ozer Grodzenski. Reb Chaim Ozer had himself received the *kiddush* cup as a wedding present from Rabbi Yisrael Salanter, his first wife's grandfather.⁵

Upon moving to Bnei Brak, Rabbi Dessler had wanted to switch to another *kiddush* cup because Reb Yisrael's was not a full *shiur* (measure) according to the *Chazon Ish*, whose rulings Rabbi Dessler viewed as determinative for all those living in Bnei Brak. The Rebbetzin, however, insisted that a kiddush cup that was good enough for *gedolei hador*, such as Rabbi Yisrael Salanter and Rabbi Chaim Ozer Grodenzki, was also good enough for the Dessler family.

In deference to her wishes, Rabbi Dessler continued using the *kiddush* cup they had received as a wedding present. The first Shabbos after Rebbetzin Dessler's *petirah*, however, Rabbi Dessler stopped the young yeshiva *bachur* who was attending him when he went to take out the *kiddush* cup and told him to bring a larger one instead.⁶

Rabbi Dessler had always trimmed his beard in keeping with the custom of Kelm. He had wanted to change this practice after coming to *Eretz Yisrael*, in accord with a passage in the writings of the *Arizal* that one should not trim one's beard in *Eretz Yisrael*. Rebbetzin Dessler, however, objected. Her father, Rabbi Nachum Velvel Ziv, had a neatly trimmed beard, and she did not wish her husband to deviate from his custom. Once again Rabbi Dessler felt that deferring to her wishes took preference over a stringency that he wanted to take upon himself. Only after her passing did he stop trimming his beard.⁷

---

5. Rabbi Chaim Ozer no doubt viewed Rabbi Dessler as the logical recipient of the *kiddush* cup because Rabbi Dessler's mother was also a granddaughter of Rabbi Yisrael Salanter and the sister of Reb Chaim Ozer's first wife.

6. Rabbi Moshe Schapiro, who was the young *bachur* in question.

7. Shortly after Rebbetzin Dessler's passing, she appeared to Rabbi Simcha Zissel Dessler in a dream, and instructed him to ask his cousin why he no longer honored her wishes. When Rabbi Simcha Zissel told this dream to Rabbi Dessler, the latter

A few days after Rebbetzin Dessler's *petirah*, she came to him in a dream and assured him, "It is good here."[8] While that dream gave him solace, the Rebbetzin's loss weighed heavily on him. Rabbi Shalom Noach Ulman, his house *bachur* after the Rebbetzin's passing, often saw him staring at pictures of her and the family, and Rabbi Dessler insisted on maintaining his modest quarters just as she had left them.[9]

In a letter to the Sassoons written more than a month after Rebbetzin Dessler's *petirah*, Rabbi Dessler gave vent to the loss he felt. Always a prolific letter writer, he told the Sassoons that except for a few lines to his friends in Gateshead, who he knew would be worried about him, he had not been able to write at at all since her death, so overwhelmed was he by grief.

Only his work in Ponevezh Yeshiva, he wrote, helped ease the pain over the loss of his wife: "On the whole, I try to throw myself into work." Complete involvement in his duties in the yeshiva allowed him "to go away for a while from [his] sorrow." Still, the relief was only temporary. Seeing the pity with which friends and acquaintances looked at him, rather than providing solace, only made him "remember [his] grief even more."

With Rebbetzin Dessler's passing, Rabbi Dessler's pace did not slacken. But he did permit himself one change of schedule. In the two years that remained to him, he twice visited his children and grandchildren in America. It must have weighed heavily on him that Rebbetzin Dessler had only lived to see her oldest grandson, Reuven Dov Dessler. And in whatever time remained to him, he was determined that Reuven Dov and the grandchildren born after him should know their grandfather.

---

replied by citing the Talmudic dictum: "One need take no account of dreams." *Rabbi Eliyahu Eliezer Dessler, the son of Rabbi Simcha Zissel Dessler*.

Though, as we have seen, Rabbi Dessler placed great stock in dreams, and at many crucial junctures in his life was guided either by dreams or the *Goral HaGra*, those instances involved issues as to how to conduct himself in areas for which guidance could not be found in halachic sources.

8. Rabbi Yehoshua Geldzahler.
9. Rabbi Nachum Velvel Dessler.

During his visit with his son and daughter-in-law in Cleveland he insisted and made sure to use every opportunity to take both Reuven Dov and Soroh Rivkah for walks, to bond and get to know them and their little *chochmos*, deriving much *nachas* from each one. It was unbelievably moving to observe him with 10-month-old Peshe Gila who from the playpen watched his every move, even as she was engaged in playful activity. The love and affection he showered upon them was in no small measure an indication how great his longing for them had been and how much he must have missed seeing them throughout the years of separation.

R' Nachum Velvel Dessler

Rabbi Dessler spent Pesach of 1952 with his daughter Hennie and her family, followed by a visit in Cleveland with Rabbi Nachum Velvel Dessler's family. The next year he returned after Shavuos and remained until just before *Elul zman*. It was to be the last time he saw his children and grandchildren. Besides his oldest grandson Reuven Dov Dessler, he also met his son Rabbi Nachum Velvel's two oldest daughters, Soroh Rivkah (Schiff) and

Rebbetzin Miriam Dessler

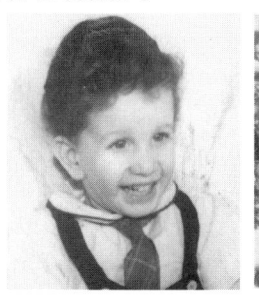

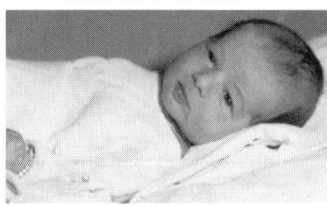

Top left, Reuven Dov; top right, Soroh Rivkah; and left; Peshe Gila Dessler, at the time of R' Dessler's visit.

Chapter Twenty-one: The Final Years / 343

With R' Yehoshua and Hennie Geldzahler, holding Moshe and Doniel

Peshe Gila (Brudny), and his daughter Hennie's two oldest sons, Moshe and Doniel. The Geldzahlers' daughter Bluma (Wulliger) was born during this visit. Rabbi Dessler would sit and look at her for a long time in the crib.

The last year of his life Rabbi Dessler experienced difficulty walking due to intense pains in his legs, which the doctors attributed to circulatory problems. Those pains intensified over time and reached their height during the *levayah* of the *Chazon Ish*. Rabbi Dessler insisted on walking all the way to the cemetery despite being in excruciating pain.

Nevertheless, with the exception of a few very close students, no one knew how far his medical condition declined. And even they did not dream that his end was near. Only afterwards did they realize from some of Rabbi Dessler's comments that he himself had had some intimation that he might not have long to live.

A few weeks prior to his passing, he made an oral will concerning the distribution of all his possessions. He mentioned at that time that Rabbi Zundel of Salant, the teacher of Rabbi Yisrael Salanter, gave away everything that he owned, down to the little stick that he used to stir batter, prior to his passing. And he himself expressed the desire to reach a situation of owning nothing in the world so that even to write a letter, he would have to borrow the paper and pen.

He explained, at that time, that the more one is attached to the material world at the time of death, the harder the body — man's physical element — makes it to die. That is what is referred to by *Chazal* as *yissurei chibut hakever* (the torments of the grave). Around the same time, he also discussed with his students the concept of *shechiv merah*, a disposition of property by one who is on his deathbed.

Yet whatever his intimations concerning his approaching end, Rabbi Dessler continued to give his regular *shmuessen* in Ponevezh Yeshiva until the last week of his life. Even within the yeshiva itself, there was no awareness that he was in very grave condition.

He was still planning a trip to England. In his last letter to Rabbi Aryeh Carmell in London, written less than a month before his passing, he lamented that it would still be more than two months before they would be together again. The tone of the letter is of one still filled with energy. Rabbi Dessler describes having just completed writing over more than twenty matters from *Elul*. It was already past midnight, and Rabbi Dessler writes that he will still be awake at least another hour preparing his *leil Shabbos shmuess*.[10]

On the morning of his passing, 24 *Teves*, 5714 (December 24, 1953), Rabbi Dessler busied himself with preparations for an upcoming trip to England. Only in the middle of the morning did he tell Rabbi Yitzchak Greenberg, who was accompanying him, that the pain in his leg rendered him unable to even lift his leg to climb a step.

That afternoon Rabbi Dessler's cousin Rabbi Simcha Zissel Dessler called a specialist to examine Rabbi Dessler. At the same time, a very small group of those closest to Rabbi Dessler gathered in his room. In the midst of the examination, Rabbi Dessler told the doctor, "I'm experiencing a pain unlike any I have ever known." Yet his external

---

10. *Michtav M'Eliyahu*, Vol. IV, p. 372.

R' Yechezkel Levenstein (l.) and R' Elya Lopian (r.)

expression remained exactly the same as before, and he continued to describe for the doctor with complete calm the progression of the pain across his chest.

Then he smiled and nodded at his cousin Rabbi Simcha Zissel Dessler, closed his eyes, and did not speak again. Rabbi Eliyahu Eliezer Dessler had passed on to a higher world.

The news struck the Ponevezh *beis medrash* like a thunderbolt. Few had had any inkling of how serious Rabbi Dessler's condition was. Groups were quickly arranged to remain with the body until the burial the next day.

The next day the *levayah* departed from Rabbi Dessler's home in the Zichron Meir section of Bnei Brak. There, Rabbi Yaakov Landau, *Rav* of Bnei Brak and an uncle of Rabbi Dessler by marriage,[11] delivered the first *hesped* (eulogy), followed by Rabbi Shmuel Wosner, *Rav* of Zichron Meir. From the Dessler home, the procession moved to the courtyard of Ponevezh Yeshiva. There *hespedim* were given by Chief Rabbi Yitzchak Isaac Herzog, Rabbi Yechezkel Levenstein and Rabbi Eliyahu Lopian, close friends of Rabbi Dessler from Kelm, Rabbi Yehoshua Zelig Diskind, *rav* of Pardes Channah, Rabbi Shmuel Rabinov from England, and Rabbi Shabsi Yogel, Rosh Yeshiva of Slonim in Europe and later Rosh Yeshiva in Ramat Gan. At the grave, Rabbi Hillel Vitkind, Rosh Yeshivas Beis Yosef, gave the final eulogy.

The loss of the generation's most influential Jewish thinker, following just six weeks after the loss of the *Chazon Ish*, the *gadol hador*, left all those in Bnei Brak that dreary December day feeling that they truly belonged to an orphaned generation.

---

11. Rabbi Landau's Rebbetzin was a sister of Rabbi Dessler's stepmother.

ONE OF RABBI DESSLER'S LAST LETTERS TO RABBI SASSOON dealt with the concept of "his lips speak in the grave" — the idea that whenever the Torah insights of a great scholar are learned in subsequent generations, the lips of the one who first brought that insight into the world are, as it were, speaking from the grave. The topic was certainly a fitting one for Rabbi Dessler, for there are few indeed in recent generations whose words continue to speak from the grave to the same extent.

Michtav Me'Eliyahu

To those who were privileged to hear him, his impact has been little diminished by the passage of the years. Nearly 50 years after his passing, groups of *talmidim* continue to gather on each *yahrtzeit* in both Gateshead and Ponevezh for days of spiritual arousal. His closest disciple from the Ponevezh period, Rabbi Chaim Friedlander, according to his family, never gave a *shiur* or went a day without mentioning Rabbi Dessler. And the same could surely be said of Rabbi Aryeh Carmell and Rabbi Mordechai Miller.

But his impact has been by no means confined to the narrow circle of those who heard him in his lifetime. Through the posthumously published *Michtav Me'Eliyahu* his influence continues to grow almost half a century after his death.[12] It would be hard to name another work that has spread to so many Jewish homes since the *Mishnah Berurah*. Forty-four years after publication of the first volume of *Michtav Me'Eliyahu*, the publisher continues to

R' Dessler's kever

---

12. The name of the work emphasized its posthumous nature. It is derived from *Divrei Hayamim II* 21:12: "A letter came to [Yehoram] from Eliyahu the prophet . . . ." Rashi explains that the letter in question arrived after Eliyahu has already gone up to Heaven.

Chapter Twenty-one: The Final Years / 347

R' Dessler and R' Carmell

print between two and three thousand new sets each year. An English-language adaptation by Rabbi Aryeh Carmell entitled *Strive for Truth* has already reached six volumes and been reprinted numerous times.[13]

The first volume of *Michtav Me'Eliyahu* was prepared for publication by Rabbi Alter Halperin of London, assisted by Rabbi Aryeh Carmell, and appeared in honor of Rabbi Dessler's first *yahrtzeit*. It contained many of the essays that Rabbi Dessler himself had written and reworked many times, including his best known essays — "Discourse on Lovingkindness" and "Discourse on Free Will." The work was an immediate popular success and quickly became the mainstay for teaching the fundamentals of a Torah worldview.

It would be nearly another decade until the next volumes of *Michtav Me'Eliyahu* appeared.[14] As Rabbi Friedlander and Rabbi Carmell wrote in their introduction to Volume II, the next two volumes provided not only clarifications of the deepest issues of faith and Divine Providence, and the challenges of the times, but also a methodology for understanding the *Aggadata* of *Chazal*. The student who absorbs that methodology finds himself in possession of the key to understanding the words of the Sages, even in places not explicitly illuminated by Rabbi Dessler.

Volume II was divided into two parts. The first deals with the

---

13. The first volume of *Strive for Truth* was published by Feldheim Publishers in 1978, the second in 1985, the third in 1989, Volume IV, also titled *Sanctuaries in Time*, in 1994, and Volumes V and VI in 1999. The first four English volumes cover much of the material of the first two volumes of *Michtav Me'Eliyahu*. Volumes V and VI of *Strive for Truth* consist of essays and parts of essays drawn from Volumes III-V of *Michtav Me'Eliyahu*.

14. Volume II was published in 1963 and Volume III a year later.

Jewish calendar and the second with the lessons to be learned from the lives of the great figures of *Tanach* — *maaseh avos siman l'banim* (the actions of the fathers are signposts to their descendants). Volume III was similarly divided into two sections: the first dealing with the path of Divine service and the second with major topics of Jewish thought, such as free will, exile and redemption, and reward and punishment. A third section included 16 letters from Rabbi Dessler to his father written during his early years in England.

Rabbi Aryeh Carmell subsequently compiled two more volumes based on Rabbi Dessler's teaching: the first in 1985 and the second in 1997. Like Volume III, Volume IV was also divided into two sections: one dealing with issues of how a Jew fashions himself into a servant of Hashem and the second with general issues of faith. Both of the last two volumes include numerous selections from Rabbi Dessler's huge correspondence. Written primarily to his students, those letters capture the love that Rabbi Dessler showed his students, his constant concern with every aspect of their lives, and the sweetness of his language.

The task confronting the editors of the latter volumes was a formidable one. Most of the essays written by Rabbi Dessler himself had already been published in the first volume, and the editors were left to fashion coherent essays out of the brief notes that Rabbi Dessler left of every talk that he gave. Nearly two thousand outlines and lists of sources were available to them, approximately five hundred from the Ponevezh period and the rest from England. But those short notes of Rabbi Dessler only have meaning for those who heard the *shmuessen* for which they served as the basis.

The material fashioned by the editors into volumes II-V can be broken down into three categories. There were the stencils sent by Rabbi Dessler to his farflung students throughout the war years and up until 1947. Though these were written by Rabbi Dessler, or under his supervision, they were not designed for publication or wide distribution and still required a great deal of work before they could be published for a broader public.

A second group of essays was prepared by a small group of his closest *talmidim* in Ponevezh based on Rabbi Dessler's brief notes and their own notes of his *shmuessen*. Those essays were then circulated among a small circle of close *talmidim* in *Eretz Yisrael*. Besides Rabbi Chaim Friedlander, the circle involved in this work included Rabbi Moshe Aharon Braverman and Rabbi Dov Wein. Among those whose notes proved particularly helpful were Rabbi Simcha Kessler and Rabbi Simcha Freudiger. These essays too had to be expanded and rewritten in order to be understood by a larger audience made up of those who had not heard Rabbi Dessler themselves.

And finally, Rabbi Friedlander and Rabbi Carmell set themselves the daunting task of preparing new essays based on Rabbi Dessler's lecture notes and the notes of those who had heard his *shiurim*.

How well they succeeded is clear from the impact of *Michtav Me'Eliyahu*. *Michtav Me'Eliyahu* has not only been purchased in the tens of thousands, but read; not only read, but learned; it has not only been learned, but entered into the consciousness of the generation.

Nor is *Michtav Me'Eliyahu* merely a popular work. Rabbi Shlomo Wolbe, the senior living *Mashgiach*, says that the first place he turns when working upon any problem is *Michtav Me'Eliyahu*. One of Rabbi Yitzchak Hutner's closest *talmidim* approached him in the late '50s and told him that he was planning on going to *Eretz Yisrael* to learn in Kollel Chazon Ish. The student asked Rabbi Hutner, the other great explicator of the *Maharal* in our time, what work he recommended that he learn well in preparation for his *aliyah*. Rabbi Hutner told him: *Michtav Me'Eliyahu*.

In his heart of hearts, the student was insulted. He knew that *Michtav Me'Eliyahu* was learned in Beis Yaakov seminaries, and he had expected Rabbi Hutner to recommend some more esoteric work. Over forty years as a major Torah educator in *Eretz Yisrael*, however, that former student has had much opportunity to marvel at his Rosh Yeshiva's wisdom in instructing him to delve into *Michtav Me'Eliyahu*.

Not only has Rabbi Dessler continued to teach thousands of *talmidim* from the grave, but his influence has spread in concentric circles through his *talmidim* and their works. In the last decade, no work of *hashkafah* has been so widely studied in the yeshiva world as *Sifsei Chaim*, a four-volume work by Rabbi Chaim Friedlander, published after his death. Rabbi Friedlander pays tribute to Rabbi Dessler repeatedly throughout the work, and cites him in nearly 200 places. Those citations do not begin to capture Rabbi Dessler's influence, however. He provided the keys that allowed Rabbi Friedlander to develop into one of the premier Torah teachers of his generation.

Rabbi Mordechai Miller is another extraordinarily prolific author and influential Torah educator whose entire approach is based on the foundations he gained as one of Rabbi Dessler's closest disciples in England.[15]

Rabbi Dessler was one of the first to foresee the potential of the modern *baal teshuvah* movement. *Michtav Me'Eliyahu* (or its English adaptation *Strive for Truth*) is inevitably one of the first works of Jewish thought to which a potential *baal teshuvah* is exposed.

In recent years, there has been an outpouring of works grounded in the greatest modern Jewish thinkers — the Maharal, the Ramchal, the Vilna Gaon, and Reb Tzadok HaKohen of Lublin — yet written in a thoroughly modern idiom.[16] These works made it possible for the first time to provide a taste of the richness and depth of Torah thought to whose who lack the background or linguistic skills to approach the classical texts directly.

The indebtedness of the authors of these works to Rabbi Dessler leaps out at the knowledgeable reader. Indeed those authors might even be described as second-generation *talmidim* of Rabbi Dessler. Almost all of them are themselves the *talmidim* of Rabbi Moshe Shapiro, the youngest of Rabbi Dessler's close followers in Ponevezh Yeshiva.

Rabbi Dessler was himself a pioneer in the effort to convey a

---

15. Two volumes of his *Shabbos Shiurim* based on his classes in Gateshead Seminary and a third volume of *Yom Tov Shiurim* have appeared in both Hebrew and English.

16. Two of the most recent examples are Rabbi Jeremy Kagan's *The Jewish Self* and Rabbi Akiva Tatz's *Worldmask*.

Torah worldview to Jews with a wide sophistication in modern science and thought. And his ideas have proven to be a fertile source of inspiration for precisely such searching Jews.

When the family of Rabbi Nachum Velvel Ziv was sitting *shivah* for him, one of those who came to offer his condolences was the Russian doctor who had attended him in his final illness. The doctor was a giant of a man, and when he walked into Rabbi Nachum Velvel's house he seemed to fill the entire doorway. Coming into the room in which the family was sitting, the doctor noticed the pain on the face of Rabbi Nachum Velvel's sister Nechama Liba. He stopped, pointed at her, and said in Yiddish, "What are you crying about? Would that I were as alive at this moment as he is."

That non-Jewish doctor had absorbed more than he knew from his patient. He had echoed the teaching of the Sages that our father Jacob did not die — because as long as his descendants are alive, he is alive.

Life is not static. Life flourishes and grows. It radiates new life and infuses itself into others. This is the life of our father Jacob.

Such was — such is — the life of Rabbi Dessler. As his influence continues to grow, the numbers of his "offspring" continue to grow and the depth of their faith and knowledge influences the entire Torah world.

All this is the living legacy of Rabbi Eliyahu Eliezer Dessler.

"Would that we were all as alive at this moment as he is."

Our father Rabbi Dessler did not die.

Appendix

Meeting the Challenge

What follows is not intended as an overview or evaluation of Rabbi Dessler's thought, nor even as a summary of a few of his best-known essays. Rabbi Dessler's corpus is too large, and his startling insights so rich and varied, that no summary could do justice to the range of his thought. More importantly, the author of the present volume views such an assessment of Rabbi Dessler's thought as far beyond his competence.

At most, this appendix is intended to demonstrate the interplay between some of Rabbi Dessler's central teachings and the situation of his young, private pupils in London.

R ABBI DESSLER SOUGHT TO TURN HIS *TALMIDIM* INTO *bnei Torah* in the classical Eastern European mold. To do so, he needed to first shake them from the complacency of their comfortable, upper middle-class existences, and substitute spiritual aspirations for materialistic ones.

Uprooting Materialism

Rabbi Dessler was, as we have seen, disgusted by the materialism of the English society into which he had been thrust. His revulsion went much deeper than just aesthetic distaste. In his view, the attainment of materialistic goals must always be at the expense of spiritual ones. He quoted approvingly the dictum of *Chovos Halevavos*: "One cannot turn towards worldly desires without first turning away from the Torah."[1]

The inverse relationship between material and spiritual goals was, according to Rabbi Dessler, imbedded in the very structure of the universe. In a letter to his father shortly after his arrival in England, Rabbi Dessler describes how from the time that *Moshe Rabbeinu* threw down the first *Luchos* (Tablets of the Law), there was a Divine decree that those who learn Torah would do so amid afflictions and poverty.

The first *Luchos* were given from Above — a physical creation from *ruchnios* (the world of Spirit). As long as the physicality was from Above, it represented no contradiction to the world of Spirit. That level, however, was lost forever when the first *Luchos* were shattered. Every subsequent decline in the spiritual level of the world, writes Rabbi Dessler, has resulted in a yet higher price being exacted from one's spiritual level for every ounce of material plenty.[2]

Rabbi Dessler's efforts to convince his students to reject the prevalent materialism began with a very simple observation: The pursuit of material pleasures does not lead to happiness. The first volume of *Michtav Me'Eliyahu* begins with a letter written in 1938 to his son Nachum Velvel that captures his approach.

Rabbi Dessler surveys all the classes of society and fails to find happiness anywhere. Among the rich, "jealousies and lusts disturb their peace of mind; domestic troubles are rife; their wives are bored, their spoiled children grow away from them...." Nor is the situation any better among the middle classes. They work hard all their lives preparing for retirement and the happiness they expect to find. But by that time, "they are too old; the zest has gone out of life and they cannot enjoy their leisure. They did nothing in their lives but work, and now that they are no longer working, they can hardly find a point in living."

---

1. Quoted in *Michtav Me'Eliyahu*, Vol. I, p. 123; *Strive for Truth*, Vol. II, p. 80.
2. *Michtav Me'Eliyahu*, Vol. III, pp. 307-9.

At the bottom of the social totem pole, the workers lead embittered lives. They feel exploited by the rich, who have denied them all the good things in life.[3]

Hashem created the world, however, to bestow His goodness on Man. He did not create it to be populated by miserable, unhappy people. Man must therefore have been created with the capacity for deep and lasting happiness. What, then, asked Rabbi Dessler, is the secret of a happy life?

For him the answer was obvious: Only a life devoted to spiritual pursuits can ultimately satisfy a human being. A life absent of a devotion to such pursuits could not be considered, in his view, life at all. Such a life lacks the fundamental quality that makes us truly human.

Following the *Ramban*, Rabbi Dessler described *Adam HaRishon* as a fully ambulatory being, possessed of intellectual gifts superior to any animal, even before Hashem breathed into his nostrils. But only with that breath did he acquire a *neshamah* (soul), and thereby become a human being. Thus that Divine breath is called " *nishmas chayim* — the breath of life." Prior to receiving that breath of life, Adam was animated only by his *nefesh*, a life force belonging to animals as well as humans.

What distinguishes the human being is his *neshamah*, the element of the Divine received from above, not the superiority of his *nefesh*. By virtue of that *neshamah*, Man is imbued with the capacity for *kedushah* (holiness) and the potential for a relationship with G-d. Only the realization of one's capacity for holiness constitutes life in the human sense. As long as man lives at the level of *nefesh*, following his own desires, just as animals follow their instincts, he cannot be said to be alive in the Torah's terms. That is what *Chazal* mean when they say that the evil ones are called dead even in their lifetimes.[4]

---

3. *Michtav Me'Eliyahu*, Vol. I, pp. 1-2.

4. *Berachos* 18b quoted in *Michtav Me'Eliyahu*, Vol. I, p. 72; *Strive for Truth*, Vol. I, pp. 210-11.

Nor can those whose lives were devoid of spiritual pursuits in this world hope for anything more in the World to Come. Rabbi Dessler emphasized that death changes nothing essential about the soul. We create our eternity by our actions in this world. *Chazal* describe *Gehinnom* as "nothingness," for that is what one who spends his

Rabbi Dessler viewed the development of the *middah* of *chesed* (giving) as the key to realizing the Divine image in oneself. We are commanded to imitate Hashem in all our actions. And it is the characteristic of *chesed* that best characterizes Hashem's conduct of the world. He is a pure giver, seeking nothing in return, for He lacks nothing.

Because Man was created in the Divine image, he too is imbued with the capacity to give. Through *chesed* Man gives the highest expression to the Divine image within himself.[5] At the other extreme, one whose life centers on grasping everything within reach for his own enjoyment defiles the Divine image.

These two opposed tendencies — giving and taking — were, in Rabbi Dessler's thought, at the root of every other *middah* and action.[6] (Some of his young *talmidim* were shocked to find that the Torah demanded of them not only certain actions but a transformation of all their thoughts and emotions as well.)[7]

Man's task in the world, according to the *Maharal*, is to fulfill himself in three ways: in relationship to himself, in relationship to other human beings, and in relationship to *HaKadosh Baruch Hu*. In "Discourse on Lovingkindness" (the ideas of which formed the core of his teaching to the young men gathered around him in London), Rabbi Dessler demonstrated why each of these tasks is possible only through the development of the *middah* of *chesed* and the uprooting of all tendencies to taking.

At the individual level, the pursuit of material objects and pleasures can offer no real satisfaction. Driving the quest for material acquisition, Rabbi Dessler argued, is an inner emptiness, a feeling of incompletion stemming from a lack of connection to Hashem. Most people mistakenly identify the source of that incompletion

---

whole life chasing after material pleasures is left with. He no longer has access to material objects. He has only his own being, and that is empty of any spiritual content. *Michtav Me'Eliyahu*, Vol. I, pp. 302-3; *Strive for Truth*, Vol. III, pp. 215-16. See also *Strive for Truth*, Vol. V, p. 216.

5. *Michtav Me'Eliyahu*, Vol. I, p. 32; *Strive for Truth*, Vol. I, p. 119. See also, *Michtav Me'Eliyahu*, Vol. I, p. 147; *Strive for Truth*, Vol. II, p. 149.

6. *Michtav Me'Eliyahu*, Vol. I, p. 32; *Strive for Truth*, Vol. I, pp. 119-20.

7. Rabbi Aryeh Carmell.

with objects outside themselves.[8] Yet even when they succeed in acquiring those objects, they are not satisfied.

The objects a person acquires always remain external to him. They cannot become part of him in the same way that his arms and legs, and even more so his thoughts, are part of him.[9] As such, they can never fill the void within.

Since physical objects can never fill the void that generates the quest for them in the first place, their acquisition must inevitably disappoint. But the reason for the disappointment is rarely understood. Rather than renouncing material acquisition, most people mistakenly think that their dissatisfaction stems from having sought the wrong object or from having obtained too little. That is what *Chazal* mean when they say that no one who pursues material pleasures dies with half his desires fulfilled. If he has one hundred, he wants two hundred; if he has two hundred, he wants four hundred.[10] One who makes material pleasures and objects his goal inevitably experiences life as hunger.

In contrast to the person whose life is driven by the pursuit of yet more material objects stands "the one who rejoices in his portion." *Chazal* do not say that such a person is also a rich man, but that he is the *only* rich man. He does not live a life of hunger because he recognizes that his task in life is a spiritual one, and that whatever he has been provided at a particular point in time is what he needs for his appointed spiritual task.[11]

Only that which truly belongs to a person, the Alter of Kelm taught, can provide him with satisfaction. One cannot really own material objects; of necessity, they always remain external to the person. (For that reason, Rabbi Dessler noted, *Lashon HaKodesh* has no verb for possessing.[12]) In the final analysis, a human being possesses only his self. The first step to true happiness, then, is recognition that the source of happiness is within and not without.

---

8. *Michtav Me'Eliyahu*, Vol. I, p. 41; *Strive for Truth*, Vol. I, p. 137.
9. *Michtav Me'Eliyahu*, Vol. I, pp. 42-3; *Strive for Truth*, Vol. I, pp. 139-40.
10. *Koheles Rabbah*, 1:34.
11. *Michtav Me'Eliyahu*, Vol. I, pp. 2-3.
12. *Strive for Truth*, Vol. I, p. 158 n. 25.

Only one who is dependent on nothing outside himself is truly happy.[13]

What does it mean to be dependent on nothing outside oneself? For Rabbi Dessler the answer was clear: to focus all one's ambition on spiritual pursuits — "love of Torah, love of wisdom, love of *mussar*...."[14] Only one who does so can still the gnawing hunger that drives all those who are slaves to the pursuit of material pleasures.

Unlike material objects which can never become part of their owner, a person's spiritual achievements are genuinely his. When he overcomes a bad character trait or the temptations of his *yetzer*, he has changed himself in some fundamental way.[15] In the process, he fills the void within himself. Each such development of his character brings him closer to Hashem.

Though the person who has devoted himself to spiritual pursuits is dependent on nothing outside himself, he is, paradoxically able to enter into far deeper relationships with other human beings than the "taker." Such a person is constantly growing from within, and in that process of growth he overflows, as it were, his personal boundaries. As described by Rabbi Dessler, he resembles nothing so much as a flooding river whose life-giving waters overflow all its banks.[16] The more he succeeds in overcoming his own selfish egotism, and becomes a giver rather than a taker, the more encompassing the embrace of his heart. The boundaries between him and others blur. Rabbi Dessler describes how "one who gives his heart to others finds that his sphere of interest widens until he feels at one time all

---

13. *Michtav Me'Eliyahu*, Vol. I, p. 3.

14. *Michtav Me'Eliyahu*, Vol. I, p. 3.

15. Thus, Rabbi Dessler explained, hospitality to guests is greater than receiving the Divine Presence. Prophecy is a gift; it is not something that one creates and thus makes part of his personality. By contrast, "an act of lovingkindness deeply and permanently affects the person's whole personality." *Michtav Me'Eliyahu*, Vol. I, p. 141; *Strive for Truth*, Vol. II, p. 134.

One of Rabbi Dessler's explanations of *Chazal's* statement that "even the wholly righteous cannot stand in the place of a *baal teshuvah*" was that the *baal teshuvah* creates something entirely new by overcoming his nature. *Michtav Me'Eliyahu*, Vol. III, p. 307.

16. Rabbi Moshe Shapiro points out that *Chazal* refer to a large measure — e.g. a large *tefach* (handbreadth) — as *tefach sochek* (literally, a laughing *tefach*). They associated joy with overflowing boundaries.

the happiness occurring in the lives of many people."[17] Through spiritual striving, a person uncovers the *tzelem Elokim* (Divine image) within himself, and therefore becomes capable of recognizing it in others.

Giving enables a person to forge lasting connection to others. Ironically, that which a person gives away lasts forever in the form of the bond created between the giver and receiver, while that which one takes for himself is consumed and gone.[18]

The taker, on the other hand, is incapable of forming deep bonds with other human beings. Because he is driven by selfishness and has lost touch with the Divine image within himself, the taker cannot see it in others either. When he sees someone else acting in an apparently unselfish fashion, he is incapable of believing the evidence of his senses and attributes to him all sorts of selfish motivations.[19]

The taker's focus on the acquisition of material goods inevitably causes him to view his fellow human beings as competitors over a finite pie of material goods and pleasures.[20] By contrast, one whose focus is on the realm of Spirit is freed from the insatiable hunger for material acquisition that breeds enmity. In the realm of Spirit, people are not in competition with one another, for Spirit is infinite. Far from one person's spiritual growth being at the expense of others, each person's spiritual growth facilitates that of others.[21]

The relationship between overcoming selfishness and bonding to others was not one way in Rabbi Dessler's thought. On the one hand, he viewed becoming a giver rather than a taker as the key to all enduring relationships. At the same time, he saw a connection to others, particularly to an organic community, is one of the great antidotes to the selfishness that lies at the root of every bad *middah*. Through attachment to the community, he taught, one automatically

---

17. *Michtav Me'Eliyahu*, Vol. I, p. 152; *Strive for Truth*, Vol. II, p. 160.
18. *Michtav Me'Eliyahu*, Vol. I, p. 37; *Strive for Truth*, Vol. I, p. 129.
19. *Michtav Me'Eliyahu*, Vol. I, p. 144; *Strive for Truth*, Vol. II, p. 142.
20. *Michtav Me'Eliyahu*, Vol. I, pp. 126-7; *Strive for Truth*, Vol. II, pp. 90-1.
21. See *Michtav Me'Eliyahu*, Vol. II, p. 108; *Strive for Truth* Vol. IV, p. 139.

lifts his spiritual level. Thus on Rosh Hashanah, when we are judged according to our spiritual level at that particular moment, Rabbi Yisrael Salanter advised people to identify and commit themselves to a community.[22]

From the time of Adam's first sin in *Gan Eden*, the *yetzer hara* always speaks to man in his particularity: "This will be good for *you*, never mind about anyone else."[23] When one identifies with the community, however, one no longer speaks the language of "I," and thereby places himself on the path to overcoming his own particularity. At Sinai, when *Klal Yisrael* reached the level of "with one heart, as one man," it once again achieved the pristine spiritual level of Adam before the sin. Only then, when selfish desires had been extirpated from every heart, was *Klal Yisrael* worthy of receiving the Torah.[24]

Finally, Rabbi Dessler saw selfishness as a bar to any deep relationship with Hashem, just as with one's fellow man. He cited the *Reishis Chochmah's* comment that we shall be asked on the Day of Judgment: "Did you make your Creator king over you every morning and evening, and did you make your neighbor King over you with mildness of spirit?" The two questions are linked, said Rabbi Dessler. Only one who is able to place himself at the service of his fellow man will be able to recognize and accept Hashem as King.[25] And one who is blocked from the former by his own self-centeredness will also be denied the latter.

The root of all service of Hashem is gratitude, Rabbi Dessler taught. Thus the giving of the Torah begins with the words, "I am the Lord, your G-d, Who took you out of the land of Egypt," in order to instill feelings of gratitude as a prelude for the receipt of the Torah. The "taker," however, is incapable of gratitude. He views

---

22. *Michtav Me'Eliyahu*, Vol. I, p. 119; *Strive for Truth*, Vol. II, p. 71.
23. Prior to the sin of *Adam HaRishon*, the *yetzer hara* was external to man. It spoke to him from the outside, "You should do such and such ..." But with Adam's sin, the *yetzer hara* became internalized. It speaks to man in the language of his own selfish ego: "I want...." *Michtav Me'Eliyahu*, Vol. I, p. 143; *Strive for Truth*, Vol. II, p. 139.
24. *Michtav Me'Eliyahu*, Vol. I, p. 120; *Strive for Truth*, Vol. II, p.72.
25. *Michtav Me'Eliyahu*, Vol. I, pp. 141-2; *Strive for Truth*, Vol. II, p. 136.

everything in the world as his by right. He can no more be grateful to Hashem than to his fellow man. That is what *Chazal* meant when they said, "Whoever is ungrateful for the good done for him by his friend will eventually prove ungrateful for the good done to him by the Holy One, Blessed is He."[26]

Combating Superficiality

DEPTH OF THOUGHT AND SERIOUSNESS OF PURPOSE WERE THE hallmark of Kelm. Rabbi Dessler sought to instill some of that seriousness in his young charges, and to remove them from a world in which people "kill time [lest] they be compelled to confront themselves and realize that they are ... *nothing*, that their lives are worthless — a constant round of preparation ... for what?"[27] Rabbi Dessler, of course, did not expect his charges to be transformed overnight into products of the Kelm Talmud Torah. He was prepared to let the ideas of Kelm sink in gradually over time.[28]

The dichotomy between "external/superficial," on the one hand, and "inward," on the other, recurs throughout Rabbi Dessler's teaching.[29] *Mitzvos*, for instance, can be either inward or superficial. The former are called "life" itself; the latter are referred to as *levushim* (apparel). "Life" refers to those *mitzvos* that come only after some inner struggle with the *yetzer hara*. Such *mitzvos* create a new point of *kedushah* that did not formerly exist, and that *kedushah* is, as we have seen, the Torah's definition of life.[30]

"Apparel *(levush)*," on the other hand, refers to *mitzvos* that possess only the external appearance of the *mitzvah*, without an inner purity of intention. Such *mitzvos* are not without value. They can serve as rungs on the spiritual ladder leading to *mitzvos* performed with sincere intention — "service for external motives *(shelo lishmah)* brings one to pure service *(lishmah)*" — provided that one at least has

---

26. *Midrash HaGadol* 1:8 as quoted in *Michtav Me'Eliyahu*, Vol. I, p. 50; *Strive for Truth*, Vol. I, p. 154.

27. *Michtav Me'Eliyahu*, Vol. I, p. 100; *Strive for Truth*, Vol. II, p. 14.

28. Rabbi Aryeh Carmell.

29. In evaluating world events, for instance, Rabbi Dessler taught his students to discern the "inner spiritual purpose" concealed behind the "outward garb" of events.

30. *Michtav Me'Eliyahu*, Vol. I, p. 224; *Strive for Truth*, Vol. III, p. 43.

the goal of eventually achieving a congruence between the inner service of G-d and its outward expression. But in and of themselves such *mitzvos* confer no merit.

Only that part of a *mitzvah* performed without any admixture of worldly motives earns a person reward in the World to Come.[31] To the extent that a person's *mitzvah* performance is motivated by something other than the desire to do Hashem's will, he is separated from Hashem.[32] At some level, such *mitzvos* even demonstrate contempt for Hashem: The one performing the *mitzvos* in such an outward fashion does not really believe that Hashem is aware of his every thought.[33] The *yetzer hara* does not even resist such *mitzvos*. "On the contrary, it is only too pleased to have a chance to blind the person ... so that he can appear to himself a good and upright person."[34]

Rabbi Dessler's continual emphasis on *bechirah*, the exercise of free will, conveyed to his disciples the high seriousness demanded of them at every moment. At a time when the very existence of free will was being denied by pseudoscientific determinists, he stressed (following the *Ramchal*) that the exercise of free will is the very purpose of life.[35]

The manner in which we exercise our free will, Rabbi Dessler taught, defines us as a human being and is the source of our humanity. Our very relationship with G-d is a function of our

---

31. *Michtav Me'Eliyahu*, Vol. I, p. 107; *Strive for Truth*, Vol. II, p. 36, quoting the *Rambam* and Rabbi Moshe Chaim Luzzato.
32. *Michtav Me'Eliyahu*, Vol. I, p. 228; *Strive for Truth*, Vol. III, p. 50.
33. *Michtav Me'Eliyahu*, Vol. I, p. 134 quoting Rabbi David Kimche (*Radak*); *Strive for Truth*, Vol. II, p. 110.
34. *Michtav Me'Eliyahu*, Vol. I, p. 73; *Strive for Truth*, Vol. I, p. 213.
35. *Michtav Me'Eliyahu*, Vol. I, p. 116; *Strive for Truth*, Vol. II, p. 61.

Those who deny the existence of free will and view all human action from a deterministic perspective, wrote Rabbi Dessler, do so because they have never chosen positively. They do not believe man is free because they themselves are not free. They have enslaved themselves to their *yetzer hara*. *Michtav Me'Eliyahu*, Vol. I, p. 112; *Strive for Truth*, Vol. II, p. 52.

Rabbi Dessler was wont to explain particular beliefs as reflection of the heart of the one expressing that belief. For instance, those who deny *Olam Haba* (the World to Come) do so because they have lost contact with that which is eternal within them, their holy souls.

bechirah. Any true relationship must be based on the individuality of both parties — on what is intrinsic to them and not compelled by circumstances beyond their control. Only because we are capable of defining ourselves through the exercise of our free will do we exist as individuals capable of relating to G-d.

Free will, as described by Rabbi Dessler, is found precisely at that point where the individual's perception of truth is equally balanced against the temptation of his *yetzer hara*. By definition every act of *bechirah* involves an inner struggle. Whatever a person does automatically, without the sense of being pulled in two competing directions, confers no merit. Sometimes, Rabbi Dessler observed, the *yetzer hara*, realizing that it has no power to prevent a person from performing a *mitzvah*, withdraws entirely so that the *mitzvah* entails no struggle, and therefore lacks "life."[36]

Every person has free will. People differ from one another only in the level at which their *bechirah* comes into play. *Bechirah* cannot be said to exist with respect to those matters that have already become fully integrated into one's moral behavior pattern; nor can it be said to exist with respect to those positive actions so completely beyond a person's moral grasp that he cannot even fathom why anyone would do such a thing.[37] No matter how elevated one's actions, if one has been trained to act in such a way, the actions cannot be properly described as one's own. One's education determines the starting point at which one's *bechirah* begins to function. But it cannot confer merit by itself.[38] Rabbi Dessler provided many spatial metaphors for the exercise of *bechirah*.[39] In one of the most powerful of those metaphors, he

---

36. *Michtav Me'Eliyahu*, Vol. I, pp. 225-26; *Strive for Truth*, Vol. III, p. 46.

37. *Michtav Me'Eliyahu*, Vol. I, p. 10; *Strive for Truth*, Vol. I, p. 53.

38. *Michtav Me'Eliyahu*, Vol. I, p. 115; *Strive for Truth*, Vol. II, p. 58.
   The Alter of Slabodka proved this point from Lot. Lot was not saved from Sodom on the merit of risking his life by bringing strangers into his home. He had learned the supreme importance of *hachnasas orchim* in Avraham's house. He merited being saved for an action that seems to us trivial by comparison: his failure to reveal to Pharaoh that Avraham and Sarah were married. Revealing that fact would have constituted a betrayal by Lot of the one to whom he owed everything. Still Lot confronted a test, for if Pharaoh had executed Avraham, he would have inherited his wealth. For that test, Lot had no models before him, and thus the decision was "his" in a way that inviting strangers into his home was not. *Michtav Me'Eliyahu*, Vol. I, p. 116; *Strive for Truth*, Vol. II, pp. 59-60.

39. See Introduction for the metaphor of a battlefield.

portrayed the space between the individual's intellect and his heart, the seat of his will, as the arena in which *bechirah* is exercised. The test of *bechirah* is whether one's intellectual apprehension of Truth will be realized in action. In the vacuum between head and heart, which intellectual knowledge must traverse, lurks the *yetzer hara*. The *yetzer's* chief weapon is the imagination, which he uses to conjure up images of all the sensual pleasures of the world.[40]

Only by filling the emptiness between head and heart with a countervailing force — the most effective being the desire for the wisdom of the Torah — can man hope to prevail.

Free will, then, is a choice between acting upon the perception of Truth and allowing that perception to become clouded. Even the wicked are not denied the perception of Truth at the level of the intellect. That is what the *Gemara* means when it says, "The wicked are full of regrets" (*Nedarim* 9b). But nevertheless they remain wicked because those intellectual perceptions are not translated into action; they remain encapsulated in the mind, without penetrating the inner being.

When Esav, for instance, asked his father Yitzchak how to take *ma'aser* from salt and straw, he was not being a complete charlatan. (The Torah does not record lies.) Esav truly experienced promptings of holiness in the presence of his father, and genuinely wanted to know at those moments. But because those promptings were inspired from outside, without being translated into action, he remained Esav, the Wicked One.[41]

Rabbi Dessler believed that in every Jewish heart is found an irreducible point of holiness, of *lishmah*, which forms the basis of the Divine promise that we shall never be utterly destroyed. That inner light, however, is prevented from shining out forth from the heart because the *yetzer hara* has succeeded in encrusting the heart. Every time we choose material over spiritual pleasures, the heart becomes blocked.

On the other hand, every time we choose positively, a little bit of blockage is removed and an opening is created for the inner point of

---

40. *Michtav Me'Eliyahu*, Vol. I, p. 212; *Strive for Truth*, Vol. III, p. 20.
41. *Michtav Me'Eliyahu*, Vol. I, p. 234; Strive for Truth, Vol. III, p. 65-6.

truth to illuminate the battleground between head and heart. Be it ever so small, that ray of light — the inner point of *lishmah*, unsullied by external motivations — has the power to push away much darkness.[42]

Rabbi Dessler's doctrine of *bechirah* was rigorous and demanding. At every moment, his disciples had to ask themselves: Are we ascending or descending spiritually? Have we expanded the points of Divine light in the ourselves by choosing Truth over Falsehood, or have we further obscured that light by letting the *yetzer hara* cloud our hearts?

By keeping his *talmidim* focused on the choice confronting them every moment, Rabbi Dessler prevented them from slipping into the easy self-satisfaction that might have come naturally to boys who were, by virtue of their parental upbringing, much more observant than almost all their peers. He enabled them to choose well.

Against the Worship of Science

SOMETHING AKIN TO A CULT OF SCIENCE EXISTED IN RABBI Dessler's day. Science was viewed as on the brink of answering all life's questions, and the scientist was revered as the fount of wisdom.

That reverence posed a direct threat to the Torah commitment of many of Rabbi Dessler's *talmidim*, several of whom were drawn to careers in science and most of whom had more than a passing knowledge of modern scientific developments. The threat was not so much from findings of modern science that appeared to be in contradiction to the Torah. It was more subtle. The authority of science and the scientist threatened to supplant that of the Torah and *talmidei chachamim*, and the standards of science and pseudoscience to replace those of the Torah.

---

42. *Michtav Me'Eliyahu*, Vol. I, p. 213; *Strive for Truth*, Vol. III, p. 21.

Rabbi Dessler expressed this idea with a fascinating interpretation of the familiar Rabbinic dictum מתוך שלא לשמה בא לשמה. Usually this is understood to mean that through the performance of *mitzvos* with imperfect motivation (שלא לשמה) one can come to performance for no other reason than the sake of the *mitzvah* itself (לשמה). Rabbi Dessler himself often employed this standard understanding. But elsewhere he interprets the phrase differently — within the *lo lishmah* enters the *lishmah*. The smallest ray of *lishmah* — a perception of Truth realized in action — transforms and softens the *lo lishmah* all around.

Most dangerous of all, in Rabbi Dessler's eyes, was the belief that science had unlocked all the secrets of the universe and that it was only a matter of time before scientists could harness all natural forces for their own purposes. That view, he felt, was nothing less than a denial of the commandment "You shall have no other gods before Me." Scientists, intoxicated with their own intelligence, attributed to themselves godlike powers to control nature.[43]

Rabbi Dessler combated the new religion of science in several ways. The first was to demonstrate how narrowly circumscribed is the realm in which scientific judgment has any authority. Scientists, he showed, had no particular insights to offer on any questions to do with the ultimate meaning of life. The ability to solve a narrow range of technical problems could not be transferred to the realm of morality where individual bias and self-interest inevitably affect all one's conclusions.

Rabbi Dessler revealed the hidden premises and bias on which the anti-Torah polemics of the day were based. "So successful did this method prove," writes Aryeh Carmell, "that one of his followers, if faced with a conflict between a widely held contemporary view and a tenet of Torah, instead of putting himself on the defensive and groping for apologetics, will immediately endeavor to bring to light the bias, individual, social, or otherwise, which has given rise to the divergent viewpoint."[44] The title of one of Rabbi Sassoon's addresses to the first conference of the Association of Orthodox Scientists of Great Britain, "The Challenge of Torah to Science," nicely captures that cast of mind.

Rabbi Dessler's critique of science, or more correctly scientism, began with an inquiry into the nature of human thought itself. Just as a scientist checks the accuracy of his instruments before embarking on a new experiment, so too Rabbi Dessler sought to determine whether human judgment is a reliable guide to the crucial decisions about the ends of life.[45]

---

43. *Michtav Me'Eliyahu*, Vol. II, pp. 41-2.
44. Carmell, "Rabbi Eliyahu Eliezer Dessler," op cit., p. 685.
45. *Michtav Me'Eliyahu*, Vol. I, pp. 52-3; *Strive for Truth*, Vol. I, pp. 161-2.

He concluded that in most cases it is not, for there is an inherent bias built into the system. Even before a person begins to consider any question affecting his life, he has certain desires. Those desires cannot help but have an impact on his conclusions. Just as a person's preexisting interests determine *what* subjects will draw his attention, so too does his self-interest determine *how* he will think about those topics.[46]

Even the slightest self-interest is sufficient to prejudice the outcome of any decision-making process. Thus a judge is prohibited from listening to the claims of one litigant when the other is not present. Having identified, even momentarily, with the first litigant, the judge is now implicated personally. He will be loathe to change his mind, and admit even to himself, that he was mistaken, however briefly. And one judgment corrupted by self-interest, of necessity, renders every subsequent judgment by that individual unreliable, for the "judge" will seek to reconcile every subsequent judgment with the earlier, tainted one, rather than confront his own bias.[47]

If even the slightest self-interest renders a person incapable of impartial, unbiased judgment, and distorts every subsequent opinion, what hope is there for a true judgment? What chance is there that a person will ever decide that he is obligated to do something which is difficult for him, and conflicts with his desires? Very little, answers Rabbi Dessler.

Only one who has purged his heart of self-interest can have any hope of reaching any truthful conclusions about the ends of life. Unless we are talking about mathematical calculations, or some other area in which the ends have already been agreed upon, character, not intelligence, is the key determinant of the reliability of the judgment.

Rabbi Dessler demonstrates the point, taking what might be a prototypical scientist for his example:

> Think of a person who, by the power of his intellect alone, wants to re-examine some fundamental problem — such as was the world created for a purpose....

---

46. *Michtav Me'Eliyahu*, Vol. I, p. 52; *Strive for Truth*, Vol. I, p. 162.
47. *Michtav Me'Eliyahu*, Vol. I, pp. 55-6; *Strive for Truth*, Vol. I, pp. 168-9.

Let us assume that the person possesses a keen intellect, is well educated and well informed. However, so far as character is concerned he is pretty average. He has never seriously tackled his moral failings. He has never worked on himself in any consistent manner to change his basic nature or correct his character faults.... If he is tempted by base desires we can by no means be sure that he will not succumb, especially if no one is ever likely to find out.

[Now let us say that] we are talking of a very comprehensive problem, the solution of which will affect the whole of his life-style.... On the solution will depend whether he will be obliged for the rest of his life to struggle constantly with his baser desires in order to meet the demands of his Creator, or whether he will be able to live without a higher responsibility with no restraints on his desires apart from those he deigns to place on them....[48]

And on the solution to this problem, Rabbi Dessler laughed derisively, "he assures us he is going to arrive at a true solution merely by the exercise of his intellectual powers."

Rabbi Dessler did not deny the power of a human being to detect his own biases and overcome them — indeed he insisted upon it[49] — but only in one who has gained mastery of his *yetzer hara*.[50]

Rabbi Dessler not only denied that scientists enjoy any advantage when it comes to determining the proper ends of life, he questioned whether all the advances in science had resulted in any increase in human happiness. What is the good, he wondered, of scientific knowledge, "if human beings cannot control it; if it breaks all bonds, joins with the evil in man, and produces results the exact opposite of those intended?" as in the case of the atomic

---

48. *Michtav Me'Eliyahu*, Vol. I, pp. 57-8; *Strive for Truth*, Vol. I, pp. 173-4.
49. *Michtav Me'Eliyahu*, Vol. I, p. 60; *Strive for Truth*, Vol. I, p. 180. See also Chapter 19, *supra*.
50. *Michtav Me'Eliyahu*, Vol. I, p. 50; *Strive for Truth*, Vol. I, pp. 176-7, quoting Rabbi Moshe Chaim Luzatto. See also, *Strive for Truth*, Vol. I, pp. 185-188.

bomb.[51] In the same vein, he questioned, whether human beings "threatened with extinction" were, in fact, any happier, on account of all the advances in wealth and power made possible by scientific discoveries.[52]

He distinguished between an arrogant knowledge, boasting of its own greatness, and that wisdom, which *Shlomo HaMelech* describes as bringing "life to its possessors" (*Koheles* 7:12). The difference lies in the modesty of those who possess true wisdom. They treat it as a gift from G-d, carrying with it an attendant responsibility to employ it only in the service of those ends laid down by G-d.[53] Those who do not acknowledge their intelligence as a Divine gift, on the other hand, feel little constraint in employing it for their own selfish purposes, and are as likely to bring destruction as benefit in their wake.

Rabbi Dessler's most audacious intellectual tack, however, was to deny the "reality" of science's very bailiwick: nature itself. Rabbi Dessler feared that with all the fanfare surrounding the rapid expansion of scientific knowledge, the "laws" of nature would increasingly seem to comprise the only reality.

He did not deny the existence of apparent "laws of nature," but he asserted that, in the final analysis, those laws are no less a mystery than the miraculous suspension of those laws. We observe, for instance, that seeds placed into the ground degenerate and give forth new grain. But we ultimately cannot explain why that takes place. Because we have observed the phenomenon so many times, we assume some process of cause and effect, but, in truth, we have no explanation of why seeds behave as they do.

If we think about it carefully, said Rabbi Dessler, we will realize that a seed giving forth new grain is no more or less a miracle than a dead body placed in the ground coming back to life. What leads us to call one miraculous and the other nature is nothing but the frequency with which we have observed the phenomenon. But we know no more about why the grain sprouts than we do of *techiyas*

---

51. *Michtav Me'Eliyahu*, Vol. I, p. 65; *Strive for Truth*, Vol. I, p. 196.
52. *Michtav Me'Eliyahu*, Vol. I, p. 67; *Strive for Truth*, Vol. I, p. 199.
53. *Michtav Me'Eliyahu*, Vol. I, p. 65; *Strive for Truth*, Vol. I. pp. 196-97.

hameisim (the resurrection of the dead.) Underlying both, Rabbi Dessler insisted, is the Divine will — nothing else.[54] Rabbi Dessler rejected the view that G-d created the laws of nature, and then left nature to run its course, with some intermittent interventions in the system when a special need arises.[55] Rather the whole system we term nature is sustained at every moment by a new infusion of the Divine will. The continuity of nature is but an illusion, akin to that created by a movie. A movie consists of hundreds of thousands of individual frames run at high speed to create the impression in the viewer of continuous action. Similarly, nature consists of innumerable discrete decisions by G-d to re-create the world.[56]

A number of important consequences flowed from this insight. At the immediate practical level, recognition of Hashem's constant involvement in every aspect of the world inevitably raised the question of how much worldly endeavor is appropriate to earn a living. Rabbi Dessler discussed this issue at great length.[57]

---

54. *Michtav Me'Eliyahu*, Vol. I, pp. 177-78; *Strive for Truth*, Vol. II, pp. 239-240.
55. *Michtav Me'Eliyahu*, Vol. I, p. 177; *Strive for Truth*, Vol. II, p. 238.
56. *Michtav Me'Eliyahu*, Vol. I, p. 183; *Strive for Truth*, Vol. II, p. 253.
57. *Michtav Me'Eliyahu*, Vol. II, pp. 187-212; *Strive for Truth*, Vol. II, pp. 262-303.

But the most profound consequence of Rabbi Dessler's analysis lay in the impetus it gave to Torah learning. For if all reality is a function of the Divine will, and that will is by definition directed toward spiritual ends, then the highest possible human activity is the study of ends of Hashem's will in the Torah. Torah is the true science for unlocking the purpose of life. Every other intellectual activity pales by comparison.

Glossary

aggadata . . . . non-halachic, *esp.* narrative, portions of the Talmud
baalebatim . . . . (*lit.* householders) laymen
bimah . . . . the podium from which the Torah is read, usually located near the center of the synagogue
chaburah . . . . study group, usually of advanced scholars
chiddush . . . . novel Torah thought or insight
Elul zman . . . . the yeshivah academic term which precedes the High Holy Days
Kabbolas Shabbos . . . . . . (*lit.* accepting the Sabbath) a prayer recited on Friday, just before the evening service
mashal, (pl. *meshalim*) . . parable
mussar . . . . study of proper ethical conduct
Shalosh Seudos . . . . the third Sabbath meal
shidduchim . . . . matrimonial match
shmuess . . . . discourse on ethics and philosophy
shtender . . . . lectern used for prayer or study
treifah . . . . non-kosher
yahrtzeit . . . . anniversary of a death

This volume is part of
THE ARTSCROLL SERIES®
an ongoing project of
translations, commentaries and expositions
on Scripture, Mishnah, Talmud, Halachah,
liturgy, history, the classic Rabbinic writings,
biographies and thought.

For a brochure of current publications
visit your local Hebrew bookseller
or contact the publisher:

Mesorah Publications, ltd

4401 Second Avenue
Brooklyn, New York 11232
(718) 921-9000
www.artscroll.com

North Suburban Synagogue Beth El
Library
1175 Sheridan Road
Highland Park, IL 60035